The Marketing Research Process

Fourth Edition

Margaret Crimp and Len Tiu Wright

Prentice Hall

London New York Toronto Sydney Tokyo Singapore
Madrid Mexico City Munich

First published 1981
This edition published 1995 by
Prentice Hall International (UK) Limited
Campus 400, Maylands Avenue
Hemel Hempstead
Hertfordshire, HP2 7EZ
A division of
Simon & Schuster International Group

Typeset in 10/12 pt Sabon and Helvetica
by Keyset Composition

Printed and bound in Great Britain at
the University Press, Cambridge

Library of Congress Cataloging-in-Publication Data

Wright, Len Tiu.
    The marketing research process. – 4th ed. / Len Tiu Wright and
Margaret Crimp.
        p.   cm.
    Previous eds. by Margaret Crimp.
    Includes bibliographical references and index.
    ISBN 0-13-202839-5
    1. Marketing research. I. Crimp, Margaret. Marketing research
process. II. Title.
HF5415.2.C73 1995
658.8'3–dc20   94-45024
                                                    CIP

British Library Cataloguing in Publication Data

A catalogue record for this book is available from
the British Library

ISBN 0-13-202839-5

---

1 2 3 4 5   99 98 97 96 95

Contents

Preface

In the previous Preface for the third edition, Margaret Crimp wrote that,

> the impact of new technology on the marketing research process was anticipated in the second edition . . . techniques once innovative have become commonplace. Changes in the techniques used to gather data and the ways in which data are used to generate marketing information, have necessitated considerable re-writing.

In this spirit, the fourth edition carries on from the previous editions in two main ways. First, the continuing impact of information technology on marketing research is implicit throughout the book and clearly stated whenever there is discussion of computerised techniques to access or analyse data or to make predictions. Second, the book follows the marketing research process in the style of asking questions, exploring the market, examining the techniques for gathering and generating data, planning the research design, testing a product or a market, media selection and evaluation of performance.

The fourth edition also includes three important appendices, the last two from John Bound and John Davies on the principles of analysis and statistical tests respectively. The late Margaret Crimp's orientation of the book has been retained.

There are notable exceptions too. The fourth edition has been re-written and brought up to date on many changes within the marketing research environment as in the provision of contemporary sources and an expanded Appendix 1, and on what research and media organisations offer. The concerns of prior readers have been addressed with clarification of the research process and the inclusion of new chapters written by practitioners in their specialist fields. New ideas, more in-depth analysis and the wider scope of the book all add to the contribution that the book now makes to the discipline of marketing research.

Acknowledgements

I wish to thank the many people who have helped and encouraged the preparation of this book. The late Margaret Crimp's contribution to the application of marketing research from the earlier editions has provided the fertile ground on which it has been possible to build the fourth edition. Julia Helmsley, Acquisitions Editor at Prentice Hall, deserves the credit for her perseverance in commissioning and marketing the fourth edition.

Valuable contributions to the specialist applications and scope of the fourth edition have been made by the individuals in the order in which their chapters appear in the book: Carol Coutts (international marketing research); John Bound (new data sources and Appendix 2); Rory Morgan (modelling techniques); Nicholas Evans and Richard Webber (CCN 'MOSAIC'); Steven Ashman and Kenneth Clarke (advertisement research); Phyllis Vangelder (quality issues); and John Davies (Appendix 3). My thanks to these authors who have enhanced the book with their chapters and their help.

I am deeply indebted to Michael Warren (MRS), John Kelly (AMSO) and Michael Waterson (NTC Publications) for their permission to reproduce some of the material used in the fourth edition.

The names of the authors and organisations whose work has been cited in the book are too numerous to thank in a short Acknowledgements section but I can mention a few individuals for their assistance: Karina Mellinger (CACI); Louise Putt (Research Business International); Carine Barker (TABS); Jean Wong (NRS) and Philip Mason (The Royal Mail).

I am extremely grateful to Christopher Goard, Brian Roberts, and Sue Homeyard of TN AGB for their material and advice in updating the book. I am also very grateful to Christopher Harris (Millward Brown) for organising the chapter on advertisement research for the book.

My thanks to both Miriam Catterall (University of Ulster) and Malcolm Kirkup (Loughborough University) for their contributions and support. Finally, Kathleen Gibson's patience and effort in typing the manuscript deserve much special appreciation.

Readership

The Marketing Research Process has been written as a text which can be used on university undergraduate courses and foundation courses at Master's level in Business Studies. It is also suitable for diploma and certificate courses in marketing, international marketing and marketing research since various elements of the marketing mix and research strategies for domestic and international markets are covered. Fresh insights are provided in the book which practitioners in business life may also find of use.

Len Tiu Wright
August 1994

Notes on contributors

Steve Ashman first trained and practised as a graphic designer. He served as marketing services director at Granada Television Rental before joining Direct Line Insurance as marketing manager. He became Direct Line's associate director of marketing. In May 1994 he moved to Ionica as Head of Marketing.

John Bound was a marketing researcher in fast-moving consumer goods manufacture and taught Marketing at the University of Strathclyde. Since then he has been a visiting researcher at the London Business School and currently at the South Bank University. He has been a member of the Councils of the Royal Statistical Society and of the Market Research Society. He has presented papers to the Conferences of the Market Research Society and of the European Society for Opinion and Marketing Research, and in 1992 with Professor Andrew Ehrenberg read a paper to the Royal Statistical Society.

Ken Clarke, as an Oxford PPE graduate, served at BMRB for six years before joining Unilever. Here he held a number of market research, sales and marketing appointments, chaired the company's research managers committee, and also led studies into the econometric effects of advertising, promotional methodology, etc. After Unilever, he ran a food company's multiple retail operation before going to Millward Brown seven years ago.

Carol Coutts has worked in the market research industry for over twenty-five years. Up to the early 1990s she was the founder and chairperson of the Research Business International based in London. This is now a part of the Research Business Group. She has published and worked extensively on domestic and overseas market research.

Margaret Crimp worked as a research executive, account executive and account director for three London advertising agencies. She taught marketing research at Ealing College of Higher Education, City of London Polytechnic and Hatfield Polytechnic, as they were then known. She was for many years a reviewer for the Market Research Society. She retired and passed away towards mid-1993.

Though she was not able to write the fourth edition of *The Marketing Research Process*, the foundation which she provided is present in the book as explained in the Acknowledgements.

E. John Davis BSc(Econ) CStat has worked in Marketing and Market Research since 1951, with Gillette, British Overseas Airways Corporation, Television Audience Measurement, the British Market Research Bureau and J. Walter Thompson. In 1974 he joined Henley Management College as Director of Marketing Studies. He is the author of *Experimental Marketing*, *Practical Sales Forecasting*, and (with Douglas Foster) *Mastering Marketing*, as well as numerous papers. He was awarded the Gold Medal of the Market Research Society for his work on test marketing, is a Fellow of the Marketing Society and an Assessor for the Market Research Society Diploma Scheme. Since retiring in 1987 he has remained active in marketing education and consultancy.

Nick Evans is Head of Analysis and Modelling and is also an Associate Director of CCN Marketing, having degrees in geography and statistical modelling. Since joining CCN Marketing he has been responsible for developing its analysis resource that now specialises in providing a range of retail modelling, segmentation and consumer modelling services.

Rory Morgan began his career in market research in 1972 when he joined Research Bureau Ltd, part of the Research International Group of worldwide companies. Equipped with a degree in Psychology and Physiology from London University, Rory has worked since in a variety of roles within that organisation, and has been involved in projects spanning a wide range of product areas, both consumer and specialist. A main board director of the company, his particular specialisms include computer modelling techniques, multi-variate analysis and pricing research.

Phyllis Vangelder has been professionally involved with market research for over twenty-five years. She was Managing Editor of the Market Research Society's publications, editing its monthly *Newsletter*, *Journal of the Market Research Society*, *Yearbook*, *Survey* as well as editing and abstracting the twice-yearly *Market Research Abstracts*. She is now an Editorial and Communications Consultant, remains Managing Editor of the *Journal of the Market Research Society* and Editor/abstractor of the Abstracts as well as editing *Newsbrief* for the European Society for Opinion and Marketing Research (ESOMAR). She is co-editor with Robin Birn and Paul Hague of *A Handbook of Market Research Techniques* published by Kogan Page in 1990.

As Secretary of the Research Development Foundation she edits their proceedings and has reported and written extensively on seminars and conferences connected with marketing research. She has sat on numerous committees associated with the industry, is a member of the MRS Awards Judging Panel and an Honorary Member of the Market Research Society.

Richard Webber is Managing Director of CCN Marketing having joined the company in January 1986 from CACI. He has been involved in the use of census statistics for targeting for the last twelve years and was one of the early pioneers in the development of the geodemographics industry in the UK, having developed both the ACORN and MOSAIC segmentation systems.

Len Tiu Wright is a Lecturer in the Department of Commerce at Birmingham University. Prior to this she was a Lecturer in Marketing and Market Research at

Loughborough University of Technology and a Senior Lecturer in Marketing at Coventry Polytechnic. She has also held teaching posts and visiting lectureships at other educational establishments. She has been employed in marketing in a variety of industries. She has a doctorate in marketing and has carried out overseas research with marketing directors and senior managers of multinational firms in Britain, Japan, the United States and the Far East. Her main interests have centred on international marketing, management and marketing research.

CHAPTER 1

An introduction to the marketing research process

This introductory chapter explains the marketing research process and the organisation of the chapters in the book. Background on the market research industry and the contribution of information technology are also given.

1.1 What is marketing research?

The Market Research Society (MRS) explains research as:

> the collection and analysis of data from a sample of individuals or organisations relating to their characteristics, behaviour, attitudes, opinions or possessions. It includes all forms of marketing and social research such as consumer and industrial surveys, psychological investigations, observational and panel studies. (MRS 1994:8)

The American Marketing Association (AMA) views marketing research as:

> Marketing research is the function which links the consumer, customer, and public to the market through information – information used to identify and define marketing opportunities and problems; generate, refine, and evaluate marketing actions; monitor marketing performance; and improve understanding of marketing as a process. Marketing research specifies the information required to address these issues; designs the method for collecting information; manages and implements the data collection process; analyses the results; and communicates the findings and their implications. (*Marketing News* 1985:1)

It can be seen from the above explanations that the terms market research and marketing research have become interchangeable in their scope and coverage of information about customers and the marketplace. That is, they cover the processes by which information on customers and their product needs and usage is gathered and analysed by research suppliers on behalf of their clients.

The primary contribution of marketing research is the acquisition and analysis of information pertinent to managerial decision-making in the appraisal of markets. As more organisations embrace the marketing concept with its focus on organisational resources and activities to satisfy the needs and wants of customers, so the scope for marketing research increases. When market conditions change, as with the application of technologies in the evolution of products and their servicing requirements, these changes have implications for the market research industry and its clients.

Market conditions can change due to a variety of reasons, such as changes in consumption patterns and consumer purchasing levels, entry or exit of competitors from markets and the impact of new technologies on the evolvement of new products. Research and development by companies on the 'convergence' of different technologies in telecommunications, computing, television, information and publishing (multi-media) will affect not only these industries but also other industries and customers using the products emerging from multi-media developments. Marketing research performs an important function in supplying organisations with up-to-date information on customer needs and dynamic market conditions.

The nature of marketing research will vary between different types of organisations, and between the non-profit and profit sectors. As an example, members of universities and medical foundations will pursue basic (fundamental) research to further their frontiers of knowledge on marketing related issues whilst profit-motivated companies will 'apply research' in order to examine the implications of management decisions taken in the marketplace. The methods of research and data gathering have to be capable of being validated to avoid bias and subjective evaluations of customers and markets (Chisnall 1992; Kinnear and Taylor 1991). This is because mistakes are costly for organisations in their time and resources spent on product development and services, and on supporting them in the marketplace. So the marketing research process is designed with the purpose of providing information which can be useful in all its stages to client organisations in their decision-making about their markets.

1.2 Synopsis of the marketing research process

Figure 1.1 sets out the framework for the marketing research process and the type of activities associated with each of the stages. It should be borne in mind that while the activities have been shown in 'stages' for the organisation of the book and are intended as a guide, organisations vary in the efforts which they expend on marketing research.

A typical starting point for the research process is the problem definition stage

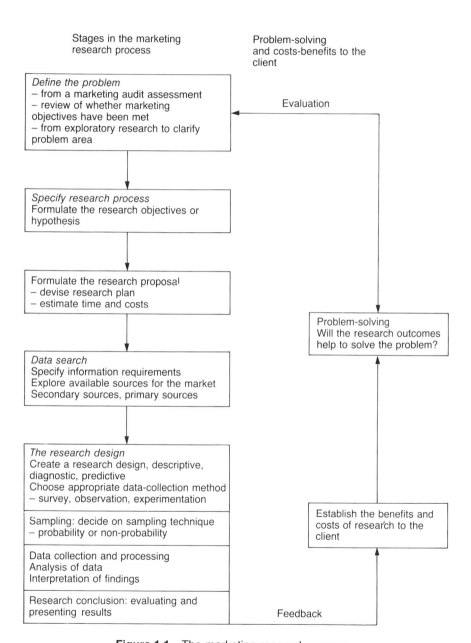

Figure 1.1   The marketing research process

which sets out what choices an organisation is faced with in its marketing activities in a particular situation and what it wants to achieve or to solve. Exploratory research can be used to assess whether marketing objectives have been met.

Most companies have periodic and systematic formal marketing audits which are undertaken to give an assessment of their internal and external business environments (for descriptions of marketing audits see Berkowitz *et al.* (1994) and McDonald (1992) in Further Reading). A strengths, weaknesses, opportunities and threats (SWOT) analysis can supplement the audit to determine the strengths and weaknesses of the organisation commissioning the research and to identify opportunities and threats to its business from external environmental forces (e.g. political, economic and social forces). Such activities assist companies commissioning market surveys to clarify the problem areas for research and to set out their research objectives.

Problem definition does not necessarily have to be about identifying threats to a company's business and how to resolve them. A company can be faced with how to plan its growth because of the desire to diversify into new products or new markets, or to acquire new brands and new distribution outlets by merging with or acquiring other companies. Such changes to a company's marketing efforts or operational status will require new studies of its market to be carried out since previous information may become inadequate or inappropriate in the changed circumstances. In this context, new research objectives will have to be set. These should be clear, measurable and achievable.

An example of a research objective can be to establish whether there is an opportunity for a new brand in a particular product field. Research investigations can then be carried out on a brand name for a product and the associations which potential customers can make towards the brand image. The brand image can then be developed in advertisements and in all the other communications associated with the product, including its packaging for the market. The research proposal will contain an outline of the research requirements and the proposed creation of a systematic and logical research process including time and cost inputs. Careful planning in the initial stages of the research process will be of benefit in guiding decision-makers in problem-solving. The data search stage is important to determine information requirements critical to the problem at hand: why the information is sought for in the first place, where it may exist within the organisation and outside of it, and whether questions asked can be answered from the research outcomes. Sources of information are considered at length in Chapters 2, 3 and 4.

The research design consists of choosing the survey method to be adopted, sampling, data collection, analysis, interpretation and evaluation of findings and the presentation of research work to a client organisation. The research design stages are set out at the beginning of Chapter 5 and explained there.

The cost and benefits of the research to the client company can be evaluated and monitored over time to see whether the research outcomes have significantly aided the client company or organisation in its problem-solving. The monitoring function is important because it is aimed at reducing uncertainty when plans are being made (whether these relate to the marketing operation as a whole or to individual components, as in advertising) and keeping an account of performance after the plans have been implemented.

Evaluation of the research outcomes is an important part in helping to assess whether the financial and human resources used have met the expectations of the decision-makers from the client organisation. If the research activities have been useful in helping them in various ways (e.g. meeting the objectives for problem-solving, re-formulation of marketing plans and strategies, adaptation of their marketing campaigns for segmentation, product differentiation and positioning purposes in the effective application of the elements in their marketing mixes), then the process of research would have been invaluable.

1.3 What role does marketing research have?

These activities enable marketing research to perform several key roles within the marketing system. These roles are descriptive, diagnostic and predictive.

1. Descriptive research provides historic and current data on consumer and organisational markets and their marketing environments. For example, descriptive data are provided on the market sizes and sales turnover of firms, emerging technologies, competitor profiles and changes in market environments (e.g. Mintel's periodic publications on the machine tool industry).
2. Diagnostic research gives new insights into problem-solving such as cause and effect relationships on the impact of marketing strategies and their marketing mixes on target markets. For example, manufacturers of food and drink products commission market research agencies to assess the effectiveness of their promotional campaigns on their consumers, or they can buy into omnibus surveys. The Target Group Index Survey in this field is an example. Consumer attitudes, lifestyle needs, purchasing behaviour and disposable incomes are researched.
3. Predictive research seeks to identify new opportunities in the marketplace and to forecast the outcomes of planned marketing decisions. For example, predictive research into new customer requirements can be undertaken for new products and services developed for the health and fitness, electronic video games and cellular telecommunications markets. New industries with emerging technologies require a reorientation and refinement of market analysis modelling and research techniques.

The marketing research process is important because information on customers and conditions in the marketplace has to be gathered and evaluated. Normally the collection and feedback of information is an ongoing necessity for companies and is carried out by their marketing departments and sales forces. Organisational data such as accounts and orders plus feedback from sales representatives are useful sources of market intelligence, especially in industrial markets where there is a heavier reliance on personal selling rather than on mass advertising. However, information derived from a company's existing sales records and its own representatives' reports will not in themselves be enough to enable an organisation to focus effectively on the following:

- The behaviour, attitudes and needs of the consumers in its market.
- The behaviour, attitudes and needs of the intermediaries on whom it relies to make its goods available to consumers.
- The activities of competitors and the response of consumers and intermediaries to these activities.

This is because whilst the managers of an organisation can control its marketing mixes, there are forces in the external environment (listed in section 1.4) over which they have little control. Managers can vary the price, product, promotion and place (distribution) elements in their marketing mixes, but changes in the marketplace will occur as old customers drop out and new ones enter due to changes in their customers' circumstances, such as changes in consumption and purchasing patterns. Marketing research has an essential role to play in providing managers with vital information which will help them to focus their marketing planning efforts and to understand the environmental forces which influence their company's target markets.

1.4 Focus on the market

The health of the company largely depends on the capacity of its management to interpret the needs, attitudes and behaviour of its consumers and industrial buyers who make up its markets. Moreover, in a mixed economy the capacity of a company to raise funds by public subscription to finance its activities is dependent on investors' confidence in its present market performance and its future business projections. By using marketing research to diagnose the needs and wants of its customers, the management of a company can alter the company's marketing mixes in response to marketing intelligence reports on changes in the marketing environment, which can have good, indifferent or determined effects on its business. If research and marketing are fully integrated, radical and unexpected changes of plan can be avoided.

External forces beyond the control of a company include the following:

- Economic trends.
- Government action.
- Changes in the law.

- Technological developments.
- Social and cultural changes.
- Demographic changes.
- Competitors' activities.
- Physical terrain, geographical dispersements of population and climatic changes.

These are sometimes listed as political, economic, social and technological forces, from which the convenient mnemonic PEST may be derived.

The challenge, then, for a firm is to recognise the potential effects of these external forces and to interpret their impact on its business. This helps a firm to be more 'proactive', that is, to anticipate customer requirements and to focus its marketing efforts more effectively in the marketplace, as opposed to being 'reactive' to market developments. The reactive approach can mean a firm losing its competitive advantage to an aggressive competitor which is forging ahead to gain market share at its expense.

1.5 Consumer and organisational markets

What information do organisations need about their markets and from whom do they gather their information? Most companies depend on buying decisions made by a large number of individuals spread over a wide area, increasingly in more than one country. Companies will be in direct contact with these individuals if they use mail order, or direct door-to-door selling methods such as those used by Avon Cosmetics and Great Universal Stores. For many products sold to mass markets, intermediaries are used. For example, all the competing chocolate manufacturers in the British market, i.e. Cadburys, Mars and Rowntree-Mackintosh (Nestlé), sell their chocolates through similar retail multiples such as Woolworths.

Companies can sell direct to retail organisations, such as Tesco and Curry's which control the outlets where their products are bought. They can also sell via wholesalers or voluntary groups of wholesalers, such as Mace and Spar, which break bulk and pass goods on to their members' outlets. By using feedback in their supply, distribution and retailing facilities, companies gather vital socio-economic and demographic information about their customers through their intermediaries and through their own marketing and sales functions. They also gather information about the way their products are bought and used, and how their customers perceive their companies' corporate image and brands.

Companies can also commission market research agencies to design market experiments and to build marketing models to test the frequency with which products are bought (this is explained further in Chapter 10). Consumer goods may belong to the category of those which are used up quickly, such as ice-cream, detergents and toothpaste, in which case they are classified as fast-moving consumer goods; or they may be more durable and infrequently bought such as motor cars, washing machines and power tools for DIY, and thus classified as consumer durables. For fast-moving consumer goods repeat purchases are a very important consideration, as well as ensuring the products are tried by a large number of buyers.

Industrial goods fall into three categories:

1. Materials (e.g. timber) and parts (e.g. timing devices).
2. Capital items (e.g. generators).
3. Supplies (e.g. lubricants) and services (e.g. advertising and transport).

Businesses are also interested in the frequency with which goods are bought when planning research in industrial markets. Success in marketing goods in categories (1) and (3) depends on repeat purchase as well as penetration, while items in category (2) are infrequently bought by any one customer. The nature of derived demand is such that in an industrial market the ultimate consumer may be some stages away but there are industrial markets in which the ultimate consumer is close at hand. Therefore companies need to study the behaviour of consumers who are end-users as well as the behaviour of their major industrial customers. The effective demand for timing devices is influenced by the dynamics of demand for motor cars, cooking stoves or washing machines, all of which incorporate timing devices in their mechanisms.

Non-profit-making organisations such as universities, local authorities, government corporations, major charities such as Oxfam and consumer watch-dog bodies such as the Consumers' Association also need to have information concerning their markets and how their products and services are received by their customers. Consumer perceptions of quality of service and value for money affect the levels of their voluntary donations to charities, or in the cases of taxpayers, the number of election votes cast for political parties. Public accountability therefore involves non-profit-making organisations in making quality assessments of what they provide (e.g. the Conservative Government's Citizens' Charter 1993) (*Economist* 1993). Trade associations carry out regular surveys on their industries for their members, for example, the Motor Industry Trade Association and the Machine Tool Technologies Association. The Confederation of British Industry takes soundings from its members and publishes annual updates on business confidence which are printed in the media. Both profit and non-profit-making organisations require feedback from their customers, members or their publics making marketing research important in helping them to improve upon their levels of provision of products and services.

The following sections on the stages in the marketing research process will be helpful to some as a map of the route to be followed in this book. However, the overview is condensed and others may prefer to proceed to section 1.7 on the market research industry.

1.6 Overview of the book

The focus of the book is on the marketing research process as indicated in Figure 1.1 and the activities associated with it. In addition there is the benefit of contributions from authors in their specialist fields. Chapter 1 sets the framework and the broad scope for the marketing research process, and provides the background material with reference to the market research industry and developments in information technology. Chapters 2, 3 and 4 look at the issues and considerations involved in designing research for domestic and overseas markets, the type of data required and the sources of data available. Chapters 5, 6 and 7 concentrate on the terms and techniques used in investigating markets and designing samples and questionnaires. Chapters 8 and 9 examine segmentation and geodemographic profiling for investigating and targeting prospective customer groups in order to reach them with the appropriate products and services. Chapters 10, 11 and 12 present the specific methods for pre-testing markets under experimental conditions and modelling applications. Chapters 13 and 14 take the research process to the final stage of reaching, informing and persuading customers through the media with the examination of media planning, the sources of media data available and the evaluation of pre-testing and post-testing in advertising research. The book concludes with a consideration of quality issues in the provision of products and services with examples of the benefits of research in improving customer satisfaction.

Exploring the market and data search (Chapter 2) This chapter on exploratory research considers the methods of data collection and in what detail topics need to be treated at the initial stage of the research process. The method adopted to collect the data will largely depend on the nature of the data required, the characteristics of the survey population, budget and time available.

International marketing research (Chapter 3) From the domestic to the international environment, this chapter examines the environmental variables and issues in the research process for international markets. The reader is taken through the design and stages of research work which show the practical application.

New data sources for marketing research (Chapter 4) This is concerned with information technology and its importance to the marketing research process with a wide use of examples drawn from government and industry sources.

Research design procedure and choices (Chapter 5) A summary of the research design choices is given secondary and primary investigations which include methods of observation, laboratory and field experimentation. Methods for the gathering and analysis of data are explained, as are the stages in the research design process; this is followed by examples of applications in the field.

Sampling in survey research (Chapter 6) It is necessary in survey research to know how the population can be stratified and whether some strata (groups) are more meaningful for various research activities than others (e.g. using quota sampling). If a minority group looks as if it will be significant, the sample must include a sufficient number of its members to justify singling the group out for separate consideration. Stratification which takes into account the relative business import- ance of groups based on volume of production or turnover for organisational markets is also considered.

Questionnaire design (Chapter 7) Asking the 'right' kind of questions and designing an appropriate questionnaire for the survey to be undertaken are of critical importance to the research outcome. This chapter looks at how question- naires can be designed and the 'art' of asking questions.

Developing a branded product or service (Chapter 8) The importance of the pre-testing stage for developing a branded product or service under experimental conditions is examined with practical examples. Ideas, or concepts, for products to meet the need that has been located are tried out on target groups using qualitative and quantitative methods. Ways of advertising the brand are likely to be tried out at the same time.

Establishing the brand identity and pre-testing the whole (Chapter 9) In consumer markets advertising is the most important means of communicating the characteris- tics of the new brand to prospective buyers and users. Other means of communication are public relations, promotions and, particularly significant in industrial markets, the sales force. We concentrate on advertising research in this chapter because here the need to reduce uncertainty is greatest and considerable value to a brand can be added. Repeat purchase data derived from consumers' panels enable market simulation models to be established and brand-share predictions to be made.

Modelling techniques for product prediction and planning (Chapter 10) A consideration of the issues in product prediction and planning with the use of micro behavioural models is presented. The strategic implications for new product development in estimating demand potential, positioning and forecasting product volume are discussed along with the research methods for mini-tests, laboratory tests and calibrated tests.

Segmenting markets (Chapter 11) The importance of market segmentation in the research process is to define and locate a target group of consumers or users who have an unsatisfied need which could be met by a branded product. Classifications of consumer and product groups are discussed and their significance for marketing activity.

Geodemographic profiling: MOSAIC and EuroMOSAIC (Chapter 12) MOSAIC is a sophisticated geodemographic system based on the electronic analysis of census and other government data. This chapter contribution from CCN explains in practical terms how geodemographic analyses with MOSAIC and EuroMOSAIC are used to define target groups in markets and to specify the characteristics of customer types within these groups for product purchases and usage, with strategic implications for organisations.

Media planning for conveying the brand message to markets (Chapter 13) The wealth of shared-cost data for media planning relating to the main media categories (television, newspapers, magazines) and the support media (radio, outdoor and cinema) are discussed.

The effectiveness of the research effort for developing the media plan cannot be measured until the advertising campaign has been launched. Syndicated retail-audit data are also discussed as a guide to making channel decisions.

Optimising advertising effectiveness (Chapter 14) This chapter focuses on how a market research supplier (Millward Brown) and its client organisation (Direct Line Insurance) created and positioned a new brand with a unique price advantage in the market. Through the case study method, the research programme incorporating quantified pre-testing, modelling and 'tracking studies' of advertisements are detailed to show how advertising effectiveness can be optimised through research.

Quality issues in market research (Chapter 15) The book concludes with a chapter on the measurements of quality perception and customer satisfaction. With the increasing sophistication in research techniques and the way in which products and services are presented to customers (as shown in the earlier chapters), formal recognition of quality standards and customer satisfaction as organisational necessities have also become more important. This chapter addresses many of the issues in this field.

1.7 The marketing research industry

1.7.1 Size and scope of research activity

Organisations buy research data from different types of market research suppliers and commission research work in a variety of ways. Syndicated continuous panel services and other large-scale shared-cost surveys will typically be bought from one of the member companies belonging to the Association of Market Survey Organisations (AMSO). AMSO was founded in 1964 and is the largest trade organisation for market research companies in the United Kingdom.

1.7.2 Sales turnover and areas researched

Companies have been amalgamating in the research field, and the marketing research (MR) industry includes some very substantial operators offering a wide range of research services. In 1992, the largest companies in AMSO had turnovers

Table 1.1   AMSO's 'league table' for 1992: research
turnovers by company

Rank order by UK turnover	1992 turnover £000s	Change % 1991–2
1. Taylor Nelson AGB plc[1]	49,867	−0.9
2. Nielsen[2]	43,732	+14.0
3. MAI Research Ltd	31,952	+2.0
4. Millward Brown	27,400	+17.4
5. Research International Ltd	26,272	+23.4
6. BMRB International Ltd	18,938	+6.2
7. Research Services Ltd (RSL)	14,155	+39.6
8. The Research Business Group Ltd[1]	12,078	+27.8
9. MORI	10,138	+12.0
10. The MBL Group plc	7,383	+18.4
11. The Harris Research Centre	6,874	+8.4
12. Infratest Burke Group Ltd	5,294	+4.1

exceeding £5 million as shown in Table 1.1 from the Association of Market Survey Organisations (AMSO) Annual Report 1993.

Table 1.1 shows the 1992 sales turnover of the twelve leading market research companies together with the percentage change in turnover compared with 1991. The relative positions of the larger companies in the 'League Table' remained unchanged except for Taylor Nelson, owing to its acquisition of AGB at the end of 1991. Member companies of AMSO make up the major part of the UK research industry and many of their employees are also members of the Market Research Society. In 1992, AMSO members earned £239.3 million from domestic research (8.1 per cent up on 1991 earnings) and £53.7 million from overseas research (11.3 per cent up on 1991 earnings).

As shown in Table 1.2, research commissioned by organisations in the fast-moving consumer goods (fmcg) sector for food and non-alchoholic drinks provided the strongest source of revenues for AMSO members at £47.4 million in 1992.

While some marketing research companies provide a wide range of services, others specialise in particular marketing applications: for example, in product, packaging, pricing or communications research, an organisation (as the client) may have occasion to commission one of these specialist market research companies. The client organisation may choose to plan its own research programme and then buy fieldwork from a specialist market research company. The data may then come back to the client organisation as computer print-outs from an agency specialising in electronic data processing. Translating the data into a report and recommendations is then the sole responsibility of the client organisation.

The two data-collection methods most commonly used in qualitative research are depth interviews and group discussions. These are also used in industrial and other 'non-domestic' enquiries where the interviewer is often seeking information

Table 1.2 Areas researched by
AMSO (1992)

Food and non-alcoholic drinks (−9%)
Media (+9%)
Public services, utilities (+15%)
Health and beauty (+16%)
Alcoholic drinks (+5%)
Government public bodies (+29%)
Pharmaceuticals (+25%)
Financial services (+9%)
Vehicles (+1%)
Business and industrial (+11%)
Advertising agencies (+7%)
Household products (+38%)
Retailers (+24%)
Travel and tourism (+31%)
Household durables, hardware (+80%)
Tobacco (+8%)
Oil (−17%)
Other direct clients
Within AMSO companies*
Mainly sub-contracted fieldwork

Note: *the percentage in brackets for
1992 denotes the rise or fall from 1991
figures.
Source: AMSO (1993) Annual Report
(reprinted with permission).

Table 1.3 Data-collection methods by value

Personal interview 54%

Telephone interview 16%

Hall test 11%

Group discussion 10%

Self-completion/postal 9%

Source: AMSO (1993) Annual Report (reprinted with permission).

from an expert. This use of these methods has not significantly changed by 1994
since the personal interview method is most commonly carried out in the United
Kingdom and in Europe, in contrast to the United States where telephone
interviews are widely used. Around 13.5 million interviews are carried out each
year in the United Kingdom by AMSO members and the data-collection methods
are shown in Table 1.3.

The services offered by research agencies are set out in the Market Research
Society (MRS) *Yearbook* (1994). The *Yearbook*, updated annually, is a wide-
ranging and essential source of information about the market research industry. It
will be seen that all the large companies include syndicated services in their product

line. These make a major contribution to turnover (as shown in Table 1.1) contributing to the leading performance of companies such as Taylor Nelson Audits of Great Britain (TN AGB) and Nielsen, the latter a subsidiary of Dun and Bradstreet.

Data collected during the course of retail audits, consumer panels, tracking studies and omnibus surveys (all of which feature in this book) constitute rich databases. In-house computer terminals linked to a host bureau's mainframe computer, make it possible for a client organisation to access a number of databases provided that it subscribes to the services filed in the host's databank. Donovan Data Systems provides such a service to advertisers.

1.8 Impact of information technology

1.8.1 Acquisition and examination of research data

Computerisation has speeded up enormously the gathering, examination, storage and retrieval of research data. The cost of computer hardware has decreased while both the proliferation of computer hardware and business software applications by firms have increased.

Major innovations will be met as this book follows the marketing research process, but the following are some examples of the impact of information technology on the market research industry.

- The use of interactive television/telephone/cable/satellite technologies has ushered in the development of interactive optical media, videotex, ceefax, teletext, video phone, multimedia home banking and shopping by video link to enable customers and companies to make contact with each other in addition to the traditional ordering systems by post and telephone. Market researchers have to make the effort to keep up with developments in telecommunications and information technologies as they affect both their clients and their clients' customers in these industries, and also the speed, accuracy and handling of the market researchers' information.
- Computer-assisted telephone interviewing (CATI) and push-button handsets (peoplemeters) are effective examples to illustrate how widespread access to the telephone and television have enhanced the gathering and recording of market research data. Instead of ringing code numbers manually on a questionnaire, the use of CATI means that the interviewer reads the question on the computer monitor over the telephone and the respondent's pre-coded answers are keyed straight into a computer. Peoplemeters capture the television viewing habits of the individuals in a household, saving the individual viewer on a panel from the need to keep a diary, thus reducing error and accelerating data capture.

- Bar coding of products with electronic point of sale (EPOS) systems means that retailers are able to record on a daily basis the products and their value sold through their checkouts. By using the cash register to enter the value and by passing the bar-coded product over the scanner at the check-out, the retail sales assistant is feeding information to a control computer. This records the sale for stock checking and calculation of the customer's bill with change given for cash transactions released automatically. Taylor Nelson Audits of Great Britain (TN AGB) and Nielsen make use of electronic data capture of coded products sold across scanners in major grocery outlets which is then matched to consumer purchasing panels. Their work provides key insights into the seasonality of purchases, competition between companies and their products, the effects of changes in prices, costs and promotions, and customer traffic density in stores.
- The computer makes it possible to relate together data from diverse sources. Using the postcodes recorded on computer files, it is possible to 'flush out' and locate consumer targets in a market. Electronic data processing has made possible the rapid scrutiny of relationships between the many population variables, for example, census data (the last census was in 1991).
- Customer database planning is driving the way in which companies market and service their products. For example, financial services institutions have the benefit of possessing their own databases containing highly detailed information personal to their existing customers. In addition organisations can also subscribe to commercial databases, e.g. the Target Group Index (TGI) to help them identify customer characteristics from the most profitable market segments, and prospect for new customers with similar characteristics. The TGI operated by the British Market Research Bureau (BRMB) draws on samples of more than 24,000 adults a year to ascertain the product usage of heavy, medium, light and non-users for a wide range of products in many markets. Companies subscribing to the TGI's services buy in the information they need relating to their own markets.
- The computer's capacity to handle calculations and relationships between data types enhances the superimposition of geodemographic classifications. These are geographical locations combined with population characteristics and lifestyle categorisations of customers. Such computer software information or geodemographic classifications are regularly updated and widely available from computer databases held by media owners, market research companies and software bureau providers. For example, geodemographic systems are produced by CACI's classification of residential neighbourhoods (ACORN), Pinpoint's Finpin, CDMS SuperProfiles and CCN's MOSAIC.

The benefits of information technology for organisations include:

1. *Efficiency*. Making more efficient use of the valuable resource in customer data for storage, electronic access to retrieval and updating of customer information, matching customers' purposes to a company's products and cross-selling for other products.

2. *Problem-solving*. Enhancing a faster response time to demand, handling of orders and resolving customer and supplier problems.
3. *Improved marketing*. Facilitating the improved positioning of products to customer targets to enhance short-term sales and profits.
4. *In the long term*. Achieving long-term competitive advantage through the integration and control of critical information relating to the customer interface with an organisation's operations to make it easier and speedier for customers to do business with it and vice versa.

1.8.2 The MRS code of practice

The issue of customer confidentiality has to be treated sensitively to avoid infringing on the rights and privacy of individuals and organisations. Members of the Market Research Society are expected to abide by the MRS Code of Conduct (1994) (extract in Box 1.1 reprinted with permission) which provides an ethical basis by which the privacy of members of the public and the confidentiality of organisations are respected.

The Code of Conduct provides useful guidelines because market research depends on the collection and storage of personal information provided by individuals which is protected by the Data Protection Act of 1984. This Act relates to 'any file of personal data capable of being processed automatically' – 'personal' meaning any information relating to a living individual which allows you to identify that individual. Further, a 'data user' is anyone who controls the contents and use of personal data. It is as well for the MR industry that the habit of protecting the individual's privacy is well ingrained. In fact the Act is more beneficial to the industry than it is harmful, for it makes it more difficult for bogus organisations to sell under the guise of conducting research.

1.9 External liaison

The MRS liaises with a number of associations representing special research interests. For further particulars please see the 'Useful addresses' section of the *MRS Yearbook*. For example, the Market and Social Research Liaison Group consists of the representatives from the Market Research Society and from the following:

- Association of British Market Research Companies (ABMRC).
- Association of Market Survey Organisations (AMSO).
- Accounts Planning Group (APG).
- Association of Qualitative Research Practitioners (AQRP).
- Association of Users of Research Agencies (AURA).
- Social Research Association (SRA).

Box 1.1 The MRS Code of Conduct

This Code of Conduct was agreed by the Market Research Society to be operative from January 1993. It is an amended version of a self-regulatory code that has been in existence since 1954.

The Code of Conduct is designed to support all those engaged in marketing or social research in maintaining professional standards throughout the industry. Assurance that research is conducted in an ethical manner is needed to create confidence in, and to encourage co-operation among the business community, the general public and others.

Relationship with the Data Protection Act
Adherence to the Code of Conduct will help to ensure that research is conducted in accordance with the principles of data protection encompassed by the Data Protection act. It is a requirement of membership of these bodies that researchers must ensure that their conduct follows the letter and spirit of the principles of Data Protection from the Act. These eight principles are:

The first principle The information to be contained in personal data shall be obtained, and personal data shall be processed, fairly and lawfully.

The second principle Personal data shall be held only for one or more specified and lawful purposes.

The third principle Personal data held for any purpose or purposes shall not be used or disclosed in any manner incompatible with that purpose or those purposes.

The fourth principle Personal data held for any purpose or purposes shall be adequate, relevant and not excessive in relation to that purpose or those purposes.

The fifth principle Personal data shall be accurate and, where necessary, kept up to date.

The sixth principle Personal data held for any purpose or purposes shall not be kept for longer than is necessary for that purpose or those purposes.

The seventh principle An individual shall be entitled:

a)   at reasonable intervals and without undue delay or expense:
  i)   to be informed by any data user whether he/she holds personal data of which that individual is the subject;
       and
  ii) to access any such data held by a data user; and
b)   where appropriate, to have such data corrected or erased.

The eighth principle Appropriate security measures shall be taken against unauthorised access to, or alteration, disclosure or destruction of personal data and against accidental loss or destruction of personal data.   →

From time to time guidance notes applying to the Eight Principles are published by the Data Protection Registry – Guideline 4 is of particular relevance to market research and fair obtaining of data.

Members should note that as from 1990, there is now an exclusive Method 2 Purpose for registering systems used for holding and processing any applicable data under the heading of Confidential Survey Research. Members using this new Purpose will need to write in the exact wording shown below in the appropriate place on the registration form. Confidential Survey Research is defined as:

Confidential survey research
Academic, market or other survey research including the collection and analysis of personal data, with no disclosure of identifiable personal details about survey respondents to any third party (including any client for the research) and no use of the personal data for anything other than statistical and research purposes.

Full details of how to register or re-register under this new Purpose are available from the MRS. Members should note that registration under the Method 2 purpose 'Confidential Survey Research' will exempt a company from its obligation to fulfil the Seventh Principle.

In order to help members keep within the Data Protection Act, a Guide to Good Practice is also available from the MRS.

Relationship with other codes
This code is compatible with the codes of AMSO (Association of Market Survey Organisation), and the ICC/ESOMAR International Code of Marketing and Social Research Practice.

1.10 Membership of the MRS

Most of those who work in market research are members of the Market Research Society. The Society is a professional body based on individual membership. It is not a trade association. The MRS was founded in 1947 and now has around 7,000 members. One or more types of data-collection method used by researcher suppliers include, for example, computer aided research, continuous consumer panels, executive interviewing, face-to-face interviewers, hall tests, observation, omnibus surveys, postal panel surveys, qualitative methods, retail audits, telephone interviews, and viewing facilities for in-door experiments and focus group discussions.

1.11 The MRS Diploma and Certificate

Details of both the Diploma and Certificate entry requirements, syllabus contents and examination details are available from the MRS approved centre at the Leicester Business School, Bosworth House, DeMontfort University, The Gateway, Leicester, LE1 9BH (Tel: 0533-551551) (Phillips 1994).

Over 12 per cent of the MRS total membership and a third of new members are diploma holders. For anyone studying or working in market research, the 'publications' of the MRS are given in Appendix 4.

References

Association of Market Survey Organisations (1993), Annual Report, pp. 4–5.

Chisnall, P. (1992) *Marketing Research*, Maidenhead: McGraw-Hill, p. 6.

The Economist (1993) 'The Britain audit: government', March/April, pp. 26, 29.

Kinnear, T. and Taylor, J. (1991) *Marketing Research*, USA: McGraw-Hill, p. 6.

Marketing News (1985) 'AMA board approves new marketing definitions', 1 March, p. 1.

Marketing News (1987) 'New marketing research definition approved', 2 January, pp. 1, 14.

Market Research Society (1994) *Code of Conduct*, January, pp. 3–5, 8.

MRS Yearbook (1994).

Phillips, H. (1994) On the MRS Diploma and Certificate courses at De Montfort University, verbal statement to one of the authors.

Further reading

Berkowitz, E., Kerin, A., Hartley, S. and Williams, R. (1994) *Marketing* (4th edn), Itaska, IL: R. Irwin, pp. 630–2.

Financial Times (1993) 'Computers in manufacturing', Survey, 18 October.

Financial Times (1994) 'A–Z of Computing', Survey, 26 April pp. 1–20.

McDonald, M. (1992) *Marketing Plans: How to prepare them, how to use them*, Oxford: Butterworth Heinemann.

McKiernan, P. (1992) *Strategies of Growth*, London: Routledge, pp. 3–15.

Tapscott, D. and Coston, A. (1993) *Paradigm Shift: The new promise of information technology*, USA: McGraw-Hill.

CHAPTER 2

Exploring the market and data search

The exploratory phase sets the stage for a company to investigate its assumptions about its market and the level and topics of consumer interest relevant to these assumptions. It is possible to have the best of both approaches: to collect the ideas at the exploratory stage and then to design a survey which quantifies the significant ones.

2.1 Why the exploratory stage is important

The exploratory stage is important because it is necessary to establish what is already on record about the market of interest and the kind of product envisaged. As we shall see, most markets are well documented: there is a wealth of information, both statistical and literary, stored in databanks, while on-line information systems make it possible to access these data without long and laborious searches through journals, published reports and newspapers. However, the available data may not focus closely enough on the product market in question and the decision may be taken to commission an *ad hoc* survey. For example, banks have their own extensive customer databases but *ad hoc* market research is still required to give feedback to the banks on the advertising and promotion of their products, their corporate image and to enable the banks to develop new products.

When Midland Bank launched a 24 hour, 365 day banking facility through its subsidiary, First Direct in 1989, it established the United Kingdom's first person-to-person tele-banking service. Exploratory market research to find out what customers wanted from such a service included the use of postal questionnaires sent to employed professional men and women on its database. The findings helped the bank to design a more efficient, convenient and better value facility to conduct its savings, mortgages, loan accounts and payment systems for customers of First Direct. Exploratory market research had helped the Midland Bank to successfully establish a new market niche and at the same time to satisfy customer perceptions about its advertised corporate image as 'the listening bank'.

A case study example of market research into advertising campaigns conducted by Millward Brown on behalf of Direct Line, a UK leading motor insurer and subsidiary company of the Royal Bank of Scotland, is included in Chapter 14. A *Financial Times* article (1994b:24) reported that with pre-tax profits of £40.5 million by May 1994 representing a nearly three-fold increase from the previous year, Direct Line's growth was attributable to its competitive price rating structure and marketing activities.

In exploratory research, in order to describe the varying habits and attitudes of different groups in the population, it is necessary to break the sample down. If a minority group looks like it may be of particular interest, then the sample design must provide for the collection of data from a sufficient number of consumers in this group. Statistical data are required about the population in order to design the sample.

Similarly with the topics of interest, in order to design the questionnaire or any other data-collection instrument, it is necessary to have explored consumer behaviour and attitudes with regard to the type of products and brands available and the context in which these are used, such as motoring, clothes washing, do-it-yourself, etc. The designer of the survey risks two 'sins': the *sin of omission* – not treating a topic in sufficient detail, or failing to include sufficient respondents in a group which has marketing significance; and the *sin of commission* – collecting data which prove to be immaterial or unactionable, or breaking the sample down to a wasteful extent. It would, for example, be wasteful to provide for a breakdown of the sample into four social classes where two would be sufficient, as in many fast-moving product fields. Companies do not have the means to cover the entire national population, that is, to conduct a census. In any case, a well-constructed sample can bring in results which are as relevant to a company's needs as those of a census.

What information requirements should be included in the design of a cost-effective survey? Exploratory research will indicate what available data relating to the following are needed:

- The parameters of the survey population.
- The ideas held by this population about the product field.
- Ideas about the brands available in the product field.

In order to define the parameters of the survey population, quantifiable data are required relating to geographic, demographic and socio-economic variables. For example, in industrial markets data are required about the location, concentration and dispersion of organisational establishments, their economic activity, size and composition. Likewise in consumers' markets, data are required about the location, types of dwelling and the composition of households with reference to income, occupation, age, sex, race, education and religion. A sample based upon a representation of the population to be surveyed can then be constructed.

The attitudes held by a sample of the population about a given product field, for example, fast-moving consumer goods, can be investigated. It is essential to obtain quantitative data about the perceptions, motivations and purchasing behaviour of the family and industrial decision-making units. Data can also be gathered concerning the types, costs and numbers of products bought or consumed.

The ideas about the manufacturers' brands available in the industrial or consumer market can be investigated through analysis of the customer purchases, behaviour, use of and attitudes to specific brands; their susceptibility to advertising, personal selling, discounts or sales promotions; the level of complexity in their buying decisions and their patronage of outlets selling the particular branded products.

A decision-making unit in an industrial establishment typically consists of a buyer or initiator, user, specifier and budget holder. For a household a decision-making unit is the head of household or the members of a household who normally undertake the control of the buying process for the specific product in question.

In their *Principles of Marketing*, Kotler and Armstrong give a definition of the marketing research process which takes into account the importance of informed conjectural and systematic procedures in research design:

> The Marketing research process consists of these four steps: defining
> the problem and research objectives, developing the research plan,
> implementing the research plan and reporting the findings. (1994:110)

In order to clarify and define the problem area and the research objectives, the research planner undertakes exploratory research or investigates a fertile opportunity to obtain information in order to arrive at 'a set of assumptions' which can be employed to build the model on which the research design will be based. Within the model (see Figure 2.1) assumptions are made about the factors relevant to a given situation and the relationships of the variables. It is apparent that the more thorough the explanation and the better the quality of the information obtained, the firmer will be the assumptions made. The model depicted in Figure 2.1 examines the interrelationships between the independent variables (causes) and the dependent variables (effects). It also identifies the marketing mix decisions (controllable responses) and factors in the marketing environment (uncontrollable influences) which determine buyers' decisions. The information needed by marketing managers is obtainable from internal company records, marketing intelligence and marketing research.

2.2   The exploratory process

In our well-documented society it is difficult to envisage a market about which there is no information available in addition to the company's own records.

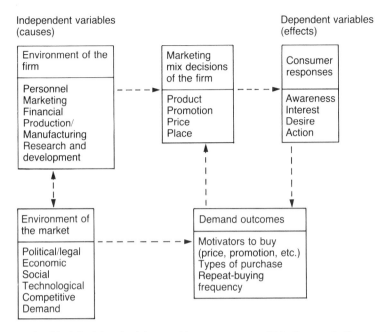

Figure 2.1 Model of the decision-making processes within the marketing system

Available information is called secondary data, while that derived from a new research study is called primary data. Since a search of secondary data takes place before the collection of primary data, use of the terms 'secondary' and 'primary' can be confusing.

The advantages of conducting secondary research first are that it avoids repeating work which may already have been carried out by others. It is unobtrusive research and is relatively inexpensive compared with primary or field research. Therefore, secondary research initially takes place before the collection of primary data in order to assess the availability of information and to arrive at the assumptions or hypotheses for primary research. It builds upon previous records and information, employing the wealth of data held in libraries and in the Department of Trade and Industry's 'Company House' in London or Cardiff. For a list of available sources of information and publications see Appendix 1 near the end of the book.

Exploratory research includes all or some of the following activities in the secondary and primary data searches:

1. *Secondary data search*:
    (a) examining internal organisational sources (e.g. organisational records);
    (b) finding available external publications, including statistics from government and syndicated sources.

2. *Primary data search*:
   (a) consulting experts who have their specialist knowledge about a particular industry;
   (b) observational studies monitoring behavioural patterns with or without the respondents' knowledge;
   (c) in observational studies;
   (d) consulting people in the market (by holding focus group discussions and by conducting depth interviews;
   (e) buying into an omnibus survey, as one of several firms contributing questions for survey research.

Let us take each of these exploratory activities in turn.

2.3 Secondary data search: internal sources

Internal sources can be divided into two categories: the company's operating records which Kotler called the internal accounting system (1994) and examining the reports on file, including research previously carried out by the company.

2.3.1 The operating records

These will cover subjects ranging from the cost of raw materials if this is a manufacturing company to sales of the company's output. Ex-works, transport costs, sales costs, advertising and other promotional expenditures are marketing costs to be set against sales revenue. Packaging and warehousing costs may also be regarded as marketing costs.

Whether or not the operating records are kept in such a way that they can be used to allocate marketing costs to specific branded products, and to help to monitor marketing performance, indicates whether the company is truly focused on the market. Records of this kind were originally designed to enable accountants to account for costs incurred and the sales manager or sales director to control the sales force. The detail and analysis needed for these purposes are not the same as the detail and analysis needed by a marketing director or brand manager striving to predict the contribution to profit likely to be made by a particular branded product or service.

Bar coding, the acquisition of computers and the availability of software systems developed by companies specialising in office automation can considerably improve the planning utility of a company's internal records. Many hardware and operating systems include IBM-type mainframe and personal computers and Apple Macintosh personal computers run desktop software such as Microsoft Windows and Lotus 1-2-3 for business use. For example, Verimation formed by Volvo in

Sweden in 1984 and in the United Kingdom in 1987 offers 'Memo' for electronic forms, work-flow management, bulletin boards and scheduling facilities. Unlimited licence for an IBM MVS mainframe costs £34,500.

Compulink Information Exchange, a UK company formed in 1987 offers a public bulletin board, conference system and electronic mail service, enabling users to send faxes from their personal computers with access to the worldwide 'Internet' service. While the 'paperless office' might still be far from reality for many companies, a *Financial Times* survey (1994a:12) reported that the market for 'groupware' (a combination of products covering the main office requirements of finding, using and communicating information) worth US$2.5 billion in products, consulting and training was set to rise.

Market research personnel, increasingly faced with developments in information technology, have to keep pace with the need to access data on-line at computer terminals from secondary sources at diverse company locations. Early office automation has progressed from word processing to far more complex products such as groupware, as *Financial Times* survey stated:

> The automatic storage and retrieval of document images by any
> number of people at the same time is a desirable part of many
> applications; incoming correspondence, forms, drawings and other
> documents which cannot be keyed in through word processor systems
> are scanned in to be held on disc and called to a screen in seconds
> rather than hunted down in a filing cabinet or on someone's desk.

2.3.2 Analysis by region

In consumer markets it is helpful if sales records can be related to television areas such as Central or London Weekend Television even if the company is not a television advertiser. Large companies tend to be television advertisers and the data generated by syndicated services (retail audits and consumer panels) are generally presented in this way. So are the statistics relating to readership of newspapers and magazines. In the case of industrial markets, sales are best recorded by standard regions for comparison with the wealth of information published by the Government Statistical Service.

2.3.3 Analysis by industrial application

Focus on an industrial market is sharper if sales and costs are recorded by the use to which the industrial consumer is putting the product. If this happens to equate with a standard industrial classification, then the figures derived from internal records can be related to a wide and international range of statistical data. Such data can be derived from sources such as the International Monetary Fund (IMF), and the UK's Central Statistical Office publications (e.g. on exports and balance of payments).

2.3.4 Analysis by size? or by numbers?

For industrial and trade customers, how they group by output, sales or turnover is more significant when designing research than how they group by the number of industrial establishments, or the number of shops, in a category. On the other hand, for consumers it is the number of individuals in a particular group that we are interested in.

2.3.5 Where internal records fall short

The company's own sales figures do not tell us about the following:

- How big a customer is.
- How much business the competitors are doing with our customer.
- What our potential sales targets can be.

Reports from sales representatives and from staff belonging to technical and professional bodies convey intelligence about competitive activity. This can provide a starting point before researching secondary data. However, we now need to extend the search to include data deriving from sources outside the company.

The advantage of secondary data is that there is much that is 'published' and therefore non-confidential. Much internal data held by organisations include 'confidential material'. These relate to documents concerning company property, personnel, meetings, plans, financial statements, research and development, production, and transactional details of clients, suppliers, distributors, debtors, creditors and investors. Bought-in secondary data to supplement managerial knowledge about customers, competitors and developments in their industries can greatly enhance their abilities to make marketing decisions.

External secondary data on information already collected by individuals and organisations specific to their purposes are usually available in the form of reports, books and periodicals. For example, libraries take out subscriptions for government and industry publications and these are made accessible and free to library users. Such sources can be quoted (for extensive quoting, permission is normally sought and as a matter of courtesy) and they are used as 'authorities' to sanction or support research objectives and recommendations.

2.4 Secondary data search: external sources

We will consider this large subject under three headings: government statistics; other published sources; and syndicated services. Appendix 1 (near the end of this book) lists the more commonly used sources. Companies operating in industrial markets will rely on the first two when making research plans. Consumer companies are likely to make use of syndicated sources if they operate on a large enough scale to warrant the cost.

2.4.1 Government statistics

The most prolific source of secondary data is the Government Statistical Service (see Box 2.1) with addresses given in Appendix 1.

The reference to 'all major departments' reminds us that government statistics are collected for the purpose of government: they do not always fit a particular marketing purpose, but every effort is made to meet business requirements, and data additional to those published are often made available on request.

A list of GSS publications is available from the address given in Appendix 1. The *MRS Yearbook* includes a useful review of GSS output by department. Two offices are of particular interest to market researchers: the Business Statistics Office of the Department of Trade and Industry and the Office of Population Censuses and Surveys.

The Business Statistics Office processes returns made by samples of industrial establishments, retailers and suppliers of services and these are published in a series of regularly updated Business Monitors. There is a production series, a service and distributive series and a miscellaneous series. The last covers a range of subjects such as motor-vehicle registrations, cinemas, finance and overseas travel. The monitors are published monthly and quarterly.

The validity of these published statistics depends on the care with which businesses make their returns. The anonymity of businesses supplying data is carefully safeguarded, and the Business Statistics Office does not tell companies who their competitors are.

The work of the Office of Population Censuses and Surveys is particularly

---

Box 2.1

The Government Statistical Service (GSS) comprises the statistics divisions of all major departments plus the two big collecting agencies – Business Statistics Office (BSO) and Office of Population, Censuses and Surveys (OPCS) – and the Central Statistical Office, which co-ordinates the system.

relevant to the planning of surveys because it is concerned with the size and distribution of the UK population by age and social grade, with the way in which the population is housed and the amenities it has or does not have, including telephones and a range of durable goods. The last census was taken in 1991. Census data, together with other 'lifestyle' statistics collected by the OPCS, constitute the computer input of geodemographic systems such as CCN's MOSAIC described in the latter part of this book. The OPCS carries out two continuous surveys which illuminate social trends: the Family Expenditure Survey and the General Household Survey.

The CSO databank holds macro-economic statistical data. This is more immediately relevant to researchers concerned with industrial products and services than to those in fast-moving consumer markets. The following approach to government statistics may help the business studies student engaged on exploratory research for a marketing project:

- Write for *Government Statistics: A Brief Guide to Sources*, free from the CSO (see Appendix 1 for address).
- Consult the *Guide to Official Statistics*, published annually by the CSO.
- Consult the cumulative and recent list of government publications.
- Familiarise yourself with the *Monthly Digest of Statistics, Economic Trends* and *Population Trends* (quarterly).
- Take note of the classifications used for population, production and distribution.
- If there is a Government Bookshop near you, visit it.
- If you are in London, make use of the Statistics and Market Intelligence Library (see Appendix 1 for the addresses of the Government Bookshops and the Market Intelligence Library).

2.4.2 Industry publications

Marketing information is also published by banks, stockbrokers, trade and professional associations, media owners, local authorities and government agencies. Appendix 1 lists commonly used sources, including sources of information about overseas markets.

It would be tedious to discuss these sources individually: it might, however, be helpful to mention NTC publications (e.g. annual yearbooks and pocket books on advertising and consumer statistics). *Retail Business* (Economist publications) and *Mintel* are both published monthly. The annuals and journals summarise data from government and trade sources relating to a wide range of markets. They can be found in some libraries with a marketing section, but it is possible to avoid library research by subscribing to commercial on-line systems such as those provided by Mintel.

Ours is indeed a well-documented society, but published data do not always fit requirements and they are often out of date. It is essential to find out how the original data were collected.

2.4.3 Syndicated sources

A consumer marketing company of any size is more likely to consult the trend data supplied by the research agencies who operate retail audits and consumer panels. This syndicated research enables comparisons to be made between estimates of own sales because the data derive from *samples* of retail outlets or consumers, and those of competitors (evaluation of performance usually being based on brand share). A panel is a sample maintained over a specified time so that trends may be observed.

The traditional retail audit records sales to consumers through a panel of retail outlets. Auditing is a method of data collection based on observation. The estimate of consumer sales is arrived at as follows:

Opening stock for period (checked last audit)	+	Net deliveries since last audit	−	Stock held at present audit	=	Sales to consumers during period

As well as estimating consumer sales, the retail audit monitors the distributive, selling and merchandising programmes associated with brands in the product field. The number of brands recorded in the reports bought by subscribers depends on their individual requirements and on the amounts subscribed above a minimum, i.e. the size of the 'all others' category varies. Nielsen, Retail Audits and Stats MR are substantial operators in the retail field (MRS). Electronic point of sale (EPOS) obviates the need for most manual point-of-sale auditing, for example automatic services such as Nielsen's Scantrack can take over. Scantrack reduces the reporting interval from bi-monthly to monthly.

The consumer panel records estimates of consumer purchases and gives useful information about the characteristics of those who buy and about their buying habits. The data yielded by retail audits and consumer panels are compared in Table 13.6. For a survey designed to describe consumers in a product field, consumer-panel data make a big contribution to informed assumptions. Most panels relate to products purchased frequently but panel data relating to a wide range of durables are available (e.g. the Taylor Nelson AGB's SuperPanel launched in 1991). Fast-moving purchases are recorded by means of an electronic capture device which scans the panel member's bar codes on the products from the grocery shopping. We need to distinguish between three types of panel:

1. The household panel: a record of housewife purchases, the most widely used being SuperPanel.
2. The individual panel: a record of purchases made by individuals for their own use; e.g. the TN AGB's 'Impulse Panel'.

3. The special-interest panel: a panel such as the Motorists' Diary Panel operated by Forecast (Market Research), a Unilever subsidiary. This panel is devoted to the recording of petrol and engine oil purchases, plus information on accessories, servicing and car insurance.

The range of the data available from consumer panels relating to repeat-purchase products is summarised as follows:

*   Trends in the total volume and value of consumer purchases in the product field.
*   The demographic characteristics of those buying in the product field, such as age, social class, size of family.
*   Buying behaviour in the product field: average amount bought, frequency of buying, and, since these data record individual purchasing of individual brands (i.e. the data is 'disaggregated'), repeat-purchase and loyalty patterns can be established.
*   All this information is recorded within net BARB television areas and by the type of retail outlet at which purchases were made.
*   Seasonal patterns can be seen.

But data derived from consumer purchasing panels do not answer either of the following:

*   How products and brands are used.
*   How buyers perceive brands in a product field.

For both retail audits and consumer panels 'back data' may be available if the company is not already subscribing. The range of these data will relate to the requirements of subscribers, but important product fields and major brands in those fields will have been covered.

The first purpose of audits and panels is to monitor the effect of marketing programmes while the accumulated trend data constitute important inputs to diagnostic predictive models (Chapter 12).

The British Market Research Bureau's (BMRB) Target Group Index (TGI) serves a strategic planning purpose. The TGI annual reports, based on a sample of 25,000 adults, relate individual product field and brand purchases to media consumption. The 86-page questionnaire (placed by interviewers for self-completion) covers 4,500 brands in 500 product and service fields, as well as the respondent's media habits and attitudes. Questions are also asked about attitudes towards, for example, drink, diet and health, home and do-it-yourself items; and a lifestyle system called Outlook, useful for segmenting markets, is based on the answers.

Postcodes are recorded and so it is possible to relate the product-media data to specific locations (see Table 6.2 in Chapter 6) It is also possible to relate TGI data to the traditional ACORN classification of neighbourhoods based on the Census of

Population and on lifestyle indicators included in the census data. Taylor Nelson Audits of Great Britain's consumer panels and BMRB's Target Group Index generate very substantial databases. Given an adequate research budget, it is possible to explore most consumer markets in considerable detail.

2.5 Consulting experts

If a company is considering entry into a new product field, the research planner may feel the need to seek expert advice. Much depends on how thoroughly he/she has been briefed. The expert may be on the staff, say, a research chemist in the research and development (R&D) department or a home economist in the test kitchen. Or it may be necessary to go for outside help to consult a heating and ventilating engineer or a paediatrician, to quote two possible outside experts.

In a consumer market there is a clear distinction between seeking the advice of experts and seeking to add to the secondary data statistics by encouraging individuals in the market to talk, either alone in 'depth' interviews or in groups. In industrial markets the distinction between 'experts' and 'buyers' is muddled by the industrial buying process. The industrial buyer is often buying at the behest of company experts. Indeed, as we shall see, determining just who makes the buying decision presents a problem when designing industrial marketing research surveys (who should be asked the questions?).

2.6 Observational studies

Strictly speaking, audits and diaries represent data collection by means of observation. Here we consider observation as an exploratory aid for the research planner.

If the product field is unfamiliar it may be advisable to go out and observe, for example, the following:

- How motorists behave on the forecourt of a filling station.
- How housewives buy bread.
- How retailers shop in a cash-and-carry wholesaler's.
- How customers behave in a do-it-yourself (DIY) centre.

It all depends on the nature of the product and the planner's experience as a consumer.

At this exploratory stage we are not collecting statistical data. Our purpose is to get better acquainted with what goes on in the market as part of the business of arriving at our 'set of assumptions' (see section 2.1).

2.7 Consulting people in the market

If the market is reasonably well documented, the search so far will have told us what demographic variables are likely to affect the behaviour of consumers with regard to the product field. We will have a good idea whether age is a critical variable, or whether social class, having or not having children, living in the north compared with living in the south, going out to work or being a housewife full time, and so on, are important criteria.

We have to take account of the distinction between 'who buys' and 'who uses' in this market when deciding on what sort of consumers to consult. Electric razors and male toiletries are often bought by women for men. But who determines the kind of holiday the family takes, the model of family car, or the kind of bicycle a child shall have?

We need to know as much as possible about consumers, and users, in the market because we are going to encourage a limited number of consumers to talk freely and at length about their behaviour in the product field, their attitudes towards what is available in the way of products (or services), their wants and their preoccupations.

We shall either contact them as individuals or bring them together in groups of about eight, a number small enough to encourage general discussion and large enough to make it likely that the group will have a good variety of ideas. This kind of research, which seeks to illuminate the motivation behind consumer behaviour, is described as 'qualitative'; as compared with the 'quantitative' type of research study, designed to produce statistics.

2.8 Qualitative research

Individual, intensive or 'depth' interviews and group discussions are the two most commonly used qualitative research methods. It would be possible to conduct a sufficient number of lengthy, unstructured interviews to draw statistical conclusions, and indeed this is sometimes done. The more cost-effective approach is to do enough *qualitative* work to reveal most, if not all, of the ways in which consumers behave in the market and of the attitudes they hold, then to use this rich data to design a *quantitative* study of a sample sufficiently large to allow conclusions to be drawn as to *how many*, and *what sort of*, consumers behave and think in the ways shown by the qualitative study.

In industrial and other 'non-domestic' markets, where information is often being sought from experts and a formal questionnaire can be out of place, individual, intensive or 'depth' interviews are frequently used, as are group discussions.

The 'depth' interview and group discussion are both clinical methods. Depth interviews in market research are shallower compared with the interviewing techniques used in psychotherapy. 'Extended' or 'intensive' is a better description but 'depth' is still in common use. Individual, depth or intensive interviews are used when the subject might prove embarrassing or if it is necessary to avoid interaction between group members. The interview may be 'non-directive' or 'semi-structured'. In the first case the interviewer, having established a relaxed atmosphere, leaves the respondent free to come up with an experience, attitude, need or idea that bears on the subject which, at the exploratory state, is likely to be broadly defined as, for example, 'feeding the family'. For a semi-structured interview, the interviewer is equipped with an agenda or check-list designed to ensure that specific aspects of interest are covered.

Group discussions have cost and time advantages. A group of consumers with an interest in common, such as motoring, child-rearing, taking holidays or DIY, can develop a synergy so that more ideas are discussed over a shorter time than would emerge from the same number of depth interviews, however skilful the interviewer is at establishing rapport. The type of group most commonly used is described here. Groups based on syndicated and brainstorming techniques (Sampson 1986) are more appropriate to new-product development.

The number and make-up of the groups depend on the variability in the consumer market shown by the secondary data search. If the market is not sufficiently well documented a limited number of questions in an omnibus survey will establish the main variables. Any variable which is known to be significant is allowed for in the design of the groups, not forgetting regional differences. The groups can either be of like (homogeneous) or be of unlike (heterogeneous) types. A mixture of types in each group could reveal a greater variety of experience and ideas. It could also have the opposite effect. In many product and service markets, social grade is no longer a discriminator where buying behaviour is concerned, but in the United Kingdom it is still usual to distinguish between middle class (ABC_1) and working class (C_2DE) when designing groups.

Discussions are tape recorded and they are often filmed so that body language may be observed. (Should participants not be told about this recording beforehand, their permission to use tape and film must be sought after the session. This is in the MRS Code of Conduct.)

2.8.1 *Risk of bias*

Group discussions are recorded on tape and later transcribed. Statements expressing habits, attitudes and wants are listed verbatim. The lists are cut up into individual statements and the statements are sorted into piles. Then the discussion is summarised, using the respondents' own words as far as possible.

In qualitative work of this kind there is clearly a risk that the results may be biased:

- Group members may not be representative of the market.
- The interviewer may influence the course of the discussion.

- The content analysis may not truly represent the experience and attitudes of the group.
- The report writer may impose a doctrinaire psychological interpretation on the content.

2.8.2 Value of qualitative work at later stages

Qualitative methods are used extensively in the search for product and advertising ideas and in the development of concepts arrived at during the exploratory stage. The validity of qualitative work depends on the recruitment of suitable market members and the choice of suitable stimuli to enable members to formulate and express their own thoughts and motivations in group discussions. As Miriam Catterall, University of Ulster puts it:

> Group discussions are the most popular method of qualitative marketing research. An interviewer recruits 8 to 10 people with similar characteristics who meet in a relaxed informal atmosphere, usually during an evening in the interviewer's home, for a discussion that can last up to two hours. The discussion is convened by a moderator who will introduce the subject matter and encourage the participants to discuss the key issues identified during the briefing with the client.
>
> The quality of the discussion is largely dependent on the accurate recruitment of participants and the skills and experience of the moderator. Participants should be recruited to specification. For example, if a discussion is planned with heavy users of a service and one or two of the recruits are non users, this can disrupt the atmosphere and flow of the discussion as these recruits probably have little to contribute.
>
> A group moderator is responsible for leading the discussion in a non-directive manner and ensuring that all the discussion objectives agreed with the client are met. Generally, people who have never before participated in a group discussion are recruited. They are not sure what to expect so the moderator needs to establish discussion ground rules at the outset and these will include:
> - a simple and brief explanation of the purpose of a group discussion, that it is not a question and answer session and, participants do not need to wait to be invited by the moderator to express their views.
> - discussions concentrating on participants' opinions rather than their knowledge of the subject matter. This is to encourage participants with different and sometimes opposing views to speak.
> - explanations that the discussion will be tape recorded since it is difficult for the moderator to listen to what people are saying and take notes at the same time.

- setting a time limit for the discussion to end. Participants will have been informed on recruitment of the time involved.

The moderator needs to ensure that everyone has an opportunity to speak as early as possible in the discussion. Moderators use a variety of ice-breakers. One of these involves dividing the group into pairs. Each pair learns something about their partner and then introduces their partner to the rest of the group. So everyone is introduced quickly in a relaxed atmosphere.

Summary points are useful during discussions. At appropriate points the moderator summarises the main points to emerge from the discussion and invites participants to confirm and add to these. This provides an opportunity for the moderator to move the discussion on to a different issue or theme which is useful where the discussion has started to wander off the subject matter.

Finally, few people ever have the opportunity to talk at such length or depth about a single product or service.

2.9 Buying into an omnibus survey

The Market Research Society's monthly newsletter carries a regular feature in which research suppliers advertise their omnibus surveys. The research *supplier* draws the sample, administers the questionnaire, processes the data, reports results, while the research *buyer* takes space in the questionnaire, pays according to the number of questions asked and the statistical breakdowns required. The number of questions one can include in an omnibus questionnaire is limited, but sufficient to establish basic market characteristics; the market may be the subject of a specialist omnibus. There are, for example, motoring omnibuses and baby market omnibuses as well as the more general omnibus surveys based on a sample of all the adults in Great Britain, or on a sample of all the households. Omnibus surveys relating to countries or geographical regions can also be found.

The samples are specified and carefully drawn. The omnibus survey is an important item in the research supplier's range of products. The surveys are conducted at regular intervals and are relied on for a regular contribution to revenue. An omnibus survey would, for example, be a good way of establishing what sort of people are in the DIY market, their DIY equipment and their most recent DIY job done.

A shared questionnaire is likely to range over a number of subjects so that it is difficult to engage the respondent's attention in more than a superficial way. This does not apply quite so much to the specialist omnibus, but the questionnaire still represents the interests of a number of sponsors. With the development of computer-assisted telephone interviewing (CATI), it is now possible to capture and process omnibus data very quickly, e.g. 'Questions by Friday noon, results by Monday'.

2.10 Importance of informed assumptions

It is unlikely that all these exploratory avenues will be followed in any one piece of exploratory research. The objective can be reached by a variety of routes and the objective is to gain sufficient certainty about the following in order to design a cost-effective research study:

- The structure of the population to be sampled, whether this be one of individuals, households, firms or retail outlets.
- The topics that are relevant to the marketing problem.

We need to be sufficiently well informed about the population to be able to design a sample which takes account of those variables likely to lead to marketing action. For an example, see Box 2.2.

Here again, we have to avoid sins of both omission and commission, as the example in Box 2.3 shows. The answer will affect the design of the questionnaire, the time taken to answer (or fill it in), the complexity of data processing and the cost of the survey.

Box 2.2

If AB class behaves in a markedly different way from C_1 in this market, then we are going to have to ensure that our sample includes enough ABs for us to have confidence in the representativeness of the AB results. If AB and C_1 behave in much the same way, then making a separate provision for AB would be wasteful. But we must avoid the risk of getting results in and finding we want to make recommendations about AB as a separate group, but cannot (or ought not!).

Box 2.3

Qualitative work has given us a list of statements expressing motorists' attitudes towards driving a car. We want to quantify these attitudes by putting them to a sample of motorists. Do we need to distinguish between how he/she feels about driving the car when going to work, ferrying children to school, taking grandparents for a run; or is it sufficient for our purpose to establish how the motorist feels about driving in general?

2.11 Conclusion

This chapter assumes company interest in a particular market and considers how this market may be explored. The time spent on the preliminary investigations reviewed here will depend on the company's familiarity with the market.

We have seen that there is a wealth of published and syndicated data available. These data, together with some qualitative work, may fit our particular interest so well that there is no need for further data collection. We are, however, more likely to find that the data, while illuminating about the general characteristics of the market and of the distributive channels serving it, are not focused closely enough on the habits, attitudes and requirements of the consumers we are interested in to meet our purpose. Exploratory research has put us in a better position to define research objectives and to design primary research, tailored to our objectives.

References

Catterall, M. (1994) 'Focus group discussions in qualitative market research', University of Ulster.

Financial Times (1994a) 'Software at work – spring 1994', Survey, 10 March, p. 12.

Financial Times (1994b) 'Direct Line surges to £40.5m', 12 May p. 24.

Kotler, P. (1994) *Marketing Management, Analysis, Planning and Control* (8th edn), Englewood Cliffs, NJ: Prentice Hall.

Kotler, P. and Armstrong, G. (1994) *Principles of Marketing* (6th edn), Englewood Cliffs, NJ: Prentice Hall, p. 110.

Organisations Providing Market Research Services in Great Britain, London: Market Research Society, updated yearly.

Sampson, P. (1986) 'Qualitative research and motivation research', in *The Consumer Market Research Handbook* 3rd edn, Amsterdam: North-Holland, ch. 2.

Further reading

Appendix 1 of this book.

Birn, R., Hayne, P., and Vangelder, P. (1990) *A Handbook of Market Research Techniques*, London: Kogan Page.

Government Statistics: A brief guide to sources, London: Central Statistical Office.

Assignments

You are employed in the research department of a chain of food stores with national (but rather uneven) distribution.

1. You have been asked to report on developments in the market for wine consumed in the home. How would you tackle this problem?
2. Write a report drawing on the sources you have consulted (the consumer market for wine is well documented).
3. How would you proceed if you were asked to report to management on the distribution of wine to the retail trade in Great Britain?

CHAPTER 3

The international marketing research process

Carol Coutts

3.1 International marketing

3.1.1 The international marketing environment

International brands offer immense opportunities to those companies prepared to take on the challenge of the marketing tasks involved. There are great potential rewards, but equally, large risks have sometimes to be taken, and substantial investments are frequently at stake. In working across countries, the international marketeer faces a complex network of differing legal requirements, trade barriers, pricing and distribution structures, and also a variety of different cultural environments.

It is for individual consumers to decide whether or not to buy a product or service offered by a company based on the other side of the world. But for most marketing companies, whether multi-national or not, there is little choice involved in whether to participate in the world of international trade. With the exception of those still protected by commercial barriers, most companies are now working in a global environment where they must seek out new markets to maintain success, or at the very least prepare defensive strategies in their home markets against invading foreign competitors.

At the supra-national level, countries are forming themselves into groups by pulling down long-established political or trade barriers. The development of the European Economic Community, once formed of six countries, now grown to twelve, is an obvious example of such a transformation. Europe is not the only arena for these kinds of changes – in the Far East too, closer trade and political links are being forged between countries such as Australia, Japan, Indonesia and Singapore.

More and more companies now operate successfully across a wide range of countries and markets. Indeed some of these companies, such as General Motors, have annual turnovers which far outstrip the Gross National Product of entire countries. Some companies have become household names the world over – think of Coca-Cola, Sony, McDonald's and Toyota.

The factors driving companies towards increasing internationalism in marketing are complex and interrelated. There has been a gradual erosion of the extent of competitive advantage achievable by marketing companies in purely product performance terms. With relatively few exceptions the major technologies on which consumer products are based are available to most, if not all, major global competitors. Equally, early advances in this area are often relatively short-lived, as the lead-times required to 'catch up' both with the technology and with the necessary production and distribution capacities become narrower. In short, it is becoming increasingly unrealistic to expect to 'steal a permanent march' on competitors in all but the very highest technologies. The very basic principle which follows this scenario is that most products and/or services cannot expect to establish, nor particularly to maintain, a sufficiently large, stable and profitable consumer franchise on the basis of explicit product superiority.

For the traditional manufacturing-based businesses there is the critical additional spur of their lack of influence on several key factors which increasingly may determine the consumer's experience of and responses to their products. The costs of raw materials, supplies of components and services, and especially the whole area of distribution from fmcg consumer retailing to the business-to-business context – all are critical influences on the consumer's or end user's ultimate desire to purchase the product at a given price – the equation which determines the commercial success or otherwise of the business.

These pressures (among others) have accelerated the pursuit of economies of scale associated with larger international marketplaces where all research, development, production, distribution and media costs are more likely to make commercial sense provided products and services can be marketed with a sufficient degree of homogeneity in the various elements of product formulation, packaging, distribution, consumer positioning and marketing communication – in short (to some degree at least) as international brands.

3.1.2 Strategic planning on an international basis

In this international environment of increasingly rapid change and fierce competition, it is vital to provide brands with a strategic direction which is both coherent and relevant to the marketplace. It is also necessary to manage international brands so that effective responses can be made to new or changing factors, whether they are concerned with consumer trends, market structures or competitive activity.

This is the stuff of strategic planning. Its objectives should be as follows:

1. Identification of the brand's current position (where are we now?).
2. Evaluation of new opportunities (where could we be?).
3. Development of a strategic plan (how do we get there?).

Current international management thinking suggests that most international organisations face broadly similar issues in terms of strategic planning. These issues relate largely to the challenges inherent in any large organisation's attempts to operate successfully in a number of different countries, and can be summarised as follows:

1. *Diversity of markets.* The markets themselves can be diverse and complex, both within and across borders. Planning is necessary to decide how much standardisation is appropriate for the organisation given potential economies of scale and individual market opportunities.

2. *Market saturation.* In the current world economic climate, many markets are saturated, and earlier misguided investment policies have resulted in significant over-capacity in production. International organisations need therefore to decide which markets represent genuine opportunities and whether to maintain, expand, close down or re-direct various production resources.

3. *Investment priorities.* Even assuming a healthy situation in terms of market growth and production resources, strategic decisions will still be needed to determine priorities in terms of investments. Potsch and Limeira (1986) demonstrate clearly how growing international organisations have to work out a path of development by deciding whether to extend their operations through diversification, vertical integration or geographic expansion.

4. *Market fragmentation.* Increasing affluence and the growth of individualism in many markets have brought about what seems like a constant process of fragmentation among hitherto stable consumer groups. This fragmentation demands greater customisation of products and a more tightly targeted approach to marketing, both of which run counter to the large organisation's interest in exploiting economies of scale. Decisions are therefore needed on whether to service newly appearing consumer segments and market niches.

5. *Centralisation* versus *decentralisation.* As international organisations develop, fundamental choices must be made on whether to have centralised or decentralised control of operations and activities. This is a complex issue involving all manner of possible organisational structures. 'Mixed modes' – with centralisation of certain functions and decentralisation of others – are by far the most common pattern.

6. *Organisation and motivation of staff.* Organisations operating across cultural boundaries have one further tough challenge – to co-ordinate their human resources, overcoming the barriers of language, distance, culture and intra-organisation politics. Recognised as a key requirement by most international organisations, human resource development can to some extent be handled by training, whether internal or external (Coutts 1991). However, the development and integration of staff and management on a truly international basis call for deliberate fostering of a management culture that is itself cross-cultural.

Fiat, as just one example, have set a priority in 'training young people to aim for positions that will involve permanent international relations' (Agnelli 1990:59). Jacobs-Suchard, in its strategic planning for Europeanisation, believe it is necessary 'to start with committed champions who overcome the attitudinal, linguistic, social and cultural difficulties' (Jakob 1990).

Setting and performing international tasks call for careful organisation and management in order to avoid misunderstanding, lack of involvement and the 'not-invented-here' syndrome. As one example, Jacobs-Suchard have involved a system of mixed nationality working groups to study international strategic issues (Jakob 1990). Another successful approach to international teamwork is described by Naeve (1986).

These issues and requirements of international marketing and strategic planning are broadly common and well defined. However, the ways in which organisations address these issues vary greatly, influenced by their inherent structural differences.

3.1.3 Typology of international marketing organisations

The classic stereotype of international marketing organisations tends to be of a multi-national, profit-making company, with establishments in several countries and a complex management structure involving centralisation of certain functions and decentralisation of others. In the author's experience, such organisations are by no means the only players in the international arena.

The variables in organisational structure which tend to affect the management of international marketing can be summarised as follows:

1. *Ownership* – the organisation may be owned by one person or group of shareholders, or may be a federation of separately owned organisations.
2. *Dedication* – all the establishments in the organisation may be dedicated solely to that organisation's goals, or some (e.g. distributors, agents) may be involved with other organisations as well.
3. *Size* – the 'organisation' may consist of only one person (e.g. a management or marketing consultant) or may have a staff of thousands.
4. *Multi-country presence* – the organisation may have its whole establishment in just one country, or may have various establishments (sales/service offices, factories, administrative functions) located across a number of different countries.
5. *Operational structure* – the organisation may be structured by product sector, by region, by function (e.g. marketing, production), or by some matrix combination of all three (see Potsch and Limeira (1986) for a full analysis of possibilities).
6. *Degree of centralisation* – the organisation may or may not retain central control of its various functions.

7. *History* – the organisation may have grown organically from a one-country to a multi-country operation; alternatively it may have been formed through acquisition of, or decision to federate by, previously individual organisations.
8. *Dominant culture* – through the accidents of history, ownership or location, the organisation is likely to be dominated by the local and business cultures of one particular country; these cultures vary enormously and lead to major differences in corporate style and practice.
9. *Level of evolution* – the organisation may be established or new and may be in a state of maturity or growth or decline; few international organisations ever seem to stand still in this respect and it is perhaps salutary to think of international organisations as being in a virtually constant process of change and evolution, on all the variables described above.

This variability in international marketing organisations is as nothing compared to the dynamism and complexity of the consumer environment in which they operate.

3.2 The consumer worldwide

3.2.1 Cultural similarities and differences

> The nature of men is always the same; it is their habits that separate them. Confucius (551–479 BC)

The existence of cultural similarities and differences between groups and individuals has long been appreciated. Culture has been defined as 'the collective programming of the mind which distinguishes one group or category of people from another' (Hofstede 1991). Factors at work in differentiating cultures include the following:

- Nationality.
- Regionality.
- Ethnicity.
- Language.
- Religion.
- Gender.
- Generation.
- Social class.

The international marketing process calls for a particularly close study of the nature and extent of these similarities and differences (see Case History 3.1).

Case History 3.1:   The razor-blade opportunity

Some years ago, a major razor-blade manufacturer wished to research the opportunities for his product in West Africa. The plan was to use a questionnaire covering the obvious criteria which apply in getting a good shave. But a researcher involved in the work felt that it might be advisable to carry out a small exploratory pilot before going ahead. Journeying intrepidly to rural areas of Nigeria and Ghana, he discovered that the most important requirement of a razor-blade in those parts was that it should be good for skinning animals! Collapse of standardised questionnaire. Revelation of new marketing opportunity – the company then successfully marketed their blades in this region by offering with each pack a patent blade-holder which made it easier to use for this specialised function.

3.2.2 The globalisation debate

Theodore Levitt has argued that consumers are becoming increasingly 'global':

> A powerful force now drives the world toward a single converging commonality, and that force is technology. It has proletarianized communication, transport, and travel, making them easily and cheaply accessible to the world's most isolated places and impoverished multitudes. Suddenly no place and nobody is insulated from the alluring attractions of modernity. (Levitt 1983)

In summary, Levitt argues that the case for globalisation lies in the following:

- The homogenisation of the world's wants.
- People's willingness to sacrifice specific preferences in product features for lower prices at high quality.
- Lower prices facilitated by the scale economies of production, transportation and communication.

Many of those involved in international marketing take a different view:

> The argument by Globalists for cultural convergence across national boundaries is not supported by the facts: even the international businessman, once his business suit is off, follows his national rather than an international life style. While there are related trends in behaviour across the world, they are developing very differently, and there is far more evidence for differences around the world than for any sort of cultural convergence. Nationality is a powerful emotional force, which actually gains strength from international communication, and to seek an advertising idea so deep in its appeal that it can transcend national boundaries is to work in the wrong

direction – indeed, when Coke 'taught the world to sing' an
expression of abundant American nationality travelled the world.
(Hawes 1985)

A brand is only global if the whole world wants it: the trick is to
identify a global need, around which the brand is built. But a global
brand is not the same thing as a product in worldwide distribution
with identical advertising: true global marketing takes account of
genuine local differences, and no global advertiser of any consequence
sends his advertising round the world with instructions to translate it,
run it, and refrain from arguing. (Day 1986)

Thus proponents of globalisation fight it out with the decentralists and the cultural
chauvinists because the attractions of multi-country economies of scale in
marketing and advertising vie with the fear that locally developed products and
services may still have the competitive edge.

The message implicit in all of these exchanges is that underneath the surface
differences of culture, language, race and religion, people often have very similar
needs and interests, and that the new opportunities afforded by greater political
and economic *rapprochement* and by technological advances are being put to use
to provide consumer satisfactions on a worldwide scale.

Some of the most exciting opportunities in international marketing lie in
identifying core motivations which operate across cultures and which can form the
basis of successful international brand positionings.

3.3 The role of international research

3.3.1 Aid to strategic planning

Good international research provides understanding of different cultural environments, offers information and guidance to assess and pursue the market opportunities afforded, and helps to reduce the risks involved in so doing.

Among the resources which can be used to aid international strategic planning,
market research can play a significant role. The reader may consider that some of
the challenges described above lie well beyond the normal research territory. It is
true that researchers have been backward in offering and deploying their skills in
certain areas, but that does not mean it is not possible or desirable! It is
increasingly becoming accepted that suppliers and buyers of market research
should recognise, understand and respond to the full range of strategic planning
needs of their commissioning organisations.

Jean-Louis Laborie, one of the most cogent thinkers on the future of market research, has argued that researchers can and should improve or (where necessary) change what they offer to provide information which is relevant and applicable to strategic decision-making:

> By vocation market research brings to other sectors a knowledge of their environment. It has the duty, where and when it is necessary, to bring to decision-makers the knowledge that they need, in such a way that they are fed on a permanent and regular basis with reliable and directly applicable information to adapt their policies to the new context. . . . Without sacrificing anything that is our strength [researchers should] go further in order to adapt to a new world in which speed of reaction is paramount, and what is decisive is the recommendation to the client and the diffusion of the results within the client organisation. (Laborie 1989)

In a fast-moving, complex world research can offer the quintessential advantage of *anticipation*, helping organisations to be one step ahead of events. Nowhere is this role more significant than in the international arena, where the risks and rewards involved in strategic planning multiply to a dramatic degree.

3.3.2 Not just a load of data

To do full justice to the potential usefulness of international research it is necessary to go beyond a conventional description of its functions. It is usually thought to deliver vast quantities of information on markets and consumer behaviour, with no user-friendly directions and no immediate relevance to strategic issues. Even worse, the information is about the past, and what good is that, in a chaotic changing world, for predicting and responding to the future?

Sadly, some commissioning organisations never seem to get anything more from their international research programmes than what is described above. But this view of research takes into account only the *content* that is presented, and ignores the *process* involved, which the author believes offers significant value in its own right (if appropriately pursued) as a means to discovery, learning, debate of significant issues, and development of international teamwork. Importantly too, the conventional view of research, whether of its content or its process, is as something essentially *inert*, with no capacity to interact or pro-act, for example, in proffering recommendations, advice or guidance.

Potentially, therefore, international research should be seen to offer a good deal more than meets the eye. Figure 3.1 indicates the 'conventional' and less well-recognised functions, and further descriptions of the four areas are given below.

POTENTIAL FUNCTIONS OF RESEARCH

Content	Process
1. Conventional view	3. Less well recognised
2. Less well recognised	4. Least well recognised

Figure 3.1 Potential functions of research

3.3.3 Unique picture of similarities and differences

Even taking the conventional view (quadrant 1 above), international research can have considerable value in strategic planning. If the data have been collected and presented on a properly comparable basis, these 'inert contents' can offer a unique picture scanning across all markets, charting the nature and degree of differences between and within countries and spotting the patterns of similarity. The true extent of market similarities and differences is often a matter of fierce debate within international organisations, with national chauvinisms lined up against the forces of standardisation and economies of scale. Good international research can help to quell this debate by settling the arguments objectively. Naeve describes the importance of such information because 'it helps to temper the "our market is different" belief that otherwise exists in almost any multi-national marketing organisation' (1986). More importantly, such information can pave the way towards identifying international consumer segments which, though too small to develop on a single country basis, represent a viable opportunity when known to exist in larger numbers across a number of countries (see Case History 3.2).

Case History 3.2: A niche in the European bath foam market

Segmentation of bath foam users

A European toiletries manufacturer wished to explore opportunities for brand diversification in the bath foam market. A six-country quantitative segmentation study on attitudes and behaviour uncovered a hitherto unrecognised group of 3.3 million women who had a particular set of characteristics and needs. 'Ms Exotic Thrill', as she was dubbed, was particularly likely to bathe (rather than shower) and wanted a product with a luxurious, strong, masculine fragrance. She was particularly likely to be found in France, Belgium or Portugal. The company developed a strongly fragranced variant to satisfy her needs and thus made a success of an international opportunity which would have been too small in any one country to justify the investment.

3.3.4 Anticipating the future

A more active type of research information should also be sought (quadrant 2 of Figure 3.1). There is as yet no crystal ball for international organisations to see into the future. However, for all those on the waiting-list for such a marvel, certain kinds of information can be obtained, which – if carefully evaluated – will provide valuable clues. These kinds of information fall into three main categories:

1. Extrapolating likely future developments from historic market information.
2. Testing and exploring likely consumer response to new products and marketing approaches.
3. 'Trawling' for hitherto unidentified trends in consumer attitudes and behaviour.

All three categories represent more active approaches to the use of research content. Although not foolproof, such information provides a picture of likely future scenarios based on the most relevant data available. When obtained on a multi-country basis, these kinds of information are especially valuable since the usual gut-feel of planners and marketing people in these matters tends not to work when a range of countries beyond their native homeland is involved.

3.3.5 The value of the basic research process

Even in its most basic form (quadrant 3 of Figure 3.1), the *process* of research can have benefits for international organisations. The simple disciplines of preparing the brief, planning the project, managing the fieldwork, and analysing and presenting the findings all serve to focus the diverse interests involved and clarify the real issues. Planning international research projects often provides the first real opportunity for the various managers involved to discuss their common interests and objectives. When tackling new markets – a situation not at all uncommon for international organisations – even the apparently simple process of defining the sample can often uncover unidentified marketing issues of the utmost importance.

Witnessing fieldwork, even via translation, can prove a stimulating process, being one of the few ways in which international marketing people can experience their consumers at first hand.

3.3.6 Getting more from the research process

If the people involved manage the research process actively (quadrant 4 of Figure 3.1) and are alive to the further benefits it can yield, then the process can serve to enhance the value of the research well beyond its function of information-giving. The realisation of these benefits rests largely on seizing the opportunities inherent in the process for bringing together key groups of people involved in the project and making use of both the information-stimulation and the neutrality afforded. Such opportunities present themselves at several stages – notably at briefing and planning meetings, and at verbal presentations of findings. These occasions can be used to exchange views and experiences, to establish common goals, and to debate strategic issues.

Meetings in the early stages of project planning can be used to uncover and resolve relevant issues specific to one country or to certain members of the project management team. They can be used to involve people hitherto unfamiliar with the needs and goals of the project and hence help to generate a structure for future teamwork. Far more than simply the means to plan and organise the research, these meetings can serve to elucidate the real marketing needs and to consolidate good working relationships between all parties involved – outcomes which are often difficult to achieve in international organisations.

Meetings convened to present findings have the obvious benefits and attractions inherent to any occasion where information new and relevant to the audience is to be conveyed. With international research they also represent one of the few opportunities where the management team finds it justifiable to meet physically, despite the time, distance and cost penalties involved. Moreover, the occasion is (largely) neutral, and unstressful from the audience's point of view. Using the information as a springboard, the audience can discuss freely and fully the implications and alternative options, gaining stimulation and instant feedback from other team members. Presenting information to a well-motivated team in this way can often lead to discussions which prove highly creative, generating fresh ideas and solutions to the questions in hand.

It will be apparent that the presenter of the research, especially if external to the commissioning organisation, must play a particularly sensitive role if such further benefits are to be gained from presentations. As Burgaud (1986) has described, the researcher in such a context must demonstrate flexibility, credibility and neutrality. To these qualities must be added: communication skills; readiness to make recommendations; and skill in mediating questions and stimulating discussion.

Commissioning organisations need to manage these aspects of the research process well to achieve the benefits described. Such meetings need to be planned and prepared well in advance, the right people invited, and the right atmosphere engendered. Practical issues also need to be addressed, for example, possible language problems, and the timing of meetings to avoid wear-out and missing of planes!

3.4 Commissioning and managing international research

3.4.1 Key differences

The major differences in approach to international research management relate to two key aspects:

Co-ordination

		Central	Local
Management by:	Research function	1	3
	Marketing function	2	4

Figure 3.2 Typology of approaches to international research management structure

1. Whether the project is co-ordinated centrally or handled separately in each country.
2. Whether the project is managed primarily by the organisation's researchers or by the marketing team involved (in the author's experience, international commissioning organisations do not necessarily appoint researchers to this role – the supplier's point of contact can sometimes be an international marketing or advertising manager or an export director).

A typology of four main approaches then emerges, as shown in Figure 3.2.

3.4.2 *Advantages and disadvantages of central co-ordination*

Centralised co-ordination tends to have the following advantages for the management of international research:

*   The objectives of the research programme will be clearly defined to the researcher.
*   The reporting chain and the hierarchy of authority will be clear and short.
*   The methodologies chosen will tend to be standardised, or at least comparable.
*   The data will be capable of being presented on a comparable basis, thus allowing for the detection of genuine similarities and differences across countries.
*   Economies of scale are achieved (by both client and supplier) in the planning and management of the research process.

The disadvantages inherent in central co-ordination can be quite serious, and all the more so because they often go undetected. They can be summarised as follows:

*   The objectives set, while disarmingly clear, may well fail to take into account important issues and relevant country variations, through insufficient consultation with local colleagues at the planning stage.

- The methodologies chosen, while apparently comparable, may be unsuitable or inappropriate for certain countries.
- Centralisation of a project's management tends inherently to alienate those involved at local levels (Kern *et al.* 1989:526); local management can be forgiven for scepticism about the project's value and recommendations ('how can those foreigners possibly know about my customers?').
- Research findings tend to be presented to a restricted central management team only (even if reports are more widely disseminated at a later stage); local managers who will have to implement resultant strategies never get the chance to hear the findings at first hand or take part in the accompanying debate and decision-making.

3.4.3 *Advantages and disadvantages of local co-ordination*

It is to be hoped that local co-ordination will ensure the formulation of an appropriate and relevant research brief for each country concerned, and the use of appropriate methodologies. Involvement of all parties in the research process, with the accompanying benefits described earlier, is also much easier to achieve in one country than in a multi-country context.

Problems arise with the approach if (for any reason) there is a need to plan or use the research on an international basis. Even if dealing ostensibly with the same brief, for example, testing a new product, locally organised projects are likely to end up with different objectives and different methodologies. The resultant reports, when brought together to form the international picture, usually prove to be a nightmare in terms of non-comparability. It is not possible to determine whether the similarities and differences observed are real or just a result of differences in approach. This makes fertile ground for the perpetuation of market myths and prejudices and the fomentation of inter-country politics – a shameful travesty of the way in which research should ideally function (see Case History 3.3).

Case History 3.3:   The squeaky clean Belgians

In planning the segmentation study described earlier (Case History 3.2) available market statistics were gathered from each of the local client offices on the incidence of bath-taking in their respective countries. A first look at the data suggested that the percentage of Belgian women who took baths was far higher than in any other European country. A second, closer look revealed that the basis of compilation was different; in Belgium the percentage estimate derived from the question: 'Have you taken a bath *in the last seven days?*'; in all other countries, the question had been: 'Have you taken a bath *in the last three days?*'

The information had not been collected on a comparable basis.

Fortunately on this occasion, the truth was uncovered before it was too late, but one shudders to think how often such non-comparable information finds its way into international planning, leading to inappropriate strategies and decision-taking.

As a small practical point, locally organised research tends naturally to be planned and reported in the local language. Unless time and resources are made available for translation, the benefits to all but the most polyglot of central staff are thereby severely hampered at the most basic level, in terms of both the content and the process of the project.

3.4.4 *Advantages and disadvantages of management by the research function*

When the commissioning organisation chooses a researcher to run the project, there is a reasonable assurance that the research will be carried out objectively to a good standard and that technical issues will be well managed. Researchers also represent an excellent corporate memory bank, and by their nature will endeavour to ensure that both central and local users' needs are canvassed and met. Moreover, they will be sensitive to the needs of the research suppliers and ensure appropriate co-ordination of activities during the course of the project.

Sadly, however, there is a well-known tendency for researcher-managers to become swamped or over-involved with the data and the technical processes – certainly an ever-present temptation or risk given the vast amounts of material which international projects can generate. Lachmann, himself a client researcher, describes this problem amusingly, criticising his fellows for their 'introverted habits, data fixation and lack of concern for the company's problems' (1988).

Working currently as a supplier, the author too questions the work priorities often observed among research managers; there seems to be too much time spent on monitoring the basic research process and not enough on internal communication. As Lachmann puts it: 'we need an active engagement of the researchers in the marketing of the company' (1988). And where is the cost efficiency in keeping a dog and barking yourself?

3.4.5 *Advantages and disadvantages of management by the marketing function*

Marketing folk earn their keep by asking the right questions – especially ones that never got asked before – and taking appropriate action when they get the answers. This skill also means that they are good at formulating the questions which they want the research to answer, and good at demanding coherent recommendations from the researcher. Thus the briefing and use made of a research project can often be to a higher standard under marketing management than under research management.

There are of course disadvantages in the relative lack of specialist experience in managing and interpreting research, although one would hope that a professional research supplier would be able and willing to take on both these roles. A more serious problem lies in the political aspect of the marketing function. Vested interests in maintaining or killing off particular brands or marketing programmes may (often unwittingly) override the neutrality required in the management and use of research. International marketing is particularly prone to this problem, with both local and central interests vying for attention and priority, and the temptation at hand – even if unconscious – to manipulate the research in favour of a desired outcome.

3.4.6 An optimal approach to international research management

The advantages and disadvantages inherent in the different approaches described in the previous section serve to illustrate that there is no simple method by which to ensure good management of international research.

Perhaps the key recommendation is that an appropriate team should be appointed *from the start*, involving all parties – users, client researchers and research suppliers – at both central and local levels. Lines of authority and communication should be clarified, ideally in a memo that is circulated to all concerned. A model of an ideal team structure is shown in Figure 3.3.

This model takes into account the need for all parties to communicate and consult with their internal and external partners. However, in the interests of avoiding anarchy, it restricts the lines of authority quite severely, while still recognising that degrees of autonomy among local operating companies can vary a lot. It is strongly recommended that diagonal lines of consultation or authority are not permitted! For organisations which have little or no formalised central management responsible for the project area, the recommendation is that one of the local groups should be voted to take on this function – again in the interests of communication efficiency.

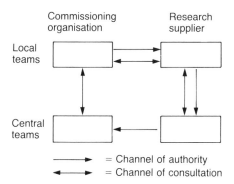

Figure 3.3 Model for an ideal international research management structure

3.5 Comparability

3.5.1 *Importance of comparability*

What do marketing companies gain by having consumer information which can be evaluated for cross-country comparability as well as an individual country basis? Only with information which is genuinely comparable is it possible to do the following:

- To identify the relative size of the business opportunities.
- To assess the extent and nature of similarities between countries.
- To understand the extent and nature of differences between countries.
- To establish inter-country investment and marketing priorities.
- To evaluate company performance across countries on a consistent basis.

Comparability of information should in fact be welcomed not only by the globalists but also by the anti-globalists. If markets have latent similarities, comparable research should reveal them; but if markets really are different, there is no better way to demonstrate the fact than by revealing the differences in a comparable context.

If we accept that comparability is generally reckoned to be 'A Good Thing' in international marketing circles, how do we go about achieving it? This question has no simple answer, and at the very least involves great difficulty and great cost – which sometimes makes you wonder – is it worth it? (One is reminded of the wisdom of a senior marketing man who said, 'You should never embark on a piece of market research if it is cheaper to make a mistake.')

Let us assume, however, that some mistakes, especially in international marketing and advertising, can be prohibitively expensive to make, and that data comparability is judged to be of value.

3.5.2 *Achieving comparability*

3.5.2.1 Meaning of comparability

Comparability means finding differences and similarities between countries which are genuine, and not the result of differences in research techniques or interpretation. It rarely means the simultaneous application of the same sampling and questionnaire techniques in a number of countries, with the emergence weeks or months later of a neat set of tables with the countries at the top and a standard list of attributes down the side. Nor should it mean trying to iron out the nasty little differences between countries such as differences in language or social class divisions so as to achieve a perfect uniformity of data collection. If we could only get all respondents to speak English, or even Esperanto, if only all countries had the same social and economic structure, if only the sun would shine for exactly the same number of hours everywhere, all our problems would disappear.

To ignore these differences in the interests of spurious comparability is a cardinal sin – because it effectively takes a technique rather than problem-oriented view of research and its application. Certain research requirements can arguably be tackled by using the same sample design and questionnaire in all countries, but frequently the imposition of a rigid research structure on a number of different countries may defeat the very objectives that the research is trying to achieve.

To achieve genuine comparability in international market research at the key stages of data collection and interpretation, two different principles must be kept in mind: the principles of *co-ordination* and *flexibility*.

3.5.2.2 Co-ordination

Co-ordination should mean not a rigid unresponsive approach to all research matters, but rather a centralisation by one or other of the researchers involved of certain key functions, namely *planning*, *control* and *interpretation*.

International research projects can very easily flounder through lack of a central co-ordinating function. If this function is not addressed, there is a very real danger of failing to maintain control and comparability through the planning and execution of a project, and ultimately failing to fulfil the client's original brief.

The best way to avoid these potential problems is to set up, for every project, one individual, or one small team, to take responsibility for the central management functions for the whole exercise. With this approach the original requirements of the research are far more likely to be kept in view than by handing on and spreading out responsibilities across disparate individuals and countries.

Similarly, any issues and problems which arise in the course of the project are known and dealt with by the co-ordinator, and not overlooked or ignored simply because they seemed unimportant to the local researchers involved.

Co-ordination not only ensures good control and direction of a project; it generally entails considerable economies of scale in both the planning and execution of international research when compared with a more loosely controlled approach on a country-by-country basis. A co-ordinated approach usually involves preparing only one major set of briefing documents, questionnaires, etc., rather than one set for each country. Processing and analysis of data, whether qualitative or quantitative, can also be more cost-efficient when co-ordinated in one place by one small team of researchers, not to mention the greater comparability of interpretation which can also be achieved in this way.

3.5.2.3 Flexibility

Over-zealous co-ordination can sometimes lead to a lack of flexibility in international research. Despite the need for comparable information, markets are simply not the same. The principle of flexibility should therefore provide the counterpoint to the principle of co-ordination. It should involve paying close attention to local differences, and may well require the use of different techniques in the interests of achieving comparable results.

It is important to adopt a creative, pragmatic outlook in designing, conducting and interpreting international research; not to impose a Procrustean bed of standardised research techniques but to find out and decide on the best approach on a country-by-country basis. In this context, it is always a good idea to seek the advice of local researchers before making commitments concerning objectives and plans. To achieve this, consultation of local research agencies should be made an integral part of the planning of the project.

Any silly ideas or misconceptions that may have arisen through lack of local knowledge will then get shot down in flames, and an improved, more soundly-based plan will finally get hammered out with the approval and support of all parties. This process also encourages the emergence of good ideas which can be used on the project from a wide range of researchers, not just those making up the central co-ordinating team.

In summary, careful application of the two principles of co-ordination and flexibility will go a long way towards achieving comparability, at both the data-collection stage and the interpretation stage. At the practical level, there is a need for both co-ordination and flexibility at all stages of research; planning, fieldwork, analysis and reporting.

3.6 Planning

3.6.1 Sensitivity to all the issues

Good planning is half the secret in international research, and it does help to have time to sort out the various requirements and constraints. The keynote is consultation, but the list below details the various ramifications, both large and small:

- Obtain all relevant needs and viewpoints from research users.
- Obtain agreement on research objectives and methods.
- Obtain views and use experience of local colleagues/research agencies.
- Clarify lines of communication, authority and reporting.
- Ensure comparability of approach/methods/techniques.
- Take care over all translation work involved.
- Check out timetables and logistics with all concerned.
- Check out costing (what is/is not included, exchange rate issues).

It is at the planning stage where local differences should be carefully

---

Case History 3.4:   Beer – a hard or a soft drink?

In the United Kingdom, Germany and Scandinavia, beer is generally regarded as an alcoholic beverage and the factors underlying its consumption are similar to those underlying the consumption of other alcoholic beverages: in Greece, Spain or Italy beer is regarded as much more like a soft drink such as Coca-Cola or orangeade. A survey designed to aid a beer manufacturer in the determination of his/her marketing strategy in Europe had to be designed to obtain information on behaviour and attitudes in relation to soft drinks in some countries and in relation to alcoholic beverages in others. However, quite apart from the expense involved, there would be little point in obtaining information about both soft drinks and alcoholic beverages in all countries covered by the survey. Orangeade just does not compete with beer when it comes to a drinking session in an English pub, and very few Spaniards would consider beer as a serious alternative to whisky.

---

considered (see Case History 3.4). Key areas of possible difference to check on should be as follows:

- Differences in actual and potential target groups.
- Differences in ways in which products or services are used.
- Differences in criteria for assessing products or services.
- Differences in marketing conditions.
- Differences in economic and social conditions.
- Differences in cultural values.
- Differences in market research facilities.
- Differences in market research styles.

There are numerous examples of how the design of a multi-country survey can be affected by differences in attitude or behaviour patterns between one country and another. A German housewife, for instance, asked about her use of bar chocolate for cooking or on sandwiches would – to say the least – be somewhat surprised: however, in France cooking is an important use for bar chocolate, and in Italy it is quite common for children to be given a bar of chocolate between two slices of bread to eat during the school break.

Moreover, the criteria by which products are judged may differ considerably from one country to another. There is little point in asking about the suitability of a food product for snacks in Italy, since most Italians just do not eat between meals: just over the border in Austria, however, many of the impressive briefcases one sees carried around are bulging with an assortment of sandwiches, sausages, apfelstrudel and other delicacies, and in England some people live on a continual diet of snacks between one Sunday dinner and another.

Completely different circumstances may result in a different universe having to be covered in each country, as shown in an eight-country survey amongst doctors on an ethical pharmaceutical product. In The Netherlands general practitioners are very restricted in the drugs they are allowed to prescribe, and there was no possibility of the product under examination being included in the Dutch national insurance list. Interviews were therefore limited to hospitals and specialists. In Belgium, general practitioners have considerable freedom in the drugs they prescribe, and most of the interviews were, therefore, carried out with this group. The problem was the same in both countries, namely to establish the acceptability of the product amongst the medical profession. There would have been no point, however, in interviewing general practitioners in The Netherlands, or concentrating on specialists in Belgium. Comparability at the interpretation stage was achieved insofar as the relative acceptability of the product in the two countries was established, but the target markets selected were very different.

These examples indicate that it is possible to achieve genuine comparability in international market research if sufficient attention is paid to national differences at the early stages of planning and design.

3.6.2 Languages and translation issues

Did you hear the story about the translator who was asked to render the phrase 'out of sight, out of mind' into Mandarin Chinese? When his version was back-translated, it came out as 'invisible, insane'! The dictionary defines 'translation' as: 'to turn from one language to another, preserving the meaning of the original', but sadly there are a good many cases in international research, not to mention marketing and advertising, where inanities of this kind occur.

International research involves a great deal of translating and translation-checking, from multi-language questionnaires and briefing documents through to reading or listening to foreign language group discussions and depth interviews, checking of concept material and delivering debriefs or reports in languages other than English.

Carrying out such translation work well is critical to the good conduct of international research. It is not just a question of sending things off to the nearest translation agency – the translator there will not have been party to the research objectives nor to the development of the material, and cannot be expected to understand the cultural communication and research issues involved. This is one of the reasons why strong linguistic abilities are vital in international research.

Simply having good linguists in-house does not amount to an adequate system in itself. The ideal approach is to ask a 'native' speaker – usually someone working in the local supplier company – to make the first draft of translation. That person is selected to be familiar with research terminology – in both languages – and should be fully briefed on the background, the issues and any subtleties that must be respected or given careful attention. His/her translation is then back-translated by a member of the central project team, who is also familiar with those same issues.

In this way, any divergence from the original English version can be identified and further checked, corrected and resolved (see Case History 3.5). If necessary or

---

Case History 3.5: The missing engagement ring

A supplier of diamonds wished to investigate the size of the potential market in various countries for diamond engagement rings. The obvious question to ask of the samples of unmarried women was: *Are you engaged to be married?*

At the pilot stage of the survey, results seemed to show that a far higher proportion of Italian women were engaged than was the case in any other country.

Now the Italian word used for 'engaged' was *fidanzata*, but this word had changed in significance over the years. An Italian girl will tell you she is *fidanzata* even if her boyfriend has only just bought her an ice-cream for the first time! This difference of meaning explained the higher figure, and led to a more careful translation in the interests of comparability. The phrase eventually used in Italian back-translated as: *Has your hand been asked in marriage?*

This was certainly more old-fashioned, but met the requirement for comparable meaning and hence comparable market estimates.

---

requested, local staff of the client's organisation can also be asked to check on the appropriateness of the translation. This can be particularly helpful when the subject matter is technical or a bit out of the ordinary run of normal vocabulary.

It is not safe to rest easy until the final version of the document has been prepared and given a last once-over, as the annals of Guinness show. A new Guinness television advertisement had been prepared for use in a country in West Africa. The lingua franca was a language little known outside those parts, but the local ad agency there undertook to handle the translation and recording of the voice-over. No one at head office was able to check this local version, but it sounded great, with the word Guinness being mentioned recognisably in apparently appropriate places. Now it just so happened that someone was passing through head office at the time who did understand the local language and apparently the back-translation showed that the text extolled the virtues, not only of Guinness, but also of a certain 'Ali's bazaar' in the local capital! Full marks for West African business enterprise, near miss of egg on face for Guinness.

The moral is, as with most things in international research, not to take anything for granted; to check and back-check until you are quite sure of every last phrase and the Tower of Babel has been well and truly dismantled.

3.7 Fieldwork

3.7.1 Ground rules

Do not think of fieldwork as the time you can take a breather while you wait for the data to roll in. There are too many dangers – and too many opportunities – at

---
Case History 3.6:   The fragrant Italians

A fragrance manufacturer wished to understand what types of fragrance were preferred by men in various European countries. Group discussions were undertaken in order to explore attitudes and perceptions in depth.

The researcher sent out to Italy from the central team experienced some dissonance in her observations. Although the Italian respondents waxed lyrical about their preference for subtle, delicate fragrances, her nose (she was sitting in the group discussion room) gave her strong contrary evidence – so much so that she almost passed out from the overpowering fragrances they were actually wearing.

Had she listened to tapes or read transcripts only, her conclusions would have been very different; hence the value of 'being there'.

---

this stage to be ignored (see Case History 3.6). Key aspects to watch out for are the following:

1. Consider the value of piloting for quantitative work, and the roll-out or lead-country approach for qualitative.
2. Specify clearly what is expected from local research agencies:
   (a) method agreed;
   (b) form of data required;
   (c) when and how delivered;
   (d) involvement *re* analysis/reporting.
3. Take opportunities to experience fieldwork at first hand.
4. Monitor progress and any problems.
5. Keep copies of all data which are to be posted/couriered.

3.7.2 Issues in qualitative research

How can comparability of data be applied to the unstructured nature of qualitative research? Differences in cultures and temperaments are obvious, even looking beyond the traditional stereotypical view of national characteristics, so that a group discussion in Paris or Madrid may give the appearance of no more than a mass of flailing arms to a Japanese moderator who is accustomed to the reserve and restraint of her typical respondents.

Often these differences are more complex than they appear on the surface. Even in markets where consumers are seemingly laying their innermost thoughts out on the table for all to view, such as in Southern Europe or North America, their responses cannot necessarily be taken at face value. They may appear more animated and more candid, but deeper motivations often still remain hidden.

Straightforward, direct questioning will freely reveal answers at rational or cognitive, and even to some extent emotional, levels, yet can fail to uncover important issues relating to deeper motivations of which consumers may not themselves be fully conscious or which they may prefer not to reveal. At the other extreme, the more reserved natures of, say, the Northern Europeans or South-east Asian consumers can mean that self-expression is more restrained, and the problems of social constraints and etiquette can elicit misleading responses. These extremes of behavioural patterns also demand a means of accessing the more covert and emotional motivations at work in consumer habits and reaching beyond the inhibitions and social barriers.

Projective techniques are vital tools to the international researcher in helping to overcome these problems in that they offer a standardised, comparable means of reaching beneath surfaces which may be diverse and multi-faceted. Different though these cultures may be, all respond well to the probing of the inner, unconscious world of the consumer which is achieved via projective techniques. The insight which this offers is often key to identifying a powerful motivation which lies hidden beneath apparent rational differences on the surface.

In the simplest of terms, projective techniques are games; games which reach beyond defences and social constraints, which give consumers the verbal and visual 'vocabulary' to help them access their deeper feelings and which create an environment in which they can express thoughts and feelings which they would not necessarily regard as part of their conscious views, or which at least give them 'permission' to express their views in a less direct way. A group of very smart, very rational German businesspeople can often be transformed into a classroom of playful schoolchildren when their imagination and creativity is unleashed via projective tasks such as collage-making or drawing.

Not all projective techniques are suitable for multi-country research. Clearly, it is preferable in centrally co-ordinated research that the techniques used should be of a central design, so that all moderators are working with the same set of tools. They need to be easy to administer and should require little or no adaptation to individual markets in order to ensure comparability. Techniques which 'travel' best are as follows:

1. *Brand mapping*, where respondents are presented with a variety of competitive brands and asked to group them into categories; a useful technique to understand how consumers view the market, to identify gaps, or to understand the positioning of a particular brand.
2. *Word association*, a widely familiar technique presenting few problems applied internationally. Word association is useful in discovering brand imagery, product attributes and consumer vocabulary. It is quick and easy to administer on either a group or individual basis.
3. *Personification*, a verbal technique with which most moderators are familiar. Respondents are asked to imagine brands as people and describe their appearance, personality, lifestyle, and so on. There are few problems in

administering this technique (provided the group is suitably relaxed) but care has to be taken in interpretation. It is important, for example, to be aware of aspirational or non-aspirational descriptors which may differ from country to country. Driving a Golf GTI may denote a yuppie in the United Kingdom but a fairly ordinary chap in Germany; holidaying at Club Med may say something pretty good about a brand in the United Kingdom, but denote a rather more down-market image in France.

4. *Bubble drawings*, a technique whereby the respondent supplies the thoughts and feelings of an individual shown in a rough-drawn situation. Care must be taken internationally to ensure that the situation depicted is relevant. For example, a typical shop-front might differ from country to country or a drinking scenario would have to be shown as a pub in the United Kingdom but a bar elsewhere. In practice, however, these problems do not often arise since the drawings are very simple and adaptable.

5. *Collages*, visual material in the form of picture boards made from scrap art. This kind of material works particularly well in multi-country research because it provides a common body of projective stimuli, thereby producing comparable data for analysis, and it allows quick access to underlying thoughts and feelings since it provides respondents with a ready-made set of symbols and images to talk around.

   These picture boards are particularly valuable in exploring user imagery and brand imagery. Each board shows a broad range of, say, people, lifestyles, occupations, environments, objects, usage occasions, or whatever is appropriate, which respondents can use to explain their feelings about a brand – why this kind of woman might be attracted to it, why this one would not, and so on. This gives us a great deal more depth and furthermore will reveal common symbols or typologies across countries.

   In designing picture boards for multi-country work, care must be taken to ensure that the final mix of images has sufficient relevance to all the countries concerned. There are many cases, even within Europe, where a particular symbol has different meanings, or the same value is represented in different ways.

   Housing is an obvious problem area; house styles and their relative values differ greatly from country to country and it is usually necessary to produce specific country boards rather than one common board. Food is another area where thought must be given to ensure that relevant symbols are used: basic, everyday fare might need to be shown as meat-and-two-vegetables in the United Kingdom but as a plate of pasta in Italy and a dish of raw fish in Japan.

With careful advance planning, the incorporation of these kinds of projective materials and techniques into multi-country studies is easily achieved, and will give greater depth to the data without compromising comparability or control, surely a worthwhile benefit.

In the case of qualitative research projects involving group discussions, there appears to be some divergence of opinion on the relative merits of using local moderators versus moderators from the central team. Arguably it is not a good idea for members of the central team, however fluent in the relevant languages, to conduct groups in other countries; unless they live as regular natives of the countries concerned they cannot hope to be tuned in to the latest issues, slang, television programmes, etc., to the degree one would consider desirable. It does, however, help immensely in carrying through international projects involving group discussions for members of the central team who speak the relevant languages to brief the local moderators and attend the groups personally, to guide and intervene if necessary, and to debrief the local moderator personally to ensure optimal fulfilment of the information brief.

3.7.3 Issues in quantitative research

Managing quantitative fieldwork internationally calls for much the same discipline as for single-country projects. Careful briefing (whether in person or by telephone/fax) and close monitoring are even more important given the higher risks of misunderstanding and unforeseen circumstances.

Even the seemingly mechanical task of quantitative questionnaire coding requires extra care in international projects. Despite its unpromulgated role in the data processing operation coding represents an important stage which demands meticulous attention to detail if it is to produce a valid and serviceable foundation to the research findings.

An international code-frame clearly plays a vital role in establishing the basis for comparability and for highlighting country differences. Its significance should be acknowledged by assigning one or more multi-lingual research executives, forming part of the core team, to construct the frame, working from verbatim originals from each country. This approach is infinitely better than creating separate code-frames for each country; the latter will be maddeningly non-comparable and can serve only to reveal differences, not similarities.

A centrally formulated code-frame takes full account of the survey objectives. At the same time, it accords equal weight to each country's responses while providing the flexibility needed for the range of emerging answers.

A piece of advertising researched quantitatively across Europe provides us with a simplistic example of the value of this. The advertisement in question elicited identical responses to one particular question from a large proportion of both French and German respondents. It was perceived by both to contain an abundance of information. However, to the rational German respondent, swayed by concrete facts and detail, this was a positive feature. To the French respondent, whose responses are governed more frequently by emotions and influenced by more abstract forces, this was a positive turnoff! In this case, therefore, two separate codes needed to be created.

3.8 Analysis, interpretation and reporting

3.8.1 A synthesised approach

All international research clients want to be able to compare findings from one market to another, and most also want a synthesis of findings in order to understand the broad patterns pertaining across markets as well as within them. It can be strongly argued that it is not possible to achieve a well-balanced or meaningful synthesis of findings if analysis is carried out separately in different countries by different researchers, however good those researchers may be as individuals (see Case History 3.7).

It is more appropriate to have the data analysis carried out by a central team of linguist researchers using a common approach and framework for the task. In this way, comparisons between countries can be more closely weighed and evaluated, and similarities and differences can be seen in their full context. This is not to say that you should not ask local suppliers for their views and help in interpretation. Far from it. But in international research the whole makes up more than the sum of its parts and clients' requirements are best met by offering a fully integrated picture of findings from all markets rather than a disaggregated (and often non-comparable) series of local reports.

3.8.2 Harmonisation of data

3.8.2.1 Need for a planned approach

To achieve an integrated picture from quantitative data requires careful pre-planning of all aspects of survey work from the outset (see section 3.6 on pages 56–9). If data are to be genuinely comparable, the research must ensure comparability, as far as possible, in the following:

- Samples.
- Sampling.
- Questionnaire design.
- Interviewing techniques.
- Code-frames.

International data, all neatly tabulated, can often appear genuine and interestingly comparable, but the user must be wary and check that the material has been properly collected and compiled as described in this chapter.

Case History 3.7: The Freudian fur-coat

A manufacturer of fur-coats wished to understand women's motivations for purchase and ownership. It was felt that the subject required the involvement of the best qualitative researchers to be found in each country, and an identical brief was accordingly given to twelve separate chosen individuals, one based in each of the relevant countries.

When the twelve reports finally came in, the client found that most women, across all the countries in the study, seemed motivated primarily by factors involving status and fashion. However, it seemed that women in France were very different, since their main motives were to do with the Freudian, sexual connotations of fur.

The client was left wondering where the real difference lay – were the women of France so very different from their European counterparts or was it the French researcher who had the difference of outlook?

3.8.2.2 Differential response tendencies

Collection of attitude data by means of scaled measures is nowadays commonplace in many countries and for a whole range of topics, from brand imagery to political polling. For example, a five-point scale is used, with the points representing: agree strongly, agree a little, neither agree nor disagree, disagree a little, disagree strongly. Although simple for everyone to use, these scales do present a problem in international research because different countries have been found to use them in different ways. Italians are more inclined to use the extreme points on such a scale, while Germans are more inclined to use the middle positions; hence 'differential response tendencies' (DRT).

There are ways of correcting for DRT and one is described in Box 3.1. This approach is particularly helpful in large-scale segmentation studies. Although typically the final corrections to be made are not very great, they do solve the problem and there is a resultant improvement in comparability.

3.8.2.3 Tabulation of data

The value and usefulness of international surveys can often be compromised by inappropriate or inadequate tabulations of data. The researcher must decide on and plan the layout. Should the data be presented separately by country (albeit comparably), or should country totals be shown side by side? Is there a need to weight the data in order to represent differences in population or market sizes? What language(s) should be used for the table headings and explanations? Graphic and colour presentation can be immensely useful in giving clarity and focus to the often complex and vast amount of data generated in international research. But make sure that your client is not colour-blind!

Box 3.1   Example of correction for DRT

1. Calculate means and standard deviations for each country separately and for the global total:

	Country A	Country B	Global
Agree strongly (5)	10,000	7,000	17,000
Agree a little (4)	10,000	7,000	17,000
Neither/nor (3)	5,000	7,000	12,000
Disagree a little (2)	5,000	7,000	12,000
Disagree a lot (1)	5,000	7,000	12,000
Mean	3.43	3.00	3.21
Standard deviation	1.40	1.41	1.42

2. Produce standardised scores for each country:

Country A	Country B
$(5 - 3.43 \div 1.40) = 1.12$	$(5 - 3 \div 1.41) = 1.42$
$(4 - 3.43 \div 1.40) = 0.41$	$(4 - 3 \div 1.41) = 0.71$
$(3 - 3.43 \div 1.40) = 0.31$	$(3 - 3 \div 1.41) = 0.00$
$(2 - 3.43 \div 1.40) = 1.02$	$(2 - 3 \div 1.41) = 0.71$
$(1 - 3.43 \div 1.40) = 1.74$	$(1 - 3 \div 1.41) = 1.42$

3. Multiply standardised scores by a global standard deviation (1.42):

Country A	Country B
1.59	2.02
0.58	1.01
−0.44	0.00
−1.45	−1.01
−2.47	−2.02

4. Add global mean (3.21) to these scores:

Country A	Country B
4.80	5.23
3.79	4.22
2.77	3.21
1.76	2.20
0.74	1.19

5. As a final check, apply these new scores to the data for each country. **Each** country will be found to have:

mean	3.21
standard deviation	1.42

3.8.3 *Summary of requirements*

To summarise the needs at the stage of analysis and interpretation the international researcher should do the following:

1. Allow sufficient time for the process. The author is only too aware of the time pressures inherent in international marketing programmes. But time must be scheduled carefully for fieldwork, analysis and reporting, taking account of the labyrinth of national holidays and organisational constraints.
2. Insist on comparable approaches. There will always be plenty of reasons why it is more appropriate/easier/cheaper/faster to have the research handled separately in each country. But the full value of international research projects cannot be realised unless comparability is achieved. Only then is it possible to discern the true nature and extent of similarities and differences across countries, and avoid bias to one country.
3. Insist on a proper synthesis of findings. Good international research does not consist only of a set of single-country reports, even if the research has been conducted on a comparable basis. Someone – ideally the co-ordinating research supplier – should prepare the data and reports in such a way that you get a valid picture of the whole rather than just the sum of its parts.

As a final, but vital element in the process, consider the best ways to approach presentation and reporting:

1. Break the language barrier. There is nothing more futile than a research presentation or report which cannot be understood by its potential users for reasons of language mismatch. And there are several ways to tear down this particular wall: choose research suppliers who have good linguistic abilities, both spoken and written; arrange for translators for team members who would otherwise be cut off from the communication process; encourage presenters to be as clear as possible in their visual and verbal expression.
2. Plan for relevant and creative reporting. Depending on user needs, it should be decided in advance what kind of reporting is needed. Presentations and/or written reports? Separate country reports as well as interviews? Full teams at presentations or central and local groups separately? (There is no ideal in this respect as approaches need to be tailored to specific organisational and project requirements.) Plan for discussion time at presentations, and encourage research suppliers to make their presentations stimulating.
3. Use the research process to achieve motivation and good teamwork. When set against the typical background of cultural barriers, international research projects offer a significant opportunity to motivate the disparate groups involved. The discipline of planning, the experience of fieldwork and the sharing of information all bring the team together in a constructive and creative environment.

3.9 Conclusion

The world is getting smaller every day. Marketing and media companies need more understanding of both the similarities and differences among countries if they are to develop their products and services successfully in an international world.

International research, when it is conducted with professionalism and credibility, can make an important contribution to the process of international marketing by providing objective, comparable and constructive market information, and by helping clients to interpret and use it well.

References and further reading

Agnelli, U. Dr. (1990) 'Guidelines for the manager of the 1990s', *The International Management Development Review*, vol. 6, p. 59.

Burgaud, P. J. (1986) 'The research at the service of decision-making in collective build-up of the enterprise's project', 39th ESOMAR Congress, pp. 599–619.

Coutts, C. (1991) 'The use of research to develop a new concept in international management services', ESOMAR Seminar, Ljubljana, pp. 85–95.

Day, B. (1986) 'Successful long-term branding: the advertising ingredients', *Admap*, January.

Hawes, C. (1985) 'Global marketing and global agencies', *Admap*, September.

Hofstede, G. (1991) *Cultures and Organisations: Software of the mind*, New York: McGraw-Hill.

Jakob, H. J. (1990) "From national to European – how to make it happen?", *The International Management Development Review*, vol. 6, pp. 65–70.

Kern, H., Wagner, H.-C. and Hassis, R. (1989) 'European aspects of a global brand: the BMW case', 42nd ESOMAR Congress, p. 526.

Laborie, J. L. (1989) 'What 1992 means for market research', Market Research Society Annual Conference, Brighton.

Lachmann, U. (1988) '7, 8, 9 out! Could this be the future of market research in companies?', 41st ESOMAR Congress, pp. 811–22.

Levitt, T. (1983) 'The Globalisation of Markets', *Harvard Business Review*, May/June.

Naeve, D. (1986) 'Integrating multi-country research into marketing strategy decisions – a case history', 39th ESOMAR Congress, pp. 621–36.

Potsch, L. E. and Limeira, T. M. (1986) 'The implications of the strategic-organisational dynamics of companies for the patterns of action of market research agencies', 39th ESOMAR Congress, pp. 559–75.

CHAPTER 4
New data sources for marketing research
John Bound

4.1 How does information technology affect marketing?

Information Technology has not only speeded day-to-day operations: it has also opened new sources of information, enabling marketers to contact individual people about whose behaviour and circumstances information is already stored in a databank. This is not a new idea. The old-fashioned grocer would send a calendar each year to the people on his/her list of good customers. Firms such as mail-order houses in direct contact with their consumers have always been able to do this, even when they have become very big: computers have just made their card-indexes of customers easier to work.

What is new is the application of direct marketing to other types of business. In the past businesses selling to consumers whom they did not know personally in this way have had to aim their marketing efforts at those groups of people who seemed the best targets, rather than named individuals. Marketing research has been the way these groups were identified. Information technology has now enabled marketers to record and keep detailed data about millions of people. Such data, which are described below, come mostly from outside the traditional sources of marketing research.

4.2 How does information technology affect marketing research?

For many years marketing researchers have used computers to process data. The new information technology applications are different, and are upsetting the well-established patterns of research data collection.

The problem for marketing researchers is that they have traditionally collected data from the public under the guarantee of anonymity and the promise of no sales contact. Now data sources not giving these guarantees can provide marketing information, as well as fulfilling a primary purpose of sales promotion. The collection of such data makes the marketing researchers' guarantee of anonymity less credible and less valuable. Indeed, it is claimed that the new data sources save consumers from irrelevant and annoying sales approaches and that consumers do not necessarily see **relevant** sales approaches as a nuisance at all.

At the time of writing, marketing researchers find themselves uncertain about these new sources which are being exploited mainly by other practitioners who operate in database bureaux, direct marketing agencies and management consultants.

Information technology enables large quantities of data to be brought together. These data as individual sets may not be of use to marketers or any challenge to privacy. Combined, however, they may do both. If, to take a imaginary example, the manufacturer of a slimming diet were able to look at records of consumer grocery purchases made by customers using debit cards to find the names of those who bought any form of slimming diet, many would feel this intrusive.

Worries about the possible accumulation in single databanks of data about individuals have led to legal protection for individuals in Britain under the Data Protection Act, and to the restriction of laws elsewhere. Paradoxically, these laws have made life more difficult for the traditional marketing researcher collecting anonymous data.

4.3 Whatever the source, the data need analysis

The actual assembly and processing of the data by computer to the stage at which the marketer has to decide what analysis will help him/her is a highly technical subject. The techniques are changing rapidly. The most useful service for readers of this chapter is to describe the different data sources and the way in which they are being brought together in the United Kingdom at present. When the data are assembled, their tabulation follows the principles set out later in Appendix 3. Indeed, the sheer volume of data and complexity of possible tabulation mean that a clear strategy for analysis is needed. The database itself must be structured with a view to its later analysis.

4.4 Where do these data about individuals come from?

Large mail-order companies, utilities and other organisations dealing direct with the public have a number of sources of information available to them. The most obvious is about their own customers' names and addresses, and purchasing history. Data from another database of another organisation's customers or lifestyle data may also be added, within the limits permitted by the present Data Protection Act.

Lifestyle data are now collected and sold on a large scale. Three companies are operating in this way at present. The databases these firms collect and maintain are essentially lists of names and addresses with details of media usage, purchasing habits, interests and other classificatory detail. Large quantities of such data are collected by mailed questionnaires, purchase registration forms included with consumer goods, questionnaires inserted in periodicals, market-research style interviews, telephone help-line records, and so on.

The collection of the data is done in much the same way as in market research, with the important differences that there is no guarantee of anonymity, and that the data are intended to be used to find sales prospects.

4.5 How is the database information used?

Decisions as to whom to send mailing-shots, for example, may clearly be made on the basis of such data. A mail-order company wishing to promote a special offer of lawnmowers, for example, might target recent customers who have made purchases of household goods from them, or who have expressed interest in gardening in response to a lifestyle questionnaire. Typically the best prospects for many products are those who have purchased the product previously.

If a firm has a large customer database, it may well find that quite a few of them also appear in a particular lifestyle database. For these people the firm will then have details of both their lifestyle responses and their purchasing history. The number of these matches is clearly unlikely to be sufficient to make individual sales approaches to these people worthwhile, but they may well be used for general study as described below.

The decision about making sales contacts may also use more general data about the area in which people live, but which does not identify individuals. In the lawnmower example, the target might also include people who live in geodemographically classified areas (how this works is explained below) where homes generally have gardens. More complicated rules for deciding whom to contact may be derived by the modelling described below.

4.5.1 Using data about groups of people to add to individual data

The postcode of each customer is now an important link which enables individual customers to be classified using data about the particular small area in which the customer lives. Each postcode covers some twenty homes (more in rural areas). Each large mail user has a unique code.

The postcode address file (PAF) is regularly updated and available commercially. It seeks to list every postal address in the United Kingdom, distinguishing business addresses from personal, and to give the postcode of each. A list of postcodes summarising the coverage of each address is also readily available.

The PAF is now widely used for drawing samples of addresses from which to conduct interviews (although a list of premises rather than people as is the Electoral Register, it is for that reason more complete and accurate). But the ability of the PAF to link addresses and postcodes has other uses with which we are now concerned.

Sources such as geodemographic databases (as explained below) or the Census of Population give information broken down by individual postcodes. If we know someone's address, we can deduce by using the postcode quite a lot about that small area in which that person lives.

4.5.2 Using the census

The way this works for the Census of Population is as follows. The 1991 census makes available for every enumeration district (ED), in which there are about 160–200 homes in each, a wide variety of information about the households and people in that area, as returned on the census forms.

There is an elaborate system for ensuring that information about individuals may not be deduced from the data or their cross-tabulation. These precautions restrict the breakdowns available.

The postcodes contained in each enumeration district in the 1991 census are recorded, so that for any postcode it is possible to attach information derived from processing census data from the enumeration district in which the postcode lies.

4.5.3 Using geodemographics

The other main source of local data is geodemographic systems, often referred to as ACORN, after the first such system. These systems are now available from several firms. By performing cluster analyses on census data these organisations have divided all the enumeration districts into a number (40 to 60) of clusters or types each of which contains districts similar in characteristics of marketing interest, such as type of housing, possession of cars, size of family, education level, and so on.

They have further attached to each postcode the cluster identifier of the ED in which it falls, so that a marketing researcher who has access to the database may for any address determine the postcode, and the cluster identifier (or ACORN group, if that system is being used). The identifier number may then be used as a classification variable in all the different types of quantitative analysis.

These identifiers often discriminate clearly between purchasing levels of products, though this effectiveness is limited since the identifier refers to the neighbourhood rather than the individual or household. A respondent may, for example, be living alone, and yet live in a district where most families have many children. Thus, he/she would not be interested in products for children, as the geodemographic identifier attached to him/her would suggest.

4.5.4 Using data about individuals for general information

This is the way marketing research has traditionally operated: the names and addresses of respondents are discarded and the data they have provided are treated as representing the market as a whole. In the same way the individual information from customer or lifestyle databases may have the names and addresses removed, thus being depersonalised. The data may then be used for more general marketing understanding rather than for addressing particular consumers. Removing the individual names and addresses for the data respects the privacy of the individuals, while still enabling their data to be used.

The most obvious application is to treat such data, or a sample of them, as a sample of the population just as though the data had come from an ordinary sample survey. The sampling process is unlikely to have been random, but by adjusting the proportions of various groups by the statistical process of weighting, the effect is of a large sample perhaps of sections of the population normally hard to find, such as lapsed readers of a particular journal. If details of people for whom a match of lifestyle and purchasing information has been achieved as described above, the sample of this quite small number may be very informative about customers in general.

The ability to provide large samples for a particular area may also help advertising media planning for products or retail outlets with localised catchment. Country-wide surveys such as the National Readership Survey can provide only small local samples. Omnibus surveys can similarly provide larger local samples from their databases accumulated over time.

Another use of the de-personalised data is for statistical modelling, as in constructing a scoring system. The various characteristics of customers are given different weights, so that for each person the aggregate of the weights represents that person's potential as a future customer, or perhaps credit risk. These rules or scoring systems may then be applied to everybody in the customer base. People who normally pay their gas or electricity bill promptly may, for example, find they are given more latitude if they forget a particular payment than people with a consistent record of bad payment.

4.6 Database use by retailers

Retailers have both special research needs and sources of data. They normally do not have a customer database such as that described above, but do nowadays have a vast database derived from electronic point of sale (EPOS), that is to say from bar-code data from check-outs. Although such data do not normally identify the purchaser, they enable supermarket operators to model the effects of promotions, price changes and store lay-out. Such data may be combined with experimental alterations of, say, price within a store. Straightforward tabulation of rates of sale aids decisions on product ranges.

In addition to their own data, retailers also have available all the area data from geodemographics and the census, as well as lifestyle data for whatever areas interest them. If, for example, a defined area around a proposed new store is taken, the number of individuals in a lifestyle database will often be great enough to estimate a profile of consumer demographics and media exposure.

4.7 Store location research

The main research problem special to retailers is store location. What volume of business would be attracted to a particular new store location, and what would the effect be on existing stores? One way of defining effective customer catchment areas is by using drive times. A survey or previous experience might say that people would be willing to shop at a store if they could travel to it within twenty minutes. From a map using estimates of average speed or experiments on the ground the area implied by this drive time may be defined.

This area may then be studied using small area geodemographic lifestyle or Census of Population data to show what sort of people live in it, and from this, the estimated potential sales volume. Since there are other stores nearby, some sort of model sharing the potential between the existing and projected stores is then needed. A gravity model is sometimes used, in which consumers' probability of going to a store is a function of its distance from them, but the problem is complex and successful practitioners seem unlikely to reveal their methods.

4.8 Summary of database applications

Richard Webber in a conference paper has summarised some of the main purposes of these different sources in Table 4.1.

4.9 Data fusion

There are limits to the amount and type of information which may be gathered from an individual respondent whether by a single one-survey questionnaire, or by

Table 4.1 Applications of databases from various sources

Source			
Surveys	Customer databases	Geo-demographics	Lifestyle databases
For what purpose:			
National market brand share measures	Credit risk	Planning door-to-door promotion	Local brand share measures
New product positioning	Actuarial analysis	Local press evaluation	Profiling detailed segments
New product development	Promotional response measurement	Local market size measures	
Attitude and value research	Catchment area measurement	Local brand potential estimation	Store catchment area measures
Pricing research	Profiling detailed segments	Profiling detailed segments	
TV and National Press advertising research			
For what types of business:			
All	Financial Mail order	All	Fast-moving consumer goods
	Public utilities		Direct marketing
	Retail		Selective coupon
Distribution			

Source: adapted from Webber, 1992.

other ways of collecting data. It has proved very difficult to collect both purchasing and media exposure data from the same person.

Data fusion has therefore been developed to combine information from two different surveys as though individual respondents had given information on both sets of topics. This is done by taking an individual respondent A from the first survey and finding a respondent B in the second survey who has very similar characteristics to A. It is then assumed that A would have answered about the second topic in the same way as did B.

Another respondent from the first survey is then taken, and a match similarly sought from the second survey, and so on, until as many as possible of the respondents in the first survey have been matched. An artificial data bank has then been created that may be analysed as though respondents had answered on both topics.

The matching process depends on the collection of similar demographic data in each survey, and on those demographics being able in combination to predict the sort of answers provided by the respondents in each survey. The rules for doing this, and deciding when a match is good enough or when no match can be made, have to be decided, and computer routines for applying them set up. There is no guarantee that the results will be as assumed.

The best-known example of the technique is the combination of TGI data about household purchasing and BARB data about television viewing. BARB'S operations will be described in Chapter 13. The fused data enable television viewing to be analysed according to the purchasing of particular products. The fusion procedure was tested by an enquiry carried out by the Market Research Development Fund in 1989, when by elaborate methods similar data were collected from the same respondents about both topics. The results from this experiment were found to accord well with the results of fusing the same data ends.

Further reading

Since this is a new and developing field, definitive accounts in it are few. The author is indebted to a number of practitioners for unpublished communications. The following papers enlarge upon or update material in the chapter.

'Data Fusion: proceedings of a Market Research Development Foundation Seminar, November 1989'. London: Market Research Society.

Leventhal, B. (1993) 'Geodemographics comes of age', *Research Plus*, December, London: Market Research Society.

Webber, R. (1990). 'Prospering together: synergy between survey research and deodemographics', in 'Database Marketing and Market Research: ABMRC Conference Proceedings, Stratford-on-Avon, October 1989', London: Association of British Market Research Agencies.

Westlake, M. (ed.) (1993). 'Relational databases: tutorial papers on the relations model selected from a SGCSA Conference on Relational Databases in Survey Research', Chesham, Bucks: Association for Survey Computing (formerly Study Group for Computer Survey Analysis.

CHAPTER 5

Research design procedure and choices

Exploratory research may yield results that are sufficiently conclusive to obviate the need for a descriptive survey of the market population. In this chapter, however, we assume the following:

- Exploratory research has put us in a position to formulate hypotheses about the characteristics of the population we are interested in.
- The extent to which these characteristics of habit and attitude are held is open to question.

This chapter is designed to give a general view of the decisions which have to be made, and the choices of research procedure available, when markets are described. Sample design and data-collection methods are considered in more detail in Chapters 6 and 7.

5.1 Stages in the survey procedure

The order of events from review of marketing objectives to provision for monitoring performance is illustrated in Figure 5.1. The diagram shows an example of the functional responsibilities and tasks needed to provide the resources for the implementation of each stage by the chart organisation and the supplier of research. The inputs from the 'marketing' and 'marketing research' functions of the client organisation are shown alongside those of the 'supplier'. The supplier of research is the external research agency commissioned or brought in to conduct the research effort. The examples shown in stages in Figure 5.1 are as follows:

Stage 1 Marketing objectives are fully discussed with those responsible for designing research and the discussion includes consideration of possible courses of action *before* the research plan is made. In Figure 5.1 the supplier may be a research agency offering a range of services or an organisation specialising in one research function, e.g. data collection or data processing (see section 5.2). The client company may proceed direct to (3) with the research design work carried out by the supplier. However, exploratory research in (2) can benefit the client company.

Stage 2   Figure 5.1 illustrates a procedure which provides for second thoughts about the nature of the marketing problem after exploratory research has been carried out. Had research been ordered without due discussion of marketing objectives and possible courses of marketing action, the client organisation would not be in a position to judge whether the research problem could be better defined. Research objectives are not a repetition of marketing objectives. The marketing objective might be to enter the market for accelerated freeze-dried convenience foods and the marketing problem the definition of the launch range.

The research objectives will then be to establish clearly the demographic characteristics of those using the main categories of convenience food, to define their attitudes towards products they had tried, how they had prepared them, when they had used them, and whether existing competitive options available fell short of requirements.

Stage 3   The research proposal specifies when, where and by whom the survey is being carried out. It summarises the research proposal, specifies the method of data collection, sampling procedure and how the data is going to be analysed, and estimates the personnel, time and cost involved.

Stage 4   The research design and sampling procedure are described. The possible choices are reviewed later in this chapter. Cost is an important constraint. The research agency (as the supplier) has the responsibility to create its research design, based on choice of data collection and sampling methods and to keep within agreed time and cost constraints with the client organisation.

Pilot work is trying out the proposed design – the questionnaire or other recording device it is proposed to use together with the selection of respondents for questioning, or observing. Pilot work is not the same thing as exploratory research. Exploratory research helps to determine the research design. Pilot work tests the design and helps to determine costs. For example, in the early days of pet-food marketing, a research agency underestimated the cost of fieldwork. Pet owners like to talk about their pets and, in the event, interviews took longer than had been anticipated. If sufficient pilot calls had been made, this problem would have been averted.

Stage 5   In consumer surveys it is unusual for a client organisation to carry out its own fieldwork of data collection. Using a research agency helps to ensure that competitors are not alerted to a company's intentions for a new product development on a product launch.

In a large organisation which has significant marketing and marketing research functions or departments, the research agency will present the analysis of its findings to managers in these departments who would in turn feed back the findings to senior managers through the organisation's management hierarchy. A

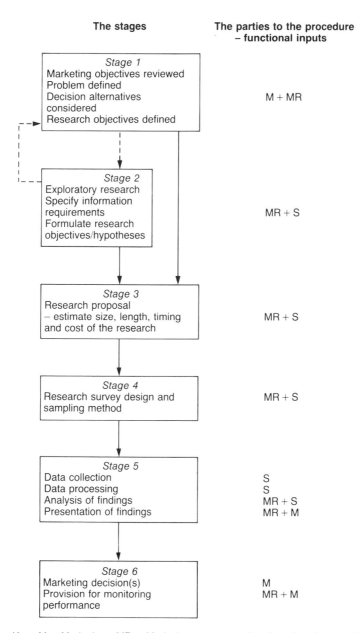

The stages   **The parties to the procedure**
                                  – functional inputs

Stage 1
Marketing objectives reviewed
Problem defined
Decision alternatives   M + MR
considered
Research objectives defined

Stage 2
Exploratory research
Specify information
requirements   MR + S
Formulate research
objectives/hypotheses

Stage 3
Research proposal
– estimate size, length, timing   MR + S
and cost of the research

Stage 4
Research survey design and   MR + S
sampling method

Stage 5
Data collection   S
Data processing   S
Analysis of findings   MR + S
Presentation of findings   MR + M

Stage 6
Marketing decision(s)   M
Provision for monitoring   MR + M
performance

Key: M = Marketing   MR = Marketing research   S = Supplier of research

Figure 5.1   Functional responsibilities and tasks for stages within the MR process

small to medium-sized company may not have established marketing research and marketing departments. Marketing intelligence reports in these firms could be disposed and held by various individuals or groups, say in sales, distribution, production and finance (McDonald 1992). In such cases, it is likely that the marketing/sales directors and managing directors would commission the survey work from the research agency and the agency would report direct to these senior managers.

The types of input from a firm to the survey procedure can therefore vary accordingly to the resources and organisation of the firm so the parties to these procedures as shown in Figure 5.1 are intended as only a guide.

Stage 6   Marketing decisions can be made by building upon the recommendations of the research agency and the company's capabilities. Implementation of these marketing decisions needs to be accompanied by some mechanism or provision for monitoring the effects of these decisions. For example, a car manufacturer or a financial services institution may be spending heavily on an advertising campaign to promote a particular product to a specific market segment. The impact of this advertising campaign needs to be evaluated and assessed for its effectiveness in reaching sales and profit projections.

5.2 Parties to the procedure

The initials set against the stages in Figure 5.1 stand for the marketing and the marketing research functions within the client organisation and the supplier which is the external market research firm. The extent to which research work is 'put out' varies. At one extreme the sponsor's marketing research department may collaborate with an outside research agency at the exploratory stage, then commission the agency to cover all stages from research design to presentation of findings. At the other extreme, the marketing company may merely commission fieldwork and electronic data processing – handing over the questionnaire, specifying the sample and receiving back computer printouts of the analysis.

If the working relationship between marketing and marketing research is a good one, interpretation of the findings will be a joint operation so that the significance of the findings is fully (marketing) and properly (marketing research) exploited. What do both parties reasonably expect from this relationship? Box 5.1 presents a check-list from the Market Research Society (*Yearbook* 1994) as a guide to the commissioning of market research for both parties: the company commissioning the research and the market research agency as the supplier.

Clearly, within a two-way relationship there must be a good element of co-operation. However, managers in client organisations may not wish to give too much internal marketing information to a research agency. Reasons for this can include any of the following:

1.   The desire not to influence or to prejudice the outcomes of the agency's work.

Box 5.1 A guide to the commissioning of survey research

This guide has a very simple purpose. It is intended to help potential buyers of survey research in the selection and briefing of a supplier. However, although the purpose is simple, its resolution is not. Many organisations which undertake a considerable amount of survey research divide this work among a number of suppliers. There is no one supplier which is the best for every project, and selecting a supplier for a particular piece of research is not a simple matter.

Notes of this kind can be only broad guidelines to the sort of things that should be considered when selecting a supplier. The three sections which follow attempt to set out a check-list of things that should be covered in your contract.

1. **What the supplier can expect from you** lists things which you should do to ensure that you give the supplier the opportunity to contribute fully in the resolution of your problem.

2. **What you can expect from the supplier – general** lists the areas that should be considered in evaluating the overall competence and standing of the supplier and thus should be used in deciding whether or not to approach the supplier on a specific problem.

3. **What you can expect from the supplier – specific** is intended to cover the points a supplier should include in his/her specific proposals and upon which final decisions in the choice of a supplier should be made.

1. **What the supplier can expect from you**
   a) A statement of the research problem, preferably in the form of a written brief.
   b) A setting of the problem in its general background and context, in some cases, users may be able to define their overall problem within its generalised context but not have the experience to define it in research terms.
   c) An opportunity to meet and discuss the problem and its background.
   d) An indication of the sorts of decisions that are likely to be influenced by the research results and the uses to which the results are to be put (e.g. whether publication is envisaged).
   e) A broad indication of the budget available for the research project.
      A research supplier cannot be expected to provide satisfactory and comprehensive research proposals in the absence of the above; it is therefore in your interests to supply them. There are three other things a supplier can reasonably expect, though of themselves they will not necessarily affect the quality of research proposals.
   f) That you should only approach suppliers on a formal basis when there is a reasonable probability that the project under commission will actually be commissioned.
   g) It is the type of project which you feel should be the subject of tenders, that you should restrict the suppliers you approach to a reasonable number (say 2–4), and then inform them that they are in a competitive situation.
   h) If you should submit a project to tender in this way, the suppliers can reasonably expect an opportunity to meet you to discuss your reaction to the approach suggested in their research proposals before you make your final choice of supplier.

→

Suppliers will often spend a considerable amount of time in the preparation of research proposals. It is desirable that this practice should continue but this will only be the case if suppliers perceive their investment has some chance of paying off.

2. **What you can expect from the supplier – general**
   The first check-list details the criteria which can be used to assess the supplier's general level of competence and will help in the decision as to whether, in principle, a particular supplier will suit your requirements.

   a) Evidence of the background and quality of his/her research executives.
   b) Details of any specialists (psychologists, statisticians) employed full-time and/or on a consultancy basis.
   c) Evidence of experience that may be relevant to your particular situation; work on similar kinds of problems; work within the same market; experience of using relevant research techniques.
   d) Details of the filed operation; selection and training of interviewers; level of supervision; checks on quality and accuracy.
   e) Details of editing, coding and purchasing operations; quality and training of staff supervision of these functions; checks on quality and accuracy.
   f) Details of analysis and tabulation; computers and machinery used; restrictions on numbers and types of tabulations.
   g) Details of normal standard of reporting; the style and content of reports.
   h) Details of accounting and legal aspects; normal billing procedures.

3. **What you can expect from the supplier – specific**
   This second check-list sets out the specific points you can expect a supplier to include in its proposals for a particular project.

   a) Demonstration, in its statement of the research objectives and of the scope of the inquiry, that the supplier understands your problem.
   b) Detailed descriptions of the research design including:
      i) A statement of the scope and nature of any preliminary desk research, qualitative work, or pilot studies.
      ii) For any quantitative study a statement of the data collection technique (how the information is to be obtained); the universe to be sampled (who is to be interviewed); the size of the sample (how many are to be interviewed); the method of sample selection (how the individuals are to be selected).
   c) A statement of the cost of the project and a clear indication of the assumptions on which it is based and what is included, e.g. assumptions made about length of interview; assumptions made about degree of executive involvement; whether personal briefing of interviewers is included; number of copies of report envisaged; approximate number of tabulations envisaged; whether there will be a written interpretation of the tabulations; whether visual presentation of results is included.
   d) A reasonably detailed timetable for the project and reasonably firm reporting date.
   e) A statement of the specific executive(s) responsible for the project.

Extract reprinted from the *Market Research Yearbook 1994* with permission.

2. The desire for the agency to uncover new information through its own work to add to the marketing intelligence effort.
3. Some information regarded as confidential may be difficult or time consuming to separate out from reports to give to the agency.
4. The agency may take on work for another company which is a competitor once its work for the client organisation is finished.

The attitudes of both parties to the research, the resources available for conducting the research, the cost-benefit implications and the potential usefulness of the research findings are useful considerations to take into account for the appraisal of whether a marketing research project should be conducted.

Research agencies need to generate results to demonstrate the financial values of their research outcomes which can be clearly communicated to their clients. However, clients also need to involve researchers in their decision-making processes and provide them with adequate funds 'to do the job' if clients are to do their part in ensuring a successful outcome to their research effort.

5.3 Design choices

Research design has been mentioned within the context of the description of the marketing research process in Chapter 1. The data collection and sampling methods in this section will be the product of the choices set out in Box 5.2. Selection of the data-collection and sampling procedures will depend on the research objectives and the funds available for research from the sponsoring company. In this chapter we are focusing on the use of surveys to describe markets but we might have decided to take a qualitative rather than a quantitative approach. Qualitative work is invaluable, indeed essential, at the exploratory stage. But when market description is going to affect marketing decisions involving substantial expenditures, findings based on statistically significant numbers of cases carry more conviction than those based on small numbers of cases, even though the data yielded by the few are likely to be richer in ideas and detail than those collected in a large-scale survey.

It is possible to have the best of both approaches; to collect the ideas at the exploratory stage and then to design a survey which quantifies the significant ones. An example of this is given in Box 5.3.

We must not underrate the importance of qualitative work, for the qualitative approach is widely used in the search for new product ideas to formulate new brands, and to create and develop advertising campaigns (Berkowitz *et al.* 1994). We are now going to review the design choices set out in Box 5.2 before focusing more closely on sampling techniques and on questionnaire design.

There are four main ways of collecting survey data: by observing behaviour, using existing material, questioning respondents and experimenting. In practice, the distinction between them is by no means cut and dried.

Box 5.2 Design choices

Data collection

Observing	*Using existing material*	*Questioning*	*Experimenting*
personal diary	secondary data	personal telephone	laboratory
instrumental	primary data	postal	field
electronic		computer	

Sampling

Probability (random)   *Purposive (non-random)*
simple random   quota
systematic random   judgement
stratified – proportionate   convenience
       disproportionate
cluster – one stage
       two stage
       multi-stage drawn
       with pps*   random location

*drawn with probability proportionate to size of population (see section 4.2)

Box 5.3

Example of a research design for qualitative research into retail merchandise assortment strategies

Defining the problem and the marketing objective

This study developed from the growing speculation on supermarket saturation attributed to market share domination by the UK 'Big Three' retailers, Sainsbury, Tesco and Argyll; the increasing number of new supermarket outlets; and lower than expected food expenditure by consumers. Similarities in supermarket merchandise ranges and the retailers need to differentiate led to the formation of the *marketing objective* for this research. This was to establish what additional product ranges could be sold in a supermarket. A consumer survey to determine market needs and preferences might be limited to product types currently carried in a supermarket. However, an alternative route to explore retailers' views on range diversification could reveal what, if any, constraints existed to prevent the introduction and success of a new range.

Research objectives
1) To establish the strategic reasoning behind deletions and expansions of merchandise ranges;
2) To determine the constraints on range diversification, and
3) To identify retailers' perceptions of the extent of diversification.

Secondary data search

A search of secondary data proved fruitless. Although sales data could be accessed this would not indicate the causes for a range's growth or decline or why that range was first introduced. A search of existing academic and trade articles identified that although the food multiples were expanding and diversifying, many mixed retailers and variety stores were by contrast rationalising their ranges. However, more qualitative detail of the reasoning behind these moves was required and few companies divulge or make public their strategy behind their successes or failures. It became necessary to conduct a primary data search.

Research design

A purposive sample of senior managers covering key roles in the selection and buying process of new product ranges was chosen. Trading directors, marketing managers, senior buyers and merchandisers were selected from five major food retailers, representing 40 per cent of the market, with five mixed retail businesses for comparison. This latter group of companies were important because they had already experienced diversification and were now rationalising a number of product categories. Their reasoning combined with the food retailer information would provide a detailed picture of the extent of supermarket range diversification. The data were obtained from twelve semi-structured 'depth' interviews which allowed the respondent flexibility to talk, and also facilitated comparisons.

Presentation of results

Sixteen hours of taped interviews were transcribed and content analysed. The transcriptions were coded and the most frequent responses to key open-ended questions were weighted. The results were first presented aggregately and following further analysis comparisons were made across retail sectors. This qualitative study has given valuable insight into retailer perceptions of range diversification, and has generated a number of hypotheses which can now be tested through a major quantitative survey.

Source: Cathy Hart (1994) Loughborough University Business School.
The Canadian and European Institutes of Retailing and Services Studies
Conference, Banff, Canada.

5.4 Observing

From time to time motorists are held up while traffic is funnelled past an observation post. This post is manned by observers with recording instruments and clipboards. The passage of all vehicles is recorded but every nth vehicle is stopped. The driver of the nth vehicle is asked where he/she has come from, is going to, the purpose of the journey and, perhaps, some questions designed to show if this is a one-off journey or a routine one.

This example illustrates the strength and limitation of observing as a method of data collection. The strength is its objectivity. Given that the recording instrument is in order and that traffic is sufficiently slowed down for the necessary observations to be made (e.g. commercial vehicles, passenger cars, etc.), risk of bias is reduced to a minimum. The data are not influenced by how questions are asked nor by the respondent's capacity to answer. But the weakness of the data is that they will tell us nothing about the purpose or frequency of journeys unless a sample of commercial vehicles and cars is stopped and questions are asked.

It is sometimes claimed that data derived from observation are more objective than those derived from questioning. This holds good if the data are automatically recorded by instruments, providing the sample being observed is a representative of the population concerned.

In the television-audience research carried out by TN AGB for the Broadcasters Audience Research Board (BARB), meters attached to panellists' sets automatically record whether the set is switched on and, when on, what station is being received. But in order to know the size of the television audience it is necessary for individual viewers to record their presence in front of the set. Peoplemeters (press-button handsets of key pads) have taken the place of diaries for this purpose. It is less onerous for the viewer to press a button at the start and at the finish of a viewing session; the risk of human error is reduced (but not eliminated) and passage of the data from viewer to databank is accelerated.

Diaries are used for a wide variety of marketing purposes. They have long been the means by which consumer purchases are recorded. Most are so designed that the respondent is only required to mark coded positions and the data are electronically 'mark-sensed' when the diary is returned to the research company. As the choices being offered to consumers proliferate – manufacturers' brands, retailers' 'own labels', generic products, varieties within brands, special offers – it is easy for the wrong position in the diary to be marked or for a purchase to be overlooked.

Observation and recording of the passage of goods along the distributive channel now generally rests on the electronic scanning of bar codes. Nielsen's syndicated Scantrack service is based on a panel of retail outlets with check-outs equipped to read bar codes so that data may be recorded electronically instead of by manual audit. There has been considerable development in the application of electronic methods outside this country, and major research suppliers, such as TN AGB and Nielsen, operate internationally.

There are two approaches to be considered; in the first case, an interviewer keys in the panellist's answers to a structured questionnaire; in the second, the panellist is equipped by the research company with a modem, together with an electronic device to read the bar codes as the shopping is being unpacked. The modem connects the domestic telephone to the company's mainframe computer and the data are transmitted as the bar codes are read. The second approach appears to be the more efficient. It is, for example, being used by McNair Anderson's Brandscan service in Australia.

Distribution checks are also used to observe retail selling prices. The observations may be made by the marketing company or by a research agency offering trade research services. The distribution checks may be made regularly to yield trend data or on an *ad hoc* basis. This use of observation is cheaper than the continuous audit based on a panel and it gives a marketing company the chance to conceal its interest from the retail trade, but the data yield is limited to what can be seen at the point of sale.

Human observation is also used in comparison shopping. Retailers are as interested in comparing consumer prices as are the consumers themselves. The John Lewis Partnership's claim to be never knowingly under-sold is supported by observation research of this kind.

When observations are being made by people, reliability of the record will be affected by whether the observer has anything else to do at the time. When self-service was first introduced to the petrol station forecourt the behaviour of motorists was observed to see if they had difficulty in following the instructions on the pump. The behaviour of those being observed may be affected by the fact that they are being watched, however discreetly. When the observer is disguised, say as a forecourt attendant, he is liable to be distracted from the business of recording observations. Hidden cameras get round this difficulty, but the rules of the Market Research Society require that the subject be informed before use is made of data collected in this way (MRS 1994). However, cameras placed in retail stores ostensibly to deter shoplifters and to provide security also record shopping behaviour.

The use of observation as a method of data collection has been stimulated by developments in the electronics field. 'Mechanical' methods are used in the development of pack designs, in the pre-testing of advertisements and in the measurement of television viewing. The use of 'impersonal' methods is discussed in these contexts, and in the context of retail auditing in this book.

5.5 Using existing material

The use of primary and secondary data has been discussed in Chapter 2 and sources of information and publications provided in Appendix 2 at the end of the book. It is important for researchers to be able to use existing material where relevant to their research purposes in terms of time and cost savings and validation of effort.

5.6 Questioning

We can ask questions in a personal interview, by telephone, through the post or by computer. The choice depends on the following:

- The subject of the survey.
- The nature of the survey population.
- The research budget.

Surveys vary in the ease with which the required type of respondent may be contacted and in the length and complexity of the questionnaire. In deciding between personal, telephone and postal interview the criterion is the cost of each *satisfactorily* completed questionnaire. This must, of course, be estimated in advance, the estimate being based on the prior experience of the research agency or of the marketing company and on the results of pilot work (see section 5.1).

5.6.1 *In a personal interview*

Face-to-face interviewing is still the commonly used method of collecting survey data in this country, whereas in the United States telephone interviewing has largely taken over. Research suppliers in Britain conduct 13.5 million interviews each year of which approximately 16 per cent are telephone and 54 per cent are personal interviews (AMSO 1993:5). But personal interviewing is labour-intensive and costly. During the 1990s economic pressure and intensification of competition have stimulated marketing companies to demand faster and cheaper data. The development of computer-assisted telephone interviewing has helped research suppliers to meet this demand, as has the use of computers to enhance the role of market research (Whitten 1991) and extend analysis (Freeman 1991).

For a questionnaire of any length or complexity, satisfactory completion is most likely to be achieved in a personal interview. Given proper training, an interviewer has the opportunity to establish rapport with a respondent and to achieve this without biasing answers to questions. In addition, the face-to-face interview offers the opportunity to show supporting material, such as cards listing all possible answers to multi-choice questions or scales to help respondents rate how strongly they feel about a subject. And it is possible to include open-ended questions which demand verbatim written answers. Computer-assisted telephone interviewing does not lend itself to open-ended questions. Finally, as we shall see, interviewers play a critical part in the selection of respondents for the quota sampling widely used in survey research.

We discuss the design of questionnaires, including the risk of interviewer bias and the Market Research Society's interview quality control scheme in Chapter 6.

5.6.2 *Use of the telephone and CATI*

Before the development of computer-assisted telephone interviewing (CATI) conducted from a central location, the telephone offered little, if any, advantage in cost and time over face-to-face interviewing. Box 5.4 contains an explanation of why CATI is used, in this case by Audience Selection, part of TN AGB. The developing popularity of telephone interviewing is due to the following:

- The demand for information *now*. CATI makes it possible to collect, analyse and despatch research findings within a day.

Box 5.4 Computer-assisted telephone interviewing (CATI)

The advantages of CATI are:

- Sample management i.e. excellent for sequential sampling, tight quotas, limited sample universe, instant sample status reports during fieldwork.
- Overall quality, e.g. all filtering and routeing are automatically conducted by the computer, ensuring standardisation and consistency. This also frees the interviewer to concentrate on the interview with the respondent, rather than worrying about which questions should be asked, etc. Supervisor has immediate access to view and listen in to interviews. Also repeat waves of interviewing, e.g. a tracking study, will be entirely consistent.
- Statistical validity enabling random allocation of sample plus management of available telephone numbers helping to reduce non-response.
- Speed of data delivery which means that data are available at the touch of a button – ideal for when results are required immediately subsequent to interviewing.
- Cost saving where interviewers tend to be more productive when using CATI and where the need for printing and punching questionnaires is also eliminated.

Audience selection uses CATI for: PHONEBUS – fastest UK consumer omnibus study. We run it every weekend. Questions are input on a Friday morning, interviewing takes place over the weekend and results are out to the client by Monday lunchtime.

We also use CATI on an *ad hoc* basis where suitable. The main constraints against using CATI are:

i)   where the questionnaire contains predominantly open questions, and
ii)   where the sample is not easily available on disk/tape ready for insertion into the CATI system.

The costs for keying in a sample can escalate the final price of a project.

Technology which links into the CATI system is a fairly recent innovation, for example with automated dialling, whereby the telephone number is selected and dialled by computer.

Source: Homeyard, S. (1994) *Audience Selection*, London.

- The spread of telephone ownership. There is a high proportion of adults available on the telephone.
- Increases in fieldwork costs and the reluctance of interviewers to work in certain areas and in the evening.
- The improved and more cost-effective control of fieldwork when telephone interviewing is centrally located.

- The opportunity to record and process results as questions are answered. The interviewers read the questions and enter the respondent's selection of the multiple-choice answers.
- The ability to avoid clustering in nationwide surveys (see Chapter 4).
- Where fast-moving packaged goods are concerned, buying habits are much the same for those without as for those with telephones.

Electronic and telephone connections in trade centres (e.g. at large, purpose-built exhibition centres in Birmingham and Wembley) have meant that data at trade shows can be gathered by electronic means by market researchers. With direct computer interviewing, on-site interviewing computerised stations or rooms can be set up with several personal computers which link via telecommunications equipment into a mainframe computer. The collection of data for the National Readership Survey (see Chapter 23) uses CAPI (computer-assisted personal interviewing).

In the United States interviewers can key in their responses at computer keyboards in shopping malls in response to questions shown on the computer screens. Trend data and omnibus surveys can be updated with the use of CATI and self-administered computerised interviewing. However, they are not cost-effective for small samples.

With telephone interviewing, the demands of structured questionnaires with pre-coded answers does not lend itself to long questionnaires. Ideally a telephone interview should not last longer than fifteen minutes, questions asked should not be too complicated, and should be designed to be quickly introduced and understood by respondents. In 1987 the Market Research Society's Development Fund (MRDF) published the research on the use of telephone interviewing and telephone availability (MRDF 1986; 1987). Analyses and answers to the question 'Have you your own telephone?' put to adults aged fifteen and over in the National Readership Survey (a meticulously designed probability sample representative of the adult population of the United Kingdom) showed the following:

- The telephone was readily available to A, B and C social grades, but a sample drawn from telephone directories would not give due weight to D and E grades:

Social Grade	A	B	C_1	C_2	D	E	Total
Adults %	98	96	94	85	74	55	82

- Telephone penetration varied by region:

ITV regions (adults %)

Highest	London (88)	Southern (87)	Anglia (86)
Lowest	Lancs., Yorks., Tyne, Tees (all 78)		Border (74)

The MRDF findings based on carefully matched samples and defined population differences still have important design implications for face-to-face and telephone interviewing for researchers today. Telephone interviewing lags behind face-to-face interviewing which is still the most popular method in the United Kingdom and Europe (MRDF 1986) with indications being that respondents find face-to-face personal contact as a more rewarding experience.

When the MRDF research was conducted in the mid-1980s there were four television channels and twelve ITC regions in the United Kingdom. The pace of technological change in this market has been rapid. By 1993, there were thirty television channels with the entry of satellite and cable television networks and fourteen ITV regions (*Economist* 1993a:30). Many more homes have telephones and some telephone companies are merging with cable television companies to develop multimedia technologies (*Economist* 1993b:87–8).

It is clear that to represent the general population by a sample available and willing to respond on the telephone involves *weighting* not only by region, sex and age (a common practice whether the sample be a probability or a purposive one – see Chapter 4), but also by social grade, to ensure due representation of the habits and attitudes in the population sample. The telephone is a useful means of reaching business respondents. Here the problem is one of deciding who should be asked the questions. Who makes the decisions? The professional buyer? The managing director? The chief chemist? A committee? The telephone has a useful screening function and it is also used to ask straightforward questions; in more searching business enquiries the telephone call will precede an interview. The renting out of lists of decision-makers derived from databases can create the risk of an irritant factor when key decision-makers are being contacted at considerable frequency.

The convenient storage and rapid retrieval of data now possible encourages marketing companies to make marketing use of the telephone, for example, to locate targets for goods and services. Companies have to weigh the benefits of improved direct responses and prompt evaluation using computerised methods such as CATI against the start-up costs involved. The rewards are potentially greater with larger samples for CATI than with traditional telephone interviews. Research comparisons of live and automated surveys (Havice and Banks 1991) have looked at the productivity of human interviewers against automated techniques. The indications are that while start-up costs of automated techniques are higher, productivity can be higher also with the larger samples. There is a danger of overkill, particularly when the target is a non-domestic one. Sugging (in which the voice on the telephone pretends at first to be conducting a research enquiry) is a dubious form of telemarketing frowned on by telemarketers as well as market researchers.

5.6.3 *By post*

The response rate achieved by a postal survey is likely to be low (30–40 per cent), unless the survey population consists of members of a special interest group: e.g. new car buyers, fellows of the Royal Horticultural Society, members of the

Wire-haired Dachshund Owners' Association. Here we can expect a better than average response to a postal questionnaire, provided the questionnaire is about new cars, gardening or wire-haired dachshunds.

For a subject of more general interest, mailing questionnaires may prove more expensive than anticipated. It is necessary to take into account the following considerations when comparing costs with personal interviewing:

- The number of completed questionnaires returned.
- The cost of follow-up letters and other inducements to stimulate response, e.g. a ball-point pen to fill in the questionnaire.
- The cost of reply-paid envelopes.
- Possibly the need for some personal interviews, for the responses may add up to what appears to be a biased sample.

A postal questionnaire may be read from beginning to end before questions are answered, so that the particular interest of the company sponsoring the research is revealed from the outset, instead of gradual introduction. In addition, we cannot be quite sure that the answers recorded represent the respondent's own habits and attitudes with regard to the subject of the enquiry. See Chapter 7 on questionnaire design.

There are occasions when a family or household response is required and the postal questionnaire gives all members a chance to join in. It may be necessary for documents to be consulted in order to answer the questions: for example, to consult the log book in an enquiry about motor cars.

There may be a case for combining data-collection methods. If the questionnaire is long, or if the respondent is being asked to keep a diary record, the questionnaire or diary may be placed during a personal interview. The introductory interview will add to the research costs but it is likely to secure a higher response rate so that cost per satisfactorily completed interview may be improved. Today mailed questionnaires have to compete with an ever-increasing volume of direct mail.

5.6.4 By computer

There have been considerable developments in computer-aided interviewing since the mid-1980s. As an example, Frost International have built up a substantial business based on data captured in computer-driven self-completion interviews (Gofton 1986:6). Here, our concern is with the different ways in which questions may be administered, and Frost's Sandpiper procedure is a good example of computer-aided interviewing (see Box 5.5).

Logistical and cost factors are likely largely to confine computer-assisted interviewing to shared-cost operations for some time to come. It is in the syndicated area that the big research money is made. As another example, the

---

Box 5.5

The Sandpiper questionnaire relates to a particular market, say the market for private cars, and to the attributes consumers associate with them. (The attributes are generated by exploratory research as described in Chapter 2.) The respondent sits facing a microcomputer screen either at home or in a hall. Cars and the attributes on which the respondent is going to rate them are displayed on the computer screen.

Netherlands Gallup poll operates a consumer panel in which the respondent is provided with a home computer with a disk drive, a modem and a diskette with an interview and communication programme.

5.7 Experimenting

The direct contrast between laboratory and field experiments is that laboratory experiments take place within internally controlled environments (humidity, heat, light or darkness can all be set and controlled) and field experiments are conducted externally in market environments. Pre-market lab and field tests are explained further in Chapter 8. Interesting examples of both field and laboratory research into the 'sleep pattern' of adults have been presented in publications by Horne *et al.* (1994) and Marjee and Horne (1994).

Most market research work is done in the field with the realism generated by relating causal relationships to external settings. Field experiments therefore have a stronger claim to external validation compared to laboratory experiments which have strong internal validation (through a closer study of selected dependent and independent variables under controlled conditions). Research data gathered from laboratory experiments would use experimental and control groups to study the compared behaviour of, for example, a specific calorie-controlled slimmers' diet or sleep patterns amongst young adults, over a specified time period under controlled conditions. Field experiments include test market studies, for example, manipulating individual elements of the marketing mix (price, promotion, place and product). The experimental treatment could be conducted within selected retail stores within certain regions of the country such as testing the impact of special offers and sales promotions. Alternatively the whole marketing mix could be tested in a limited way when a test product is launched.

Before going into the field it is necessary to have met the following preconditions:

- Formulated objectives and set criteria against which results are to be judged.
- In most cases the ultimate objective is increased profit contribution but the immediate objective is likely to be seen in terms of sales.

- Decided where the experiment is to take place, on what scale and for how long.
- Set in motion a research programme designed to monitor happenings in the market as well as to measure effects of the experiment.

However, obstacles to external validity in field experiments can occur with any of the following situations:

1. Variables in the marketing environment beyond the control of the market researchers conducting the field experiment: for example, competitors may intensify their fight for market share in the same market as the product types under trial.
2. In a laboratory test it is possible to ensure that the treatment is introduced to experimental and control groups in exactly the same way. This is not always the case with field experiments: for example, in an experiment at the point of sale the positioning of items (packs/merchandising material) may well be altered unwittingly during the course of the experiment so that experimental and control groups do not receive exactly the same treatment.
3. It is sometimes difficult to isolate the effect on sales of one particular element in the mix from the effect of others: for example, measurement of the effect on sales of an increase in advertising weight may be contaminated by differences in the merchandising performance of sales representatives, one area being better served than another.
4. There is a risk of 'hothousing', particularly in the case of an experimental launch when reputations are at stake and there is the temptation to show too much management interest, and for sales representatives to be unduly zealous.
5. The financial commitment is greater in a field than in a lab-type experiment. Anxiety to show a return encourages hothousing and may cause the experiment to be stopped too soon. When it looks as if an experiment is proving successful, considerations of 'opportunity cost' may prompt too rapid an extension of the experiment to the wider market.

It is, however, possible in a well-designed experiment to ensure that obstacles to a valid result are anticipated and so allowed for. Given an adequate budget, the research programme will monitor competitive, and own, activity at the point of sale. A marketing intelligence system can be organised to ensure that environmental happenings are noted. Use of a control group, essential in field experiments, and, where possible, replication of the experiment, make it possible to calculate margins of error and show how precisely results may be interpreted (see Appendix 3, Statistical tests).

Most experiments in the field relate to individual elements in the mix or to relationships between elements, as explained in the following:

1. Experiments related to an established brand are likely to be focused on individual elements in the mix – on price/packaging/advertising/sales promo-

tion, and so on, or on the relationship between two elements. This could be the effect on profit contribution of different ratios of advertising to sales-promotional expenditure not forgetting that, once a brand is established, manipulation of elements in the mix takes place in the context of the image created by its marketing history.

2. For a new introduction the experimental treatment in the field is likely to be the whole mix, but the experimental launch may be preceded by a pilot launch with the product packaged, named and priced. This is designed to ensure a smooth transition from the production line through the distribution channel to the consumer.

3. Some elements in the mix lend themselves to field experimentation on a limited scale, whereas others demand a more extended environment. The effect of a change in pack design can be assessed by comparing sales achieved in two matched and comparatively small groups of retail outlets. To measure the effect on sales of a change in the level of advertising expenditure may involve comparison between sales achievement in two television areas.

Before setting up a field test, we need to have considered the criterion against which the effect of the treatment is to be judged. It is desirable that the possible benefit to be derived from the manipulation of mix elements be estimated in advance for two reasons:

1. Account has to be taken of two kinds of cost: out-of-pocket costs and (given success) opportunity costs.

2. In order to determine the size of the matched samples we are going to use we need to know not only what proportion of those in the market are likely to respond to the treatment but also the precision with which results are to be considered. The results will be estimates. That is, what margin of error can be accepted around the estimates? (See Appendix 3.)

These considerations determine the scale of the experiment: in how many retail outlets to put the experimental pack; through how many doors to put the promotional offer; how many people to ask questions on product awareness and performance, and so on.

A real-life simulation adds to research costs; to avoid the learning effect the design would need to be a monadic one with groups of testers matched. An experimental design can get as close as possible to real life under the following conditions:

• Advertising and pack are 'finished' – they may not be final but they appear so.
• The pack is of a size it is intended to market.
• The target consumer tries the product where it would normally be used (e.g. kitchen, bathroom, garage, workshop, etc.).
• Sufficient time is allowed for a thorough trial by all who might share in the use of the product.
• The brand is introduced as being on the market elsewhere.

In addition to asking questions on the 'likelihood of buying', questions can be asked about the product, the kind of people who would use it, how the product would be used and 'acceptable' price levels both at the concept stage (i.e. before it has been tried) and after trial.

Sales predictions, given various levels of marketing costs, will almost certainly have been made at stages on the road to market. It will be known that, for the proposed mix of marketing costs, a specified sales minimum must be achievable. The formula:

$$\frac{\text{Sales}}{\text{revenue}} = \frac{\text{Variable}}{\text{costs}} + \frac{\text{Contribution to}}{\text{fixed costs}} + \frac{\text{Contribution to}}{\text{profits}}$$

involves critical business decisions because sales are required to do the following:

- Make the required contribution to company profit.
- Cover costs associated with the production and marketing of the brand (variable costs).
- Make a contribution to company overheads (fixed costs).

5.8 Probability (or purposive) sampling

A glossary of sampling terms is given at the end of the book. Whatever the type of design, the object is to draw (or select) individuals from the population in such a way that the sample represents the population being surveyed, whether this be one of consumers, retail outlets, industries or organisations.

We want to ensure that the sample is large enough to pick up variations in behaviour and attitude which are relevant to our marketing plans, and to be reassured that these variations appear in much the same proportions in the sample as in the survey population. (The expression 'in much the same proportions' is used because the statistics driven from samples are estimates. One can be pretty sure that a properly designed and managed survey will yield sample estimates which reflect population values but one cannot be 100 per cent sure.)

5.9 Probability (or random) sampling

It is possible to calculate how close to population values the sample estimates are likely to be, and the statistical procedure is described in Chapter 4. But, strictly speaking, this procedure should only be used if the following apply:

- Every individual or item in the population has a known chance of being included in the sample.

- The draw for the sample is made using a random procedure so that human judgement does not enter into the selection or rejection of individuals or items.

To meet these requirements it is necessary to be able to locate every individual in the survey population on a list. For some populations this is an easy matter. For the student body of a university, polytechnic or other academic institution, for the membership of a professional body such as the Chartered Institute of Marketing or for the account or budget customers of a retail store, suitable sampling frames are readily available.

Each individual on the list is identified by means of a number and numbers are drawn at random until the sample has been filled. This is a simple random sample. For example, a telephone directory can provide a convenient sampling frame. Every seventh name can be picked out of the directory on a simple random basis. If the survey population is of any size, we may decide to adopt a systematic procedure.

Box 5.6 is a systematic sample and the drawing technique is generally used in probability sampling. We have to be sure that the names are recorded on the sampling frame in a sufficiently random order, and that there is no periodicity in the listing. Application of the fixed interval to a list recorded in a hierarchical way, say, the *Army List*, could produce a biased sample.

For a national survey the register of electors is likely to be used as a sampling frame. (There is, in fact, a separate register for each polling district.) The Post Office's postcode file may also be used to solicit a frame of addresses. When the postcode file is being used in probability sampling, it is necessary to list individuals living at the randomly drawn addresses, to number them and then to make the final draw.

When the survey population is large and widely dispersed a probability sample will commonly be drawn in more than one stage – this is multi-stage sampling. It would be possible to draw a sample of 3,000 adults from the adult population in the United Kingdom in one stage but the following problems could occur:

- The sample members might well be found to live at addresses scattered throughout the United Kingdom without regard to region or population density.

Box 5.6

Let us assume we need to draw 500 individuals from a survey population of 5,000: the sample members will amount to 1/10 of the survey population. We draw the first numbered individual at random, say this is the individual numbered 5. We then program a computer to generate the names of the individuals numbered 15, 25, 35, and so on, until the sample is filled: i.e. to add 10 four hundred and ninety-nine times.

- Dispersal of calls would make it difficult to organise fieldwork and to supervise investigators.
- Scattered calls would add to the time taken to complete fieldwork and so to the cost of the survey.

Stratified random sampling contains proportionate and disproportionate sampling techniques. The samples chosen by using either of these techniques prevent the occurrence of a skewed sample which does not give a fair representation of the population. Simple random sampling does not allow for an adequate representation of members from 'each group' since the population members may be made up of diverse groups of varying sizes (e.g. religions and ethnic groups). In stratified random sampling, the chosen sample will contain units from each stratum or segment of the population. The units can be selected from each stratum 'proportionate' to the total numbers in the station or related to the 'disproportionate' (varied size) of the units within the station.

A cost-effective procedure is to divide the population into geographic groupings (geographic stratification) which take account of region and population density, and to draw the sample in more than one stage. We might, for example, draw a sample of constituencies within regions at the first stage, and of electors from the registers for the selected polling districts at the third stage. A procedure for selecting non-electors at random is described in Chapter 6 where multi-stage drawing with PPS is considered in more detail.

A sample is drawn in more than one stage in order to cluster calls. This improves administrative efficiency and reduces fieldwork costs, but if calls are unduly clustered we may end up with a sample which does not represent the variety in the population as a whole. The decision as to how many constituencies to draw and then how many polling districts, is based on informed judgement. If we were using the postcode file as a sampling frame we would have to decide how many postcode areas, and sectors within areas, to draw.

The national census tells us a good deal about variation in the geodemographic distribution of the population, how locations vary by levels of unemployment, types of house tenure, enjoyment of basic housing amenities such as baths and toilets, and size of immigrant population. Census data is used to classify residential neighbourhoods and ACORN was developed as a market-analysis system by CACI as the first geodemographic classification for this purpose (Webber 1977).

As a market-analysis system, ACORN applies published census statistics and classified areas of about 150 households (census enumeration districts) into 54 different neighbourhood types. The ACORN classification takes into account different variables encompassing demographic, housing and employment characteristics (CACI 1994). This is shown in Chapter 11. Competing systems such as ACORN, Pinpoint, MOSAIC and SuperProfiles all use census data. Use of CCN's MOSAIC analysis in sample design is developed in Chapter 12.

The census is taken every ten years and the last one took place in 1991 (Marsh 1991). Postcodes are now routinely collected in large-scale research operations and the postcode provides a link between different sources of data. This is given in more detail in section 6.3.4. The Post Office address file and central postcode directory are the main unit of spatial location (Royal Mail 1994).

It is common practice for research agencies to use a master sample of first-stage units for all their survey work. The field force will be recruited and supervised in randomly drawn constituencies, administrative districts or postcode areas representative of the distribution and environmental circumstances of the population as a whole. Fieldwork might, for example, be concentrated in 200 out of 635 constituencies. Samples will be drawn in these constituencies as required. A random procedure may be used up to and including the selection of respondents, or up to and including the selection of sampling points, as in random-location sampling.

In random-location sampling final selection of respondents is based on quotas. Quota samples are widely used in marketing research: cost-benefit analysis favours their use. In probability sampling, the randomly drawn individual must be interviewed. A one hundred per cent response is difficult, if not impossible, to achieve, but at least three calls must be made at the address, and sometimes interviewers are instructed to make more than three. The cost of call-backs is added to the cost of drawing respondents from a sampling frame. The fieldwork for a national survey is likely to cost twice as much when probability methods are used throughout the drawing of the sample.

A probability sample design has two particular advantages:

1. Random drawing of the sample from the population makes it possible to establish a statistical relationship between the sample estimates and population values.
2. If names and addresses are drawn by a random process there is less danger of the composition of the sample being affected by the interviewer's likes and dislikes.

The reports published by the Office of Population Censuses and Surveys are based on probability samples. Government departments have to be prepared to answer politically loaded questions about sample estimates. It helps to be able to establish the statistical significance of the findings and to know that human judgement has not entered into the selection of respondents.

Psychologists and sociologists tend to use probability methods. They work in areas where motivations are often obscure and this makes it difficult to control the purposive selection of respondents.

Probability methods are also used to set up and maintain panels of consumers for the collection of trend data relating to buying behaviour or media habits. This is done on a shared-cost basis and the use of a probability method to draw a pool of panel members encourages confidence in the findings. The panel is stratified to mirror the major demographic characteristics of the population as shown in official statistics, and members are selected from the randomly drawn pool as required.

5.10 Quota sampling

In marketing research it is common practice to use quota samples. In developed countries a good deal is known about the structure of populations whether these be consumer, trade, industrial or organisational populations, and the records are regularly updated. Governments collect and publish statistics, as do professional, industrial and trade associations (see Appendix 1, 'Access to secondary sources'). A quota sample takes account of this wealth of statistical data.

Let us assume that we are going to select a quota sample from the adult population of the United Kingdom: first, we stratify the population by region. We may use the Independent Television Commission's fourteen television areas. These are often used in marketing surveys because of the importance of television as an advertising medium. Second, we can stratify the population by social-class group and by age group. These variables are used for market segmentation purposes, and are described in more detail in Chapter 11.

Classifying people according to social classes has always been one of the most dubious areas of market research investigation, but is also one of the most widely used classification systems. Along with age, the use of 'social class' is generally seen as a control in the selection of requirements for quota sampling. A great deal of unsuccessful effort has been put into developing a classification system that is easy and simple for the interviewer to apply in the field with a reasonable degree of reliability and validity. The current convention is to use a socio-economic grouping, based on the occupation of the Chief Income Earner of his/her household as explained by the National Readership Survey Ltd (NRS 1994:3). (See pages 234 and 271 on the change in social grade classification.)

An interviewer's daily assignment may be anything from ten to twenty calls, depending on the nature of the survey. (Length of questionnaire is critical.) For the sake of simplicity let us assume that a quota has been set based on a hundred calls for five days' work. The interviewer is instructed to contact seventeen ABs, twenty-two C_1s, thirty-one C_2s and thirty DEs. Among these one hundred interviewed, twenty are to be within age group 15–24, seventeen within age group 25–34, and so on. The social class and age controls are independent of each other. The interviewer might end up with a group of calls showing a distorted relationship between age and social class, so it is better practice to set the quota with interrelated controls, but this adds to the cost of fieldwork.

It may be possible to combine groups so that the interviewer's task is simplified, saving time and cost. It may not, for example, be necessary to distinguish AB class (upper-middle) from C_1 class (lower-middle) or the 25–34 age group from the 35–44 group (see Table 5.1 as an example). These decisions depend on the nature of the product field or service being surveyed and the extent to which exploratory research indicates that behaviour and attitudes vary by social class and age. For most fast-moving packaged goods, class is a weak discriminator and a breakdown of the sample by three social-class groups – middle class, skilled worker and unskilled group – would be relevant for planning and control. In Table

Table 5.1 An example of a sample quota taking a spread of four age groups and three social-class groups

Social class	Age				
	15–24	25–44	45–64	65+	Total
ABC_1	7	23	11	7	38
C_2	6	10	9	6	31
DE	6	10	9	6	31
Total	19	33	29	19	100

5.1 it is assumed that four age groups and three social-class groups will adequately reflect the variability in the population.

Quota samples are often controlled by social class and by age because other relevant data are classified in this way, an important example being the continuous surveys on which media planning is based. Media planning is discussed in Chapter 13. But other controls may be relevant, such as size of family and whether a housewife works outside the home. In a survey relating to convenience foods or to durables the interviewer is likely to be required to collect data from a laid-down proportion of 'gainfully occupied' housewives (22 per cent of housewives work full-time, and 21 per cent work part-time). In other words, the selection of respondents is purposive. They are chosen to fit a quota designed to mirror relevant characteristics in the population. They are not drawn from the population by a random procedure. This is the essential difference between purposive and probability sampling.

A quota sample is as reliable as a probability sample in practice, though not in theory, when the following requirements are met:

- Up-to-date statistics relating to the structure of the population are available.
- The quota is set in such a way that important population characteristics are interrelated, such as age and social class, age and size of family, or age and working outside the home.
- Classification questions are carefully designed so that, for example, the occupation of the head of the household is established with some certainty.
- The interviewer's choice of location is restricted. This is not always possible but where the decision as to which door to knock on is taken out of the interviewer's hands, the main criticism of quota sampling is removed.
- The selection of respondents features in the interviewer's training programme.

5.11 Proportionate or disproportionate sampling?

This is an important decision when making design choices. It is likely to affect both the cost of a survey and the validity of the sample estimates derived from it. In

---

Box 5.7

Let us assume we are going to survey the habits and attitudes of adult males with regard to shaving. We are interested in all males of shaving age but have a particular interest in the 15–19 age group because males in this group are developing their shaving habits and attitudes. But the group represents a small percentage of the male shaving population. If we use a uniform sampling fraction we either end up with too few interviews in this group and about the right number in other, larger groups; or we provide for a sufficient number in the 15–19 age group and conduct many more interviews than we need in the larger groups. Obviously, we would deploy the research budget to better effect if we used a variable sampling fraction, 'over-sampled' the small group and restored their weight to the larger groups when the data relating to all men were processed by the computer.

---

asking the question 'Proportionate or disproportionate sample?', we are implying that the population can be divided into groups (or strata) whose relative weight is known. We consider three commonly used stratification factors when describing the selection of a quota sample of adults from the British population: region, social class and age.

In a proportionate sample each stratum has its population weight:

$$\frac{n \text{ (number in the sample)}}{N \text{ (number in the population)}} \text{ is } \textit{uniform} \text{ for all strata}$$

In a disproportionate sample we over-sample small-sized strata at the expense of large-sized strata, but restore their due weights in the population when we come to consider total results or proportions of the total results:

$$\frac{n \text{ (number in the sample)}}{N \text{ (number in the population)}} \textit{ varies} \text{ from one stratum to another}$$

For the proportionate sample we used a uniform sampling fraction and for the disproportionate sample a variable sampling fraction (see Box 5.7 for an example). Exploratory research will have cleared our minds as to which strata in the population should be considered as separate and individual groups.

Disproportionate samples are often the most cost-effective. (Questions of sample size and of confidence in sampling estimates are dealt with in Chapter 4.)

In a stratified sample, whether a uniform or a variable sampling fraction is used, the risk of sampling error is reduced. If we drew the sample of adult males at random, without stratification, we might find ourselves with a 15–19 age group whose sex did not equate with official statistics. By ensuring that each group is given due population weight we remove a possible source of error.

There are more opportunities to use stratification in the design of purposive samples than in the design of probability samples. Any reliable statistical data about the structure of the population, relevant to the marketing objectives, can be used to stratify a purposive sample. For a probability sample it is necessary to be able to identify individuals within the strata in order to be able to make a random draw.

If we are going to use the register of electors as a sampling frame we can stratify geographically before making the draw because the registers tell us where people live, but social class and age of the respondent (to quote two commonly used ways of classifying respondents) are not known until *after* the interview. We can stratify after the interview and re-weight in accordance with official statistics.

5.12 Judgement sampling

Box 5.2 on 'design choices' has shown two types of purposive sample: quota and judgement. We have seen that judgement enters into multi-stage probability sampling as well as into purposive designs. But the description 'judgement' is particularly applicable to industrial and trade research sampling.

In industrial and trade research we are concerned to sample output or sales turnover. Our base for sample design is output or turnover and not the number of establishments or shops in a particular industry or trade. For example, there are a vast number of retail outlets selling food in Britain but the leading food stores which have control of national chains of supermarkets are as in alphabetical order: Asda, Gateway, Safeway, Sainsburys and Tesco. When we consult secondary data sources at the design stage (see Appendix 1) we soon realise that in many fields there are a few concerns so large that, if they were excluded from a sample in a probability draw, sample estimates would be unlikely to represent values in the real industrial or trade world. Any survey of the manufacturers of paints should include ICI Paints and any survey of the grocery trade should include Tesco. In this circumstance our sample design is:

Census of dominating firms + Sample of the rest

If no one concern is so dominant that it must be included in the sample, we are likely to find that a comparatively small proportion of the industrial or trade population we are surveying (say 20 per cent) does a substantial proportion of the business (say 80 per cent): the '80–20' rule. Stratification by volume/value is accordingly an important factor in the design of industrial or trade surveys.

The official statistics provide information about the structure of industries and trades, but firms return this information on the understanding that names are not published. Fitting names to strata requires skilful judgement in the use of secondary sources.

Where it is possible to establish a complete list of firms within strata a probability design is theoretically possible (an example is given in section 5.3), but purposive selection of firms within strata is the more general practice. Survey design calls for the exercise of judgement.

5.13 Convenience sampling

As this name suggests, a convenience sample is picked on the basis of convenience. As examples of convenience samples, companies can use their employees to evaluate new product or prototypes developed by their R&D departments. Universities and colleges can carry out market research surveys on students and visitors to their campuses (Bound 1987:12). Convenience sampling lends itself to exploratory research where consumer information can be obtained fairly quickly, inexpensively and effectively from 'convenient' population samples which are accessible and close to hand.

5.14 Conclusion

In survey research cost-effective allocation of often scarce resources depends on the following:

- Close collaboration between those who are commissioning the research and those responsible for its design and execution, both while the research proposal is being developed (section 5.2) and when the findings are interpreted.
- Estimating what proportion of questionnaires (or other means of collecting data such as diaries) are likely to be satisfactorily completed before deciding whether to contact respondents in a personal interview, over the telephone or through the post (section 5.6).
- Using quota samples when the parameters of the survey population are well documented, provided sampling points are specified and the selection of respondents is controlled (section 5.8), and there is proper provision for the training and supervision of the field force.

To use a probability sample when a quota sample would be suitable is to incur opportunity costs. That is, to use the opportunity within the research budget either to enlarge the sample or carry out further research.

References

AMSO (1993) *Annual Report*, p. 5.

Berkowitz, E., Kerin, A., Hartley, S. and Williams, R. (1994) *Marketing* (4th edn), USA: R. Irwin.

Bound, J. (1987) 'The use of socio-economic grading', *MRS Newsletter*, Dec., p. 12.

CACI Market Analysis (1994) *Users Guide*.

Economist (1993a) 'Bad Show', 6 Nov., p. 30.

Economist (1993b) 'Multimedia's yellow brick road', 4 Dec., pp. 87–8.

Freeman, P. (1991) 'Using computers to extend analysis and reduce data', *Journal of the Market Research Society*, vol. 33, no. 2, pp. 127–36.

Gofton, K. (1986) 'Using a model approach', *Marketing*, 6 Feb.

Havice, M. and Banks, M. (1991) 'Live and automated telephone surveys. A comparison of human interviewers and an automated technique', *Journal of the Market Research Society*, vol. 32, no. 2, pp. 91–102.

Horne, J., Pankhurst, F., Reyner, L., Hume, K. and Diamond, D. (1994) 'A field study of sleep disturbance: effects of aircraft noise and other factors on 5,742 nights of actimetrically monitored sleep in a large subject sample', *American Sleep Disorders Association and Sleep Research Society Journal*, vol. 17, no. 2, pp. 146–59.

McDonald, M. (1992) *Marketing Plans: How to prepare them, How to use them*, Oxford: Butterworth Heinemann.

Marjee, V. and Horne, J. (1994) 'Boredom effects on sleepiness/alertness in the early afternoon vs. early evening and interactions with warm ambient temperature', *British Journal of Psychology*, 25 Jan., psy 847, pp. 1–17.

Market Research Society *Code of Conduct* (1994).

Marsh, C. (1991) 'Microdata from the 1991 Census of Population in Britain: applications in marketing research', *Journal of the Market Research Society*, vol. 33, no. 4, pp. 275–84.

MRDF research projects (1986) 'Comparing telephone and face-to-face interviews'.

MRDF research projects (1987) 'Telephone availability'.

MRS Yearbook (1994).

NRS (1994) Bulletin no. 31, Feb. 23, 3.

Royal Mail (1994) 'The complete guide to postcodes', Stoke-on-Trent.

Webber, R. J. (1977) 'The national classification of residential neighbourhoods: an introduction to the classification of wards and parishes', *PRAG Technical Papers*, Nov.

Whitten, P. (1991) 'Using IT to enhance the roles of market research', *Journal of the Market Research Society*, vol. 33, no. 2, pp. 113–25.

Further reading

Economist (1994) 'America's information highway', 25 Dec.–27 Jan., pp. 65–8.

Sparrow, A. (1993) 'Improving polling techniques following the 1992 General Election', *Journal of the Market Research Society*, vol. 35, no. 1, pp. 79–89.

Wright, L. (1991) 'Research in concert', *Marketing Education Group Conference Proceedings*, University of Cardiff, July, pp. 1386–404.

Assignments

1. 'The design of a survey, besides requiring a certain amount of technical knowledge, is a prolonged and arduous intellectual exercise' (Oppenheim). Discuss.

2.   Faced with the following assignments, what method of data collection would you
     propose in each case? List main topics of interest and explain your choice of method.
     (a) A survey of voting intentions at a general election.
     (b) A survey to establish where and in what way gardening tools are selected by the
          population of an expanding town in the south-east, a town served by a variety of
          traditional and modern retail outlets.
     (c) A survey to establish car accessories in use on the vehicles of private motorists,
          together with those not on the vehicle but desired.
     (d) A survey designed to show regional differences in the use of equipment by
          commercial laundries.
     (There is also a question on sample design, given these assignments, at the end of
     Chapter 6.)

3.   A company marketing a premium brand of cooking oil has to decide whether to adopt
     a revolutionary new bottle closure. The closure, which acts as a pourer, is more efficient
     and hygienic than those in general use. However, its adoption would increase the price
     of the brand to consumers by at least 3p a bottle, irrespective of size. (The current
     prices are 110p for 1 litre and 68p for the 1/2 litre size.)
        The marketing director is anxious to get in first with the new closure but has to
     show what effect its adoption would have on profit contribution. A research agency is
     asked to establish the effect on consumer sales of price increases of 3p and 5p on both
     sizes. The research budget is 'flexible' but a time limit of six weeks is set.
        The research agency is told that the company's brand is the leading premium brand
     in most parts of the country, but the consumption of premium cooking oil is higher in
     the south than in the north.
     (a) Does the research agency need a fuller brief? If you think so, make informed
          assumptions using secondary sources if necessary.
     (b) Specify the research design(s) you would use to arrive at a projectable answer in
          the time available.
     (c) Explain your choice of design(s).
     (d) Assume adoption of the new closure and a decision in favour of a rolling launch
          with television advertising demonstrating the convenience and efficiency of the
          closure. How would you monitor acceptance of the change? (Media planning is
          discussed in Chapter 13.)

CHAPTER 6

Sampling in survey research

This chapter carries the discussion further into the standard procedures and empirical applications of the sampling techniques described in Chapter 5. The techniques for probability sampling provide two particular advantages:

1. Human judgement does not enter into the selection or rejection of respondents.
2. It is possible to measure the extent to which values in the population may vary from the estimates yielded by the sample.

The application of probability theory to sampling in consumer and in non-domestic markets is examined in this chapter.

6.1 Taking a census or a sample

In any survey of a population, unless a census is conducted, random (probability) sampling or some form of clustering is essential. Consumer research is usually based upon sample survey techniques. However, it is possible within an organisation or a small locality to use a census approach. Census surveys of employees, for example, can be undertaken in a small or a large organisation where all employees are given the opportunity to express their feelings and preferences. This census method has the following benefits:

- All employees are seen to have been consulted in the interest of good labour relations.
- Employees feel included by senior managers in the decision-making processes of the organisation.
- It avoids criticism of why some employees could have been chosen for a survey and others were not.

- Contributory or root causes to problems, anxieties and complications in human relationships can be made more apparent.
- Importantly, unlike consumer research, commitment from the highest management levels drives the research programme itself to ensure a successful response outcome.

As an alternative, a sample survey can be constructed using a mixed approach to include a sample of employees from the big departments and a census of those from the small departments. Weighting of the resulting data could be necessary to make it representative of the survey population. Research International's booklet on 'Employees Attitude Research', Position Paper 14 lists four main data-collection techniques for quantitative employee surveys:

- Individual self-completion.
- Group session self-completion.
- Face-to-face interviewer administered.
- Telephone interviewer administered.

National censuses present a different scenario. Most organisations large or small do not have the financial and manpower resources to conduct them for their own use, nor do they necessarily want to. For instance, multinational companies such as Procter & Gamble produce many different types of product ranging from toothpaste, soap, detergent, deodorants, coffee to disposable baby nappies. Within each product range, the company will have different brands as for detergents (Ivory, Snow, Dreft, Tide, Joy and Bold). Market research may be required only at any one time, say, for one brand of detergent bought by a small sample of a population rather than for the whole product range.

More importantly, most organisations do not possess the legal authority to enforce participation in market surveys, unlike agencies of government, for example, in the requirements for household returns collected for the United Kingdom population census in 1991 or company returns for the Central Statistical Office and Company House. There exist many published, validated and accessible sets of data, some free, which are available to organisations and individuals (see Appendix 1 for information sources). Therefore, researchers do not need to 'reinvent the wheel' if they can use published information which has some relevance to their survey populations.

Secondary information can be of use in sampling design, for example, in giving a general indication of population size, characteristics and locations. The market researcher proceeds to sampling because detailed data on the characteristics, nature of demand and behavioural patterns of survey populations specific to a particular market for an organisation's products are not available. They are needed for problem-solving and marketing planning.

The market researcher does not need to draw large numbers of the population into the sample provided that a smaller sample size and the method by which it was drawn (given the nature of the population) can be validated. Samples of 2,000 or less are commonly used to represent a population of over 45 million adults in Britain. Sampling therefore constitutes a cost-effective and efficient method in survey research.

6.2 Sample estimates and population values

Validity of the sample estimates depends on the following:

- The size of the sample in relation to the variability in the population where the subject of the survey is concerned (if habits and attitudes were uniform throughout the population, the responses of one individual would suffice).
- The care with which the sample has been drawn.
- There being an adequate number of respondents in any one group which is to be considered in isolation.
- Avoidance of 'non-sampling errors' when the data are being collected and analysed, errors such as 'interviewer bias' and use of ambiguous questions (see Chapter 7).

There are many possible samples of 2,000 in a population of 57 million in Britain. Can we be confident that the sample we happen to have drawn is a representative one? We cannot. But we can take individual sample estimates and establish what the relationship between sample estimate and population value is likely to be. Box 6.1 summarises notation in common use and gives the formulae referred to in this section. This is followed by explanations of the mean, standard deviation and the standard error.

6.2.1 The mean and the standard deviation

Let us consider a population value, say, the foot sizes of adult women. Plotting the normal distribution of female foot sizes, see Figure 6.1, is of importance to shoe manufacturers. If we were to plot foot sizes, one by one, on a piece of squared paper we would see a pattern emerge. In due course the plottings would be seen to be symmetrically distributed around their mean. If we outlined the shape of the distribution, as shown in Figure 6.1, we would see that the foot sizes filled the area beneath a normal curve.

Distance from the mean is measured by the standard deviation, which takes account of the variability in a population. A normal distribution would show the following characteristics:

- Sixty-eight per cent of the areas occupied by our plottings of shoe sizes would lie within −1 and +1 standard deviations from the mean.

Box 6.1 Survey research, sampling: basic statistics

Notation

	Population (values)	Sample estimates
Number of items	N	n
Mean	μ or X	X
Standard deviation	σ or S	s
Standard error of the mean	–	s_x or s.e. (x)
Proportion	π or P	p
Standard error of the proportion	–	s_p or s.e. (p)

Sampling formulae

See section

Standard deviation $\sqrt{\dfrac{1}{n}\Sigma(x-x)^2}$ 4.2.1

Standard error of the mean $\dfrac{s}{n}$ Applies variables   4.2.2

Standard error of the proportion   Applies attributes   4.2.4

$$\sqrt{\dfrac{p(1-p)}{n}} \quad \text{or} \quad \sqrt{\dfrac{p(100-p)}{n}} \ \%$$

q is the proportion
without the attribute

$$\text{or} \quad \sqrt{\dfrac{pq}{n}}$$

To estimate sample size: 4.2
Let Z stand for the number of standard errors
required by the confidence level (in market   4.25
research it is usual to work at the 95 per
cent confidence level, i.e. to set limits of
±1.96 (or 2) standard errors around the   4.26
sample estimate); let E represent the range of
error around the sample estimate acceptable to the
decision maker; then the formula for estimating sample size is –
  for variables using the standard error of the mean

$$n = \dfrac{s^2 \times Z^2}{E^2}$$

for attributes using the standard error of the proportion

$$n = \dfrac{pq \times Z^2}{E^2}$$

Source: C. A. Moser and G. K. Kalton (1971). *Survey Methods in Social Investigation*. 2nd edn (London; Heinemann Educational Books).

Box 6.2

- Draw the ten possible samples of 2 from the five women with foot sizes ranging 3, 4, 5, 6 and 7.
- Average the foot size of each sample of 2.
- Take the mean of the ten averages.
  The answer is 5, which is the mean of $3 + 4 + 5 + 6 + 7$.

- Ninety-five per cent would lie within -2 and $+2$ standard deviations (or, to be exact, ±1.96).
- Ninety-nine per cent would lie within -3 and $+3$ standard deviations (or ±3.09).

Provided we are considering a sample of at least thirty people and the sample has been drawn using a probability procedure (as in Box 6.2), we can use knowledge of the normal distribution to relate our sample estimates to values in the population as a whole.

It is possible to prove mathematically that the means of all the possible samples in a population equal the population mean. If we were able to draw all the possible samples of women from a population and to plot the average shoe size of each sample, we would find that the distribution of our plottings of means took the same symmetrical shape around the mean of all the average sizes as that shown in Figure 6.1.

Mini-exercises apart, we are not going to be able to draw all possible samples from the survey population, so how do we use this finding to calculate how much confidence we can have in an estimate given by our one sample?

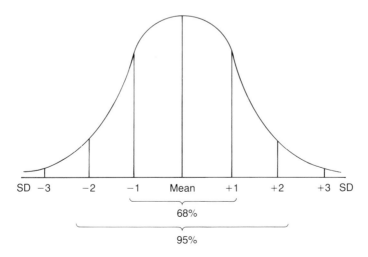

Figure 6.1 A normal distribution

6.2.2 The standard error of the mean

We do not expect our sample estimate to be exactly the same as the population value. We are going to make an allowance for possible error and the size of the allowance will depend on the following:

- Variability in the population – if all women had the same foot size there would be no risk of error.
- The size of the sample.
- The confidence level we choose to work at.

Variability in the population is measured by the standard deviation. Without a census, we do not know how foot sizes vary in the population as a whole, but we can consider the distribution of foot sizes shown by our sample and calculate the standard deviation of these. We know the size of our sample, and we choose at what level of confidence we want to work.

Research data relate to amounts spent by samples of the population on a variety of items, such as rent, rates, holidays, car insurance, petrol and, perhaps most frequently, food and other fast-moving necessities (see Box 6.3).

But in choosing the 68 per cent level of confidence we run a one-in-three risk of our sampling mean being outside the range of all possible means covered by the ±1 standard deviation. If we allow for ±2 standard errors of the mean, the risk is reduced to one in twenty (see Box 6.4).

We have increased confidence at the cost of precision. To achieve a more precise estimate at the 95 per cent level it would be necessary to increase the sample size. However, to halve the allowance for error it would be necessary to multiply the sample size of four. The 95 per cent level is common practice in marketing

---

Box 6.3

Let us assume that the average daily amount spent on food and necessities by a sample of 400 households is £6 and that the standard deviation from the mean shown by the 400 budget totals is £1.60 or 160p. Then the standard error of the mean is given by:

$$s_i = \frac{s}{\sqrt{n}} = \frac{160p}{\sqrt{400}} = \frac{160p}{20} = 8p$$

If we choose to work to the 68 per cent level of confidence we allow for a possible sample error of ±8p and conclude that the sample estimate of £6 represents a population value lying between £5.92 and £6.08.

Box 6.4

At the 95 per cent level of confidence our sample estimate of £6 represents a population value lying between £5.84 and £6.16.

---

research. The cost of working at a higher level of confidence is out of proportion to the benefit received. In any survey of human behaviour and attitudes there are possible sources of error other than those which can be statistically measured.

6.2.3 *Categorising variables*

In marketing research we often consider attributes and variables. Attributes, such as being able to drive a motor car, are either present or not present whereas variables, such as the amounts spent on petrol, have a range of values. For example, variables can be reduced to means/averages and attributes to proportions/percentages.

The dichotomous (binary) variable is the simplest categorial variable denoting the presence or absence of some attribute, e.g. attitude towards a product (good/bad) or intention (will vote 70 per cent, will not vote 30 per cent). Polytomous variables have more than two categories using a range, e.g. rating scales (excellent, good, moderate, bad, worse) and age (under 10, 11–17, 18–24, 25–40, 41–59, 60+). Survey variables can be categorised or classified into mutually exclusive groups for examination rather than be further measured on a continuous scale. Exogenous variables which are quantifiable on continuous scales are not categorised, e.g. as measured on a mileage clock or a centigrade/fahrenheit scale (Bagozzi 1994).

The numbers of observations (attributes) sorted into each category of a variable can be shown in a frequency distribution (see Figure 6.1). A joint frequency count representing the combination of two or more categorised variables can be represented in a cross-tabulation. The simplest form of a cross-tabulation or contingency table is conventionally represented by a 2×2, $r \times c$ table showing the rows (categories of the predictor variables) and columns (categories of the dependent variables). Applying the chi-square tests a multi-way table (categorising multi-variate data) can generate estimated expected counts for each cell so that comparisons can be made between them and the corresponding observed counts for the goodness of model fit. The chi-square test is suitable when the desirability is to establish a significant difference between one distribution and another where the expected values in all cells of the tables are greater than 0.5.

Methods of analysis and statistical tests of data are explained further in Appendices 2 and 3.

6.2.4 *The standard error of a proportion*

The distribution of a population according to whether or not its members have a particular attribute is called 'binomial distribution' from bi-nomen meaning two names; for example, adults in Great Britain can be called 'drivers' or 'non-drivers' according to whether or not they hold a driving licence.

Let us assign the letter P to the drivers (using a capital letter because P relates to drivers in the population and not to drivers in a sample of the population). Then let us assign the letter Q to the non-drivers; $P + Q = N$ (the population). If we are working in proportions N is 1, or 100 if we are working in percentages. So Q is either 1 minus P or 100 minus P.

If we were to draw all possible samples from the population, the proportions shown to be drivers would vary, but distribution of the sample ps in relation to the population P is known and so, as with the standard error of the mean, it is possible to make allowance for sampling error. The standard error of a proportion takes account of n, the number in the sample and p the proportion with the attribute (see Box 6.5).

Most market research data are presented in the form of percentages rather than proportions so we use percentages in the example in Box 6.6.

Box 6.5

If p is the percentage or proportion with the attribute and q the percentage or proportion without, the standard error is calculated as follows:

$$s_p = \sqrt{\frac{pq}{n}} \quad \text{often written as} \quad \sqrt{\frac{p(1-p)}{n}} \quad \text{or} \quad \sqrt{\frac{p(100-p)}{n}}\%$$

Box 6.6

A survey shows that 40 per cent of the women in a town drive cars. The estimate is based on a sample of 600. How precisely can this estimate be interpreted at the 95 per cent level of confidence?

$$s_p = \sqrt{\frac{40 \times 60}{600}} = \sqrt{4} = 2\%$$

At the 95 per cent level of confidence, a likely range of error is $\pm$ twice 2 per cent. The sample estimate of 40 per cent indicates that the true proportion probably lies between 36 and 44 per cent.

6.2.5 *Estimating sample size*

The formulae given in Box 6.1 suggest that in order to estimate sample size we need to put figures to the following:

- The standard deviation anticipated for individual variables (s).
- The proportion/percentage likely to hold each attribute (p).
- The number of standard errors required by the confidence level (Z).
- Action standards set by the marketing department, the acceptable error (E).

The data needed to estimate s and p are an important product of exploratory research (see Box 6.7). If secondary sources do not give the necessary clues, an omnibus survey may be used (see section 2.8).

Since surveys cover a variety of characteristics, and we are likely to want to consider these for a number of sub-groups within the total sample, the full statistical procedure is unduly laborious.

It is, however, essential to have decided in advance how the results of a survey are going to be analysed and what measurements will be the most important. It is unfortunate if a particular estimate arouses marketing interest, and this estimate is found to be based on the habits or attitudes of so few individuals in the sample that a conclusion cannot be drawn. In determining sample size it is common practice to ensure that there are at least fifty, and preferably one hundred, individuals in the smallest sub-group likely to be considered in isolation.

Sample size is often constrained by cost. We start with a budgetary allowance sufficient to buy a certain number of interviews. In the example given in Box 6.8

Box 6.7

When exploratory research has suggested that p is 40 per cent, the range of acceptable error (E) is $\pm$ 2 per cent and the confidence level requires allowance for $2s_{p1}$ then:

$$n = \frac{pq \times Z^2}{E^2} = \frac{40 \times 60 \times 4}{4} = 2,400$$

Were we prepared to tolerate an error of $\pm$ 4 per cent the required sample size would be 600:

$$n = \frac{40 \times 60 \times 4}{16}$$

Doubling the allowance for error makes it possible to quarter the sample size. (Conversely, in order to halve the standard error, it is necessary to quadruple the sample size.)

Box 6.8

A population of 50,000 persons is distributed over three areas: 10 per cent live in area A, 40 per cent in B and 50 per cent in C. Exploratory research has stimulated marketing interest in an age group which accounts for 20 per cent of the population in each area. We want to be able to consider the habits and attitudes of this age group in relation to the population as a whole. Given that we can afford 1,500 interviews, and that we are required to use a probability design, how should we proceed?

Design using a proportionate sample

Area	Population		Sampling fraction	Sample	Special-interest group of 20%
	N	$N\%$	N/n	n	(n)
A	5,000	10	33.3	150	30
B	20,000	40	33.3	600	120
C	25,000	50	33.3	750	150
Total	50,000	100	33.3	1,500	300

Note that with a proportionate design we have an unduly small number of the age group in region A and a generous allocation to B and C.

Design using a disproportionate sample

A	5,000	10	10	500	100
B	20,000	40	40	500	100
C	25,000	50	50	500	100
Total	50,000	100	33.3	1,500	300

We make a judgement decision to allocate 1,500 interviews in total which we can afford, giving 500 to each region so using a variable instead of a uniform sampling faction. This gives us a satisfactory number of interviews in each of these regions with the age group we are particularly interested in. We shall, of course, have to restore their due weight to the three regional populations when calculating total results for the three regions as a whole. Had we not been committed to a probability design, we could have sampled disproportionately by age as well as by area, setting quotas to achieve the following allocation of calls:

Area	Population	Sample	Special-interest group of 20% (n)	Remaining 80%
	n	n		
A	5,000	500	250	250
B	20,000	500	250	250
C	25,000	500	250	250

The computer would be programmed to restore due weight to totals by area and by age, and a more cost-effective design would be achieved.

we can afford a total of 1,500 and we compare the efficiency of a design using proportionate stratification with one using disproportionate stratification (see section 5.7).

6.2.6 *Effect of design on sampling error*

The basic formulae given in Box 6.1 relate to simple random samples. In a simple random sample all the individuals in the population go into the draw and the sample is drawn in one stage.

If we stratify the population and draw a simple random sample from each stratum, we reduce the sampling error. If we sampled a population of polytechnic students without prior stratification we might, by chance, draw too many engineers and too few business studies students, or too many full-time students and too few part-time ones. In a survey relating to courses we might need to be sure that engineering and business studies were duly represented, while for a survey about amenities we might want to ensure that the attitudes and behaviour of part-time students carried due weight. There is here a clear case for stratification, whether we are considering courses or amenities, and we can use a probability design because the student records enable us to assign students to strata.

If we draw in more than one stage, with probability proportionate to size of population, we increase the sampling error. The multi-stage procedure has the effect of clustering the members of the population included in the sample. The effect of this has been investigated using estimates drawn from simple random sampling as the criterion. The standard errors arrived at using the formulae given in Box 6.1 are corrected for design effect by multiplying them by a design factor of between 1.0 and 2.5. Even the National Readership Survey, recognised as having a particularly good sample design (Collins 1988), had been estimated to have a design factor of 1.4. It had a CAPI-based system introduced in July 1992 (*The Magazine of MRS* 1993:4). The size of the design factor depends on the closeness with which calls are clustered when the sample is drawn. Clustering has a stronger effect on sampling error than stratifying.

If the sample embraces 10 per cent or more of the population (as might occur in a survey among students), we apply a correction factor, known as the finite multiplier, $\sqrt{(N - n/N - 1)}$. This has the effect of reducing the standard error, but surveys are usually based on smaller sampling fractions.

6.2.7 *Weighting samples*

We have seen that in both probability and purposive sample designs, data derived from reliable sources, such as the Government Statistical Service, are used to stratify the population *before* individuals are drawn/selected for interviewing. But some of those drawn/selected may be unavailable for interview, or they may refuse to be interviewed. In telephone interviewing a substantial proportion of those approached may refuse (section 5.6.2). The sample we achieve may be unbalanced when compared with the population as known. 'Weighting' aims to rectify this. The procedure is described by Ehrenberg:

> If an unstratified sample of 10 has given us 6 boys and 4 girls and we know that boys and girls are 50:50 in the population, the results in each stratum can be 'weighted' to bring the sample into line with the population proportion (e.g. by multiplying all the girls' readings by 1.5). This kind of 'posterior' stratification is usually less effective than prior stratification. The weighted portion of the sample has an undue effect on sampling errors (e.g. an untypical girl would count for 50% more than an untypical boy). (1975:291)

Weighting by region, sex and age is standard procedure in a sample drawn from the general public. In the case of telephone surveys 'telephone-accessible weighting' is used. These are up-weighted (together with the oldest and youngest age groups). Ehrenberg's caveat is relevant here. The MRDF's methodological survey ('Comparing telephone and face-to-face interviews') found that those with a telephone may behave differently from those without. Today's accessibility to households for sampling in telephone surveys can be hampered by the wider spread of unlisted telephone numbers (ex-directory) and the use of answering machines (answerphones).

Specification of 'any weighting methods used' is among the 'relevant details' which members of the Market Research Society are required by the Code of Conduct to provide to clients. Computerisation makes possible the programmed application of weights. This may reduce vigilance to 'an undue effect on sampling errors'.

6.3 Drawing procedures

6.3.1 Drawing with probability proportionate to size (PPS)

The PPS procedure is associated with multi-stage sampling. For example, let us assume that the first-stage sampling unit is the constituency. The 633 parliamentary constituencies in Britain (excluding the seventeen constituencies in Northern Ireland) are first stratified by region using the Independent Television Commission's fourteen ITV regions. The order in which the constituencies are listed within regions is important because we are going to draw the first constituency at random and then take a systematic interval.

Every individual in the population must have had a chance of being included in the sample when we get to the end of the drawing process, but first of all we want to ensure that the regional distribution of constituencies, together with their varying population densities, are duly represented in the sample. Having stratified by region we may take account of population density by sorting each region's constituencies into four groups in each region. Thus far the ordering of the list of constituencies is as follows:

Region 1
Conurbation constituencies
Other 100 per cent urban constituencies (but non-conurbation)
Mixed urban and rural constituencies
Rural constituencies

Region 2
Conurbation constituencies
Other 100 per cent urban constituencies
Mixed urban and rural constituencies
Rural constituencies
And so on until all the regions have been covered.

We have four strata relating to population density within each of fourteen regions (assuming we are using the ITV regions). Within each of these strata (or cells) it is quite usual to list the constituencies in descending order (see Table 6.1) according to the percentage of Conservatives to the total of Conservatives and Labour votes cast at the most recent general election. This is done because voting tends to correlate with social-economic class. The final list is therefore stratified by an approximation to social economic class as well as by population density and regional distribution. This is implicit stratification, i.e. stratification is 'implied' in the way in which the first stage sampling units (in this case constituencies) are listed.

Quota sampling based on updated socio-economic variables (class, age, sex) should be regularly carried out and updated from sources, e.g. the census and the National Readership Survey, with monthly or even weekly sampling points, if possible.

In order to draw with PPS, it is necessary to accumulate the electoral populations of the constituencies, so that each constituency is represented by a range of numbers equal to the size of its electorate (see Table 6.1 and Box 6.9).

The procedure used to draw first-stage sampling units with PPS is illustrated in Table 6.1. The twelve Birmingham constituencies are listed in the order of the percentage of Conservatives to the total of the Conservative to Labour votes cast at the 1992 general election in each constituency, then electorates are recorded and accumulated. If we were drawing from the complete list of 633 constituencies in Great Britain (the UK total is 659; there are seventeen constituencies in Northern Ireland), Birmingham's twelve would be well down the list in region 7, and a substantial number of electors would have accumulated before Hall Green was recorded. However, for the purpose of this example, we start with Sutton Coldfield and this constituency is represented by the range 1–71,410.

Table 6.1   Twelve Birmingham constituencies listed for drawing of three with PPS

Constituency	% Cons. to total Cons. + Lab. votes[a]	Electorates[b]	Electorates accumulated[c]	
Sutton Coldfield	81.3	71,410	71,410	1st number drawn
Edgbaston	56.6	53,041	124,451	at random is
Hall Green	54.6	60,091	184,542	135,000
Yardley	49.7	54,749	239,291	
Northfield	49.3	70,533	309,824	2nd number drawn
Selly Oak	47.9	70,150	379,974	is 325,000
Erdington	42.7	52,398	432,372	
Perry Barr	40.7	72,161	504,533	3rd number drawn
Hodge Hill	40.4	57,651	562,184	is 535,000
Sparkbrook	27.9	51,677	613,861	
Ladywood	27.8	56,970	670,831	
Small Heath	27.7	55,213	726,044	

Notes
[a]These are listed in order of the percentage of Conservative to the total of Conservative and Labour votes cast at the 1991 general election.
[b]This is the total number of adults eligible to vote in each constituency.
[c]The three constituencies selected with probability proportionate to their electoral populations are Edgbaston, Northfield and Hodge Hill.

Box 6.9

N/N = 40 million over 200 = 200,000.
Draw a number at random between 1 and 200,000, say 135,000. The constituency with this number in its range is the first drawn. Add the sampling interval of 200,000 to 135,000 – 335,000. The constituency with this number in its range is the second drawn, and so on. The sampling interval of 200,000 is added on 199 times.

At a second stage wards or polling districts may be listed, their electorates accumulated and a second draw made using PPS (see Box 6.10 for an example). There is less risk of undue clustering if respondents are selected at the second stage, that is, after the constituencies have been drawn, but this would still produce rather a widely dispersed sample.

6.3.2 *Variability in opinion polling – lessons learnt*

Savings in cost and improved supervision have to be weighed against undue clustering of sampling locations. Take some examples from the results of the 1970, 1987 and the 1992 UK general elections:

● In 1970 most of the national opinion polls predicted a Labour Party victory but the victor was the Conservative Party led by Edward Heath.

Box 6.10

Let us assume that we are drawing a sample of 3,000 people using a master sample of 200 constituencies. The varying sizes of the constituencies have been allowed for in the PPS procedure so we have to make fifteen calls in each constituency. The extent to which we cluster the calls will depend on the subject of the survey and the extent to which habits and attitudes vary where this subject is concerned. We could, for example, draw five names from each of three polling registers or three names from each of five registers to get our fifteen per constituency, for here again variation in the size of polling districts will have been taken into account in the PPS drawing procedure.

- One reason given for this was the late turnout of voters for the conservatives after the national polls had completed their findings at the weekend before the start of polling day (Waller 1992).
- In 1987, the 'poll of polls' was taken which averaged the results of the national opinion polls throughout the election campaigns. The BBC commissioned a 'Newsnight' panel of voters in marginal constituencies and an eve-of-election survey from Gallup. The BBC's prediction of 26 seats and ITN of 68 seats for the Conservative Party led by Margaret Thatcher were far lower than its actual majority of 102 seats (Moon and McGregor 1992).
- In 1992, out of fifty national published polls, thirty-nine polls suggested the likelihood of a hung Parliament (if the results were converted into seats), eight predicted a Labour victory and three predicted a Conservative victory. Three exit polls (the ICM poll for Sky television, Today newspapers and the *Sun* newspaper; the NOP poll for the BBC; and the Harris poll for ITN) were indicative of hung parliaments (Hutton 1992:12–13). In the event, the Conservative Party under John Major was returned to office.

Even with well-designed samples, there is an inherent difficulty in measuring public opinion despite any seemingly unpopular record of a political party in power. Nowhere is this fickle nature shown more so than with electoral samples where the voting intentions of the electorate can change right up to the time they cast their votes. Big and late swings from one party to another particularly in key marginal constituencies can, as the previous examples show, lead to a different political outcome. For some background on the British system of opinion polling, see Worcester (MORI) (1991, 1992), the nature of constituency polling by Waller (Harris Research Centre) (1992), and Moon (NOP) and McGregor (BBC) (1992) on developing a methodology for exit polls.

The MRS enquiry into the performance of opinion polls in the 1992 general election found that 60 per cent of the difference between the final polls and the election outcome could have been accounted for by three factors: late changes in voting intentions; failure to reveal voting intentions amongst disproportionately conservative supporters; and a small impact from the deregulation of voters.

The Economist (1994:35) pointed to two serious sources of error uncovered in the MRS report: the 'spiral of silence' where those who thought their party was not fashionable refused to tell the pollsters that they would vote for it (in this case the Conservatives); and a sample quota based on old social-class definitions. 'Secret ballot' questionnaires are now used by some market researchers to avoid the problem of respondents refusing to disclose voting intentions for an unfashionable party. The European elections in June 1994 to elect members for the European Parliament presented an opportunity for market researchers to get their predictions in their polls close to the outcomes through adjusting results to check their representations with past elections, as MORI has done.

The predictive nature of opinion polling at the constituency level was regarded as 'very patchy' by Waller (1992) since people were interviewed in certain areas at certain times taken in the days, weeks or months prior to the day of voting. Even the eve-of-election polls (on the evening immediately preceding the day of voting) could be affected by the last-minute differential turnout of party supporters. Sample sizes for constituency polling needed to be large (1,000 respondents if possible). Moon and McGregor's support for the accuracy of exit polls was that such last-minute differential turnout could be circumvented by interviewing electors at polling stations from the time the polls open to the time they close (Moon and McGregor 1992).

Such methods were adopted by Harris for ITN and the BBC's exit polls. The National Opinion Poll's sampling strategy was to aim for maximum coverage of the maximum variability. Variability in this respect refers to variations between polling districts, between hours of the day, and time of day between polling districts. Since polling takes place in polling stations, these stations would be the primary sampling units (PSUs) chosen for exit polls, rather than the polling districts. In cluster sampling, the following are alternative choices of PSUs:

1. A random selection of population size with a constant sampling interval so that bigger PSUs could generate more interviews.
2. PSUs proportionate to population size with a varied sampling interval to produce the same number of interviews in each PSU.

Since population sizes between polling districts vary greatly, the first choice would be uneconomic if a constant sampling interval set large enough to generate the required number of interviews for large constituencies produced only a few interviews for the smallest polling districts. Moon and McGregor recommended the selection of PSUs with a probability proportionate to size (PPS) and varying sampling interval. PPS selection would be achieved in pre-election polls by 'the simple means of listing population size against each unit in the stratified list, accumulating population down the list and then applying a constant sampling interval' (1992). For exit polls consideration of the functions of time and place were required so that each polling station could have '15 calls in each stratified list – one for each hour of voting' (1992).

6.3.3 *The electoral register as a sampling frame*

The names and addresses of all British subjects aged eighteen and over who are entitled to vote and have registered are listed in the register of electors. The returns are made in October and the register is published in February of the following year. From the marketing point of view the main weakness of the register as a sampling frame is the fact that it excludes young adults and immigrants. There are procedures for including 'non-electors' in the sample but let us first draw the electors. An example of this is given in Box 6.11.

We stop at this point if the intention is to interview electors, but our interest is more likely to be in all adults, 'non-electors' as well as 'electors'. The following procedure makes it possible to extend the draw to non-electors while giving every adult a known (and non-zero) chance of being included in the sample:

- A name and address are drawn from the register using the method described above.
- The interviewer works to a sample issue sheet: all the electors at the same address as the selected electors are listed in the order of the register on the sample issue sheet.
- The selected elector is starred.
- The total number of electors at the address is the sampling interval.
- Suppose there are e electors at the address of the starred elector, then starting with the starred elector every eth name following is starred. The added starred names (if any) will all be non-electors and they constitute the non-elector sample.

This procedure cannot determine the number of non-electors in the sample in advance, but the probability of selecting a given non-elector is the same as the chance of selecting any given elector, provided he/she lives in a household where there is an elector!

Box 6.11

Let us assume that we are making five calls in each of the three polling districts drawn with PPS. In one of these three polling districts there are 845 electors listed on the register and numbered 1 to 845 ($N/n = 845/5 = 169$). We draw a number at random between 1 and 169. Let us say this is 109. By adding the sampling interval onto the random start we draw the following respondents:

    109 Marks, Ann M., 10 Bran End Road
    278 Low, James W., Brambles, The Spinney
    447 Fellows, Jean B., 40 Garden Fields
    616 Crisp, Elizabeth M., Mill Cottage, Rosemary Lane
    785 Humphreys, Christopher A., 12 High Street

6.3.4 *The postcode address file (PAF) as a sampling frame*

The procedure of drawing a sample in more than one stage with PPS is applied to the postcode units in the same way as to parliamentary or local government units, or as with constituencies and wards and polling districts. These different units are best explained by taking a typical postcode (Royal Mail 1994), e.g. LE11 3TU.

The first half of the postcode (LE11) is the outward code which indicates to the accepting office where mail is to be directed and the second half (3TU) is the inward code for the sorting office near to the point of delivery so that letters and parcels can be correctly delivered.

LE	11	3	TU
Postcode area (i.e. Leicestershire)	Postcode district	Postcode sector	Postcode unit

The introduction of postcodes dates back to 1857 when Sir Rowland Hill split London into postal areas (e.g. NW and SW). Following this, cities such as Birmingham and Sheffield introduced postal districts up to 1932. Numbers were added to the initials in World War I. In the 1950s, automatic sorting systems were introduced – as well as the Alpha Numeric format of coding. The United Kingdom was fully coded by 1974 followed by the coding of Guernsey, Jersey and the Isle of Man by the early half of the 1990s, see Table 6.2. There were 180,000 large users each with their own postcodes and the Royal Mail computerised postcode address file (PAF) can be purchased on standard computer media, that is, compact disk, floppy disks and magnetic tape (Royal Mail 1994).

The PAF system provides an up-to-date database resource for use by other organisations to check and add to their databases, this includes:

- Geodemographic profiling by market researchers.
- Postcode mapping software for transport companies.
- Geographic information for service centres and major retailers to select profitable locations for new service and retail outlets.
- Property coding for crime prevention.
- Credit referencing for insurance companies for assessing risk and insurance premiums.
- Hospital billing using National Health Service area codes.
- Direct responses promotion and sales targeting by firms to other businesses and to households.

It will be readily appreciated that, with the postcode file as a sampling frame, it is possible to draw a national sample in more than one stage, stratifying by postcode areas, treating districts and sectors as first- and second-stage units, and arriving at a sample of postcodes (i.e. groups of on average seventeen homes) at the

Table 6.2 1994 postcode figures

Postcode areas	122
Postcode districts	2,807
Postcode sectors	9,114
Postcode units	1.6 million
Addresses	24.5 million
Delivery points per code	15 (av)
Large user codes	180,000 with 50 items per day
Guernsey	Fully coded
Jersey	to be fully coded by Summer 1994
Isle of Man	Fully coded

Source: Mason, P. (1994) The Royal Mail Postcode Centre, Stoke-on-Trent.

third stage; the draw at the first and second stages being made with probability proportionate to the number of addresses in each district or sector.

The postcode file is used by Taylor Nelson Audits of Great Britain (TN AGB) as a frame for their syndicated home audit of consumer durables, based on a large sample of households, in which 30,000 are audited quarterly (the sample has to be large because durables are infrequently bought). Taylor Nelson Audits of Great Britain draw in two stages: having stratified by postcode area, they draw sectors at the first stage and postcodes at the second. Their interest is in households. To use the postcode as a frame for adults it would be necessary to list all the individuals at selected postcodes and then draw the required number of respondents or to interview every adult at each of the seventeen addresses covered on average by each selected postcode. A more efficient method would be to select postcodes at random and then select respondents to fit a quota relevant to the subject of the survey, i.e. to use a random-location design.

6.4 Geodemographic stratification

In Chapter 3, for multi-stage drawing and the clustering of calls, we recognised the importance of ensuring that the sample represented the population's variety of habit and attitude where the subject of the survey was concerned. In this chapter in section 6.4.3, we also recognised that the decision as to how many constituencies to carry out fieldwork in was based on informed judgement. There are available statistical data to show how the population varies. Geodemographic systems such as ACORN (explained in more detail in Chapters 11 and 12) are based on these data.

The first geodemographic system using census data to cluster its population into neighbourhood types was CACI's ACORN (a classification of residential neighbourhoods). Richard Webber, who pioneered the ACORN system for CACI, set up CCN systems and the classification system MOSAIC (CCN systems is

---

| **Box 6.12** |

At the first stage
Standard Region 1
Classified residential neighbourhood (CRN) types listed in order of, say, affluence.
Enumeration districts listed within their CRN group.

Standard Region 2
As above. And so on, until all ten regions and 125,000 enumeration districts are
covered. The populations of the enumeration districts are accumulated and districts
are drawn for the sample with PPS following the standard procedure, random draw
and systematic interval.

At the second stage
Electors or their addresses may be drawn using the registers covering the selected
enumeration districts. Or streets may be drawn from within the selected enumeration
districts with probability proportionate to the number of addresses in them, and
quotas set relevant to the subject of the survey. This second case is a random-
location sample.

---

owned by Great Universal Stores). The CCN system is explained in a case study
(see Chapter 12). The marketing needs of mail-order operations have stimulated
development in the geodemographic field. In addition to the variables derived from
the census, MOSAIC multi-variate analysis takes into account length of residence,
as shown by changes in the annual registers of electors, together with financial
standing, as shown by bankruptcies and appearances in debtors' courts.

Fifty-four types of residential neighbourhood classifications are produced by
ACORN analysis. SuperProfiles offers an *à la carte* service as well as a
general-purpose classification (or menu). Subscribers are encouraged to order
classifications tailored to their particular marketing needs and to access the
system's computer file direct. SuperProfiles uses 'affluence rankings' to identify
prospective types of customers.

Pinpoint analysis was launched in 1983. Pinpoint's PIN (Pinpoint identified
neighbourhoods) is a classic example of the benefit to be derived from the
electronic marriage of data from disparate sources. In a joint venture with the
Ordnance Survey, and in co-operation with the Post Office, large-scale Ordnance
Survey maps were 'digitised' and used to define postcode boundaries. Postcodes
and enumeration districts may be matched via the national grid references making
it possible to target individual households within the census's household-
enumeration district blocks. Pinpoint's FINPIN is targeted at the financial services
industry to identify prospective types of customers and wealth indicators.

It is possible to draw a probability sample of households using geodemographic stratification. Taking enumeration districts for the first-stage units, the
listing for the draw might be as that in Box 6.12.

We have been considering the procedures used to sample consumer markets. Most consumer markets embrace a large number of households, or individuals, and these are distributed over such a wide area that it is necessary to cluster class while ensuring that the geographical distribution of the population is represented in the sample. When drawing a probability sample it is, at the same time, necessary to ensure that every household/individual in the population has a known chance of being included in the sample.

In non-domestic markets the situation is different. Here a limited number of manufacturers or traders may account for a substantial proportion of output or turnover and it is necessary to recognise their importance in the market when designing a sample. However, opportunity to apply probability methods is limited while, working with often imperfect information, construction of purposive samples requires judgemental skill.

6.5 Sampling 'non-domestic' populations

The description 'non-domestic' is useful because it reminds us that practical considerations affecting the sample of manufacturing industries also apply to the distributive trades, government departments, local authorities and the service industries.

In section 6.3.8 we stressed the need to exercise informed judgement when designing 'non-domestic' samples and said that, where it is possible to establish a complete list of firms within strata, a probability design is theoretically possible, but purposive selection of firms within strata is the more general practice.

In this section we look more closely at stratification of 'non-domestic' markets by volume/value of output or turnover, at the problem of establishing a complete list of establishments and consider the relevance of probability methods.

6.5.1 Stratification by volume/value

In consumer markets the individual purchaser has, with rare exceptions, little effect on total sales. In non-domestic markets, where one or two firms may dominate, these dominating firms must be included in the sample if sampling estimates are to reflect the behaviour and attitudes of the industry as a whole. In any non-domestic market there is going to be sufficient variation in the demand of different-sized establishments for it to be desirable to design a sample which attaches due weight to variations in size.

Table 6.3 illustrates a situation in which 79.2 per cent of establishments account for only 13.3 per cent of gross output while 1.4 per cent account for 40.7 per cent. The eighty-four establishments which constitute the 1.4 per cent make a contribution to gross output out of all proportion to their numbers. Let us assume

Table 6.3 An example of the constitution of a sample

Employees N	Establishments N	%	Gross output %	Sample n	%
1–99	4,532	79.2	13.3	27	13
100–199	452	7.4	8.1	16	8
200–499	459	8.0	17.7	37	18
500–999	281	3.1	14.0	29	14
1,000–1,499	50	0.9	6.2	13	6
1,500+	84	1.4	40.7	84	41
	5,731	100.0	100.0	206	100

that we decide to draw a sample in which the eighty-four are self-selecting and all size categories are represented in proportion to their contribution to gross output, the constitution of the sample would be as in Table 6.2.

There is a wealth of statistical information available about the structure of manufacturing, distributive and service industries. The standard industrial classifications (SIC) used by the Government Statistical Service are broad (Table 6.3 is based on order III), but around thirty SIC orders are sub-divided into nearly 200 headings and some of these are further divided into sub-divisions. The closeness with which the SIC definitions fit marketing requirements varies. The mass industrial market will embrace a number of classifications. But the official statistics usually make it possible to define a non-domestic population in terms such as those used in this example.

The official statistics enable us to set quotas, and the chances are that we will decide to proceed on a purposive basis, using names of establishments derived from internal records, directories and business associates to fill the quotas.

To draw a probability sample we would need to acquire a complete list of establishments: a sampling frame. It is clearly desirable that we should be able to assign firms to strata before we draw: to stratify after drawing is likely to be wasteful of effort, time and money.

6.5.2 Sampling-frame shortcomings

In order to draw a sample at random we need a list which is complete, up to date and without repetition of items. None of the generally used non-domestic frames quite meets these requirements (see Box 6.13). They are useful sources of names for a quota sample but are likely to be inadequate for a probability sample.

Knowing the size structure of a market and being able to relate establishments to the size structure are crucial to sound estimates of market size.

Box 6.13

The financial directories (e.g. the *Stock Exchange Yearbook* and *Dun & Bradstreet*) define the overall worth of an enterprise but may not record separately that part of the enterprise in which we are interested. They give 'no indication of the geographical location, size or activity of individual plants'. (Waller, 1992)

Kompass Register relates enterprises to standard industrial classifications, but subsidiaries may be omitted and information relating to financial standing and to size may be inadequate for the purpose of stratification.

Trade directories vary in their effectiveness. Omissions within and duplications between directories occur.

Trade associations are not necessarily supported by important enterprises.

The classified Yellow Pages computer file is invaluable when it comes to making contact with establishments selected for the sample, but it does not include information about the size of establishments. To use the *Yellow Pages* file as a sampling frame necessitates telephone screening.

Records built up over time from representatives' reports, the financial press, industry and trade association sources together with previous research are valuable sources of marketing information. But they are unlikely to be sufficiently complete for a probability sample.

It is possible to project from sample estimates to the real world with confidence in the results if the following conditions are met:

- The market in question fits the SIC classification system.
- There is a complete, up-to-date and unduplicated listing of establishments available.
- The source of information has been located within establishments.
- Unambiguous answers have been given to survey questions.

There are usually a good many 'ifs' and 'buts' attached to the projections: so much so that, particularly in a market extending over several industrial classifications (e.g. heating and ventilating equipment), there may well be a case for the sequential approach:

1. Decide what return (e.g. in terms of return on investment or contribution to profit) is required to make the venture viable.
2. Translate this into minimum demand for the product or service.

3. Estimate its potential popularity in terms of market share, taking account of viable marketing expenditure.
4. Sample the market until sufficient potential has been located.

6.6 Conclusion

Use of a probability procedure to draw a sample of individuals, householders, firms or other 'unit of enquiry' has two advantages:

- It makes it possible to measure sampling error when translating sample estimates into population values.
- It ensures that human likes and dislikes do not influence the selection or rejection of units for the sample.

It is possible to cluster calls while ensuring that every item in the population has a known (and non-zero) chance of inclusion in the sample. Drawing in more than one stage with PPS reduces fieldwork costs and makes for improved supervision, but this procedure, as we have seen, is quite a complicated and lengthy one.

The procedure when it is used to draw a master sample is likely to be cost-effective in consumer markets and there are certain non-domestic markets of a 'mass' nature offering opportunities for the use of a master sample drawn in more than one stage with PPS.

Drawing in more than one stage makes it possible to concentrate the sampling frame for the final draw, for example, to draw from a comparatively small number of registers. This concentration is particularly valuable where non-domestic surveys are concerned, because sampling frames do not come ready-made in non-domestic markets. It is usually necessary to construct them.

The advantages to be derived from probability sampling are dearly bought. In non-domestic surveys it is usually necessary to compromise and in consumer survey work there is a cost-effective case for drawing sampling locations at random and then setting quotas relevant to the nature of the enquiry.

References

Bagozzi, R. (1994) *Advanced Methods of Marketing Research*, Cambridge, MA: Blackwell, ch. 3.

Collins, M. (1988) 'Sampling', in *Consumer Market Research Handbook*, Amsterdam: Elsevier Science Publishers, ch. 4.

Economist (1994) 'Opinion polls', 9 July, p. 35.

Ehrenberg, A. (1975) *Data Reduction Analysing and Interpreting Statistical Data*, London: Wiley, p. 291.

Hutton, P. (1992) 'Industry issues: after the poll is over . . .', *MRS Newsletter*, May, pp. 12–13.

The Magazine of the Market Research Society (1993) 'CAPI is working, says NRS', Jan. Issue No. 320, p. 4.

Moon, N. and McGregor, R. (1992) 'Exit polls – developing a technique', *Journal of the Market Research Society*, July, vol. 34, no. 3, pp. 257–68.

MRS (1992) 'MRS Inquiry into the performance of opinion polls in the General Election', *Newsletter* July, p. 1.

The Royal Mail (1994) *The Complete Guide to Postcodes*, Stoke-on-Trent: Royal Mail.

Waller, R. (1992) 'Constituency polling in Britain', *MRS 1992 Conference Papers*, 18–20 March, pp. 63–82.

Worcester, R. (1991) *A Guide to the History and Methodology of Political Opinion Polling*, Oxford: Blackwell.

Worcester, R. (1992) 'Opinion polls in British General Elections', *MRS 1992 Conference Papers*, 18–20 March, pp. 51–61.

Assignments

Faced with the following assignments: (a) what type of sample design would you propose in each case?; (b) what data sources would you use to establish the population parameters?; (c) what breakdowns would you provide for when calculating sample size?

1. A survey of voting intentions at a general election.
2. A survey to establish where and in what way gardening tools are selected by the population of an expanding town in the South-east, a town served by a variety of traditional and modern retail outlets.
3. A survey to establish car accessories in use on the vehicles of private motorists, together with those not on the vehicle but desired.
4. A survey to show regional differences in the use of equipment by commercial laundries.

CHAPTER 7

Questionnaire design

This chapter focuses on 'question and answer' as a means of finding out about the habits, awareness and attitudes of consumers *vis-à-vis* the products and services available to them and the needs these products and services are designed to meet. The chapter proceeds from a general discussion of types of questionnaire and kinds of question to a detailed examination of the stages in the development of a questionnaire and consideration of the questions themselves, 'the art of asking questions' (Payne 1951).

Methodological research funded by the Market Research Society suggests that more than half of the questions asked in surveys of the adult or housewife populations are attitude questions. Attitude questions are given a separate section at the end of the chapter. There are certain techniques in common use for measuring attitudes and these are best considered in isolation; for a survey, attitude questions are likely to be introduced into the questionnaire as and where relevant to questions of behaviour and awareness.

In 1993, the MRS produced a booklet backed by the Association of British Market Research Companies (ABMRC) and the Association of Market Survey Organisations (AMSO) for consistency in approach to the conduct of face-to-face interviewers (MRS 1993). The booklet gives answers to questions which are most often asked with samples of the 'interviewer identity card' and the 'market research mark'. The MRS Freefone service verifies for respondents if a research company carrying out interviews with them is a genuine market research agency operating under the MRS or related associations' codes of conduct.

7.1 Asking questions for attitude and product usage studies

The questionnaire is a very useful, flexible and far-reaching tool for the market researcher who can use it to obtain important information on the following:

- Consumer behaviour: what consumers buy, where they buy and how they use what they buy.

- Consumer awareness: how aware consumers are of available services and brands; product characteristics and the claims made for them.
- Consumer attitudes: how consumers view the relevant activity (e.g. motoring, clothes washing, shaving) and the types of product and service available for pursuing the activity.

An attitude is a learned predisposition to respond in a consistently favourable or unfavourable manner with respect to a given object. An opinion is the expression of an underlying attitude. An individual might hold the attitude that smoking is anti-social and express the opinion that people who smoke in non-smoking carriages should be put out at the next station. The distinction is a fine one and the terms are often treated as interchangeable.

Attitudes are the product of experience (what has happened to the respondent), awareness (what has been noticed and learnt) and volition (what is wanted or willed). Attitudes are recorded to help explain behaviour so that informed assumptions may be made about future behaviour. (For techniques used to elicit and measure attitudes, see section 7.5.)

The questionnaire is an indispensable tool for the market researcher since the results are critical to the research outcome. The questionnaire is a common form of collecting information on markets. Markets can be described and analysed in detail so that opportunities can be taken, company performance assessed and competitors' activities tracked.

So why do we not just ask consumers what they are going to do? As we have seen in the previous chapter on voting intentions, some people will not necessarily disclose their real intentions if the party they want to vote for or the product they want is perceived to be the 'unfashionable' one at the time. Studies are undertaken on consumer attitudes and product usage because it is important to understand what is happening in their markets. It is also important for organisations to have these insights in order to identify new opportunities which arise.

In order to aid management decision-making, *ad hoc* or 'one-off' studies can be undertaken on consumer attitudes and product usage. These are designed to aid the making of a specific and immediate decision because it is important for managers to understand what is happening in their markets at a particular point in time.

If we lack trend data we can arrive at hypotheses concerning future behaviour as follows:

1. By first asking questions about present experience of the product or service: about what is being bought, used, owned or done now.
2. We then ask questions about past experience in order to determine whether present behaviour is habitual.
3. Questions about intentions, such as intentions to buy or to invest capital can usefully be asked if sufficient data have been collected over time to establish relationships between intentions as expressed and past actions.
4. Lastly, answers to awareness and attitude questions taken together with

answers to the behavioural ones, help us to decide what the respondents' future behaviour is likely to be.

It is important for managers to develop these insights so that future behaviour may be anticipated and new opportunities can be identified.

7.2 Questionnaire types

In an industrial society, the common prevalence of the use of the questionnaire method means that it is difficult for people to avoid participating in questionnaires about themselves, for example, in applications for financial services products such as mortgages and insurance policies or to take part in direct marketing mailshots linked to sales promotions. Most people become familiar with the notion of questionnaires before they have reached adulthood having disclosed information on themselves in applications, for example, to study at educational establishments or membership of sports and travel clubs.

Consequently, there are many questionnaires put forth by organisations and individuals which vary between two basic types. These take the form of being fully structured with closed questions at one extreme to being completely unstructured with open-ended questions at the other extreme. A compromise is the semi-structured questionnaire which incorporates a mix of the two.

Structured questionnaire: The order in which questions are asked together with their wording are laid down. The interviewer must not alter or explain questions. Many questions are closed and the possible answers to most questions are pre-coded so that all the interviewer has to do is to ring a code number (for coding, see section 7.3.5) or tick a box.

Unstructured questionnaire: Most of the questions are open-ended. The interviewer is free to change the order of asking questions and to explain them. The questionnaire may take the form of a check-list for discussion. The unstructured questionnaire is used in 'depth' interviews, group discussions and in non-domestic surveys. The interview can be respondent-led particularly if the interview is with an expert in the field so that the observations and expertise of the respondent can be taken account of.

Semi-structured questionnaire: This usually constitutes a mixture of closed or fixed-response questions, quick-response ranking or rating scales for measuring attitudes, organisational and product attitudes (see section 7.3.7), and open-ended questions or spaces for respondents to fill in their comments. Semi-structured questionnaires are useful in enabling the interviewer to 'stage-manage' the interview by making sure that all questions are covered with room for the interviewee (respondent) to add comments to the specific questions already asked.

Closed questions: The respondent chooses between possible answers to a question. This may take the form of yes or no answers with a tick in the relevant box. A good example is the data collection for the government's household census in 1991 by questionnaire which contained a long and detailed list of closed questions to elicit some demographic data on heads of households and their families. Answering of the questionnaire was compulsory. The questionnaires distributed and collected door-to-door by temporary workers who could give assistance to any householder who had difficulty in answering the questionnaire for a variety of reasons, for instance, because of low levels of literacy.

In a closed question, the question is dichotomous (either/or) if there are only two possible answers (apart from a 'don't know' or 'no preference'). If there are more than two possible answers, apart from 'Don't know' the question is multichotomous. Answers to questions can be to tick the yes/no boxes or to ring the correct answers or code number, for example:

Dichotomous
    Is your mower:
    a rotary mower?   (Code No)
    a cylinder mower?   (Code No)
    (The mower has to be one or the other)

Multichotomous
    Is your mower driven by petrol?   (Code No)
    Mains electricity?   (Code No)
    Battery? (Code No)
    Human effort, unaided?   (Code No)

Coding: A numerical code is allocated to each type of response to facilitate data processing. All possible answers may be listed and coded in advance of the interview and, in surveys of any size, this is done wherever possible. When responses cannot be allocated to a range of possible answers, coding takes place after the interview (see section 7.3.5 and Appendix 2).

Open-ended questions: The respondent is left free to answer in his/her own words and the interviewer is required either to write down the answers verbatim, or to allocate the reply to a range of possible answers set out and coded on the questionnaire. Verbatim answers demand subsequent coding. Answers to the question 'Would you tell me why you chose a rotary mower?' might receive 'open' treatment.

Direct questions: The respondent is asked about his/her own behaviour without equivocation, as in the questions given above.

Indirect questions: The respondent's own behaviour or attitude is inferred from answers to questions about the behaviour or attitude of other people: 'Why do you think people have pets?' or 'Why, would you say, do people go to church?'

(Respondents reluctant to give true answers can also be overcome by using a projective technique such as 'sentence completion' or 'word association'.)

Electronic data processing (EDP) puts a premium on questionnaire 'structuring' and this has in the past been counterproductive, impeding instead of facilitating data collection: both the interviewer and the respondent have suffered from the computer revolution. The practice of recording answers on grids and scales, which are easy to analyse, causes boredom and frustration in the interview situation, unless the subject is absolutely riveting (Fabridge 1980).

By making the processing of data so fast and effortless EDP removes or weakens obstacles to the lengthy questionnaire. Using the computer to feed in and to analyse data is now a common, and to some an essential, part of the research effort. Both computer-assisted telephone interviewing (CATI) and computer-assisted personal interviewing (CAPI), described in the information technology section in Chapter 1 (see pages 1–19), have integrated the interviewing and electronic data-processing functions. Computer hardware and software have been made more accessible due to lower costs and better-designed 'user-friendly' programs such as the statistical package for the social sciences (SPSS). As this example shows SPSS was originally created in the 1960s for use with mainframe computers but has been subsequently adapted as a statistical and data-analysis package available for use with UNIX, OS/2 Macintosh, MS-DOS and Microsoft Windows. A student version of SPSS is also available through SPSS UK Ltd and Prentice Hall.

7.3 Design of a structured questionnaire

We are going to consider the stages in the development of a structured questionnaire from the formulation of research objectives during exploratory research (Chapter 2) to the pilot test in which the proposed questionnaire is tried out on members of the survey population. (The proposed sampling method may be tried out at the same time.)

The flow chart in Figure 7.1 illustrates the stages which are considered in the following sections:

1. Formulation of hypotheses.
2. Topics of interest.
3. Survey methods.
4. Levels of generality.
5. Plan of tabulations.
6. Ordering of topics.
7. Treatment of topics.
8. Questionnaire layout.
9. Pilot testing.

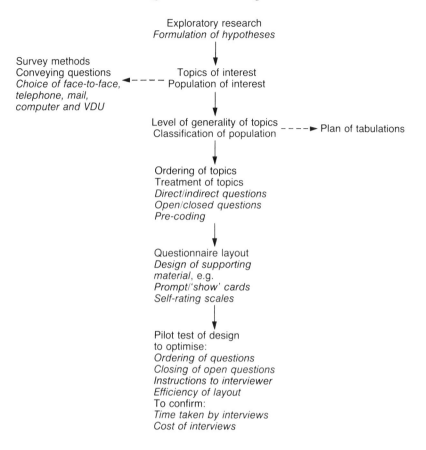

Figure 7.1   Stages in the development of a questionnaire

By the time that we come to design the questionnaire we should know what topics are relevant to the decision-making task, and from what population the sample is to be drawn. We ought to have arrived at tentative ideas (hypotheses) about behaviour and attitudes in the market, and we should be clear as to the conclusions we are going to need to be able to draw, depending on whether our hypotheses are accepted or rejected.

In order to do this we have to decide the following:

1. In what detail we need to ask questions about the survey topics – the level of generality (see section 7.3.2).
2. How we are going to relate answers to respondents – the plan of tabulations (see section 7.3.3).

7.3.1 Formulating research objectives

Considering what conclusions we may want to draw does not mean that we are pre-judging the answers. We are just making sure that when the time comes to draw conclusions, the data are available in sufficient detail for us to be able to accept or reject our conjectures about the market we are describing. The intellectual effort involved is illustrated in the case of a possible demand for works transport (see page 160).

7.3.2 Topics of interest

The research effort can be to describe a particular market from the viewpoint of a consumer. The objectives can be set around the identification of market opportunities or the solving of a specific problem, optimising the positioning of a brand or to make recommendations for a marketing mix approach to target markets.

Topics can be examined such as consumer awareness of a product or a specific brand, sources and frequency of brand purchase and use, prices paid and quantities consumed, and the attitudes and needs of consumers using the brand.

7.3.3 Qualitative and quantitative approaches to survey methods

Qualitative research usually involves a small number of sample units of individuals or groups because the qualitative approach is used to explore problems in depth and to identify root and contributing causes. Inferences can then be made about a range of respondents' experiences and their opinions. The cause-and-effect relationships in data generated can be inferred. So the qualitative approach is necessarily inductive and respondents are usually chosen on the basis of purposive (non-probability) sampling (Sykes 1991). By its nature, qualitative research lends itself to face-to-face, in-depth interviews undertaken in respondents' houses or in work environments. Semi-structured and non-structured questionnaires are normally used to engage respondents with exploration of their feelings, opinions and interest about specific issues or products.

Quantitative research provides a statistically valid picture. Larger numbers of sample units are chosen using probability sampling. Quantitative research can also be conducted by re-interviewing samples, for example, from a pool of known co-operative respondents using random-digit dialling by telephone with interviewing via a CATI system (Hahle 1992). Results can be correlated and statistically quoted with cost-benefit analysis supplied. Quantitative research is thus more applicable to self-completion postal questionnaires and electronic data-collection methods such as computer-assisted telephone interviewing (CATI) and computer-assisted personal interviewing (CAPI). Structured questions are normally used.

Short structured questionnaires are used in conjunction with shopping centre interviews or hall tests, consumer panels and in-house tests where consumers can try out a sample of products before completion of questionnaires.

There is some evidence that with the main types of survey methods – personal interviewers, telephone interviewers and postal self-completion questionnaires – the inclusion of some monetary incentive or product promotion will increase response rates (Brennan *et al.* 1991).

7.3.4 *Levels of generality*

Decisions are made not only about the topics to be included in the questionnaire but also about the detail in which they should be covered. We must be careful not to leave some critical aspect out. Relevant information collected on topics of interest need also to be related to consumers in terms of socio-economic and demographic profiles and attitude observations. Therefore the information can be usefully applied to segment markets for targeting new products, representing brands or other marketing promotion initiatives.

In designing the questionnaire it is also necessary to take into account the way in which the survey population can be broken down. When it comes to making decisions, what groups are going to be critical? The sample should be designed to yield enough individuals in each critical group for us to be confident that they represent this group in the population. On the other hand, each interview costs money. The group's behaviour and attitudes must be relevant to the decisions we anticipate having to make. The best way of deciding what classifications are relevant is to take each survey topic in turn and consider the importance of each group in the survey population in relation to it. (The relationship between topics and population is developed in section 7.3.3.) A detailed picture of the kind of decisions that have to be made by the research planner at this stage is given in the case described at the end of this chapter (see page 160).

7.3.5 *Plan of tabulations*

The topics have been listed in the required detail and the population has been classified into relevant groups (see Figure 7.1). This is a good point at which to plan the tabulations, bearing in mind that too much detail is as counter-productive as too little detail. We need to take each topic in turn and to decide which groups in the survey population warrant individual attention when it comes to discussing this topic.

The agreed classification of respondents may usefully be applied to every answer, but this is not invariably the case: we are likely to want to consider other groupings, such as those whose answers to the questionnaire show them to be alike in their behaviour.

Taking an example from the 'works transport' case on page 160, it goes without saying that we are going to put questions about a particular mode of travel, say, its advantages and disadvantages, to those who use it. But in planning tabulations we may still have to make a number of decisions. Take those who come to work by car:

- Do we put these attitude questions to all of them, passengers as well as drivers?
- To those who come all the way as well as those who come part of the way?
- Or do we focus on drivers who have used no other mode of travel to work during the period covered by the survey?

Tabulations need to be decided upon before the questionnaire is written because the wording of the questionnaire must make it clear whose answer is required for each question. This applies when an interviewer is putting the questions in a personal or telephone interview, and when the questionnaire has been mailed to a respondent for 'self-completion'. Decisions about the tabulations also affect sample size. Particularly crucial for the calculation of sample size is the decision on whether to break down the behavioural groupings by a demographic classification. Where 'getting to work' is concerned we might hypothesise that the 'shop-floor' attitude towards driving to work and type of car ownership is sufficiently different from that of 'senior managers' to warrant this further breakdown of the car drivers. The further breakdown would necessitate a large sample and the additional cost might not be justified.

It may be helpful, when considering tabulations, to set up a matrix with topics in detail down the side and standard demographic and other groupings across the top. The plan of tabulations can then be seen at a glance and we will have ensured that nothing of importance is left out. The code-frame should include a description of the question and a description of who should be answering it (MRS 1987). For a more detailed treatment of this subject, see Appendix 2 and for the data reduction approach to survey analysis, see Collins (1992).

7.3.6 *Ordering of topics*

It is good common practice to follow these principles:

- Open with one or two general, bland questions which the respondent is expected to find easy to answer.
- Explore present behaviour in the market before delving into the past, i.e. to focus on what is being done, used, bought, eaten *now* before asking about earlier experience.
- Record behaviour before putting attitude questions. Answering behaviour

questions concentrates the respondent's mind on the topic in question so that he/she is ready to express an opinion about it, or to take up a position on a self-rating scale (see section 7.5 on attitude measurement).

- Take topics in a logical order so that the respondent is not confused.
- Withhold topics that might be embarrassing until the personal or telephone interview is under way or, in the case of a mailed questionnaire, until the respondent's interest may have been aroused by the earlier questions.
- Be prepared to try more than one place in the questionnaire for the 'difficult' topic at the pilot stage.
- Try to avoid boring sequences in the questionnaire, e.g. a run of multi-choice questions or too many rating scales one after the other.
- In a personal or telephone interview, make sure that the topics are ordered in such a way that ideas influencing answers to later questions are not put into the respondent's head. The mailed questionnaire is likely, if filled in, to have been read right through first.

Classification questions are often embarrassing or difficult, but they can be left until the end in the case of a probability sample, for the respondent drawn at random must be interviewed. In the case of a quota sample, some classification questions need to be asked at the outset because it is necessary to establish that the respondent fits into the quota set.

In a postal survey classification questions can be put at the end of the questionnaire. They are unlikely to be as disturbing as they would be in an interview because the respondent is not always asked to fill in his/her name and address.

'Show cards' are often used to take the embarrassment out of age and income questions because the respondent can be asked to point at the slot they fit into. An example for age might be, depending on the requirements of the survey:

'Would you show me on this card your age last birthday?'

15–24	45-64
25–44	65+

In the case of a mailed questionnaire the respondent ticks in the appropriate box, while in a telephone interview age and income brackets, if used, must be kept few and broad.

It is clearly desirable that questions designed to classify respondents should, as far as possible, be standardised so that the results of surveys can be compared. The Market Research Society set up a working party in 1971 'to consider whether the use of standard questions in survey research should be encouraged, and if so to put forward recommendations'. The recommendations still relevant today are based on research agency practices which are summarised in *Standardized Questions: A Review for Market Research Executives* (Wolfe 1984).

7.3.7 Treatment of topics

We are going to consider the actual wording of questions in section 7.4 but, before writing the questionnaire, we need to decide whether we should treat the topics in an 'open' or 'closed' way, and in a 'direct' or 'indirect' way.

In the survey research there is a practical case for pre-coding, and also for closing as many questions as possible. The respondent is given a choice of answers plus 'don't know'. The interviewer has merely to ring the code number alongside the respondent's choice of answer. Too many closed questions may bore the respondent but interviews and data processing take less time than they would if the question were open and the answers had to be put into coding categories *after* the interview. Also the closed pre-coded question is more likely to yield valid data: there are fewer opportunities for lapses of memory on the part of the respondent and for the incorrect recording of answers by the interviewer (see Box 7.1).

We need to distinguish between questions which are pre-coded and closed (as in the car accessories example) and questions which are pre-coded but put to the respondents as if open. In both cases the respondent answers and the interviewer rings the relevant code number, but in the first case all possible answers are put to the respondent and memory is stimulated.

There is evidence that respondents react differently to the two types of question as if they are being asked to perform two different answering tasks. In the open situation the respondent is required to generate and define items relevant to the question. In the closed situation he/she has to choose or judge between relevant items already selected. It has been shown when the same question is put to matched samples of respondents, responses vary with the approach used.

The importance of this finding depends on the nature of the question being asked. In the car accessories example the respondent is being asked a strictly factual question and the closed question is clearly more likely to produce a true answer than an open one. When attitudinal or 'why' questions are being asked, there is room for doubt. This is illustrated in Belson's comparison of open-ended and check-list questioning systems (1982). See Box 7.2 for an example of this.

The check-list questioning system stimulates memory and it may put into words the ideas which the respondent was not conscious of having or to introduce new ones. The check-list also draws attention to items which the respondent might not have considered worth mentioning when asked an open-ended question. That is, the two questioning methods cannot be assumed to produce the same result. Full advantage is taken of electronic data processing when questions are closed and pre-coded. In survey work it is common practice to use the open-ended system at the exploratory stage and then to reduce the list of items and close.

We need to remember that the two questioning methods are likely to produce different data sets and that, when we reduce the list by discarding less frequently mentioned items, we are making the assumption that ideas voiced infrequently are less important in determining behaviour than those voiced frequently.

In order to pre-code questions it is necessary to anticipate the possible answers.

Box 7.1

Example
Open: 'What extras and/or accessories were already fitted when you bought your car?'

(The respondent tries to remember; perhaps goes out to look at the car. The interviewer writes down items as they occur to the respondent.)

Closed: 'Which of these extras and/or accessories were already fitted when you bought your car?' [SHOW CARD]

	Col. 9
Wing mirrors	1
Seat belts	2
Radio/tape recorder	3
Heater	4
Head rests	5
Fog lamps	6
Reversing lights	7

For standard classification questions (such as age, class, sex) or regular items such as 'don't know', 'no preference', 'anything else'/'any other', pre-coding is a straightforward matter. But in order to pre-code answers to most survey questions, prior knowledge of this range of possible answers is needed. Exploratory research will have suggested what answers are to be expected and the pilot test will confirm the completeness of the list, provided an 'anything else' is included and respondents are given time to think whether or not there is 'anything else'. A questionnaire consisting entirely of 'closed' questions is boring for both respondent and interviewer. Open questions break the monotony. But when designing a survey to describe a market as many questions as possible should be pre-coded and open questions necessitating hand-written answers kept to a minimum.

If a closed question means choosing between more than three possible answers, it can be best to list the choices on a show card. This assumes a personal interview. On a mailed questionnaire they would be set out alongside the printed question. If a topic proves to be 'difficult' or embarrassing at the exploratory stage, we may decide to approach it indirectly when it comes to formulating survey questions. In survey research we need the comfort of numbers, so our treatment of the subject must be a *quantifiable* one.

A quantifiable questioning technique used by Research International is the cognitive response analysis (CRA). This elicits spontaneous reactions to a commercial as well as an understanding of how involving the commercial is to viewers. According to worded instruction, viewers are required to write down all their spontaneous thoughts, ideas and reactions to an advertisement. They are then asked to rate each of their thoughts on a scale ranging from positive to negative.

Box 7.2 Belson's comparison of open-ended and check-list questioning systems

During survey work in five different product fields an experimental 'why' question was asked. The five samples were split so that one half received the experimental question open and the other closed. One half were required to volunteer reasons for liking, disliking or using as the case might be; the other half were given a list of reasons to study. The items on this check-list were derived from 'preliminary open-ended research'.

Example: 1,521 interviews with 'bath additive' users in Great Britain dealing with reasons for using a bath additive.

A. *The check-list system*
   'You've said you have used . . . (READ OUT ALL RESPONDENT CLAIMS TO BATH ADDITIVES USED) in your bath. I would like to know *all your reasons* for using this/these.'
   (PAUSE)
   'Here is a list of possible reasons.'
   PASS CARD AND SAY:
   'Please go through it and call out all that apply in your case.'
   WAIT FOR RESPONDENT TO FINISH WITH THE LIST
   WHEN HE/SHE HANDS IT BACK, SAY:
   'What other reasons do you have for using this/these bath additives?'

B. *The open-ended system*
   'You've said you have used . . . (READ OUT ALL RESPONDENT CLAIMS TO BATH ADDITIVES USED) in your bath. Please tell me *all your reasons* for using this/these.' (PROBE FULLY, USING PROBES SUCH AS: 'What else?'/ 'What other reasons?'/'Uhuh', followed by a waiting silence.)

Findings: The five samples yielded six experimental treatments (one sample was asked first about things liked and then about things disliked). The following findings are based on all six sets of data:

- The check-list stimulated a substantially higher overall level of response.
- Check-list respondents offered fewer 'other reasons', suggesting that the use of the check-list has a dampening effect upon the volunteering of any further items.
- The frequency with which individual reasons are given by the two halves of the samples varied (from 0.93 to 0.02), i.e. rank order is not stable between the two systems.
- Reasons quoted only once during the preliminary research scored frequently when on the check-list; from the bath additive study, for instance;

From bath additive study	Check-list	Open-ended
% endorsing/volunteering each reason	(760 cases)	(741 cases)
To ease my feet	22.1	5.4
It has a clean smell	9.3	0.1

These responses are then analysed for self-relevance and positive or negative associations. While the responses are quantifiable, the technique retains the benefit of qualitative elicitation and it adds a unique extra dimension to conventional pre-testing methods.

7.4 Questionnaire layout

Apart from the questions relating to the survey topics, we have to provide for the following:

- Identification of the job by means of a reference number.
- Identification of each individual questionnaire by means of a reference number.
- Identification of the interviewer in the case of a personal interview.
- Introductory remarks.
- Classification of respondents, plus, in some personal interviews, the respondent's name and address.

The job may be one of many being handled by a research agency. In addition, it may be necessary to identify the filed data long after the job is finished. In the case of a personal or telephone interview it is good practice to check a proportion of calls. Alternatively, quality may be controlled by comparing the answers recorded by one interviewer with those recorded overall. This can be done through the MRS Quality Control Scheme which now has a membership of fifty companies supplying research. These companies all operate above, or at least to, the standards laid down by the Scheme. All have been visited by QCS inspectors, who have required access to all their documentation relating to training supervision, quality control and the office procedures and records that are kept by each company. At the end of the inspection companies have compiled a short summary describing their field-work operation.

In a personal interview, a card (complete with the interviewer's photograph) introduces the interviewer (provided the research supplier is a member of the MRS Quality Control Scheme), but it is still important to explain to the respondent why his/her privacy is being invaded (see Box 7.3). This applies whether the data are being collected face-to-face, over the telephone or by mail. In a structured survey

---

Box 7.3

'Good morning/afternoon/evening.'

SHOW INTERVIEWER BUSINESS CARD

'I am from Researchplan. We are conducting a survey on do-it-yourself activity and the sort of jobs people do around the home, and would be grateful for your help.'

Box 7.4

The questionnaire layout must clearly distinguish questions from instructions. It is good practice to use upper and lower case letters for questions and capitals for instructions, as in the example shown below. There must be no doubt as to who is to answer the question, e.g.:

ASK THOSE WHO WENT BY AIR
'Did you get there on time?'
or, for a mailed questionnaire:
'If you went by air . . .'

---

the words used will be standard so that each respondent is introduced to the subject of the survey in the same way. These introductory remarks often appear at the beginning of the questionnaire, but if the questionnaire is mailed the introductory remarks are more likely to be the subject of a covering letter.

We discussed the placing of the classification questions and the ordering of topics in section 7.3.4. Here we are concerned with the effect of the layout of the questionnaire on the respondent in the case of a mailed questionnaire and on the interviewer in the case of face-to-face and telephone enquiries. An example of this is given in Box 7.4.
This extract from a questionnaire illustrates the following 'ground rules':

- Questions are best clearly separated from answers in the layout of the questionnaire.
- The route through the questionnaire should be immediately clear (see Q1 'SKIP to Q3').
- The interviewer must be told whether to read out the pre-coded answers (compare Q2 and Q4).
- And when to show a card (the instruction at Q4 might have been SHOW CARD instead of READ OUT).

In Box 7.5 we assume that the first four columns are allocated to classification data.

The interviewer must be left in no doubt as to whether or not to read out coded answers. By reading out the answers as coded the interviewer stimulates the respondent's memory. If some memories are stimulated and others not, bias is introduced.

Finally, in an open-ended, un-coded question ample space must be left for taking down the respondent's answer in the respondent's own words.

7.5 Pilot testing

Pre-testing a questionnaire is an important part of the research effort (Reynolds *et al.* 1993). When designing a new questionnaire, it is best to pre-test it to gauge

---

Box 7.5

Col. 5

Q1   Do you own an electric drill?
Yes 1
No 2 SKIP to Q3

Col. 6
(We assume 'Researchplan' is a member of the Quality Control Scheme.)

Q2   What brand or make of drill
do you own at the moment?

Black & Decker	1
Wolf (and so on)	2
Other	8

Col. 7

Q3   Do you use a drill in your day-to-day work?
Yes 1
No 2

IF NOT A DRILL OWNER NOR A USER
AT WORK, CLOSE INTERVIEW

Col. 8

Q4   About how often do you use some
sort of power drill?
READ OUT

Less than once a week	1
At least once a week	2
At least every two weeks	3
About once a month	4
Less than once a month	5

---

anticipated reactions from a sampled population, to check for ambiguities in the questions and level of understanding of the questions from the respondents, and to help in the elimination of bias. The initial choice of respondents has to be carefully selected so that it can incorporate fair representation of the target population to be surveyed. Careful screening avoids the time and cost of mistakes and enhances the accuracy of the findings.

7.6 The art of asking questions

Here we would overload the text if we attempted to do more than set out some generally accepted principles, together with examples. The content of the questionnaire is determined by the research objectives as laid down in a research proposal and the way in which the questions are put will be influenced by the following:

- The nature of the survey population.
- The method chosen to convey the questions to the survey population.

There is interaction between those two factors. If our research objective were to predict demand for private motor cars, we might well decide to focus our enquiry on the behaviour and attitudes of new car buyers and to send questionnaires through the post because the subject is of particular interest to this survey population. We would need to define 'new' and to take account of new cars other than outright 'company' cars, whose funding is aided by employers. It would also be desirable to repeat a survey of this kind at regular intervals to establish trends.

Having determined the topics to be covered and in what detail individual topics should be investigated, we need to ask ourselves the following:

- Has the respondent got the information?
- Will the respondent understand the question?
- Is the respondent likely to give a true answer?

7.6.1 Has the respondent got the information?

It is easy to assume that the respondent has had the experience necessary to give a valid answer to your question, but it is good practice to find out about a respondent's actual experience of a product or service before putting questions about how it is used or regarded. You can ask a respondent 'which do you prefer for cooking, gas or electricity?' and he/she may well answer 'gas', having had no experience of electricity. He/she may use solid fuel or may not cook at all.

Or the respondent may give you an opinion about packaged tours without having been on one. On the whole, respondents feel they *ought* to have an opinion. They also, on the whole, aim to please the interviewer by having an opinion to give in return for the question (Hahle 1992). The respondent may not have the information because he/she is not the right person to ask, e.g. the respondent may not know how the house is insured or the professional buyer, or purchasing officer, may not know why this particular piece of laboratory equipment is being used.

7.6.2 Will the respondent understand the question?

At the pilot stage we may find that a commonly used word is variously interpreted. Everyday words like 'lunch', 'dinner' and 'tea' can be ambiguous. 'Tea' may be confused with 'supper', 'dinner' may be a midday meal or an evening one, and 'lunch' may be a 'bite' or a sit-down meal. If you want to find out how and when bacon is used, it is safer to pin the questions to 'midday meal', 'evening meal' and 'main meal'. Words such as 'generally', 'regularly' and 'usually' are a common source of ambiguity. Faced with a question about what they generally/regularly/ usually do respondents either describe their recent behaviour or answer in terms of the way in which they like to think of themselves as behaving.

An unfamiliar word in a question either leads to misunderstanding or puts the interviewer into the undesirable position of having to interpret the question. Words such as 'faculty', 'facility', 'amenity', 'coverage' are not helpful in an 'everyday' context, though they would be appropriate if the respondents were academics, insurance brokers, hoteliers or media planners.

It is easy, but of course wrong, to ask two questions in one:

> Do you think Tide gets clothes clean without injuring the fabric?

and to ramble on, so that the thread of the question is lost:

> Do you buy your dog any dog treats – by dog treats I mean any item that is outside the dog's normal diet, is consumable at one occasion (i.e. excluding rubber toys) and is not fresh food, e.g. human biscuits or fresh bones?

Instead of trying to define 'dog treats' in the question it would be better, as recommended, to list all the items regarded as 'dog treats' on the questionnaire or a show card.

7.6.3 Is the respondent likely to give a true answer?

Given that the respondent has the information and understands the question, what are the chances of the question eliciting a true answer?
There are three outstanding hazards:

1. The respondent may find it difficult to verbalise.
2. The respondent's memory may be defective.
3. The respondent may be reluctant, or unwilling, to answer the question.

The respondent may find it difficult to verbalise   The respondent has an answer to give but cannot find the words to put it into or the respondent is slow and the interviewer records 'don't know' and moves on to the next question. This hazard is avoided when questions are closed and the respondent has merely to choose between possible answers. If the question is open but pre-coded, the interviewer may be tempted to read out the code answer categories to hurry the interview along. This is not desirable!

The respondent's memory may be defective   Memory varies from one individual to another, and with the importance of the event. Questions about the new car are more likely to get true answers than questions about the brand of motor spirit last bought. Three practical measures which help respondents to remember are the following:

1. recall can be aided by means of a check-list;

2. the respondent may be asked to keep a diary;
3. a recording mechanism may be installed, for example, the 'set meter' used in television monitoring.

The diary and the mechanical device properly belong to observation as a means of collecting data (see section 7.4). The check-list is a questionnaire component. We have met it in the form of the closed question.

By showing a card or reading out a list we are stimulating memory and we have to be sure that is what we want to do. Ask a respondent what electrical appliances there are in the house and you will probably get an incomplete answer such as forgetting to mention the power drill in the garage. However, if the respondent is shown a list of appliances and provided that the list is complete, the answer stands a good chance of being true. If we need to know what comes to mind unprompted, we can always ask the open question first (unaided recall) and then use the show card.

The respondent may be reluctant, or unwilling, to answer the question We all have ideas as to what is expected of us by other people. We all have a self-image which we aim to preserve. We do not want to give ourselves away or show ourselves in a poor light. Oppenheim (1970) quotes five barriers to true answers:

1. the barrier of awareness: 'People are frequently unaware of their own motives and attitudes';
2. the barrier of irrationality: 'Our society places a high premium on sensible, rational and logical behaviour';
3. the barrier of inadmissibility;
4. the barrier of self-incrimination;
5. the barrier of politeness.

Barriers (3) and (4) are two aspects of the same problem, the problem of reconciling our everyday behaviour and attitudes with those we consider desirable (3) and those we consider acceptable (4). For example, some respondents may fancy themselves as being able to drink large quantities of liquor but be wary of revealing their actual consumption of alcohol. The barrier of politeness (5) means that 'people often prefer not to say negative, unpleasant or critical things'. The respondent may be motivated by kindness as the interviewer 'is only doing his/her job' by a desire to get the interview over as quickly as possible or by fear of repercussion.

Oppenheim's barriers are, perhaps, more critical in social than in marketing research, but research at the exploratory stage may alert us to a sensitive area in our survey.

Projective techniques have been developed by clinical psychologists to enable their patients to express motivations which come up against Oppenheim's 'barriers'. Projective techniques are sometimes used in marketing research to uncover motivations behind the opinions expressed about products and services and the communications designed to advertise them. The more commonly used techniques are as follows:

- *Sentence completion*. The respondent is asked to complete a series of sentences without 'stopping to think'.
- *Word association*. Here the stimulus is a word and the respondent is asked to give the first word that comes into his/her head. It *might* be 'cholesterol' in response to 'butter'.
- *Thematic apperception test (TAT)*. The respondent is shown illustrations of critical situations and is asked to describe what is going on.
- *Cartoon test*. Similar to the TAT except that the characters have balloons coming out of their mouths or heads and one balloon is waiting for the respondent to fill it in.

In each case the respondent is being given an ambiguous stimulus. The stimulus is meaningful to the psychologist but not to the respondent who is being given opportunities to express his/her own behaviour and attitudes without self-censorship. Interpretation of the data collected can also be ambiguous. This also applies to the responses to 'third person' questions. The respondent, on being asked 'why do you think people . . .', may well give what he/she believes to be the behaviour or views of 'people', and fail to project his/her own.

7.7 Asking questions about attitudes

In section 7.1 we defined *attitude* as:

> a learned predisposition to respond in a consistently favourable or unfavourable manner with respect to a given object

and *opinion* as:

> the expression of an underlying attitude

We said that the distinction between 'attitude' and 'opinion' was a fine one. In this section we do not attempt to draw the distinction, using 'attitude' throughout, as in common practice.

Respondents hold attitudes about general subjects (or 'attitude objects') such as motoring and about specific objects such as a Range Rover. Where specific objects are concerned attitudes can be held about physical or functional properties, e.g. acceleration and petrol consumption or about subjective and emotional ones such as the kind of lifestyle suggested by Range Rover ownership. Attitudes are the product of the respondent's experience to date: what he/she has become aware of, and what he/she has come to want. They are influenced by the respondent's view of what society regards as desirable and this influence depends on the extent to which he/she is inclined to conform.

We ask respondents about the attitudes they hold to help us predict their future behaviour in the market. In making predictions we are careful to relate the attitudes expressed to the respondent's present and past behaviour.

7.8 Establishing the 'universe of content'

When we ask an attitude question we sample a 'universe of content': the body of ideas held by the relevant population, say the driving or maintenance of a car. 'Depth' interviews or group discussions during exploratory research will have generated a variety of statements about products or services in the market we are investigating and the contexts in which they are used. We can be reasonably sure that we have spanned the dimensions of the attitude when we no longer meet fresh ideas about the attitude object, but we cannot be entirely sure.

In order to quantify the results of this qualitative work we need to arrive at a list of statements representing the universe of content. If exploratory research has been adequately thorough we have the following in the transcribed recordings of 'depth' interviews and/or group discussions:

- The ideas held about the attitude object by the population we are going to survey.
- The expressions used by the population when talking about these ideas.

The same basic idea may be expressed in different ways by different respondents and the compilation of an attitude battery requires considerable skill. Decisions have to be made about the order in which ideas (or topics) are put, and the number and variety of attitude statements associated with each topic. It is important to recognise that, among the statements listed, some are likely to be more important to the respondent than others. A respondent might agree strongly with both of the following statements:

- Convenience foods are a necessity to the modern housewife.
- Convenience foods make it possible to give more time to the family.

However, the second statement might count for more than the first with the respondent concerned. It is also important to bear in mind the fact that, in agreeing with a statement such as 'Convenience foods are a necessity to the modern housewife', the respondent may be either expressing a belief ('I accept this as a true statement') or making an evaluation ('I identify with this point of view'). (See Belson's comparisons of open-ended and check-list questioning systems in section 7.3.5.)

7.9 Choosing the type of scale

We have now to decide in what form to administer the attitude statements to the respondent. At the simplest we put the statement, in words or in writing, and ask the respondent whether he/she 'agrees' or 'disagrees' with it, or neither:

Convenience foods are a necessity   Agree 1
to the modern housewife.   Disagree 2
                                           Neither agree nor disagree 3
                                                           Don't know 4

This is a nominal scale. We sum the responses by adding up the number in each of the four categories and for each statement, comparing the 'agree', 'disagree', 'neither' and 'don't know' numbers. We could compare the individual statement scores with the scores for the battery as a whole.

To establish the relative importance in rank order of the attitude statements we might construct an ordinal scale. If we were investigating attitudes towards biological detergents we might, for example, ask respondents to rank statements such as 'remove stains', 'saves time', 'no need to soak', 'gets clothes cleaner', 'the modern way', in order of importance. To summarise the responses we would allocate a number to each rank. Given five items to be ranked, the first/top position scores five, the second scores four, and so on, down to the fifth which scores one. The ordinal scale lacks sensitivity. The rank order gives no indication of the intensity with which attributes are viewed. The attribute ranked first may, for example, be far and away first for the respondent who may not find much to choose between the rest. This limitation also applies to the nominal scale. We have no indication of how strongly those who reply 'agree' do agree, nor how strongly those who reply 'disagree' do so. In order to get an indication of the strength or weakness with which an attitude is held, we need to construct rating scales. We are going to consider two commonly used types of rating scale:

1. Likert summated rating scale.
2. Osgood semantic differential scale.

7.9.1 Likert scales

A statement is put to the respondent and the respondent is asked 'please tell me how much you agree or disagree with . . .'. It is common practice to give the respondent the choice of five positions (1–5) on the scale ranging from 'strongly agree' to 'strongly disagree'. To avoid responses converging on the middle ground around '3' that is neither, some people may prefer a seven-point or a ten-point scale to have more response. The scale may be put to the respondent in the form of words printed on a show card, for example:

Agree strongly
Agree slightly
Neither agree nor disagree
Disagree slightly
Disagree strongly

For a postal survey the approach would, of course, need to be modified ('Here are some of the things . . .'). Whether in a personal interview or through the mail, respondents rate themselves. These are self-rating scales. As an alternative, a diagrammatic rating scale based on the Likert approach is as follows:

Strongly agree	Slightly agree	Neither agree nor disagree	Slightly disagree	Strongly disagree
0	0	0	0	0

The statement is read out by the interviewer, or written on the questionnaire in the postal survey. The respondent is invited to point at the position that expresses his/her feeling in response to the statement or to tick in the appropriate position in the case of a postal survey. In a personal interview the interviewer has the scale with him/her to show to the respondent. It is a form of show card.

The words used to denote varying strength or weakness of attitude are not immutably those quoted so far. A Likert-type scale might range from 'true' to 'untrue' or from 'a very important reason for' to 'an unimportant reason for'.

The responses are analysed by allocating weights to scale positions. Given five scale positions we might allocate 5 to 'strongly agree', 3 for the mid-position, 1 for 'strongly disagree', or vice versa: it does not matter provided we are consistent. If the scale battery includes both positive and negative attitude statements, as most do, we have to make sure that 'strongly agree' for a negative statement rates 1 and not 5.

We want to be able to compare the sample's total response to individual statements with its response to the battery as a whole, remembering that the statements have been chosen to span the dimensions of this attitude object, i.e. to represent 'the universe of content'. We also want to be able to compare the summed scores of individual statements; to see how responses to statements correlate. We return to this subject in Chapter 11 when, under market segmentation, we discuss psychographic groups.

7.9.2 Osgood's semantic differential scale

Likert-type scales are commonly used to investigate general subjects such as motoring, do-it-yourself, clothes washing. They are use to rate agreement/

disagreement with the specific attributes of individual models of motor car, makes of power drill, or brands of detergent. But in practice, scales of the semantic differential type are found to be easier to administer and more meaningful to respondents when it comes to rating responses to statements about the specific attributes of named products and services, e.g. a product or service designed to have certain desirable attributes. We want to find out whether or not and how strongly these desirable attributes are associated with our product as compared with the competition. Let us assume that our product is a Rover motor car and that we want to investigate attitudes towards power, styling, driver's image, petrol consumption and reliability in relation to our make/model and others in the market. Following Osgood and his colleagues we might construct the following double-ended scales:

Good acceleration	O O O O O O	Poor acceleration
Up-to-date styling	O O O O O O	Out-of-date styling
Thrusting driver	O O O O O O	Sluggish driver
Extravagant consumption	O O O O O O	Unreliable

The respondent is asked to rate each model in turn on these attitude dimensions. It is important that the order in which the cars are named, whether by the interviewer or on a postal questionnaire, is rotated so that the Rover car is not always considered first. Semantic scales can be either monopolar (e.g. sweet . . . not sweet) or bipolar (e.g. sweet . . . sour). With bipolar scales it is important that the two poles should be perceived as opposites. For an example of a semantic differential scale using a scoring system see Box 7.6.

7.9.3 Kelly's 'personal constructs'

A structured 'depth' interview procedure using 'cards' based on Kelly's theory of personal constructs can help respondents to express their views about individual brands, products and models:

- The product (or service) field is represented by names on cards, photographs of models or of packs, or by the packs themselves, depending on what stimulus is most appropriate.
- The respondent is handed a pack of cards and is asked to discard any brand, name or model that is unfamiliar.
- The retained cards are shuffled by the interviewer who deals three to the respondent.
- The respondent is asked to say one way in which two of the brands or models named on the cards are the same and yet different from the third.

The answer is the respondent's personal construct and it can be used to form a

Box 7.6 The semantic differential scale

Respondents may need to be probed, especially if they provide over-evaluative information, such as 'great – nice – I like it'. This information is not specific, and is therefore difficult to use as a basis of decision-making. Probing can provide a salient battery of attributes, which can then be quantified. For example, a consumer may believe the packaging is sophisticated because of its gold colour. A useful measurement technique is to use a form of attitudinal scaling which can measure both communication and functional objectives of packaging.

The *semantic differential scale* uses a series of bipolar adjectives. Both image and functional attributes can be tested. For example:

Pack A, compared to Pack B, is:

	+3	+2	+1	−1	−2	−3	
Special	–	–	–	–	–	–	Ordinary
Exciting	–	–	–	–	–	–	Boring
Dull	–	–	–	–	–	–	Bright
Hard to use	–	–	–	–	–	–	Easy to use

This can indicate the relative strengths and weaknesses of particular pack designs. It provides an overall index of packaging effectiveness, using the aggregate scores of each respondent. A frequency diagram can then be produced, as in Figure 7.2. The results would indicate that improvements are required since more people are dissatisfied than satisfied.

   An alternative use of the semantic differential scale is to measure the means of each factor for every respondent. This allows you to identify specific strengths and weaknesses. In the aggregate analysis the overall index may be satisfactory but ratings of specific criteria may not be. Therefore both measures of analysis are necessary and should also be compared to the main competitors.

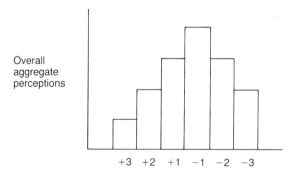

Overall aggregate perceptions

+3 +2 +1 −1 −2 −3

Source: Davies, M. A. P. (1994) 'Using the semantic differential', Loughborough University.

Figure 7.2   Frequency diagram of aggregate scores towards packaging

semantic scale. For example, faced with cards showing three shampoos, a respondent might make one of the following responses:

1. 'These two are scented, that one isn't' (monopolar semantic scale).
2. 'These two are for greasy hair, that one's for dry hair' (bipolar scale).

The shuffling and dealing of triads goes on until 'the respondent can no longer think of any reason why two items are different from the third' – the procedure is fully described by Sampson in the *Consumer Market Research Handbook* (1986).

7.9.4 Some further considerations

It has been found that too many scale positions confuse respondents and demand too much of their capacity to discriminate. However, we need at least five because there is a tendency to avoid the extreme scale positions, especially the negative ones.

Giving the respondent an even number of scale positions to choose from forces choice. There is no middle position to accommodate uncertainty. Opinions vary as to whether this is a desirable practice or not. When choice is forced, a more clear-cut verdict 'for' or 'against' is delivered but this may be dangerously misleading.

If a product or service is liked, the respondent may automatically rate it high on all attributes (the halo effect) and, in the course of scoring his/her own attitude on a large number of attitude scales, the respondent may get into the habit of going for the same position on the scale. The tendency to go for the same position on the scale is less likely if favourable (positive) and unfavourable (negative) statements are interspersed.

When attaching weights to responses to attitude statements it is important to discriminate between favourable and unfavourable statements and to maintain a consistent direction. This is illustrated by Green and Tull (1988) in Box 7.7.

The data derived from weighted responses to rating scales are used as the basis for sophisticated statistical analyses. It is important to remember the following:

- The scale positions and the weights attached to them are arbitrarily fixed.
- With the scales in common use in marketing research, distance between positions appears equal but for the respondent this is not necessarily the case. A distance in strength of feeling between 'approve' and 'strongly approve' may well be different from the distance between 'disapprove' and 'strongly disapprove', but responses are weighted as if the distances were equal.

The rating scales in common use give us useful assessments of the way in which consumers respond to attitude statements about products and services and the needs these are designed to meet. The statistical data derived from rating scales

---
Box 7.7

Example: Consumer attitude statements towards the advertising industry

Item 1: Advertising contributes very importantly to America's industrial prosperity.

Item 2: Advertising merely inflates the prices I must pay for products without giving me any information.

Item 3: Advertising does inform the public and is worth the cost.

Item 4: The American public would be better off with no advertising at all.

Item 5: Advertising old products is a waste of the consumers' dollar.

Item 6: I wouldn't mind if all advertising were stopped.

Item 7: I wish there were more advertising than exists now.

Three of these scale items (or attitude statements) are favourable towards the advertising industry (1, 3 and 7), and four are unfavourable (2, 4, 5 and 6).

A Likert-type scale is used:

Strongly approve	Approve	Undecided	Disapprove	Strongly disapprove
0	1	2	3	4

and each subject (or respondent) underscores 'the description that most suits his/her feeling' towards each statement. Green and Tull use the following weights:

   +2   +1   0   −1   −2

(The procedure is the same if weights running from 5 for 'strongly approve' down to 1 for 'strongly disapprove' are used.)

For items classified as favourable these weights are used without modification. For items classified as unfavourable, the order of the weights is reversed so as to maintain a consistent direction.

Application of the weights is illustrated in the following example, based on the responses of one subject to the seven items:

Item	Response	Weight
1	Strongly approve	+2
2	Disapprove	+1
3	Approve	+1
4	Strongly disapprove	+2
5	Disapprove	+1
6	Strongly disapprove	+2
7	Strongly approve	+2
	Total score	11

As a matter of interest, it is assumed by Green and Tull that these seven items are taken from a scale battery of one hundred items.

enable us to make comparisons and draw useful conclusions; they are not, strictly speaking, measurements.

A case example on 'the means or methods used to get to work' is given at the end of this chapter (see page 160) to illustrate the need to define clearly classifications in relation to survey objectives.

7.10 Conclusion

The questioning techniques discussed in this chapter may be applied to a wide range of descriptive surveys from a simple recording of products, services and brands in current use to the collection of data about how these were acquired, how they are used, why they are used, why they were chosen and how far they go to meet the needs as perceived by the respondents.

Asking questions remains the most fruitful way of collecting statistical data about consumer behaviour. From an examination of the relationships between habits, awareness, attitudes and needs revealed in answers to questions it is possible to arrive at a sufficiently robust understanding of consumer behaviour to formulate hypotheses as to 'what might happen next', or 'what might happen if'.

References

Belson, W. (1982) 'A comparison of open-ended and check-list questioning systems', *MRS Conference Papers*.

Brennan, M., Hoek, J. and Astridge, C. (1991) 'The effects of monetary incentives on the response rate and cost effectiveness of a mail survey', *JMRS*, vol. 33, no. 3, July, pp. 229–41.

Collins, M. (1992) 'The data reduction approach to survey analysis', *JMRS*, April, vol. 34, no. 2, pp. 149–62.

Fabridge, V. (1980) 'Fieldwork and data processing', *Supp. to the MRS Newsletter*, no. 177, Dec., Introduction.

Green, P. and Tull, D. S. (1988) *Research for Marketing Decisions*, Englewood Cliffs, NJ: Prentice Hall.

Hahle, G. (1992) 'Examining the validity of re-interviewing respondents for quantitative surveys', *JMRS*, April, vol. 34, no. 2, pp. 99–117.

The Magazine of the Market Research Society (1993) 'A very clear "Thank you" . . .', July, Issue No. 326, p. 3.

Market Research Society (1987) *Guide to Good Coding Practice*.

Oppenheim, A. (1970) *Questionnaire Design and Attitude Measurement*, London: Heinemann Educational Books.

| **Case History 7.1**   The means to get to work |

Possible demand for works transport: extracts from a case history to illustrate deciding levels of generality with regard to a survey topic, in this case 'the means used to get to work'.

The management of a labour-intensive firm with a factory on the outskirts of a large town is considering whether to provide transport for its employees.

The board wants to be able to predict who might use the firm's transport without, at this stage, committing the company to setting it up. The personnel director suggests that a 'getting to work' survey should be commissioned for publication in the house journal. The survey would describe transport used, routes taken and costs incurred together with opinions held about the transport means available.

A research agency was employed. The research officer assigned to the job observed traffic at the firm's car parks and bicycle sheds, held three group discussions, listed question topics suggested by this exploratory research and discussed the detail in which means of getting to work should be recorded. Was a two-way breakdown sufficient?

Private transport   Public transport

What about on foot, all the way? (Public transport would mean some walking!) The effect of railway strikes and of petrol cost and shortage had come up during the group discussions. It was decided that getting to work should be recorded in a less general way:

Private transport	*Public transport*
Motor car	Bus
Motor bike/moped	Train
Bicycle	
On foot all the way	

Suppose more than one means of transport were used: car to station, then train, or train then bus. And what about variations in habit? It was decided to stratify calls by day in the working week and to ask a question about getting to work today. Then to find out if today's journey had been different in route taken and transport used from other journeys to work in the rest of the previous week. Use of 'generally', 'regularly', 'usually' could then be avoided.

Observation of traffic into the car parks at the exploratory stage had revealed that lifts were given, car owners taking it in turn to act as chauffeur. The effect of increased petrol costs had, the group discussions suggested, developed the habit of sharing transport. Company cars and car allowances also came up. It was hypothesised that sharing costs and company funding might affect reactions to attitude statements on the questionnaire. It was finally agreed that data about the topic 'the means used to get to work' should be collected in the following detail:

Private transport	*Public transport*
Motor car, driver	Bus
No passenger	
With passenger(s)	Train
Company car/allowance	
Motor car, passenger	
Motor bike/moped, driver	
Motor bike/moped, passenger	
Bicycle	
On foot all the way	

There were other topics on the list. We move onto classification of the survey population. Company cars apart, was there likely to be a relationship between means of transport used and job done? Would a simple dichotomy be sufficient?

Staff	*Shop floor*

Or would it help management to decide whether to introduce a transport service if employees were classified in more detail, so that the habits and attitudes of smaller groups towards getting to work could be compared? The following classification of respondents was considered:

Staff	*Shop floor*
Management	Supervisory
Sales	Wage-earners
Clerical	Piece-workers

But it was soon agreed that the following classification would be more relevant to the survey objectives:

Staff	*Shop floor*
Itinerant, i.e.	By 'shop'/department
sales representatives	e.g. paintshop
service engineers	despatch
On the spot	

The decision to distinguish the 'itinerant' group from the 'on the spot' group was taken because it was hypothesised that those who had to get to the office every day would have different attitudes from those who came in and out at irregular intervals, while the irregular habits of the latter would confuse the overall 'staff' behaviour data.* The decision to relate 'means of getting to work' to shops or departments in the works was determined by the management's desire to know where bus or train strikes or a petrol shortage would be most damaging and should there be marked variation in habit from one department to another. (Since all employees and their jobs were recorded on a computer file, it was possible to draw a stratified probability sample, using a variable sampling fraction.) Shop-floor employees far out-numbered staff and some shops were very much larger than others, a disproportionate design therefore made more efficient use of the research allocation than a proportionate one.

*It was recognised that all the 'itinerant' group would have company cars, but so, of course, would some of those who worked 'on the spot' while the reasons for isolating the 'itinerant' group still held good.

Payne, S. (1951) *The Art of Asking Questions*, Princeton: Princeton University Press.
Seibert, J. and Willis, G. (eds), (1970) *Marketing Research*, Harmondsworth.
Reynolds, N., Diamantopoulos, A. and Schlegelmilch, B. (1993) 'Predicting in questionnaire design: a review of the literature and suggestions for further research', *JMRS*, vol. 35, no. 2, April, pp. 171–82.
Sampson, P. (1986) 'Qualitative research and motivation', in R. Worcester and J. Downham (eds) *Consumer Market Research Handbook* (3rd edn), Amsterdam: Elsevier Press.
Sykes, W. (1991) 'Taking stock: issues from the literature on validity and reliability in qualitative research', *Journal of the Market Research Society (JMRS)*, Jan., vol. 33, no. 1, pp. 3–12.
Wolfe, A. (ed.) (1984) *Standardised Questions: A review for market research executives* (2nd edn), London: Market Research Society.

Further reading

Belson, W. (1986) *Validity in Survey Research*, London: Gower.
Collins, M. and Courtenay, G. (1984) 'The effect of survey form on survey data', *MRS Conference Papers*.
Parasuraman, A. (1991) *Marketing Research*, Boston, MA: Addison-Wesley, ch. 10 and 11.

Assignments

Imagine that you are designing the questionnaire for a face-to-face usage and attitude survey of the in-home wine-drinking habit of the British population.

1. (a) Define the population of interest (the survey population) and prescribe population breakdowns taking account of the statistical data quoted.
   (b) Draft classification questions and pre-code these.
2. List topics of interest and construct a flow chart to illustrate the ordering of topics and the route taken through the questionnaire by the interviewer.
3. Draft the questionnaire including introductory comment and instructions to the interviewer.
4. Pre-code answers wherever possible.

Users of table wine (base all adults)

Heavy users	3–5 bottles a month	7.5
Medium users	1–2 bottles a month	20.0
Light users	Less than 1 bottle a month	29.5
All users		57.0
Non-users		43.0

Demographic profile (base all users)

Men	47.4	15–24	18.7	AB	23.9
Women	52.6	25–34	21.2	C_1	27.2
		35–44	18.5	C_2	29.0
		45–54	14.5	D	14.1
		55–64	13.3	E	5.8
		65 & +	13.8		

CHAPTER 8

Developing a branded product or service

8.1 Research for branding

The marketing research process has reached the point where a market of interest has been explored, described and segmented and a promising target or niche located. We now develop a product or service that appears to meet the needs which the research has uncovered. Our concern is to develop a brand:

> The ingredients in a brand constitute the product itself, the packaging, the brand name, the promotion, the advertising and the overall presentation . . . branding consists then, of the development and maintenance of sets of product attributes and values which are coherent, appropriate, distinctive, protectable and appealing to consumers . . . Advertising is a narrower function within marketing which is concerned with the use of media to inform and stimulate consumers that products or services, branded or otherwise, are available for them to purchase. (Murphy 1992:3)

This chapter considers the research methods used to specify the ingredients and the brand as a whole and how these are best packaged and priced together with the application of advertising research to the development of the brand image.

8.2 The validity of qualitative methods

During recent years great emphasis has been placed on the usefulness and validity of qualitative methods when new branded products or services are being developed: 'The findings from qualitative research should have a truth that goes beyond the research context to a truth founded in the world' (Callingham 1988). Indeed, there are those who contend that richer ideas and more meaningful decisions derive from a carefully designed programme of group discussions, extended individual interviews and other qualitative techniques than from a meticulously designed series of controlled experiments to which statistical tests can be applied.

In qualitative work the findings are derived from the experience, perceptions and ability of a small number of target consumers, say, four groups of eight individuals, or thirty extended interviews, or a mix of the two. The setting of quotas for the recruitment of these individuals is clearly critical. So are the methods used to stimulate and focus discussion, the stimulus material, the role of the moderator or interviewer and the way in which consumer behaviour and opinions are recorded and presented (see Chapter 2).

8.3 Selection of participants

If a segmentation study has been carried out, the demographics, behaviour in the product field and lifestyle of those in the market of interest can be modelled, the characteristics of a potential target group defined and a quota representative of this group set. This applies to both qualitative and quantitative sampling as commonly practised.

In a qualitative research design the setting of the quota for participants' recruitment is especially important. Indeed it is generally agreed that the validity of qualitative research rests substantially on highly purposive sampling (*MRS Newsletter* 1988).

The respondent's experience in the use of the product concerned is important when quotas are set, whether for qualitative or for experimental work. How the product is used can have a marked effect on choice as the example in Table 8.1 shows. The three brands were considered similarly by the whole sample but differently when the sample was broken down by the way they used the spirit. The 40 per cent (3.02) who took the spirit neat preferred C, which had originally been least preferred overall.

Table 8.1 Preference of spirits and relationship to use with a mixer or not

Brand	Total	Mixer	Neat
A	2.86	3.12	2.62
B	2.86	2.84	2.88
C	2.91	2.68	3.02

Source: Callingham, M. (1988) 'The psychology of product testing and its relationship to objective scientific measures', *Journal of the Market Research Society*, vol. 30, no. 3, July.

8.4 Threats to validity

Validity also rests on recruitment (Feldwich and Winstanley 1988). Suitable subjects are recruited by interviewers, who are generally required to find quota members who have not been contaminated by previous group experience. It is not easy to locate suitable participants when working to a quota which may represent only 5 per cent of the total population, while meeting standards set by the MRS and AMSO. 'Historical', 'maturation', 'instrument effect' and 'testing' or 'learning' aspects can affect research outcomes.

History: Outside events may affect the dependent variable during the course of the experiment. Clearly, the longer an experiment goes on the greater the risk of history contaminating results.

   Let us assume that we have designed an experiment to test the effect on sales of brand X paint in a home-decorating campaign. If there were a prolonged strike in the test area during the course of the experiment and if this strike affected a substantial number of workers, results of the experiment might be deceptively encouraging since enforced 'leisure' can have an effect of stimulating home decorating. In this situation, increased sales would not be attributable to the campaign and the experimental results would be spurious.

Maturation: This effect relates to change in the test subjects in the course of the experiment. They may, for example, get tired.

   If we were comparing the effects of two sales training programmes we might find that test subjects 'played back' what they had learnt better at the beginning of the day than at the end. If we were aiming to compare two training methods, and failed to arrange that both groups contained comparable proportions of 'fresh' and 'stale' subjects, the results might then be spurious.

Instrument effect: As might be expected, this relates to inconsistent or faulty instruments and in experimentation the instrument is often a questionnaire administered by an interviewer. Mechanical instruments are also used: tachisto-scopes, psychogalvanometers and projectors feature in experiments described in this chapter and in Chapter 9.

   Continuing with the sales training example, we might expect the training officer to suffer fatigue too, so that the questionnaire is administered less effectively towards the end of the day.

Testing or learning effect: This is particularly relevant to company image, public relations and advertising research.

   Let us assume that we have been commissioned to create a campaign to improve the image of a company in its employee catchment area. We decide to do a 'before and after' test: to ask a sample of local people what they know about the kind of work the company offers, the amenities it provides, and so forth; then to run the campaign, going back at a later date to see what effect the campaign has had on the experimental group's view of the company.

We cannot attribute greater awareness and changed opinions to the campaign because the respondents' attention will have been drawn to the company and its activities by the first call. What they learn at the first call may stimulate the sample to pay more attention to the campaign than they would otherwise have done, and to pick up information about the company which might otherwise have passed over their heads.

For this reason we either use an 'after-only' with control design when testing communications (see below); or we take the 'before' measurement on one group and the 'after' on a group matched to the first (i.e. we use matched samples).

Selection of test subjects: This is not just a matter of ensuring that those who receive the experimental treatment represent the target for whom the product is designed. We also have to ensure that experimental and control groups are matched. (For the role of the control group see section 8.6.) Before designing an experiment it is necessary to know what demographic and product-use characteristics are critical. Experience in the product field often acts as an initial filter: for example, if we were developing medicated bubble bath products, we would need to know whether the targeted consumers were bubble-bath users or users of medicated bath products or both. Age and class might be critical demographic variables, but when it comes to setting quotas by age within class (or vice versa) as in an interrelated quota, it adds to the time needed to recruit and to the cost of the experiment. It is common practice to sort the test subjects into age and into class strata, then to use a random process when assigning members from within these age and class strata to either the experimental or to the control group. If combinations of age and class are found to differ from the experimental to the control group, or from one experimental group to another, it is possible to standardise results by weighting, as in a disproportionate sample.

8.5 Control versus experimental groups

A control group is used in an experimental design to make it possible to discount the effect of unforeseen extraneous variables. The control group is matched to the experimental group. It is questioned, or observed, at the same time as the experimental group, but the control group does not receive the treatment, nor is it asked those questions which relate to the experimental group. Control groups are not always used in marketing experiments. Decision may be based on the responses of two or more matched experimental groups to alternative product formulations, pack designs or advertisements.

In comparative tests, especially in tests to decide product formulation, control may be exercised by setting a standard against which alternatives are assessed: for example, one group may be given the existing product and another the formulation which is thought to be an improvement on it with both products being wrapped and presented in the same way. In this case the control group receives a treatment but it is one against which the experimental treatment is judged. When two possible advertising treatments are shown to two matched groups we have a design based on two experimental groups.

However well designed an experiment may be, there is always a risk that an observed difference may be due to sampling error, and not to the effect of the treatment. The statistical procedures used to establish the significance of the differences observed are summarised in Appendix 3. Unless subjects have been assigned to groups at random, or groups to treatments, these calculations should, strictly speaking, not be made.

8.6 Experimental designs in common use

The designs set out in Box 8.1 are the basis of most of those in common use. The notation developed by Campbell and Stanley (in Green and Tull 1986) is a useful shorthand which helps to concentrate ideas about experimental procedures. The following comments relate to Box 8.1.

After-only without a control group. This is not a true experiment but it is not uncommon for an increase of sales over target to be attributed to some marketing tactic, such as a sales promotion or increased advertising, when other factors have contributed. In other words, the collection of evidence has not been organised 'so that an hypothesis may be tested'. (But it is sometimes possible to guard against spurious results by asking questions: claimed awareness of an advertisement can be validated in this way.)

After-only with control. Given that the experimental and control groups are well matched, that observations are made at the same time and that the environmental input is the same for both, we can use the control group to discount factors other than the treatment as contributing to the result shown by the experimental group.

Before-after. By observing the experimental group a suitable interval before and then after it receives the treatment we get a less ambiguous measurement than with an after-only design. However, where there is danger of the respondent learning from the pre-test an after-only design is to be preferred. But *before-after with control* makes it possible to allow for any continuation of the experimental result (as in the case of after-only with control).

Time series is an extended 'before-after' and it may be used with or without a control group (or area). In 'real-life' market tests it is common practice to take a number of observations before and after introduction of the new product, pack,

Box 8.1 Experimental designs in common use

Notation: X exposure to the experimental treatment
O measurement or observation taken
Sequence of events from left to right

Design			**Measurement***
After-only	X	O	O
After-only	X	O_1	$O_1 - O_2$
with control		O_2	
Before-after O_1	X	O_2	$O_2 - O_1$
Before-after O_1	X	O_2	$O_2 - O_4$
with control O_3		O_4	$(O_2 - O_1) - (O_4 - O_3)$

Time series**
$O_1 O_2 O_3 O_4$ $\qquad$ X $\quad$ $O_5 O_6 O_7 O_8$ $\qquad$ Mean of 4 post-treatment observations – mean of 4 pre-treatment observations***

Time series with control
$O_1 O_2 O_3 O_4$ $\qquad$ X $\quad$ $O_5 O_6 O_7 O_8$
$O'_1 O'_2 O'_2 O'_4$ $\qquad\quad$ $O'_5 O'_6 O'_7 O'_8$

$$\begin{pmatrix} \text{Mean of } O_5 \ldots O_6 \\ \text{minus} \\ \text{Mean of } O'_5 \ldots O'_6 \end{pmatrix}$$

$$- \begin{pmatrix} \text{Mean of } O_1 \ldots O_4 \\ \text{minus} \\ \text{Mean of } O'_1 \ldots O'_4 \end{pmatrix}$$

Cross-sectional

		Matched groups
X_1	O_1	$O_1 \ldots O_n$ compared
X_2	O_2	(see section 8.1.3)
.	.	
.	.	
.	.	
X_n	O_n	

Randomised block $\qquad\qquad\qquad\qquad$ (see Section 8.2)
Latin square
Factorial

* $\quad$ We assume a positive result throughout
** $\quad$ The mean of the observation is taken when the effect of a particular treatment, e.g. of a sales training programme, is being measured.
*** The number of observations taken pre- and post-treatment will not necessarily, of course, be four as here.

┤ **Box 8.2** ├

Let us assume that we need to measure the effect on sales of three pack designs.*
A supermarket chain has agreed to have the experiment staged in some of their
branches. Previous research has suggested that there may be regional differences
in consumer reaction to the three packs. We accordingly do the following:

- Stratify by region, say North, South and Midlands.
- Arrange for the test to be made in, say, three branches in each region.
- Use a random process to assign pack design to branch in each region as
  follows (T stands for treatment).

Region	*Three branches in each region*		
North	T1	T2	T3
Midlands	T1	T2	T3
South	T1	T2	T3

*The example is based on one quoted by Cox and Enis (1973).

The product is on sale in all three pack designs in each region. We are assuming
that the supermarket branches do not have distinct regional characteristics. The
statistical figure-work (analysis of variance) is shown in Appendix 3. Briefly, the
design makes it possible for us to isolate the between-regions source of error so that
we are left with a smaller residual error to take account of when considering the
between-treatments results: i.e. the design is cost-effective because we can use a
smaller sample than would be the case if we had not 'blocked' (or stratified).

---

price or advertising. The interval between observations is related to the rate at
which the product is purchased by consumers, and the data are often derived from
consumer panels. The repeat-buying rate is an important factor in brand-share
prediction.

With 'going' brands it is common practice to predict what would happen, if
the experimental treatment were not introduced, on the basis of the trend data
collected 'before'. The effect of the experimental treatment, say, a pack change, is
then measured by comparing the actual 'after' observations with the 'after'
predictions (see Box 8.2).

Cross-sectional. Different levels of treatment such as different prices, levels of
advertising and incentives to sales representatives are applied to a number of
matched groups at the same time. The main problem is matching the groups.

Randomised block. So far we have assumed that the only difference between
groups is the kind of treatment they receive: in other words that, having matched

groups on critical characteristics, the environmental effects will be the same for all groups. It may well be that previous research has alerted us to differences, for example, of region or location, which may influence results. Blocking is stratification applied to experiments. Use of stratification to reduce sampling error in survey work was discussed in Chapter 6.

Latin square. The randomised block design illustrated above controls one extraneous variable. If the product were one which sold through more than one type of retail outlet, we might have decided to use a Latin square design. The Latin square is a cost-effective design which makes it possible to allow for two extraneous sources of variation, in our case region and type of retail outlet.

In the Latin square design it is conventional to think of the two extraneous sources of variation as forming the rows and columns of a table. Treatment effects are then assigned to cells in the table randomly, subject to the restriction that each treatment appears once only in each row and each column of the table. Consequently, the number of rows, columns and treatments must be equal, a restriction not necessary in randomised block designs.

The finished design might look as follows:

Three regions, Three types of retail outlet (A, B, C), Three treatments
(T1, T2, T3)

Region	Type of retail outlet		
	A	B	C
North	T2	T3	T1
Midlands	T1	T2	T3
South	T3	T1	T2

The Latin square is an economical design for the measurement of main effects, in this case variation due to region and to type of retail outlet. Each treatment (in the case we have been considering, a pack design) is tested in each type of retail outlet and in each region. We can estimate error due to these two sources of variation using analysis of variance (see Appendix 3), but we are assuming that the treatment effects will not be contaminated by interaction between them. We allow for the effects individually but not as the one (here region) influences the other (retail outlet).

Factorial design. If it is necessary to take account of the interaction of variables, as opposed to measuring main effects, a factorial design is used. Anticipating product testing, let us assume we are developing a soft drink. We may expect that, in a taste test, there is likely to be interaction between the colour of the drink and the amount of sweetener in it: the more acid the yellow of a lemon drink, the sourer the response to tastes. Say we are experimenting with three variations of colour and three degrees of sweetness, then the factorial design would be as follows:

Sweetness	Colour		
	a	b	c
A	Aa	Ab	Ac
B	Ba	Bb	Bc
C	Ca	Cb	Cc

Every possible combination of colour and sweetness is allowed for in the design, which requires nine matched groups of testers. This can be an expensive design and we may find that we have not used a sufficiently large sample when it comes to considering the significance of results. If there is any doubt on this score the test should be replicated so that there are sufficient testers' judgements to warrant the drawing of firm conclusions. Replication may avoid the waste incurred when an unnecessarily large sample is drawn in the first instance, but it extends the time taken up by the test and there is always the possibility that time itself may affect results.

8.7 Pre-testing branded products and services

8.7.1 The whole and its parts

Market description may suggest introduction of a new product or modification of an existing one. Analysis of data about consumer behaviour and attitudes may yield tentative ideas, or hypotheses, about the kind of product required, the way in which the product should be packaged and priced, and how it should be brought to the attention of potential consumers. Before considering ways of testing these hypotheses we have to recognise that, once the product is out on the market, consumer perception will be influenced by the interaction of all four of the components, as well as by environmental factors, such as the actions of competitors and distributors, not to mention the state of the world at the time.

Product formulation, packaging, pricing and communications are likely to be the subject of separate experiments on the way to 'real-life' testing in the market of the complete offering: first, on the grounds of cost; and second, to help assess the contribution made by constituent parts to the overall performance.

With regard to cost, even a small-scale test in the market makes notable demands on resources. The product must be available in sufficient quantity to meet demand and it has to be associated with properly finished packaging and advertising.

The product concept may be introduced to the experimental group in the form of a rough advertisement before the product is tried and responses to the product both before and after actual trial are compared. Pack designs may be presented to testers along with designs for advertisements, while questions about selling price are likely to be asked at every stage. The fact that the whole may well be different from the sum of its parts has to be taken into account.

8.7.2 Having and trying out ideas

Most 'new' products or services derive from what is already available to consumers. The true innovation is rare indeed, and if successful, soon copied, as with the camcorder and compact disc products. New product development (NPD) makes considerable demands on company resources. The modification of a going brand with a view to increasing its popularity or sustaining its life may make less demand on resources, but here there is the additional hazard of putting off existing supporters.

During the development stage, choices need to be made with confidence. To rely entirely on qualitative methods demands faith in the research supplier and understanding of the rigour with which qualitative methods may be applied.

It is easier for a marketing company to have confidence in the experimental approach. The setting of quotas and the recruitment of those taking part are as critical to the design of experiments as for qualitative work. But if the standardised methods are duly followed it is possible to subject the results of experiments to statistical tests. For the decision-maker there is comfort in numbers.

Given an experimental approach the collection of data is less open to bias, and the results less open to mistakes of interpretation. On the other hand, the opportunity for a new product breakthrough may be missed; experimental data lack the stimulus of qualitative findings when the brand presentation is being designed.

In order to design experiments it is necessary to have hypotheses to test! Qualitative research is a valuable source of hypothetical ideas and the two approaches to NPD may be combined with advantage.

8.7.3 The experimental approach

To arrive at any hypothesis which is both meaningful and relevant it is necessary to have data about the consumers and products in the market. Detailed knowledge of the market makes the following more pertinent and thus effective:

- Choice of hypothesis to be tested.
- Decisions regarding the criteria to be used when measuring and analysing results of the experiment.
- Control of environmental factors.
- Selection of the subjects to take part in the experiment.

For an ongoing brand, or for a new brand in a familiar market, 'detailed knowledge of the market' is likely to be driven from previous product research and from monitoring of own competitors' achievements in the product field. Kotler's explanation of 'the experiment as a system' can be shown as a useful introduction to the forces at work in an experiment (Kotler 1994):

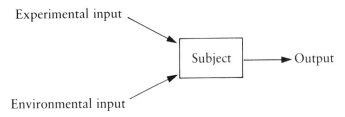

The experimental input is called the 'independent variable' and the output is called the 'dependent variable'. The environmental input is made up of extraneous variables, some of which can be foreseen, others not, i.e. some of which are controllable variables and others uncontrollable variables. The experimental input is the treatment applied to subjects whether this is one variable (e.g. sweetness, or a combination (e.g. sweetness plus colour) in a soft drink.

So how can research aid innovation? In the first instance by supplying 'background knowledge' and it clearly helps if that background knowledge is the result of thoughtful, rather than mechanistic, descriptions of consumer habits and attitudes. Research can usefully 'try the idea out' in concept tests. A 'trade-off' approach in which the respondent is asked to choose between a series of options can be applied. The trade-off technique is based on the concept that obtaining a desired product quality (say efficiency) will require the consumer to sacrifice – trade-off – some other desired quality (say, gentleness). This use of the multivariate approach has, of course, been stimulated by the speed with which a long list of 'trade-off' choices can be processed. The respondents may find the questioning procedure less tedious when operating a microcomputer.

One research stage can lead to another, for example:

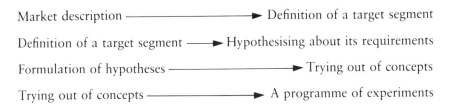

Blackett and Denton recommended the development of 'ideas into products which in their formulation, packaging, branding and general appeal offer a unique selling proposition' (Murphy 1992:73–85). This point of difference should be familiar or recognisable to consumers, needed or wanted by consumers, be true to its promise and communicated in all presentations to consumers.

Table 8.2 'Lab' versus 'field'

Laboratory	Field
Under controlled conditions (internal validity)	Under external environmental conditions (external validity)
Tested in-house (on company or agency premises)	Tested in-home (where product is used) or in test centres (where product is bought and viewed in shopping-centres)
Trial, recording and observation of controlled versus experimental groups	Trial, recording and observation of target groups
Comparative or monadic tests	Monadic tests

8.7.4 'Lab' versus 'field'

A carefully controlled experiment, conducted in 'lab-like' conditions, yields results which are unambiguous. The experiment has internal validity. But the conditions in which the test is carried out are not those in which the product would normally be chosen or used and the lab-like experiment lacks external validity.

The field or market test, on the other hand, is conducted in a real-life context. The findings have external validity but they may well have been distorted by market influences or local happenings so that they are ambiguous and difficult to interpret. The more that is known about the forces at work in the market from descriptive work, the easier it is to control them or to allow for them when drawing conclusions.

Companies which continuously engage in product testing such as Heinz, Spillers and Unilever place products with panels of consumers. Demographic and product-use characteristics of panel members are recorded and the computer is programmed to retrieve experimental and control groups suitable for the test concerned. Test products are distributed by hand, or through the post, to panel members and the proportion returning the test questionnaire through the post is usually substantial (over 70 per cent).

There is a risk that the panel members may learn from their testing experience and cease to be typical. But when the panel is a large one and the research supplier covers a wide range of product fields, it is possible to maintain the interest of panel members without running the risk of conditioning them. For control versus experimental groups, see section 8.5.

In a monadic design the respondent experiences only one test product. In a comparative test the respondent is given more than one product to try. The products may be given to the respondent simultaneously, or they may be given in sequence.

Comparison sharpens perception and so comparative tests are more sensitive than monadic tests, but the comparative procedure is further removed from real life than the monadic procedure. In real life products are usually judged in the light of current or recent experience of a similar product. In a monadic test responses to the test product are similarly based on current or recent experience in the same product field: with the critical difference that the test product is likely to be in a plain package without benefit of pack design and advertising support.

If the test programme is based on a series of paired comparison experiments, one test product can stand as a control throughout (although this may not always be the case (as in Box 8.3). The control product may be the market leader or the leader in a particular market segment. If a product is being re-launched, the existing product is the control product. If a brand is being re-positioned, it may be desirable to move closer to consumer perception of the 'ideal' brand.

Since, at the outset, all products are likely to be tested 'blind', the difference in dress and communication between the test product and a product actually on the market is obviated. If the same individuals make all the tests, sampling error is reduced (but we must ensure that learning from test experience does not contaminate results).

In the 'blind' test, products are judged on taste or performance. In the 'normal pack' test, previous experience (packaging, price and advertising message) comes into play.

In a monadic test, respondents deliver verdicts on a 'blind' product in the light of their experience and knowledge of the product field. They are often asked what brand they use and are then encouraged to compare the test product with this brand. The test product has the advantage of being new and different, but the possible disadvantages of not being supported by pack design and advertising message.

8.8 Preference and discrimination

In most product tests a definite preference is being sought. It is hoped that new *A* will be preferred to old *B*, or that there will be a significant difference between the preference score of new *A* (1) and that of new *A* (2). However, occasions arise when a product is established on the market and either substitution of another ingredient reduces production costs and so contributes to profit, or a source of supply is interrupted and an alternative source has to be found.

The substitute ingredient will not be used unless those concerned with the marketing of the product are satisfied that users will not notice the difference. Testers are reluctant to show lack of discrimination. Many are going to guess and there are two types of error to be avoided. If there is an observable difference, but the experiment does not reveal this, the position of an established brand may be undermined. If there is *not* an observable difference, and the results of the

Box 8.3

It may be possible that there is no obvious control product and a number of possible product formulations are to be compared. This situation might arise if, say, a range of prepared foods was being developed. In this situation a *round robin* would be an efficient design to choose. Given four different fillings *A*, *B*, *C* and *D* the procedure would be to test:

A versus *B*　*B* versus *C*　*C* versus *D*　*A*　versus *C*　*A* versus *D*　and　*B* versus *D*

If the tests were made by six matched groups of fifty from a sample of 300, each filling would be tried by 150 respondents.

experiment suggest that there is (a more likely happening), we pass up the opportunity to make a cost saving or to ensure supplies.

The triangular discrimination test, developed in the brewing industry, is one way of approaching this problem. There are two test products, new *A* and existing *B*. The sample is split in half. Each half is given three products to test: one gets triad *AAB*, the other *ABB*. The products are presented 'blind' with ambiguous code numbers (*A* and *B* would certainly not be used).

The respondent is told that one product is different from the other two and is asked to find the different one. It is assumed that a third of the respondents will guess right and that the measure of discrimination is the percentage correctly picking the modified product, less 33.3 per cent. If 40 per cent picked correctly, the measure of discrimination would be $[(40 - 33)/0.67]$ per cent, i.e. of the order of 10 per cent instead of 7 per cent because we have assumed that one-third of the testers will guess right.

Discrimination tests are not always triangular. Respondents may, for example, be told that, out of a group of five products, two are of one type and three of the other. This is a more severe, but perhaps rather intimidating, test of discrimination.

It follows that, as in real life, response to the product will be influenced by the way in which it is introduced. It is, of course, possible to try out more than one message and more than one pack design, not to mention price, together with a particular product formulation. The programme of tests could be rather expensive because testing or learning effects make it necessary to test each combination of elements on a separate sample, while results may be affected by the degree of finish of advertisements on packs. We return to the subject of concept testing in Chapter 9, where we focus on the procedures used to pre-test advertising messages.

The decision whether to test the components of the perceived product individually, or in combination, is a vexed one. A company such as General Foods draws on a considerable experience of product tests. By consistently following standard procedures a company accumulates normative data: it is able to compare pre-launch test results with post-launch performance and it is in a better position to construct pre-test models (see section 9.5).

8.9 Pre-testing packs

8.9.1 Function, impact and image

Packaging both 'inner' and 'outer' is a significant item in the costing of a product, and packaging research is a wide-ranging subject involving studies carried out by R&D, production, distribution and the suppliers of packaging materials, as well as those commissioned by marketing among distributors and consumers.

We need to distinguish between tests to assess the functional efficiency of a pack, its visual impact at the point of sale and the image of the product conveyed by the packaging and its label (Davies and Wright 1994).

8.9.2 Functional testing

To give a product the best possible chance of success its pack must function well in the following conditions:

- On the production line.
- As bulked quantities travel along the distributive channel to the point of sale.
- At the point of sale after bulk has been broken.
- When being used by the consumer.

The pack has to protect the product from deterioration and from pilfering. It must stand up to handling and the shape should lend itself to efficient stacking, wrapping and palletisation. At the point of sale how the pack behaves compared with the competition is important. Does it 'hog' shelf space, or fall over? When it reaches the consumer, ease of opening and of closing (if not used up at once), and of dispensing the contents, together with being steady on its feet, are critical variables to be considered in experimental design.

The suitability of the materials used and of the method of construction are tested by R&D, production and by the suppliers of containers. Suppliers such as Metal Box, who make plastic as well as metal containers, are so close to the consumer market that it serves their purpose to carry out research among consumers as well as among manufacturers and distributors.

The supplier has to satisfy the manufacturer that his/her product will not deteriorate and that it will reach the point of sale in good order. Suppliers of packaging materials are particularly interested in consumer responses when introducing an innovation, such as the aerosol and the ring-top opener for cans. The innovation is likely to involve a considerable investment: the research findings help to persuade manufacturers to adopt the innovation, as well as improving it.

Distributors' complaints and the reports of sales representatives are the usual

---

Box 8.4

When a ring-top can-opening device was introduced as an alternative to the tear-off tag, consumers were invited into a mobile van to try one against the other. A hidden camera filmed the way in which the consumers approached and handled the cans.

---

sources of information regarding the behaviour of the pack before it makes contact with the consumer at the point of sale. Here our concern is with the product as it presents itself to the consumer.

If the product is used up in one go, as with a can of beer, and the critical factor is ease of opening and dispensing, the experiment can be staged in a hall, mobile van or research centre; the data are better collected by means of observation. Some consumers get fussed when faced with an unfamiliar method of opening or dispensing, and it is necessary to create a relaxed atmosphere. This is difficult to achieve if the tester's efforts are being closely watched and recorded by an observer. A method used by Metal Box has much to commend it (see Box 8.4).

A camera can be used to record whether or not consumers read instructions, and whether one form of instruction appears to be easier to follow than another. Individuals vary in their dexterity and with tests of functional efficiency there is a case for using a comparative design, with each respondent trying both types of opening, assuming there are two to be tried. It is probably sounder to allow for the learning effect by rotating the order in which packs are tried, than totally on samples being matched not only on product use and demographic criteria but also on how they are handled, but this is a matter of opinion.

If the product is used, closed and then re-used, the experiment needs to be carried out where this goes on – kitchen, bathroom, garage, etc. – and data are likely to be collected by means of a questionnaire. In this context variations in dexterity are less critical, though still material. They are less critical because results will be based on how easy or difficult the respondent perceives the opening, closing and dispensing of the product rather than the observed behaviour.

To isolate the effect of function it is necessary to use plain packs as in a 'blind' product test. If the opportunity is taken to test 'visuals' at the same time, response to visual effects may contaminate response to functional efficiency. On the other hand, we have to remember that when the product reaches the market, consumer response will be conditioned by the visuals.

8.9.3 Visual impact

As we all know, products have to speak for themselves at the point of sale. There is usually no one around to make the introduction. The term 'impact' is used here to mean 'stand-out' value. Tests of 'stand-out' value are usually based on observation by means of the tachistoscope, or as in William Schlackman's 'find-time' procedure with a slide projector (Schlackman and Chittenden 1988).

The tachistoscope enables an image to be exposed for controlled lengths of time. Lengths of exposure likely to be used in a pack test are from 1/200 of a second up to 1/10. The respondent is either looking into a box-like instrument or a screen. After each exposure the respondent is asked what, if anything, was seen. This simple procedure is useful for comparing the visual impact of elements in a pack design, such as colour, brand name or message; it does not simulate the context in which the respondent is going to meet the pack. A closer approach is made to reality in the following conditions:

- The respondent is shown the test pack along with two or three control packs, care being taken to simulate the size of the packs as they might 'loom up' on the shelf at the point of sale.
- After each timed exposure the respondent is asked to pick the three or four packs out from a display which reproduces the company in which the pack is likely to find itself on the self-service shelf.

In a test of this kind results can be contaminated by learning and it is advisable to use matched samples. If responses to the control products are of the same order for both samples, we are reassured that the samples are matched for acuity (i.e. speed of perception and response) as well as on the more obvious criteria.

When designing experiments to measure visual impact it is necessary to take into account variations in sharpness of eyesight and the speed with which individuals respond to the image. They may, for example, be required to press a button as in the 'find-time' design described below. Organisations specialising in pack testing use standard acuity tests.

When recruiting for an experiment it would be time-consuming to take acuity into account as well as product use and weight and demographic characteristics. It may be necessary to weigh results when the acuity of matched samples is found to differ, but acuity is affected by age and familiarity with the product field, so matching on these variables may obviate the problem.

In the 'find-time' procedure (see Table 8.3) pioneered by William Schlackman (Schlackman and Chittenden 1988) matched samples are used and the respondents are allowed to familiarise themselves with a test pack. They are told that this may or may not be present in the displays which will be projected onto a screen. The procedure is as follows:

1. Some nine displays, typical of the product field at the point of sale, are photographed and the photographs are prepared for slide projection.
2. In about six of the nine slides the test pack is among its competitors, in six different positions. It is absent from the other three slides.
3. The slide remains on the screen until the respondent presses a button to signal that the test item has been found, or has not, as the case may be.
4. The measure of 'stand-out' value is the time taken to find the test pack when it is present. This is automatically recorded when the button is pressed.

Table 8.3   A 'find-time' experiment

Pack	Mean reaction time in sec	t-test value	Significance level
V2	1.77		
P	1.59	1.99	not
V1	1.98		0.001
P	1.59	3.71	
V2	1.77		
V1	1.98	2.05	0.05

In this table results are compared for the three
possible pairs. Clearly, neither new version is an
improvement on the current pack design.
For statistical tests, see Appendix 2.

8.9.4 Image of the product in the pack

The product has been designed to meet the requirements of a target group in the
market. If a segmentation study has been made, the characteristics of the group,
and the benefits wanted by it, are certainly known. The pack has to tell these
consumers that it contains a product with the desired qualities. In a programme of
image tests respondents are asked for their perceptions of the product in the pack
before they have tried it (see Box 8.5 for an example of this concept test).

When a consumer meets a new product at the point of sale, the decision
whether to try it is influenced by ideas about the product conveyed by its pack.
Having carried out this concept test, the marketing company concerned might well
have put the same questions to the test panel after actual trial. Comparison of the
responses would show whether or not the product came up to expectation. If it
exceeded expectation the pack design might need modification.

The pseudo-product test (Box 8.6) is designed to measure what William
Schlackman describes as 'symbolic transference'. Influence of the labels on taste
perceptions is further evidence of the importance of testing the whole as well as its
parts.

8.10 Testing the brand name

Marketing companies may apply the company name to all their products, as in the
case of 'Heinz', or give each branded line a distinctive name, the practice pursued
by the Unilever marketing companies and by Beecham. Ideally, the brand name
should convey or support the product concept. If the product has a unique selling
proposition (USP) the brand name should, if possible, reiterate this: for example,
'Head and Shoulders' for an anti-dandruff shampoo. If the packaging and

---

Box 8.5

At the test centre, panel members were asked what products they usually used for their main wash and for their light hand-wash. If they used a washing powder they were introduced to the experiment as follows:

'I am going to show you two different packs of washing powder called Coral. The manufacturer is considering two different versions of the product, and would like to know what housewives think about them.'

(The interviewer was instructed: SHOW FIRST PACK, THEN AN ALTERNATIVE AT EACH INTERVIEW.)

'I would like you to tell me what you think about the product in this packet by indicating where you think it would come on this scale. If you point to the largest box you strongly agree with the statement. If you point to the smallest box you think the statement applies very slightly to the product.' (There were seven sizes of box.)

The respondent then rated each pack in turn on the following criteria without having tried the product:

Suitable for all modern fabrics
Gets white nylon really white
Suitable for machine and hand-wash
Washes thoroughly but gently
Cares for delicate fabrics
Up to date
I would buy

Box 8.6 The pseudo-product test

Test items: 'A mild beverage', two labels *L* and *M*
Design: Simultaneous comparison test (i.e. two bottles were 'placed' at the same time). Four days' trial.
Procedure: Respondents were asked to use one bottle first, then, on completion, the second. Order rotated. Consumers told the interviewer would be returning to ask them about their experience.

	L	*M*	Don't know	Total
Product found most acceptable	20	75	5	100
Product which was mild	25	65	10	100
Product most bitter	70	28	2	100
$n = 200$				

Conclusion: label *M* moves the product more effectively in the direction of the marketing intention than does label *L*.

promotion are being designed to convey an emotional benefit in the context of a 'brand image', the name will be chosen to support the image, as in 'Close-Up' for a toothpaste. (For 'USP' and 'brand image' see section 9.3.3.)

Before brand names are tested for their power to communicate the nature of the brand, it is necessary to establish the following:

- The name is available for registration in the countries in which the brand is going to be marketed.
- The name has no dubious or unhelpful association in these countries.
- The name is easy to pronounce, read and remember.

Ease in pronouncing the name may be tested by asking consumers to read over a short list of names, taking note of hesitations and of any variations in emphasis. A tape recorder makes it possible to play back responses.

The 'stand-out' value of the name is likely to be tested as a component of the pack design, after the 'runners' have been reduced to a few, perhaps in a tachistoscopic test or in a 'find-time' test. The communicative power of the name is tested by establishing its associations in the mind of consumers in the following ways:

- In the first instance by means of 'free association', consumers being asked to say the first word, or thought, that comes into their head on hearing the name.
- Then by asking consumers to associate kinds of product with the brand names as these are read over.
- And/or by asking consumers to associate the brand names with product-attribute statements.

When designing research of this kind three factors need to be taken into account:

1. Respondents should be given a trial run before the critical names are put to them. This applies in particular to the 'free-association' test.
2. The order in which names and/or statements are put to respondents should be rotated.
3. The time taken to respond must be recorded.

8.11 Testing the market for price

The price at which a product is offered to the market is influenced by many considerations. These considerations include endogenous (internal) forces within the organisation and exogenous (external) forces in the marketplace.

The internal objectives of an organisation will include one or more of the following: return on investment; survival and growth; project maximisation; achievement of sales targets or increased sales volumes; defence, maintenance or exercise in market share; and market leadership. An organisation may also be concerned about its standards: interpretation; the provision of long-term employment and the staff development of its employees; its research and technological expertise; its reputation as a supplier of products and services; and its compliance with legal requirements, e.g. consumer protection acts.

Resource inputs (e.g. bought-in materials), equipment and skills, manufacturing, transport and distribution, market research, marketing, selling, and financial and administrative costs are added considerations. All these internal considerations provide a 'feel' for an organisation of the price band in which it 'ought' to charge for a given product, particularly if it is a new product. There may be little room to manoeuvre if a product is already established in a fiercely competitive market. In this case, any product improvement or innovation will have to be presented to existing consumers as significantly better than the old bundle of product attributes to either justify a rise in price or increased purchase at the old price.

However, what an organisation can charge for its product in the market depends on exogenous factors, for instance, what customers are prepared to pay and what product options are available from competitors (Doyle *et al.* 1989). Consumer perceptions of price associations with, for example, quality, value for money and image, are important constraints on the price that an organisation can charge for the product.

Pricing research is therefore a very important area in marketing research. From the 'ideas' explanation stage of what product to produce, through the stages in the new product development process (screening, business analysis, market testing and commercialisation), soundings from the marketplace are taken. These soundings are usually in the form of intention to buy questions which are related to quoted and to competitive prices. It is common for competitive organisations, e.g. financial services companies or car research companies, to use omnibus surveys. This has the advantages of bought-in market research expertise in a complex area and of protecting the anonymity of the name of the organisation commissioning the pricing research.

When the product goes on sale in a store test, or in a full market test, a credible verdict may be delivered depending on the length and sensitivity of the test. The purpose of taking soundings on the way to a market test is as follows:

- To see what kind of price consumers associate with the product and how this varies between types of consumer.
- To try out the effect on price perception of changes in the product attributes, its packaging and advertising.

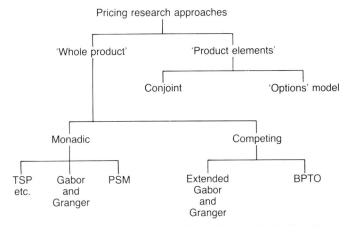

Source: Research International (1994) 'Pricing Research', Position Paper 10.

Figure 8.1 Pricing research

8.12 Pricing approaches

The willingness of consumers to buy at different prices can be used as a measure either of price elasticity in the brand field or of the value to the consumer of individual elements in the brand mix as, for example, packaging. Research International's approach to pricing (1994) given in Figure 8.1 includes methodological approaches to the problem of setting prices. It shows the relationship of pricing to the constituent product elements and to the whole (total) product.

Pricing research for the 'whole product' can take the monadic or the competitive form.

Monadic Pricing. Monadic pricing approaches vary from those which assess consumer responses to a range of manufactures prices to those where consumers themselves are asked to suggest appropriate prices for a given product. Three monadic pricing approaches (TSP, Gabor and Granger, PSM) can be considered:

1. *TSP (Try, Server, Pay/Purchase.* This is a simple approach which is based from 'definitely not buy' to definitely buy. The TSP approach is an example of scalar methods used in the early days of pricing research. The possibility that consumers would try, serve and pay/purchase a food product at a given price could be measured by looking at the distributions of responses on the sale points.
2. *Gabor and Granger.* Instead of suggesting a price, a manufacturer may want to test different prices for a product. Gabor and Granger's buy-responses model (Figure 8.2) uses price as an indicator of quality to measure consumers' likely purchase intentions. The usual procedure is as follows:
   - The range of consumer selling prices in the product field is recorded and not more than ten prices are chosen for testing.

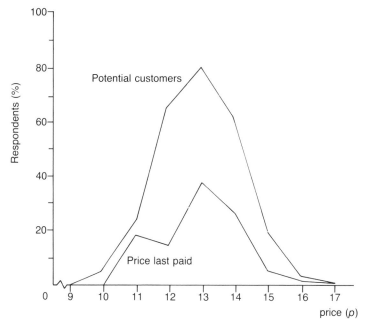

Source: A. Gabor (1977) *Pricing: Principles and Practices*, London. Heinemann Educational Books.

Figure 8.2 'Buy response' and 'price paid'

- The respondent is shown the product, its pack or its advertising and is asked 'would you buy X at . . .? The price first quoted will be near to the average for the product field. The other prices will be quoted at random so that upper and lower limits are not suggested to the respondent.
- The responses are summed for each price accepted by respondents and the acceptable prices are charted as shown in Figure 8.2. Respondents are also asked prices last paid (for existing products) and here again the distribution is charted.

The idea of price as an indicator of quality has long been associated with durables and luxury goods. Methodological research has shown it be relevant to fast-moving consumer goods. Too low a price is risky while a high price may be 'too dear'. The buy-response curve (Figure 8.2) shows the limits within which a selling price would not be a barrier to acceptance, while the shape of the curve shows where the most generally acceptable price is likely to fall. In addition, a comparison between the shape of the 'price last paid' curve and the buy-response curve may indicate an opportunity. It is possible to use the buy-response method to compare the effect on consumer price perceptions of different product formulations, different packaging and different communications.

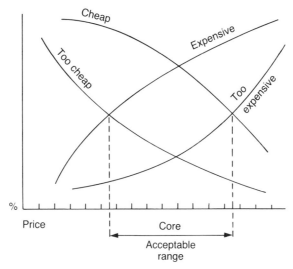

Source: Research International (1994) 'Pricing Research', Position Paper 10.

Figure 8.3 The PSM approach

3. *PSM.* The Price Sensitivity Measurement (PSM) approach is used in new product development, product line extension or product positioning research. Consumer perceptions of the most likely and acceptable prices for the new concept or product are sought with the objective of guiding a manufacturer in setting the optimum price. Each consumer would be asked at which point on the price scale a product was 'cheap, expensive, too cheap and too expensive'. Research International's development of PSM is shown in Figure 8.3. The area within the core acceptable range where the intersecting curves meet is seen as the price range where most respondents think that the new product concept or brand is not cheap or expensive and not too cheap or too expensive.

'Intention to buy' is a measure of *price acceptance* where the objective is to answer the question: Are the considered price levels for a particular product going to be accepted by a sufficient proportion of the consumer target group to make the new product viable? However, price-acceptance research is distinguishable from price-importance research in that it seeks to measure the importance to the target consumer of different levels of price compared with different levels of other attributes, e.g. a range of car prices compared with a range of miles per gallon/maximum speeds/different lengths/numbers of seats/countries of origin.

Product elements Pricing research for this involves looking at how people make trade-offs in choosing among multi-attribute alternatives.

1. *Conjoint.* The Conjoint or trade-off approach is employed to arrive at each respondent's preferred combination of product attributes. Presenting alterna-

tives in pairs is the simplest form. However, the full concepts method may be preferable to researchers who feel that two-at-a-time (pair-wise method) to product attribute evaluation is less realistic.

In the *pair-wise* method, attributes are presented in pairs to each respondent for example:

> taste versus colour
> taste versus size
> size versus colour
> and so on . . .

Normally, the pairs are presented in 'grids' and each respondent undertakes a self-completion exercise by filling in a booklet containing such grids. The pairs are ranked in order of the respondent's preferences. The task itself can become boring and repetitive and other researchers may prefer the 'full concepts' method.

Using the full concepts method, a number of combinations can be given as for size, colour and shape, for example, large or small (size), blue or yellow (colour), round or square (shape). Each respondent is asked either to rate all the possible combinations on scales or to rank them. Where there are twenty combinations or more, the task can become more complex to the respondent.

Take, for instance, a large series of cards constructed with each card representing one of several possible mixes of attributes. The respondent is then asked to order the cards from the most-liked combination to least-liked. Care has to be taken to ensure that all possible combinations of attributes are represented by the cards. However in a trade-off covering the multi-variable relationships of all product attributes (instead of just price), the number of cards can become too large for one sorting operation. In this event, a preliminary sorting of cards can take place, that is, into 'definitely like', 'neither definitely like nor dislike', 'definitely dislike', followed by rankings within each of the three groups. This helps to concentrate the mind of a respondent.

2. *Options model.* Conjoint analysis lends itself to pricing research, for example, in food products. However, the assessment of product attributes is not shown in relation to consumer budgets, an important consideration particularly where the expensive consumer durables are concerned. The Options model developed by Research International allows each respondent to build his/her own 'ideal' package (e.g. an audio/hi-fi system) via computer-aided interviewing (CAI). The computer 'introduces' the respondent to up to twenty-two product features which the respondent can build onto the basic unit. Through analysis of all the 'ideal' packages built by the sample of respondents, the options model identifies an optimum durables package which would satisfy most potential consumers.

    Pricing research approaches are now more 'predictive' than merely 'diagrammatic'. For example, if the objective is to predict actual brand share, the respondent taking part and the brands displayed should mirror the real market.

If the objective is to diagnose, say, brand-switching patterns, there is a case for drawing the sample of respondents from among those making frequent purchases in the product field and for excluding from the array of brands those which are bought infrequently (the trade-off price/response model gives useful insights into the elasticity of price changes). The predictive element is important in pricing research because the purchases psychology of consumers within a particular product or brand sector should mirror the real world as closely as possible.

8.13 Conclusion

Laboratory test conditions achieve internal validity but the conditions can, to varying extents, be unreal. It is therefore important to conduct experiments which also have external validity.

In the real world the consumer perceives the whole product formulation + packaging + price + the 'added value' of advertising. It is, therefore, necessary to devise a programme of experiments which seeks to optimise various elements, such as price formulation and consumer interactions. Pre-testing consumer responses to pricing is one of the most complex areas in market research and requires both careful application in test design and attention to detail concerning purchase intentions within product sectors.

References

Callingham, M. (1988) 'The psychology of product testing and its relationship to objective scientific measures', *Journal of the Market Research Society*, vol. 30, no. 3, July.

Cox, K. and Enis, B. M. (1973) *Experimentation for Marketing Decisions*, Glasgow: Intertext.

Davies, M. and Wright, L. (1994) 'The importance of labelling examined in food marketing', *European Journal of Marketing*, vol. 28, no. 2, pp. 57–67.

Doyle, P., Saunders, J. and Wright, L. (1989) 'A comparative study of US and Japanese marketing strategies in the British market', *International Journal of Research in Marketing*, vol. 5, no. 3, pp. 171–84.

Feldwich, P. and Winstanley, L. (1988) 'Qualitative recruitment: policy and practice', *MRS Conference Papers*.

Green, P. and Tull, D. S. (1986) *Research for Marketing Decisions*, Englewood Cliffs, NJ: Prentice Hall.

Kotler, P. (1994) *Marketing Management, Analysis, Planning and Control*, Englewood Cliffs, NJ: Prentice Hall.

MRS Newsletter (1988) 'Reliability and validity in qualitative research', Report on an MRDF Seminar, no. 268, July.

Murphy J. (ed.) (1992) *Branding: A Key Marketing Tool*, Basingstoke: Macmillan, pp. 3 and 73–85.

Research International (1994) 'Pricing research', Position Paper 10.

Schlackman, W. and Chittenden, D. (1988) 'Packaging research', in R. M. Worcester and J. Downham (eds) *Consumer Market Research Handbook*, Amsterdam: Elsevier Press, pp. 513–36.

Assignments

1. What experimental designs would you advocate in the following circumstances? How would you recruit the test subjects? What treatment would you apply to the subjects? How would you measure results? (Assume you are pre-testing.)

    (a) Acceptability of a cooked breakfast cereal which (it is claimed) does not stick to the saucepan.

    (b) Response to an addition to a confectionery counterline popular with junior schoolchildren.

    (c) Perceived effectiveness of a shampoo for cars with a protective ingredient.

    (d) Response to a range of selling prices for a new range of gourmet foods.

    (e) Alternative packaging for a range of frozen desserts.

2. 'Whatever the difficulties of interpretation, research is only relevant if it attempts to stimulate the situation in the market.' Discuss this statement, focusing your answer on the pre-testing of a branded, fast-moving consumer product/service of your choice.

3. You have been asked to design an experiment to show which (if either) of the following two courses of action is more likely to increase the total of a bank's transactions with its customers (the bank has branches in major population centres throughout Great Britain):

    (a) the offer of sales promotions incentives using discounts ranging from 10 per cent to 25 per cent for specific products, e.g. hi-fi equipment, computer games and clothes on purchases at stated major retailing outlets; or

    (b) opening times to the public to be extended from 9a.m.–4p.m. to 9a.m.–6p.m. on weekdays and 9a.m.–1p.m. on weekends.

    What experimental method would you use? How would you measure effects? How would you seek to achieve external validity?

CHAPTER 9

Establishing the brand identity and pre-testing the whole

In the last chapter we considered how uncertainty may be reduced through pricing research for a branded product which is being developed for the market. The brand – the product or service as perceived by consumers – is a mixture of intrinsic qualities (such as colour, taste, consistency) and of the way in which these qualities are packaged and priced. Consumer perception is influenced by the way in which the brand is presented in advertisements.

This chapter introduces the advertising, theory, objectives and tasks in the creative research programme. To complete the cycle of advertising research, section 9.2.4 briefly looks ahead to the advertising research role after the advertising campaign is launched. A case study approach of Millward Brown's pre-testing for an advertising programme for Direct Line Insurance is presented in Chapter 14.

The once hard and fast distinction between pre-testing and post-testing has been blurred. Greater confidence in the meaning of pre-test results, access to databanks and computer programs plus disenchantment with the cost and necessary duration of the traditional test market have stimulated interest in research approaches designed to simulate the responses of the target segment before exposure to the market, which may well take the form of a rolling launch.

9.1 The creative research programme

Communications research is a large subject. Figure 9.1 sets the scene, summarising the stages in the development of an advertising campaign and relating these to the relevant chapters in this book. The 1980s and 1990s have seen increasing emphasis on the role of the account planner in advertising agencies. The claim is made that 'the account planner creates a dialogue between the consumer and the process of creating advertisements' and that the responsibility for setting advertising in its real-life context is what differentiates the account planner from, on the one hand, the market researcher, and, on the other, the account handler (or account

191

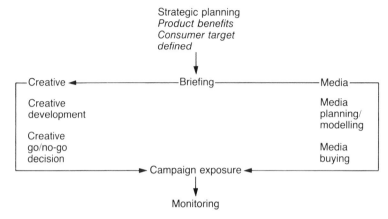

Figure 9.1 Stages in the development of an advertising campaign

executive). The market researcher is there to *answer* questions, the planner is there to ask them and to interpret the answers.

The relationship between the message and the medium used to convey it is necessarily a close one, and the most cost-effective results are achieved when creative work and media planning proceed simultaneously and with joint consultation. If advertising objectives are agreed between client and agency at the outset, and if the creative task is defined at an early stage, there are defined standards for experimental and, finally, monitoring purposes.

9.2 Advertising objectives and creative tasks

We need to distinguish between marketing objectives, advertising objectives and creative tasks. The marketing objective is, in the last analysis, to improve the contribution to profit of a particular brand or to maintain its contribution for as long as possible. The profit contribution can be achieved by improving or maintaining sales value or, in the shorter term, by reducing marketing costs, and this generally means the advertising appropriation. The relationship between marketing objective, advertising objective and creative task can be illustrated by the scenario in Box 9.1.

9.3 Stages in the advertising research programme

The cycle of planning, creative development, decision and campaign exposure in Figure 9.2 illustrates the stages in the advertising research programme. These stages are explained in sections 9.3.1 to 9.3.3.

Box 9.1

The marketing objective is to increase the market share of the brand by *x* per cent. The client's promotional budget, which embraces trade deals and consumer promotions as well as the advertising appropriation, is related to this objective. Study of disaggregated panel data shows that, among those who buy the brand, there is a group of individuals who return to the brand time and again without being entirely loyal to it. The data describe the demographic characteristics of this group and indicate that the segment is sufficiently large to warrant further attention.

The advertising objective is accordingly to stimulate the loyalty (or to improve the repeat-purchase rate) of a consumer target defined as housewives with children at home who are working full- or part-time outside the home. The social class and age classification of the segment are known and this is important to media planning.

The creative task may be determined by qualitative work among women representative of the segment. 'Depth' interviews or group discussions may suggest that, in this product field, the target consumer is anxious to maintain her home-making role in spite of the demands of outside work. The creative task might then be defined as supporting the domestic confidence of these hard-pressed women. There is, of course, more than one way of doing this in an advertising campaign!

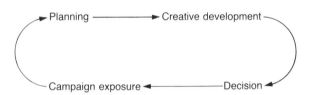

Figure 9.2   The creative programme

9.3.1 The strategic planning stage

The role of planners in advertising agencies is to help ensure that the available data are effectively digested and to act as purveyors of the relevant and stimulating findings of research. The purveyors' role is especially important when it comes to briefing creative people. To do this effectively requires a rare combination of the analytical and creative faculties. The advertising objective(s) are defined at this stage and the creative group briefed.

Data considered for planning purposes can range from the following:

- A client's sales figures.
- Trend data derived from subscription to consumer panels and/or retail audits.
- Repeated attitude surveys tracking consumer responses to brands on the tests carried out during the development of the product.

- Descriptive surveys including segmentation studies and qualitative work on file.
- Media statistics, e.g. from BARB, MEAL.

The study of consumer data in sufficient detail enables consumer or target groups to be identified. Benefits to be conveyed to these target groups are sharply defined when media and creative groups in the advertising agency are briefed.

9.3.2 The development of creative ideas

When the creative task has been defined during the strategic planning stage, the creative group has been effectively briefed. At this early stage of creative development qualitative work is commonly used to try out ideas. A limited number of target consumers are shown creative ideas in an unfinished form. Such stimulus material is conveyed by, say, a sketched layout plus headline, or perhaps a typed copy for print advertisements, storyboard or a mocked-up video treatment for a television commercial. The degree of finish is a matter of judgement.

Stimulus material is a thing, article or item that is used to convey a product, pack or advertising to the consumers or to trigger their responses to a particular area of enquiry. Stimulus materials in current use are summarised in Box 9.2. The type of material chosen to start a group discussion (or extended interview) is clearly going to influence the views expressed by participants. Choice of material, including degree of finish, demands professional judgement based on experience and training in the behavioural sciences.

The material used will relate to the stage reached in the development of the product/service, from the initial concept or idea to presentation of the brand in an advertisement. The concept may be introduced to those taking part as a simple statement on a board; the eventual brand presentation as a photomatic.

Gordon and Langmaid (1988) ask three basic questions:

1. What do consumers see when shown stimulus material? 'Consumers evaluate all research stimuli as advertisements: most find it difficult to deal with concepts or ideas.'
2. How 'rough' or 'real' should the stimulus material be? 'Consumers do not see "rough ideas" when shown stimulus material: they see a finished execution.'
3. How do consumers create meaning, or de-code, stimulus material? The material may convey an idea or message very different from the one intended: for example, the Benetton advertisement featuring a dying man with the AIDS virus in the early 1990s.

This material is used as a stimulus for discussion in groups or in individual interviews. The discussion or interview is taped so that the creative group (who should in any case be involved in the research work) can play it back. In some

---

Box 9.2 Stimulus material

Concept boards:	Single boards on which the product, pack or adverting ideas is expressed verbally and/or visually.
Storyboards:	Key frames for a commercial are drawn consecutively, like a comic strip. The script may be written underneath and/or played on a tape recorder with special sound effects.
Animatics:	Key frames for a commercial are drawn and then filmed on video with an accompanying sound track. The effect is of a somewhat jerky TV film, using drawn characters to represent live action.
Admatics:	A development of animatics, changing crudely animated story-boards into something nearly approaching the level of a finished commercial by using computer-generated and manipulated images.
Flip-overboards:	Key frames for a commercial are drawn as above but, to avoid the respondents reading ahead, are exposed one by one by the interviewer in time to a taped sound track.
Narrative tapes:	An audio tape on which a voice artist narrates the dialogue and explains the action of the commercial and describes the characters. The tape may be accompanied by key visuals.
Photomatics:	A form of animatic using photographs instead of drawn key frames, thus showing the characters and scenes more realistically.

Source: W. Gordon and R. Langmaid (1988) *Qualitative Research: A practitioner's and buyer's guide*, London: Gower.

---

agencies, videotape or one-way mirrors are used so that 'body language' may be observed by the creative staff.

No attempt is made to count heads. The numbers taking part in this qualitative work are sufficient to generate a good range of ideas and reactions, but not for statistical analysis. Content of the tapes is analysed in terms of the following:

- Ideas about the product derived from the advertising stimulus, including ideas about the kind of people who might be expected to use the product.
- The extent to which those taking part associate themselves with the product and the context in which it is shown.
- Features ignored, which may indicate either that the message is unclear or that those present are dissociating themselves from this aspect.

As with product and price testing, definition of target and benefit(s) specifies the type of consumer to be involved in qualitative and experimental work, and what consumer perceptions of the product should be used as measures of advertising effectiveness.

Debate has for a long time centred on the validity of the measures used in pre-exposure testing, measures such as the recall of advertisements and their contents and expressed intention to buy the branded product. Once a pre-tested brand is out in the real world it is possible to compare actual performance with estimated performance: to establish the relationships between recall of advertisements in the pre-test and awareness of the advertising after exposure, between expressed intention to buy and actual sales, and to arrive at correction factors which enable predictions to be made with more confidence. The estimation of correction factors is, however, a difficult and expensive exercise.

It may be necessary to give statistical support to the agency proposal or to choose between more than one approach. What is now wanted is 'a quantified measurement of future performance in real conditions' without incurring the cost of the complete marketing effort and before meeting competitors in the market.

9.3.3 Campaign exposure

Once the creative campaign is out and about in the media it becomes difficult to distinguish the effect of the creative work from that of the media selection. After exposure, advertising research is often used to see whether the opportunities to see/hear the creative message, offered by the media selected, are in fact being taken by the target consumers. Results of the recognition checks and campaign penetration studies considered in Chapter 13 are used (a) to monitor performance and (b) to refine future media scheduling, for the process is a circular one.

What we would like to be able to do at this stage is to relate the advertising costs to sales achievement. A simple cause-and-effect relationship between advertising and sales can be observed when response is direct, as in mail order. In most cases other marketing factors intervene. Has the sales force, perhaps aided by dealer incentives, been able to achieve not only distribution but 'stand-out' value for the brand? What level of competitive activity is the campaign provoking? We discuss the research methods used to help answer questions such as these in Chapter 8.

In the meantime, the grey area is shrinking with the increasing availability of disaggregated data – 'within person' and 'shop-by-shop' – and the associated development of computer programs which examine relationships between the brand and media consumption of individuals over time, while the availability of 'shop-to-shop' data will in due course make it easier to establish the effect of distributive, as opposed to advertising, tactics.

9.4 How advertising works

Ideas as to how advertising works influence the research methods used when advertisements are tested. It is now generally accepted that there can be no one all-embracing theory because advertising tasks are so varied. To take two extreme cases:

1. In 'direct-response' advertising the goods are sold to the consumer in an advertisement and delivery is direct from the manufacture/marketing company on receipt of cash or credit-card number. The Sunday supplements carry many advertisements of this kind.
2. In 'corporate-image' advertising the objective may be to protect profit growth from attack by political and social pressure groups, and the advertising task to keep the public informed about technological achievements of benefit to the community (e.g. the nuclear industry).

In the direct-response case, sales are substantially attributable to an advertisement in a particular medium (provided the print advertisement, television or radio commercial had a code attached to it, and the purchaser refers to the code!).

In the corporate-image case, the effect of the campaign is likely to be measured by asking members of the public awareness and attitude questions in *ad hoc* surveys carried out at regular intervals, say, once a year. By asking a standard core of questions in each survey it is possible to keep track of changes in the image of the enterprise held by the general public. In the direct-response case, advertising can be said to *convert*; in the corporate-image case, to *reinforce*. Let us now see how these two conceptions of the advertising task, conversion and reinforcement, arose.

9.4.1 The early models

Attention, interest, desire, action (AIDA) is one of the earliest models. This model postulates a simple relationship between advertising and selling. Provided the advertising succeeds in attracting attention, arousing interest and stimulating desire, the result is a sale:

Attention → Interest → Desire → Action

Colley's DAGMAR model is more sophisticated in its approach, but the advertising process is still seen as one of step-by-step conversion (Colley 1961). DAGMAR stands for 'defining advertising goals for measured advertising results', the goals being to achieve the following in the consumer:

Awareness → Comprehension → Conviction → Action

Lavidge and Steiner's 'hierarchy-of-effects' model (1961) draws on the theory that an attitude embraces three elements of states – cognition (knowing), affect (evaluation) and conation (action), but the advertising process is still seen as one in

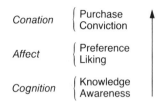

Figure 9.3 Lavidge and Steiner's 'hierarchy-of-effects' model

which, for the potential consumer, a change of attitude will precede a change in behaviour (see Figure 9.3).

The assumption that attitude change precedes change in behaviour ignores the implications of Festinger's theory of cognitive dissonance. Individuals aim to achieve consonance or harmony in their thinking and feeling. Choosing (as between products, brands and services) threatens a consumer with post-decisional dissonance (dissatisfaction after purchase). In other words, it is now generally accepted that a change in attitude may either precede or follow action: that the relationship may work in either direction.

$$\text{Attitude} \rightleftharpoons \text{Behaviour}$$

9.4.2 The reinforcement role

Dissonance theory suggests that advertising has a reinforcement role to play, for, by reassuring consumers that they have made a sensible choice, loyalty to a particular model or brand is reinforced (see Box 9.3). Ehrenberg's rigorous examination of disaggregated panel data has shown that, in many product fields, 100 per cent loyalty to a brand is rare indeed; on the other hand, choice is not haphazard.

For establishing brands, sales increases represent only a small proportion of total sales in any one period and reinforcement of the status quo is essential to the maintenance of profit contribution. But consumers die, move out of the country or

---

Box 9.3

Let us assume that a typical shopper's short list is of three brands, E, F, G: that his/her habitual pattern of buying is E, E, F, G: and our brand is G. It would clearly improve our brand share if this shopper's buying of G were sufficiently frequent in relation to E and F to create a habitual buying pattern of G, E, F, G. The advertising task might then be to reinforce the attraction of G for those who already use the brand from time to time.

Box 9.4

Example: New users (converts) are essential to the baby-food market. But this is a field in which cognitive dissonance is particularly painful, and reassurance in numbers is necessary by reinforcing the brand's advantages in advertising and sales promotions.

---

get too old for the product. Brands grow partly through attracting new buyers, partly through increased frequency of buying among existing users. The relative importance of these two roles, conversion and reinforcement, will depend on the nature of the market and the position of the brand in the market (see Box 9.4).

Finally there are situations in which advertising is used to defend a brand's position and the advertiser is satisfied if market share is maintained without any increase in advertising or other marketing costs.

9.4.3 USP and 'brand image'

These two models, the 'unique selling proposition' (USP) by Rosser Reeves and the 'brand-image' concept by David Ogilvy, were developed in New York advertising agencies in the early 1960s.

The unique selling proposition (1961). In the rare case of a product with a unique, and desirable, attribute, definition of the USP is a straightforward matter. But integral differences between brands in a product field are often marginal and a USP is likely to be suggested by study of consumer habits and attitudes in the product field: to quote a classic example, use of toothpaste + fear of bad breath = 'the Colgate ring of confidence'. The USP, once defined, must be adhered to in every communication about the brand. This is a behaviourist approach to 'how advertising works' and, as with Pavlov's dogs, repetition is of the essence. Time is needed to condition the consumer to associate the proposition with the brand.

Brand image (1963). David Ogilvy's concept of the 'brand image' has proved more fruitful in the development of creative advertising. Consumers buy brands (not products or services) and by developing a personality for the brand (as opposed to attaching a proposition to it) the brand is made more meaningful to the consumer and this added value strengthens loyalty. The consumer is treated as a rational being with conscious ends in view and a defined self-image. Brand loyalty is strong when there is empathy between the brand's image and the consumer's self-image. Recall and awareness are likely measures to use when assessing the effectiveness of a USP campaign, while attitude measurement and the tracking of changes in attitude over time are essential to 'image' studies.

9.4.4 Fishbein and buying intention

'Intention to buy' (or 'try') questions are now accepted as valid indicators of consumer response to products and the advertising associated with them. The answers have been shown to have predictive value. As a result of Fishbein's work on attitude theory and measurement, investigations into consumer habits and attitudes often include questions relating to the act of purchase (Fishbein 1967).

Fishbein postulates that behavioural intention (BI) is the product of how we feel about the act ('attitude towards the act', Aact) – and in our context the act is buying a brand – plus how we feel about society's attitude towards the act (SN, a subjective norm). In the formula given below, w_1 and w_2 are weights representing the strength of our wanting to carry out the act (buying or trying the brand) and the extent to which this might be modified by social considerations:

$$BI = Aact_{w_1} + SN_{w_2}$$

Lintas and Research International have long made a practice of asking 'intention to buy' questions. The data have been systematically filed and (where possible) correlated with actual purchase data. Experience has shown that (intention to buy) scores indicate how far the total message effect adds up to a feeling of wanting to buy the brand (as opposed to, say, just enjoying the advertisement), and this feeling is related to subsequent sales.

9.5 Verbal measures

At the pre-test stage, i.e. before campaign exposure, the most commonly used measures of creative effectiveness are the following:

- Recall, unaided and aided.
- Attitude towards the product/brand and its likely users.
- Intention to buy.

Questions relating to the respondent's habitual behaviour in the product field will often help to determine whether the respondent is a suitable participant in the test. They will also contribute to interpretation of the answers to recall, attitude and intention to buy questions. Impact is the result of the following:

- The information conveyed to the respondent (usually measured by recall).
- The respondent's emotional response to the brand (measured by attitude questions).

Box 9.5

Each step in the hierarchical advertising models has one or more measures associated with it. But 'hierarchy of effects' might apply more to high-involvement than to low-involvement products.

Cognition: Recall
                      Recognition
                      Belief strength
                      Awareness
                      Comprehensive of main copy points

Affect: Attitude regarding product's features
                      Product preferences
                      Extent of match of product with self-image
                      Internalisation of message

Conation: Purchase intent
                      Intent to try product (trial)
                      Intent to adopt product (commitment)
                      Actual purchase behaviour

- The strength of the respondent's desire for the brand (as indicated by intention-to-buy questions).

We are close to the hierarchical models with their cognitive, effective and conative components (see section 8.3.1 and Box 9.5) but with two important differences:

1. We recognise that attitude change can be the effect as well as the cause of a change in behaviour, that it can be 'post'- as well as 'pre'-action.
2. We distinguish between attitudes towards the brand and those who might use it, and attitudes towards the act of purchasing or behavioural intention.

Once the campaign is out in the real world, recognition is an important measure. Recognition checks whether or not an advertisement has been noticed. This will depend on the effectiveness of the media planning and buying as well as on the creative impact.

Awareness, *campaign penetration* and *salience* are other terms used when discussing advertising research after campaign exposure (post-testing). Awareness covers a range of responses from mere recognition to unaided recall of the attributes the advertising seeks to associate with the brand. Campaign penetration and salience measures help to establish whether the opportunities to see, view or hear offered by the media schedule are in fact being taken.

9.6 Testing before campaign exposure: three methodologies

9.6.1 The folder or reel test – a lab-type experiment

Let us assume that the creative group has come up with two possible solutions to the creative task.

The test material: Two folders or videotape reels are prepared containing a selection of advertisements with which the proposed advertisements will have to compete for attention. The competitive advertisements are likely to represent a variety of product fields. The two folders/reels are identical except for the test advertisements, assigned one to each, and placed in the same position relative to the rest of the content. It is important that the test material be of the same degree of finish as the rest of the content.

The design: Monadic, using two matched samples of 50–100 members of the target population.

Procedure: The respondents are asked to go through one of the folders or to watch one of the tapes. They are then asked which advertisements they happen to have noticed. Given that the brand is an established one (as is often the case in advertising research) the test advertisement will not stand out as being of special interest to the interviewer. Once unaided recall has been recorded, a list of the brands in the test is shown to the respondent as a memory trigger. The respondent may be asked which was most liked and which was liked least, or which 'you would most like to talk about'. Procedures vary but essentially attention is gradually focused on the test advertisement and recall of its content. Recording of aided recall must be differentiated from unaided recall, and the order in which advertisements and product attributes are mentioned is likely to be significant as a measure of salience.

Measurement of results: Applying the notation used in Box 8.1 (see page 169) we have an after-only design based on two matched experimental groups, here E_1 and E_2:

Group	Treatment	Observation	Measurement
E_1	X_1	0_1	0_1 compared with 0_2 in a controlled context
E_2	X_2	0_2	0_2 in a controlled context

The basis for comparison is not likely to be limited to recall. Attitude and intention-to-buy questions may also be asked, while behaviour in the product field will be taken into account.

9.6.2 Testing in the field before campaign exposure

If the brand is on sale it is possible to pre-test in the field by arranging for the run of a publication to be 'split', so that different areas receive issues with different advertisements, or by arranging for different transmitters to put out different commercials. Here again the context is controlled: same television programme, same publication; the independent variable being the advertisement.

Here again the measures used to determine the relative effectiveness of the alternative advertising approaches are recall (unaided and aided), attitude questions, and intention to buy (if not already doing so) in the light of experience to date in the product field.

The setting up of this kind of experiment is straightforward enough, publishers and independent television contractors offer standard packages as part of their own sales promotional activity.

The main procedural difficulties are the following:

- Contacting suitable, i.e. target-group, respondents.
- Matching experimental groups on critical product-use and demographic criteria.
- Making sure that respondents have in fact been exposed to the test material.

A question relating to editorial content of the issue, or in the case of television, about adjacent programmes, is the usual way of establishing that the responses recorded relate to the advertisements whose impact we are trying to assess. It is possible to use the media to test the effectiveness of a new advertising approach if the brand is 'ongoing' and in distribution. Were the media to be used to finalise advertising for a new brand it would be necessary to have produced the product in sufficient quantity, packed and priced to meet the demand created – and the competition would be alerted.

9.6.3 An 'after-only with control' example

When we pre-test the effect of communications we would like to be able to take a 'before' measurement and to base our conclusions on observation of the changes effected by the advertising material on the respondent's awareness, attitudes and intentions with regard to the brand. But we know that questions asked at the first interview are likely to influence responses at the second.

Validating a procedure which sidesteps this difficulty:

- Two samples of about one hundred target consumers are matched on about two demographic characteristics and, where relevant, on some aspect of brand or product field usage.

- The experimental group receives the advertising test material plus some other prompting stimulus such as a pack shot.
- The control group receives the other prompting stimulus without the advertising material.
- The two samples are questioned about the brand and the added value of the advertising material is appraised by comparing the responses of the experimental group with those of the control group.
- The design (using the notation shown in Box 8.1 on page 169) is, given X = advertising test material and Y = the other stimulus:

Group	Treatment	Observation	Measurement*
E	$X + Y$	0_1	$0_1 - 0_2$
C	Y	0_2	

*It is possible that some of the verbal measures used may not show a positive result for E, the experimental group, and that the overall result may not show value being added by the advertising.

In an 'after-only with control' design sampling error will be greater than it would be if both sets of measurements were taken on the same sample of respondents, as in a before-after design. In order to avoid the possible bias due to the learning effect, communications research relies very often on a comparison of responses from more than one group, whether these be two experimental groups, as in our first sample, or an experimental group with a control group. Matching of the groups is critical and it is advisable to ensure that test and control samples use the same interviewers in matched locations. When commercials are being tested, the location is likely to be a van, suitably equipped, or a hall.

9.7 Pre-testing with instruments

There is a good case for using mechanical means of observation when testing the stand-out effect of pack designs. For a time lab-type experiments using mechanical observation were fashionable in communications research, but the following considerations now count against the use of 'ironmongery' to measure advertising effects:

- Use of measuring devices such as the tachistoscope or psychogalvanometer restricts the venue for the experiment to a test centre or mobile van and adds to the cost of data collection, for the ironmongery is expensive and the procedure likely to be time consuming.
- Artificiality in the circumstances in which the advertising material is exposed to the respondents which reduces belief in the external validity of their responses.

- It is usual to ask questions in order to interpret the meaning of the physiological observations recorded by the instruments.

We are going to consider two devices: the tachistoscope and the psychogalvano-meter.

The tachistoscope is relevant to the testing of posters for stand-out value, and it could be claimed that the more speedily perceived of two advertisements has the better chance of being noticed in the press or during the commercial break on ITV. But, posters apart, experiments based on verbal measures are likely to produce richer and more actionable data for physiological aspects. It is always possible to combine the physiological and verbal procedures: to record the speed with which elements in the advertisement are perceived and then to ask the recall, attitude and intention questions.

As for the psychogalvanometer the case for physiological measurements rests on doubts about the capacity of researchers to ask meaningful questions and of consumers to give true answers. Response to an advertising stimulus when attached to the psychogalvanometer (or 'lie detector') is involuntary. Electrodes attached to the hands measure sweat levels, an autonomic indicator of emotional arousal. Provided the temperature of the research centre, or van, is kept stable, comparison of fluctuations with a base measurement will show how the respondent reacts to the development of a commercial, or to the sight of a press advertisement or sound of a radio commercial. The emotional responses are duly recorded but the nature of the responses, whether these are favourable or unfavourable, has to be elicited by means of questions.

9.8 Simulated test markets

Simulated test-market tests have the following features:

- They have the advantage of speed for both penetration and repeat buying are 'hothoused'.
- They provide for 'extensive diagnostic questioning'.
- They depend on neither attitude measurement scores nor the availability of trend data.
- They can eliminate the need for much of the hitherto necessary separate testing of elements such as advertising, pack and product.

As an example, Research International's Sensor model simulates encounter with the new brand at the point of sale:

- Respondents are 'recruited to central locations'.
- Respondents are exposed to advertising.

- Respondents are taken to a simulated shop display including the new brand and its competitors.
- Respondents are given coupon money to spend on products in the display.
- Those who buy the test product are given it to use at home under natural conditions.
- After a suitable interval triallists are called on and asked brand preference questions.
- Prices are discussed using the 'trade-off' procedure.
- The respondent is given the opportunity to buy the test brand using his/her own money.

Sensor estimates market share. The model assumes that the size of the market (as revealed by shop audit, consumer panel or omnibus data) will remain much the same. The marketing task in many cases is to establish a place for the brand in individual shopping baskets or purchasing repertoires and 'a measure of absolute volume sales' is needed. Research International's MicroTest model includes the inputs such as availability, advertising, brand visibility, concept acceptability, product acceptability, frequency of purchasing and weight of purchasing. MicroTest is used for predictive product testing to provide estimates of sales volume at an early stage which can be validated, based on trial and adoption measures. The predictive value of the models (Research International 1994) depends on corporate experience in the market, the existence of trend data and the care with which preliminary research, such as the hall test, is designed and interpreted. The simulated test market models are discussed in more detail in Chapter 10 on modelling techniques.

Respondents can be conveniently tested in the following locations:

- In-hall (where there is greater interviewer control of product presentation and sample).
- In-home (where respondents can consume the product according to their daily routine).
- On-site (on business premises such as pubs, wine bars and working men's clubs).

9.9 Conclusions

In order to create effective advertising it is necessary to consider how advertising can work to further the marketing objective, and so to arrive at a definition of a specific advertising objective. Given an adequate advertising appropriation, successful achievement of the advertising objective depends on a combination of effective media planning and the capacity to create persuasive advertisments. Advertising is a substantial marketing cost, especially where branded consumer products are concerned. With considerable sums at stake advertisers are not, as a rule, happy to take creative work entirely on trust; while advertising agents, including their creative staff, seek reassurance that they are on the right lines. The usefulness of qualitative work is to stimulate creative thinking and to try out ideas. The predictive value of models depends on corporate experience in the market, the existence of trend data and the care with which preliminary research, such as hall tests, is designed and interpreted.

References

Colley, R. (1961) *Advertising Goals for Measured Advertising Results*, New York: Association of National Advertisers.

Fishbein, M. (1967) *Readings: Atttitude theory and measurement*, New York: John Wiley.

Gordon, W. and Langmaid, R. (1988) *Qualitative Research – A practitioner's and buyer's guide*, London: Gower.

Lavidge, R. and Steiner, C. (1961) 'A model for predictive measurements of advertising effectiveness', *Journal of Marketing*.

Research International (1994) Position Paper 5, p. 10.

Further reading

Dunn, S., Barban, A., Krugman, D. and Reid, N. (1990) *Advertising*, USA: Dryden Press.

Hart, N. (ed.) (1993) *The Practice of Advertising*, Oxford: Butterworth Heinemann, published on behalf of the CAM Foundation and the Chartered Institute of Marketing.

Peter, P. and Olson, J. (1994) *Understanding Consumer Behaviour*, Itaska, IL: R. Irwin.

Smith, P. (1993) Marketing Communications, London: Kogan Page.

Assignments

1. 'In the advertising business we all know that the ultimate test of any advertising campaign is the sales result to which it contributes.' Does this statement imply that attempts to pre-test advertising campaigns are irrelevant?

2. 'Consumption decisions are a vital source of the *culture* of the time . . . The individual uses consumption to say something about himself and his family and his locality.' Does this statement by an anthropologist answer the question, 'What makes advertising work?'

3. A marketing company, fearing 'me too' action by competitors, is hesitating to test
    market a shampoo which includes an ingredient to improve hair 'rinsibility' after
    shampooing. You have been asked to review and evaulate the method(s) whereby the
    impact of the total mix (formulation, package, price and communication) might be
    assessed without alerting the competition. Propose a suitable research design.

CHAPTER 10

Modelling techniques for product prediction and planning

Rory P. Morgan

10.1 The role of market research in NPD

Market research has a key role in the new product development (NPD) process, partly in generating ideas and developing them, but primarily in reducing the risk, or exposure to down-side financial loss. The many hurdles that a new product must face include the following areas where market research techniques, appropriately applied, can significantly reduce this risk.

Accurate assessment of market demand. Clearly, some internal estimate must be made of the potential for a new product or service, in order to justify the NPD exercise in the first place. This assessment should not only indicate the overall total demand, but also indicate the characteristics of potential triallists/adopters, plus any significant segmentation of the market in terms of users.

Obtaining a good product fit. The product must be optimised to meet known demand, given the constraints of competition, production and cost. This may need to acknowledge some trade-offs in design/composition if the optimisation is targeted at specific user segments with a different needs profile to the population at large.

Identifying optimal positioning. In most developed markets with existing competition, some consideration needs to be taken of these competitors. Generally speaking, the positioning of the new product or service will be defined in order to maximise some declared goal. For example, in a 'cloning' strategy, the aim would be to identify and mimic a target competitor, and develop a competing product that utilises some inherent benefit in order to develop a consumer proposition with a similar profile but with an advantage, e.g. through better distribution, pricing or branding equity (or, indeed, any of these in combination). Alternatively, a strategy of distinctiveness would lead to the development of a 'unique selling proposition', possibly resulting from an identified gap in the market. However, in either case, there is a need to estimate the likely source of business from other competitors (e.g.

brand switching patterns). This is particularly true when there is a need to minimise cannibalisation from one's own brands.

Payback and profitability. Marketing is a commercial activity, and ultimately has the aim of generating profits. Hence, there is an overriding need to ensure that the stream of revenue resulting from sales of the new product will pay back the investment made in the required period, and has a good chance of sustaining profit levels in the foreseeable future. This invariably means making some estimate of the volume of sales, both in the period of growth (e.g. first and second years, in the case of many grocery products), and thereafter. The better these predictions, the more the risk is reduced.

Models using data derived from market research can be used to assist in all these areas. One feature of modern times is that the quantitative methods that have been developed have tended to become more and more specialised, and many of the better approaches use proprietary techniques developed by research agencies. It is likely that this process will continue, since even the largest marketing conglomerate finds it difficult to match the range of experience and case material available to agencies, who (in the largest companies) deal with hundreds of such exercises every year. And many of these are models in the sense that a variety of inputs both from survey research and from marketing are synthesised with the aim of making 'what if?' predictions. These are the predictive models. Others are more descriptive in nature.

The aim of this chapter is to provide an overview of the ways that market research models can assist the NPD process, both from product inception to launch. It is highly selective, since there are already a vast number of marketing models in existence, ranging from the highly theoretical (and possibly untested) to the highly practical (with years of experience and back data). I have therefore tended to concentrate on well-known services of proven stature, which are commonly available to marketing people. Even then, it is not exhaustive, but should serve to give a flavour of the area.

10.2 Sizing the potential

It is frequently thought that product forecasting takes place at the end of the NPD process, when a 'finished' product is available for production, and volume estimates are required. This is true, but often overlooked is the fact that the most critical forecasting exercise is (or should be) conducted right at the beginning. Some products *must* fail, despite high acceptance among actual users, simply because the number of users is insufficient to generate sufficient revenue to lead to profitability.

An initial assessment of demand (and therefore potential) is critical. Sometimes this is common sense – a new drug targeting migraine or asthma sufferers must take account of the simple number of such sufferers that exist. Other products, operating in fast-moving grocery areas, can make use of common patterns. The basis for a great number of marketing models was provided by Parfitt and Collins (1968), who postulated back in 1967 that brand share is a function of the *penetration* that is achieved (usually thought of as the proportion of product field buyers that have actually tried the test product), the *repeat-purchasing rate* (the proportion of triallists who buy again within a given time period), and the *buying rate index* (to take account of users of the test product using more or less than the average for the field).

Armed with this model, some preliminary 'scenario planning' is possible. For example, consider the following facts:

- In almost all product fields it is extremely rare for more than half of those who make a trial purchase to repeat purchase the product at all.
- Once the product has settled down, it is unusual for more than 15–20 per cent of triallists to repeat purchase in any 4-week period.
- Repeat buyers in most product fields purchase between 1.6 and 2.2 times per 4-week period.
- New products very rarely have a higher purchase frequency than existing products.

Thus, if financial calculations suggest that 10 m units need to be sold in a year, we can estimate the region of trial levels required to support this. Good product performance might result in a repeat-purchase rate of 15 per cent, with an average of 2 units per buyer in each 4-week period of the year. Thus, if all 20 m households in Great Britain purchased (100 per cent penetration, mind) 3 m (i.e. 15 per cent) triallists would result in 78 m units sold in the year (3 m triallists × 2 units × 13 4-week periods). We should make a fortune!

So far so good. However, actual sales will depend on a number of other factors, of which actual penetration and physical distribution are the most significant. Penetration is certain to be much less than 100 per cent. If the average penetration of the product field is 25 per cent, and we are unlikely to get more than 50 per cent distribution, then our new estimate would be 78 × .5 × .25 = 9.75 m units. Added to this the fact that we need to down-weight further, because we would not achieve 100 per cent awareness or visibility of the product, and we are now well below our action standard.

The lesson to be drawn from this simple 'back of the envelope' modelling exercise is that all of these factors trade off with each other, so that even excellent products, operating in sectors with lowish penetration, find it difficult to achieve critical volume unless they can achieve compensating higher levels of distribution, communication, or reduced costs of manufacture.

In addition, there are occasions when the forecast will need to take account of longer-term changes in the market, and particularly when the expected life of a product might be measured in decades. Examples here would include changes in the birth rate (important for manufacturers of baby products), and the gradual 'ageing' of the population. Equally, trends in the working status of women, disposable income, available leisure time (maybe resulting from the unemployment rate), health consciousness, etc., could be relevant.

Forecasting potential demand for consumer goods which have a longer purchase cycle (e.g. durables) offers different challenges, since repeat-purchase rates have less meaning.[1] This is also true for services, such as financial products. Commonly used methods here involve the synthesis of a number of different measures, some of which include formal models:

- *Industry consensus forecasts.* Many industries produce pooled estimates of the rate of growth (e.g. number of adults with bank accounts, satellite dishes, microwave ovens, etc.).
- *Econometric sales trend forecasts.* Statistical models can range from the very simple (moving averages) to the highly complex (Box-Jenkins forecasting). Much of this is conducted in-house, using commonly available statistical software, such as SPSS or SAS. However, this is a very technical field, and the novice would be well advised to seek the services of specialised agencies.
- *Analogy with related fields.* Durables manufacturers can determine the rates of penetration of analogous products. So a manufacturer of satellite dishes might be interested in the historical rates of growth of comparable products such as VCRs, camcorders, CD players, etc.).

In the case of durables, the notion of the 'park' can provide a basis for forecasting national demand. Here, we need to estimate the number of existing products currently in use (the park), the growth rate, and the replacement rate. Given these, we can build a model which says (effectively) that demand for a product at any point in time is a function of the demand from initial buyers, and the demand for replacement at that time.

10.2.1 Innovation products

'Innovation' products, or those products that are so new and novel in conception that they have no obvious competition, are the most difficult of all to forecast. Indeed, identifying the need for them in the first place (the 'latent demand') can be fairly challenging. In many cases, classical market research involving concept testing can dramatically underestimate potential, simply because respondents cannot envisage the usefulness of the product – until, at least, they see them in use. Cellular phones are a good example of this. Equally, it is said (apocryphally) that Sony Corporation pushed ahead with the development of the Walkman despite, and not because of, the market research.[2]

However, some basic principles do exist. The 'rate of diffusion' of a new idea

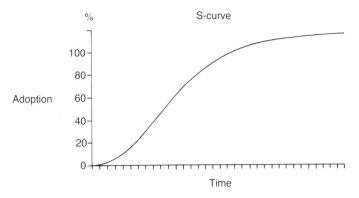

Figure 10.1   The S-shaped (sigmoid) curve

(i.e. the cumulative sales) can be broken down as the combined effect of two distinct processes:

1. *External influences* – such as communication through the media, and advertising weight. On its own, the effect of these issues is proportional to the number of potential buyers who have not yet purchased. The effect is therefore logarithmic: it is reduced as the proportion of adopters increases.
2. *Internal influences* – such as the communication of buyers and potential buyers among themselves. This could be the result of word-of-mouth communication (e.g. recommendations), or simply the effect of seeing an increasing number of products in use (e.g. cellular phones). On its own, the effect of these issues is proportional to the number of buyers to date, and is therefore exponential: its effect is enhanced as the proportion of adopters increases.

The net result of these influences is the familiar S-shaped (sigmoid) curve, as shown in Figure 10.1. To quote Mahajan and Peterson (1985):

> After the product is launched, only a few people buy. However, in subsequent time periods, an increasing number of adoptions per time period occur as the diffusion process begins to unfold more fully. Finally, the trajectory of the diffusion curve slows and begins to level off, ultimately reaching an upper asymptote, and the diffusion is complete.
>
> Although the diffusion pattern of most innovations can be described in terms of a general S-shaped curve, the exact form for each curve, including the slope and the asymptote, may differ. For example, the slope may be very steep initially, indicating rapid diffusion, or it may be gradual, indicating relatively slow diffusion.

The shape of this curve can be modelled; both the Logistic or Gompertz trends are popular here.

10.3 Meeting the demand

It almost goes without saying that any new product should, within the constraints of brand heritage, production and cost, meet the demands of its intended target customer base. This is particularly true of products that are intended to appeal to specific segments. The general rationale for segmented marketing is that by meeting a very specific set of needs, a price premium can be charged for the added value provided. For this reason, a segmentation approach based on needs is preferable.

Three situations commonly arise where there is an opportunity to develop products around changing needs:

1. Where a revolution in technology or production makes it possible suddenly to satisfy needs hitherto unmet or even unseen (e.g. pocket calculators, frozen foods, instant noodles, freeze-dried coffee, etc.). This can result in a situation known as a 'paradigm shift', where consumers are often initially unable to see the benefits to themselves, as referred to earlier. These sorts of products in effect generate their own demand (or hope to).
2. Where an advance in product delivery improves the way in which an existing need is met. Many products fit into this category, but a classic example would be disposable nappies. Note that 'need' in this instance can refer to a search for novelty, or fashion.

    Another way to think of this is in terms of developing products to overcome problems. The research requirement here is to identify problems, and then quantify their importance and frequency of occurrence. Techniques such as problem detection studies[3] help to build a scatterplot of 'problems' as in Figure 10.2. This could be regarded as an example of a descriptive model, since the analysis suggests problem areas that offer the best opportunity, i.e. they occur frequently, and have the greatest impact, and therefore could be supposed to have the greatest benefit if they were put right.
3. Where the circumstances, behaviour or attitudes of consumers change, giving rise to new needs. Changes can result from fundamental trends such as the increase of working mothers, changes in the patterns of family eating, or holidays taken abroad. Or, they could refer to more mercurial changes such as eating habits (snacking, meal times). Attitudinal topics might include health, environmentalism, and so on.

In situations where the new product is heavily dependent on patterns of behaviour (e.g. snack products consumed in certain situations), it is important for the forecasting process to quantify the opportunities for use in the target population, since this will obviously have a direct bearing on the volume consumed. A classical approach here is to use panel diary data, or alternatively to use a sample of respondents asked to recall occasions of use, to build up an item-by-use matrix as shown in Figure 10.3. This is another descriptive model, where the relative frequency of occurrence of each of the cells in the matrix can

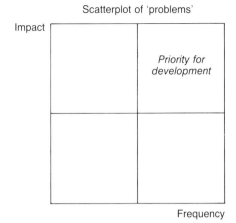

Figure 10.2 Scatterplot of 'problems'

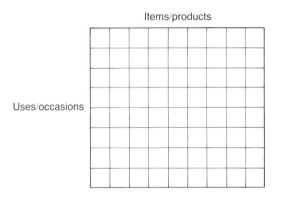

Figure 10.3 Items by use matrix

then be used to indicate the potential of new products. In a sense, this is a form of forecasting demand.

10.3.1 Conjoint analysis

Another way to optimise products in terms of the way they meet core needs, while at the same time modelling market performance, is with the use of conjoint analysis. This modelling technique has become a very important method in the NPD armoury, since it can simultaneously quantify the importance of product features, identify segments of individuals who want different features, and model the likely market shares of potential product configurations.

In essence, a main-effects version of a statistical method is known as factorial testing, conjoint analysis is known as a 'decompositional' method, since it proceeds by showing product configurations to respondents, and then asking for their degree of preference. From an analysis of all the configurations shown, the appeal or 'utility' of each of these constituent variables can be 'decomposed' and quantified. The method of administering these product configurations to respondents (and hence calculating from all the myriad combinations possible which is the best one to show next) can nowadays be done on a computer.

In practice, there is a risk of a 'combinatorial explosion'[4] with a large number of variables, and the practical limit is 12–20. Variables are expressed in terms of levels, so that a variable measuring, say, engine size, might have levels of 1800cc, 2000cc and 2300cc. Because of the nature of the exercise, conjoint analysis is best when used with relatively 'hard' product features, and therefore lends itself to consumer durables, or services. While it can be used with grocery products (e.g. product forms, packaging, etc.) it is not best at handling 'softer' image-related attributes, for which other techniques are preferred.

The 'utility values' generated in a conjoint analysis exercise can be calculated for every variable level in the exercise, and individually for every respondent. There is no space here to consider their derivation, but they are commonly thought to be one of the most accurate and discriminating ways to measure the importance of product features. They can be used in three principal ways, which are of great value in the new product development process (and, indeed, of general market studies).

Sub-group analysis. The utility values generated by every respondent for all attribute levels can be taken as a measure of the 'importance' or desirability that they attach to these features. Therefore, we can analyse this data by groupings of individuals that we suppose, a priori, might differ in terms of what they consider to be important. For example, we can look at men v. women, Northerners v. Southerners, brand users v. non-users, in short any pre-defined group that we care to specify.

Segmentation. At the same time, we can use statistical techniques such as cluster analysis to identify groupings of people who share the same notion of what they consider to be important in the product. In many respects this is the reverse of sub-group analysis, since having found groups of individuals, we then need to profile them by demographics, usership, etc., in order to find out who they are.

Segments identified in this way have a very important significance in new product development, since they can be regarded as corresponding to primary need groups in the marketplace, and therefore offer an ideal mechanism for product development, since in principle we can easily see what the product form would be that would maximally satisfy them. The problem does not end here, since we would need to know if (and by how much) they would pay a price premium for the product. However, segmentation performed upon conjoint utilities is one of the classic ways of identifying product feature opportunities.

Simulating market shares. The real power of conjoint analysis can be seen in its ability to conduct simulation or 'what if?' modelling. One of the mathematical properties of computed utility values is that they can be used predictively to estimate the degree of preference that any individual would exhibit to any array of possible product configurations.[5] Thus, we can estimate the likely appeal of a huge variety of possible product feature combinations – many more than we could possibly test through direct interviewing. Combined with cost data, we can therefore conduct an optimisation procedure that identifies a short list of product configurations that offer the best level of acceptance for the minimum cost of production.

Although primarily a tool for examining 'hard' product features, there are an emerging number of models which use the basic principles to investigate 'softer' issues – the IdeaMap system from Moskowitz Jacobs, Inc. in the United States being one of these.

10.3.2 Optimising the range

Another area where modelling can help is in the area of optimising a range of products designed to span a market (generally on a 'de luxe' to an 'economy' price-scale). This is particularly applicable to durables, where a manufacturer would like to know what product profiles his/her 'high-end' and 'low-end' products' should have to optimise appeal overall. This is frequently a tricky problem, since, for example, the best product would not necessarily have all the features that consumers prefer as the resulting product would cost too much. So, what features do we give up?

One way of solving this is by using the Options model.[6] In this, respondents are asked to complete a computer-administered task, in which they effectively build their own product from a list of costed components. So, for example, in an automotive exercise, the respondent would be told that the base car cost was £12,000, and he/she had the ability to add or take away a range of costed 'extras', which might include safety features, standard of interior trim, instruments, etc. When the respondent is happy with the final profile, and with the total cost of the package, the interview stops. The same process could occur with other product areas, e.g. hi-fi equipment, cookers, and so on. It can even be used for service areas (e.g. hotel extras, package holidays, etc.).

This procedure leaves us with a database of choices from which we can build a simple but effective selection model. For example, suppose we want to examine two possible product profiles, one 'high-end', and the other 'low-end'. We know the ticket cost of these by adding up their features and adding this to the base cost. But who would buy what? We can tell this by examining our database of choices, and selecting the better 'fit' of each product for each respondent. For example, some respondents would rule out the more expensive option simply because the ticket price was higher than their own costed choice. Overall, we therefore know who would be likely to choose what. In some cases, they would choose nothing, if both prices exceed their maximum.

In fact, we can go further than this, since we can tell by how much the product they would be more likely to choose exceeds their maximum cost. In this way, we can conduct a series of simulations, exploring changes in product configuration, until we minimise this amount. In this way, choice models of this kind help us to optimise the product to meet demand.

10.4 Optimising the positioning

In competitive markets, there is generally some need to explore the potential interactions that a new brand would have with existing brands following launch. This is partly done with the aim of controlling or targeting brand-switching behaviour in a desired direction.

Most NPD exercises will aim at developing a brand-positioning statement, around which the communication strategy will be developed. In many cases, the positioning will involve product performance issues. But increasingly, especially in Western-style segmented markets, the positioning will incorporate softer motivational-type issues (for example, trust/reliability, sophistication, fashionability, age identification, and so on). The marketing arena can be thought of as a 'map' of product qualities, some hard and some soft, on which products are positioned.

In fact, quantitative mapping techniques can be used with brand-image data derived from survey research to create 'maps' of this sort,[7] and these can be very useful in conceptualising the space, and analysing gaps in the market. However, on their own they are generally useless for the purposes of forecasting.

The big problem with these sorts of analyses is that they invariably do not take account of the underlying preferences that consumers may have, irrespective of the imagery that they have of brands. For example, I may think that Marlboro has a strong macho image, but this is irrelevant to my choice of cigarette brand if I do not find this property desirable. In fact, the brand manager of Marlboro may have a number of difficult choices. He/she may know exactly where to position the brand on a market map, but in which way should the communication message move – towards 'for real smokers', 'having special offers', 'pleasant tasting', 'suitable for all occasions', or what?

The clear message here is that in situations where the positioning involves non-functional issues (where the direction of benefit may be more clear), then image data of the current market on its own is a poor indicator of where to be. In many cases, it is simply a playback of past advertising history. This means that we need a good understanding of what drives preference in a market at any point in the NPD process.

What we are missing is some notion of what consumers find 'important'. For functional benefits, we can use conjoint analysis, and this is a useful way of giving some weight to product features. In markets where these play a large part (e.g.

durables and some services) this is one way to proceed. However, this is much more difficult in those markets where non-functional and more emotive issues not only play a large part in the decision process, but are the very characteristics on which the market is defined.

Moreover, it is very difficult to approach this directly through survey research. In general, consumer's understanding of their own motivation is poor, and many purchasing decisions are at best semi-rational. Of course, we can always use our own 'common-sense' about what is important, or even rely on qualitative evidence, but this is hardly using the principles of the systematic reduction of risk. In fact, a number of research models have been built to handle this problem. Generally speaking, the aim is to interview respondents and collect their images of brands in the market on a whole range of descriptors, using some form of scale. Like all scales, these should be unambiguous, related to preference, and discriminate between the brands rated. The modelling then consists of establishing a mathematical relationship between brand positions in this image space (similar to the mapping techniques discussed earlier), and the preference that respondents have for those brands.

The value of this is twofold:

- The process will generally give us some idea of how 'important' topics are (in the sense of influencing preference).
- The system can be used as a predictive 'what if' simulation model, in which the effects of changing image positions can be seen as directly affecting preference, and hence (putatively) market share.

It would be wrong to say that these sorts of models are specifically for the use of NPD, since they are increasingly being used to study current markets in an on-going way. However, they fit into the NPD process in the following ways.

1. For exploring current markets and identifying promising positions relative to current brands (after all, most product launches are line extensions). In addition to 'modifying' existing brands, the ability exists in most of these models to 'create' new brands with specified properties, and determine what potential levels of preference share they might attract.
2. Used with concept testing, to measure the imagery generated by concepts, and incorporate this into a market model. This will indicate the relative strengths and weaknesses of the concept, and the potential for change.
3. Used with full market mix testing, often as part of a simulated test market (see below). The value here lies in providing a good actionable base for diagnosing any problems related to failures to gain acceptance, and providing a means of determining remedial action.

There are a number of approaches here. In the Sandpiper model,[8] respondents rate brands on image statements, on which they also indicate the position of their 'ideal' brand. In the modelling, summed distances from the ideal are taken as being inversely proportional to preference. Sandpiper models tend to be built from large exercises (5,000 respondents or more), and are run essentially as panel operations. A number of databases covering a number of product fields are maintained, and to which on-line access is offered.

In contrast, the Locator model[9] uses image data collected in the user's own study, and is presented very much as the modern way of analysing image data collected as a normal part of the questionnaire. The process is also different, in that no 'ideal' data is collected, instead, respondents are asked for their brand preferences in addition to the image data, and the modelling therefore deals directly with imagery and preferences collected from the respondent. However, the model (which is very suitable for NPD exercises), operates in the same way, and can provide the user with a copy of his/her own model, running under Windows on his/her own PC.

10.5 The 'go/no go' decision – forecasting volume

As has been indicated earlier, the critical question preceding any launch decision will be 'Can I sell enough of the product to meet my profitability objectives?' The riskiest decision of all (but by no means uncommon in practice) is simply to trust to judgement and go ahead. However, it is worth restating that the function of market research is to reduce risk, and a wide range of models is available to do just that.

Historically, the first attempts to do this involved little research. Area test markets were used, which consisted of a limited sales effort in a localised geographical region where distribution and local media could be used. In the United States, with the ability to split cable television transmissions, different marketing support strategies could be simultaneously tested. However, they are becoming less frequently used, as they have a number of distinct disadvantages:

- They are costly.
- They require major production runs of product, and in-store merchandising.
- They are time consuming – competitors can counter-launch before they are over.
- They are difficult to organise (increasingly) through retail channels.
- They are not necessarily representative of other regions.
- They expose 'one's hand' at an early stage, and competitors can actually 'interfere'.
- Other methods offer good results, with fewer disadvantages.

Cut-down versions of this principle have also been used. For example, in store tests the product is sold through a limited number of outlets, and sales figures monitored. However, these suffer from similar problems, with the additional problem of accounting for matching stores carrying different marketing support strategies. Additionally, it is almost impossible to restrict media along store lines.

The pressure was on, therefore, to find acceptable substitutes, and it was this pressure that led to the development of simulated test markets, of which we can distinguish three main types:

1. *Mini-test markets*, in which a permanent consumer panel is serviced by an exclusive retail system, operated by the research agency. Here, purchasing is real.
2. *Laboratory test markets*, in which the choice situation is 'recreated' for potential purchasers with mock store shelving and product displays, including facings if required. Here, purchasing is semi-real, with respondents being given cash or tokens to exchange for products.
3. *Calibrated tests*, in which fully branded in-home product use tests are used to expose prospective purchasers to the advertising and the real product, and in which purchase-related questions are asked and assessed using empirically derived weights. Here, actual purchasing is seldom used.

Each of these then represents a trade-off between the *realism* of the task for respondents, and the *risk* to the manufacturer.

10.5.1 Mini-test markets

The controlled nature of these panel operations removed many of the problems associated with regional test markets. However, because the purchasing patterns of individual consumers could be monitored in a way that was not possible with simple sales testing, it was possible to distinguish two important diagnostic measures:

1. The proportion of potential buyers who bought the product at all in a given period (*penetration*).
2. The proportion of buyers who went on to buy again (*repeat purchasers*).

These became important diagnostic measures for manufacturers, because they indicated the source of any problems with the product. Thus, if the product's poor performance was the result of poor penetration, then more attention could be given to the concept, packaging and communication strategy. Alternatively, if poor levels of repeat purchasing were encountered, the problem lay at the door of the product itself in use. (It could also be both of these.)

However, in the early days, a problem that remained was that of the long period that a test took, since it was judged necessary to allow a considerable period before repeat-purchase rates stabilised in order to make an accurate prediction. A considerable amount of effort was made, therefore, to predict the final level of repeat purchasing from the early indications. From the work carried out (primarily by Parfitt and Collins on the Attwood consumer panel), a consistent model was developed to predict brand shares. In the event, however, these methods became sufficiently accurate for other *ad hoc* methods to be used to estimate the key parameters, with a huge impact on reduced costs of the system, and shortened timings. Additionally, there was a growing need to obtain market potential feedback from earlier on in the NPD process, possibly single concepts only, and storyboards for advertising communication. With this, the mini-test markets fell into decline. The last major operation, the RBL mini-test market, has now closed in favour of other methods.

10.5.2 *Laboratory test markets*

The aim of these methods is to expose respondents to competitive market arrays, and to emulate a choice process in which they are commonly provided with actual money or tokens in which to purchase product.

A good early example of this can be seen with the Assessor model.[10] In this, respondents are invited to a simulated shop in a central location, in which the test product is displayed alongside the rest of the market. A constant sum preference (CSP) procedure is used to measure the shares of preference for established brands which they can see (alongside advertising, if required). They are then introduced to the test product (including advertising), stated at a given price, and given a coupon with a face value that would enable them to purchase any of the items on display. Then, irrespective of whether they chose the test brand, they are given it to be used in-home for a fixed trial period. After this, respondents are then re-interviewed, and their preferences measured again with CSP, except that this time the new product is included.

From this data, two models of choice (i.e. brand) share are constructed:

1. A preference model (derived from the constant sum preference).
2. A trial-repeat model, along the lines of Parfitt and Collins' approach (1968), which uses measures of trial and repeat purchase. Trial is measured by the observed number who chose the test product, but can also include estimates of sampling. This is qualified by input estimates of awareness and availability (distribution), which are assumed to be independent. Repeat purchase is measured by a Markov process, which is effectively the new brand's share of subsequent purchases in the category among triallists.

The two models are then compared. If they are consistent, all is well. If not, typically, the trial-repeat model is investigated, and the external inputs re-examined. Generally, sample sizes are chosen to result in 200 or so triallists, although this is difficult to predict in advance (actually, it is one of the reasons for doing the study).

The Sensor model[11] follows a similar procedure, except that a third model is added, the brand/price trade-off method. This model, which is a general tool used in many other areas for the purpose primarily of pricing research, adds another important dimension to the test – that of the ability to gauge the sensitivity of the product to price variations.

The problem with these systems is that they are share based, in that they assume a fixed market of known competition, and that the introduction of the new product will not affect the total size of the market. Volumes can therefore only be calculated by taking the total market, and calculating the appropriate fraction. This makes LTMs difficult to use for innovation products, but also increasingly difficult to use where the nature of the competition is diffuse.

10.5.3 Calibrated tests

In contrast to LTMs, calibrated tests aim to predict volume, rather than share. As such they overcome many of the drawbacks of LTMs and are now, at least in the United Kingdom, the primary market prediction systems in use.

Historically, these are developments of the monadic concept-use product tests that used to be conducted as part of the optimising process in the NPD cycle. These tests are conducted in two stages: a *pre-trial* stage (in which the product in concept form is introduced to the respondent, often in a fixed location), and an in-home recall *post-trial* stage (in which reactions to the product in use are collected). For a full volume prediction, both stages are necessary, and this is normally what is meant by a full STM. However, if only the first stage is used, then a prediction can be made of potential levels of trial for a product, and most of the major systems (e.g. BASES I and MicroTest concept) have this as an option. In fact, there is an increasing tendency to encourage the use of STMs at an earlier point in the NPD process, rather than confirming a 'go/no go' decision right at the end.

In this account of calibrated tests, I will refer to two systems: Bases[12] and MicroTest,[13] since not only are these the principal systems currently in use in the United Kingdom, but they also represent quite different approaches. Both, however, aim to provide the following:

- Sales forecasts in years 1 and 2, and the on-going level thereafter.
- Sales breakdown of levels of trial and repeat purchase (called 'adoption' in the MicroTest terminology).

10.5.4 Bases

The Bases system uses aggregated data, and is therefore a type of 'macro-model'. Respondents are selected according to some criteria, and then shown a concept board bearing a representation of the product, including price (the pack is not shown at this point). Purchase intentions are then obtained on five-point scales. Likely trial is subsequently computed by weighting the points on this scale, taking into account adjustments for the category penetration and rate of growth, and the seasonality. These adjustments are normative, i.e. they are empirically derived from past cases. External estimates of awareness and distribution are also used to compute trial levels.

After a period of trial, respondents are asked for their re-purchase intention, plus other measures for value for money, and overall liking. These three scales are modelled to obtain a value of a first repeat rate, which is then converted using norms (possibly on a country basis) to a long-run weighted repeat-purchase measure.

To compute sales, the number of units purchased is needed, so the question-naire also asks about the degree to which the new product will substitute current products, and their purchasing frequency (which is also adjusted for over-claim using norms).

10.5.5 MicroTest

The MicroTest model works on a completely different principle. Instead of using macro aggregates of purchasing intention so that volumes are computed using averaged data, the modelling works at the individual level, so that the system is of a type known as a 'micro-model'. The advantages of this approach are threefold:

1. Modelling at the individual level (in essence, making a volume prediction for each person in the sample) makes no assumptions about the underlying distributions of the data, and can handle polarised reactions (e.g. where an 'average' score could result from a small number of people who like the product a lot, and a much larger number who are at best indifferent). In principle, it can never be any worse than macro-modelling, and is often much better. These techniques became available with the advent of cheap computing.
2. Individual predictions allow considerably better diagnostics, so that the profile of likely adopters can be established.
3. These systems place less reliance on norms for calibration, since as far as possible the central constructs are self-adjusting. This can be useful where norms are scanty (or do not exist for the product category, country or type of target market), or where they are old.

The fieldwork procedures are similar to those used by the Bases approach, although a wider variety of questions are used as inputs to the model. Central constructs of the MicroTest approach are the following:

1. *Visibility* – or salience in the marketplace of the product, which is taken to be a function of the level of physical distribution achieved, the weight of

advertising used (typically TVRs/GRPs, and share of voice), and the 'heritage' of the brand. This last factor caters for the fact that products launched by major manufacturers, possibly under a house brand, have a higher impact on consumers than novel products with unknown antecedents. These inputs, some from the respondent and some from marketing, are integrated using a separate model.

2. *Trial* – which is modelled as being a function of the visibility achieved, but also in terms of the appeal of the concept. The key questionnaire inputs here are the attitude towards price, and the propensity to purchase ('buy' scale). Another issue taken into account is the innate experimentalism of the respondent, as measured by his/her claimed use of new products recently launched, as well as his/her perception of the 'risk' associated with purchasing in this product category.

3. *Adoption* – which is taken in this model to be a somewhat stricter definition than simple repeat purchase, since it refers to the probability of incorporating a product into a consumer's repertoire on a long-term basis, and not just the initial period of experimentation. This is essentially the result of the degree to which the expectations created by the concept have been met in the product during test, as measured by 'pay' and 'buy' scales. At the same time, an adjustment is made for the respondent's innate *fidelity* towards new products, or the degree to which they are not simply experimental 'gadflies' – always in search of the novel.

These concepts are integrated at the individual level, and result in the computation of probabilities both of trial and adoption for the individual. However, before summing the results and projecting to the marketplace, they are adjusted by each person's *weight of purchase*, which in competitive markets is taken to be his/her frequency of purchase, and the average amount bought on those occasions.

The integration of these sub-models is shown in Figure 10.4. All calibrated

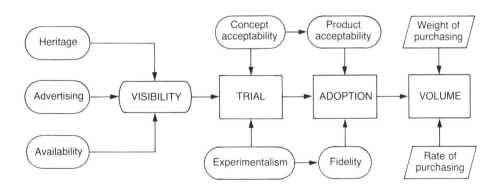

Figure 10.4   The MicroTest model

tests require marketing inputs, both for estimating trial levels, but also for projecting the results of the test to the market universe. Typically, marketing input would include:

Universe
- Market size, in terms of numbers of households, or individuals
- Seasonality
- Regionality
- Category development

Marketing strategy
- Build of awareness (e.g. quarterly)
- Build of all commodity distribution (sterling) on a quarterly basis
- Promotional events
- Competitive activity
- Likely out of stock levels, if any

10.6 Handling price

It is a characteristic of calibrated tests that they operate in a monadic way – a single sample tests a single offering, and this must therefore include a single price. However, a common marketing conundrum is that we would really like to know how volume would vary with price – after all, it may be more profitable to go for a smaller brand share, but with bigger margins, particularly if production costs are constrained, or non-linear. Strictly speaking, therefore, a number of test cells should be conducted if price itself is under investigation, but this could be a costly exercise. In order to avoid this, sometimes links are made with other models. One example of this is using the brand/price trade-off method, which can be used at the recall stage (post-trial). This system is useful insofar that it gives us a demand curve for price points. Using this system, and calibrating two end-points with test cells predicting volume, we can 'read off' the likely volumes of intermediate price points as shown in Figure 10.5.

One word of warning with all STMs. Nearly all simulated test market systems are described in terms of a single, new product being launched in a well-developed market. Life is more complicated than that, and a majority of recent NPD launches in the United Kingdom have involved range extensions, line extensions or even re-launches of existing products. These can be coped with by STMs, but they normally require some amendment for particular situations. Equally, there are important differences in the way that 'difficult' markets are modelled – for example, the universe of mothers for baby products is a constantly moving one!

How reliable are the results? In many cases, subsequent validation (where possible) has shown them to be surprisingly accurate: 80 per cent of tests falling plus or minus 20 per cent, and a good proportion within 10 per cent. The overall conclusion, therefore, is that compared with the other costs involved in NPD, the reduction in risk is well worth the effort.

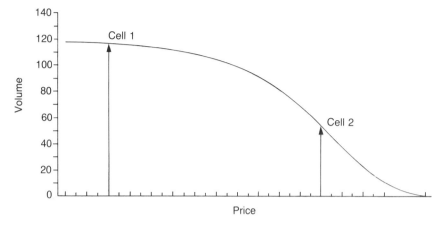

Figure 10.5   The brand/price trade-off demand curve

Notes

1. Except at the extreme. For example, the average purchase cycle of white-goods is around eight years.
2. Surely an example of poor market research.
3. Originally developed by the advertising agency BBDO.
4. So said because the number of possible combinations rises exponentially when the number of variables increases – hence 'explosion'.
5. At least, configurations made up from the features studied in the exercise.
6. Developed by Research International in 1990.
7. Multi-dimensional scaling, and correspondence analysis, are examples of this sort of map.
8. Developed by Frost International.
9. Developed by Research International.
10. Developed by Management Decision Sciences.
11. Developed by Research International.
12. Developed by Burke Marketing Research, Inc.
13. Developed by Research International.

References and further reading

Davis, J. (1986) 'Market testing and experimentation', in R. Worcester and J. Downham (eds) *Consumer Marketing Research Handbook*, Third Revised Edition, Amsterdam: ESOMAR/North-Holland.

Mahajan, V. and Peterson, R. (1985) 'Models for innovation diffusion', Sage University Paper Series on Quantitative Applications in the Social Sciences, 07–048, Beverly Hills and London: Sage Publications.

Morgan, R. (1987) 'Brand/Price Trade-Off – where we stand now', EMAC/ESOMAR Symposium on Macro and Micro Modelling, Tutzing, October.

Morgan, R. (1990) 'Modelling: conjoint analysis', in R. Birn, P. Hague and P. Vangelder (eds) *A Handbook of Market Research Techniques*, London: Kogan Page.

Parfitt, J. H. and Collins, B. J. K. (1968) 'The use of consumer panels for brand share prediction', *Journal of Marketing Research*, vol. 5, no. 2.

Wind, Y., Mahajan, V. and Cardozo, R. (1984) *New Product Forecasting*, Lexington, MA: D. C. Heath.

CHAPTER 11

Segmenting markets

11.1 Why segment?

To 'segment' is to divide into parts. In marketing, to segment is to separate from a population the individual units which are then classified into homogeneous groups according to chosen characteristics. Market segmentation involves the classification of consumer types; it is, to borrow a phrase, the deliberate putting of 'birds of a feather' in a 'flock together'.

In marketing research, it is necessary to identify the relevant characteristics of market segments or groups of consumer in that the assessment of their demand, consumption patterns and buying potential for certain types of product and service can be arrived at. The research strategy aims to do the following:

1. Locate a new opportunity, a 'gap' or unfulfilled (or only partly fulfilled) need in a market.
2. Position a brand (or brands) *vis-à-vis* competitive brands so that an organisation's brand is favourably placed within the product field.

A market researcher is likely to approach design of a segmentation study from one of two angles:

1. Collection and analysis of data relating to the habits, attitudes and needs of consumers with a view to sorting consumers into homogeneous groups differentiated by their lifestyles and buyer behaviour (consumer typology).
2. Collection and analysis of data relating to the products/services/brands available in the market focusing on how these are perceived by consumers. The intention is to sort the brands into groups of those with similar attributes as perceived by consumers so that a market researcher can identify the appeal or unique selling proposition (USP) for a product (for the purpose of product differentiation).

By meeting the requirements of those whose wants are not being satisfied or by concentrating marketing effort on a particular segment market the manufacturer can expect to create a loyalty sufficiently strong to counteract the appeal of competition brands. In addition, by consistently focusing effort on a target segment, a satisfactory relationship between marketing costs and sales revenue can be achieved.

It is therefore necessary to develop a product of service to which both consumers and distributors respond. Research funds are laid out with maximum cost-effect when the target segment and its wants have been established, for it is then possible to work to an unequivocal brief specifying both of the following:

- The kind of people to be asked to discuss ideas about a product, e.g. for concept testing and to take part in experiments to help determine final choices.
- The criteria to be used in the design of concept tests and experiments, and in the interpretation of results.

11.2 Segmentation variables

Variables used in domestic markets. In the search for a target segment we consider the ways in which variables in the market vary. These variables are summarised in Box 11.1. They fall into two broad categories:

1. Variables which are descriptive, e.g. geographic, cultural, demographic and 'behaviour in the product field' groups.
2. Variables which are explanatory, e.g. social and psychological groups.

Sections 11.3 and 11.4 present the descriptions of the main types of classification and explanatory variables which are more commonly used in segmenting domestic markets.

Variables used in organisation markets. The geographical locations, cultural characteristics, demographic distribution of population and behaviour of customers are of importance to organisations in locating and estimating market potential for their products and services. Organisational markets can be segmented according to type of activity and making into product output. The geographical location and size of the organisation, e.g. share capitalisation, sales turnover and number of employees can be included as segmentation variables. The structure, composition and behavioural characteristics of decision-making units are also important considerations for market segmentation purposes in understanding the nature of demand and how, when and why buying decisions are made by profit or non-profit organisations within specific market segments.

Box 11.1 Segmentation variables

Variables used in domestic markets

Classification variables:
Geographic
Cultural
Demographic
  Social class
  Income
  Age
  Terminal education age (TEA)
  Family life-cycle
Behaviour in the product field
  Heavy, medium, light purchasers
  Brand loyalists, switchers

Explanatory variables
Social-psychological
  Innovators . . . late adopters   }
  Reference groups   Academic origin
  Personality, standardised inventories }

Principal benefit sought   }
Psychographic/lifestyle groups   Marketing origin
Product differentiation   }

Variables used in non-domestic (organisational) markets
Includes the use of variables for domestic markets.
Activity and product output + e.g. by Standard Industrial Classification codes
Organisational buying behaviour e.g. decision-making units

11.3 Classification variables

11.3.1 Geographical and cultural

Both in home and overseas markets, geographical and cultural variables are often related together. In an advanced and wealthy economy, regional differences become blurred as a result of increased mobility and communications brought about by modern advances in transport and telecommunications. Despite this, cultural differences brought about by different language, religion, race and social behaviour remain significant considerations in understanding the markets and marketing environments of countries. For example, ethnic groups can be geo-graphically concentrated and culturally distinct and can therefore represent significant market segments for food, toiletries, cosmetics, air travel and packaged holidays.

Geodemographic systems relate population characteristics to the geographical distribution of population and the 1991 national census provides a rich database. The CACI's ACORN classification system described below uses data allowed to be accessed from the 1991 census database to build its fifty-four ACORN types. As described by CACI:

> As many as 79 different data items, carefully screened from some 9,000 items produced by the Census authorities for each of the 150,000 small geographical areas covering Britain, are incorporated in the ACORN classification.
>
> This means that all the significant factors – such as age, sex, marital status, occupation, economic position, education, home ownership and car ownership – are covered to give a very full and comprehensive picture of socio-economic status. (1993:3)

The purpose behind the range and detail offered in geodemographic analysis is to enable marketers to target people who are most likely to use their goods and services from the classification database and avoid those people who are least-likely users. For example, households in the F 'striving' category have much lower disposable incomes compared to the wealthy achievers in the A 'thriving' category, see Table 11.1. The 'strivers' are classified into social class, C_2 to DE grades while the 'thrivers' are socially graded from the AB to ABC_1.

The competing systems such as those from CACI (ACORN), CCN (MOSAIC), Pinpoint (Finpin) and CDMS (SuperProfiles) all relate population characteristics as revealed in the census to the enumeration districts from which the data are recorded. Statistical data reduce this mass of data to meaningful clusters. These systems vary in the census and other variables fed into their computer programs, in the statistical procedures used to cluster these, in the number of residential population types emerging from the statistical treatment and in the descriptions attached to these types. A comprehensive description of the MOSAIC geodemog-raphic system is provided by CCN in Chapter 12.

11.3.2 Demographic

Social class (or social grade). This occupation-based system of classification remains a much-used standard for both market and social research. The occupation-based system in common use is that used in the continuous random-sampling procedure followed for the National Readership Survey (NRS). The class categories derived from this are summarised in Box 11.2.

Table 11.1 Breakdown example of the ACORN targeting classification

6 Acorn categories and % UK populations	17 ACORN groups		54 Neighbourhood types	Corresponding social grades represent national average
A: Thriving 19%	1.	Wealthy, Achievers, Suburban Areas	5	AB, ABC_1
	2.	Affluent Greys, Rural Communities	2	ABC_2D
	3.	Prosperous Pensioners, Retirement Areas	2	ABC_2D
B: Expanding 10.4%	4.	Affluent Executives, Family Areas	3	ABC_1
	5.	Well-off Workers, Family Areas	3	ABC_1, C_1C_2
C: Rising 9%	6.	Affluent Urbanites, Town and City Areas	3	AB, ABC_1
	7.	Prosperous Professionals, Metropolitan Areas	2	ABC_1
	8.	Better-Off Executives, Inner City Areas	5	ABC_1
D: Settling 24.5%	9.	Comfortable Middle Agers, Mature Home-Owning Areas	4	ABC_1, C_1, ABC
	10.	Skilled Workers, Home-Owning Areas	3	C_2, C_1, C_2, C_2DE
E: Aspiring 13.9%	11.	New Home Owners, Mature Communities	3	C_2DE
	12.	White-Collar Workers, Better-Off Multi-Ethnic Areas	3	C_1
F: Striving 23.1%	13.	Older People, Less Prosperous Areas	2	C_2DE
	14.	Council Estate Residents, Better-Off Homes	6	C_2DE
	15.	Council Estate Residents, High Unemployment	3	DE, C_2DE
	16.	Council Estate Residents, Greatest Hardship	2	DE
	17.	People in Multi-Ethnic, Low-Income Areas	3	DE

Source: Adapted from CACI ACORN (1993), *ACORN User Guide*.

Box 11.2 Social-class classification

Social Grade	Social Status	Chief income earner's (CIE) Occupation
A	Upper middle class	Higher managerial, administrative or professional
B	Middle class	Intermediate managerial, administrative or profes-
C	Lower middle class	sional
C_2	Skilled working class	Supervisory, clerical, junior administrative or pro-
D	Working class	fessional
E	Those at lower levels of subsistence	Skilled manual workers
		Semi-skilled and unskilled manual workers
		State pensioners, widows, casual and lowest-grade earners

The social grade of an informant is normally based on the occupation of the Chief Income Earner of his or her household; if the Chief Income Earner is retired it is based on the Chief Income Earner's former occupation. Where there is no such occupation, or information about it is unobtainable, the assessment of social grade is based on environmental factors such as the type of dwelling, the amenities in the home, the presence of domestic help, and so on. Income level is not used to define social grade.

Prior to July 1992, social grade was based on the head of household or, if the head of household was not in full-time employment, or was retired, widowed or a pensioner with an income of not more than the equivalent of the basic pension obtaining at the time of interview, then the social grade of the informant was based on the occupation of the chief wage earner (CWE) of his or her household.

Source: National Readership Surveys Ltd (1994) London.

Income. Income, and more especially disposable income, is a common classification variable used. To overcome the reluctance of respondents to give the information, respondents are asked to point to a figure on a show card, or a questionnaire on a computer monitor. The main difficulty is in establishing what disposable incomes are as the standard question shows:

> Which of these comes closest to your total take-home income, from all sources, that is after deducting income tax, national insurance, pension schemes and so on? SHOW CARD

And what about mortgage, and commercial insurance repayments? It is necessary to keep the annual, monthly and weekly lists of earnings on the show card up to date. In many surveys the data, e.g. for diaries, relate to buying for a family by the housewife. Here, definition of income is further complicated by the fact that family income often derives from more than one wage packet. A full accurate investigation requires a whole questionnaire with documented cross-checks.

Age. This is an important discriminator in many consumer markets. It is a useful check on the representatives of samples, for the age distribution of the population is well documented. Two methods of establishing the respondent's age are in common use; a straight question – 'What was your age last birthday?' – or by means of a show card with age brackets. As with income, this may reduce reluctance to answer the question. However, there may well be respondents over the age of sixteen attending 'day release' or part-time vocational courses or mature students returning to higher education within a sample. So supplementary questions on education and training can be necessary.

Terminal education age (TEA). Terminal education age, type of school or college attended and examinations passed have gained in significance as segmentation variables. The standard TEA question is 'How old were you when you finished your *full-time* education?

Family life cycle and life-stage classification. With or without marriage, the family remains a basic social unit in many countries. Demand for many products and services is related to the stage reached in the family life cycle. These stages are commonly defined as:

Young	Young single, no children	Young couple, youngest child under six	Young couple, youngest child six or +	Older couple, with children 18+ at home	Older couple, no children at home	Older single

The life-stage classification mentioned above under social class, takes account of occupational database or employment in the family as well as the family's composition (number of occupants, age, sex, ethnic grouping) increasing the marketing relevance of this segmentation variable.

The geographical, cultural and demographic variables are necessarily used to locate and delimit the social-psychological groups derived from attitudinal lifestyle and life-stage studies. Most segmentation approaches involve the multi-variate computer analysis of data.

11.3.3 Behaviour in the product field

Given the adequate data, users of products/services can be divided into 'heavy'-, 'medium'- and 'light'- user categories according to amount bought and frequency of buying. This kind of analysis is best based on trend data derived from consumer panels, whether the data are recorded in diaries or by means of regular audits. We need to remember that those who buy the product are not always those who use it, and to distinguish between data based on household panels (e.g. the Attwood consumer panel and the television consumer audit) and data based on panels of individuals (e.g. the TGI's diary panel). Apart from 'heavy', 'medium' and 'light' buying it is also possible to sort the individuals on panels into 'loyalists' and 'switchers' according to how their buying moves between brands. All these 'buying-behaviour' groups can be described in geographic and demographic terms.

11.4 Explanatory variables

The segmentation variables considered so far are important for 'measurability' and 'accessibility'. They help to define the size of segments and how best to reach them through the media. All these variables are, however, descriptive: they do not explain behaviour. We can observe associations between the demographic variables and those relating to behaviour in the product field in order to infer reasons for the behaviour of consumers.

11.4.1 Social and psychological

The procedure developed and tested by anthropologists, sociologists and, more particularly, psychologists might be applied to the segmentation of consumer markets in the following ways:

- Dividing the population into innovators (2.5 per cent), early adopters (13.5 per cent), early majority (34 per cent), late majority (34 per cent) and late adopters (16 per cent) following the 'diffusion of innovations' theory.
- Establishing the kind of individuals with whom consumers sought to identify themselves following the 'reference group' theory.
- Using psychologists' standardised personality inventories, i.e. standard lists of attitude and behaviour questions designed to sort individuals into homogeneous personality groups.

11.4.2 Principal benefit sought

The 'benefit' approach to segmentation focuses on product or brand use but introduces psychological variables into the segmentation study. Consumers are grouped according to the principal benefit they seek when they make buying decisions. Table 11.2 reproduces Russell Haley's benefit segmentation of the toothpaste market. Haley (1968) pioneered the 'principal benefit' idea and this is now a classic example. Michael Thomas (1988) commented on benefit segmentation as:

The goal of benefit segmentation is to find a group of people all seeking the same benefits from a product. Each segment is identified by the benefits being sought. It is not unusual for various segments to share individual benefits. The major factor is the amount of importance each segment places on each benefit.

The 'benefit' approach to segmentation is particularly relevant to market planning for existing brands. It effectively describes, and begins to explain, the branded product field as it is. Haley's analysis takes note of segmentation variables other than benefit sought, as Table 11.2 shows, but the criterion for segmentation is principal benefit sought. As Haley (1968) points out, 'the benefits which people are seeking in consuming a given product are the basic reasons for the existence of true market segments', but consumers do not always find it easy to define the benefits they seek or to give true answers. As an example, toothpaste producers are able to use benefit segmentations to launch new brands with perceived benefits such as Crest toothpaste by Procter & Gamble building on the presentation of tooth decay with its anti-cavity protection for a unique selling proposition.

11.4.3 Psychographics or lifestyle classification

In a segmentation study, attitude statements forming the inventory (or battery) of scales are elicited from group discussions, depth interviews or Kelly 'personal construct' interviews. As a general rule the statements are put to consumers in the form of either Likert-type, or semantic differential scales, depending on whether the segmentation study is designed to type consumers or to group products according to the ways in which consumers perceive them. For example, respondents would be asked to express their attitudes towards the following:

- A relevant activity, such as leisure, feeding the family, housekeeping, shaving, insuring against risks.
- Types of product, brand, service which are available for carrying out the stated activity, that is, which were the ones that were known about, and of those used, which performed best for the stated activity or activities.

A segmentation study will necessarily include questions of a demographic and product-use nature as well as the attitude battery (Rothman 1989). The range of questions will depend on how far it is intended to explore the lifestyle of those in the market.

A company embarking on a segmentation study is likely to have a good deal of descriptive data on file and to know what kind of consumers to invite to group discussions or depth interviews. Taped recordings are transcribed, consumer statements sorted into groups according to topic, and attitude scales constructed. There may be sixty to one hundred attitude statements on a questionnaire.

Table 11.2 Russell Haley's benefit segmentation of the toothpaste market

Segment name	The sensory segment	The sociables	The worriers	The independent segment
Principal benefit sought: product	Flavour, appearance of teeth	Brightness, prevention	Decay	Price
Demographic strengths:	Children	Teens, young people	Large families	Men
Special behavioural characteristics	Users of spearmint flavoured toothpaste	Smokers	Heavy users	Heavy users
Brands disproportionately favoured	Colgate, Stripe	Macleans plus White Ultra Brite	Crest	Brands on sale*
Personality characteristics	High self-involvement	High sociability	High hypochondriasis	High-autonomy
Lifestyle characteristics	Hedonistic	Active	Conservative	Value-oriented

*i.e. on offer.
Source: Haley, R. I. (1968) 'Benefit segmentation; a decision-oriented research tool', *Journal of Marketing*, July, pp. 30–5.

11.5 Piloting a questionnaire and factor analysis

With a limited number of attitude statements it would be possible to establish associations between consumer responses by drawing up a correlation matrix, but it would clearly be difficult to 'read' a 60×60 correlation matrix (scale batteries can run to more than sixty items). We therefore need the means to deal with the interrelationship of many variables quickly by using the computer. Statistical techniques which simultaneously examine the relationships between many variables are known as multi-variate statistical procedures.

Provided it is done on an adequate scale (say 200 calls) the pilot test gives us the opportunity to use the multi-variate technique called *factor analysis* to reduce the battery of attitude statements to a small number of factors each made up of a group of highly correlated scales representing a particular dimension of the overall attitude. Box 11.3 gives an example in which four factors were found to account for most of the variability shown in the answers of respondents to questions about saving.

Box 11.3

Exploratory stage: Depth interviews generated a list of some twenty-five attitude statements.

Pilot stage: These statements were put to 130 members of the public in the form of scales, and weights were attached to their responses.

Factor analysis: Multi-variate analysis for the scores derived from the responses of the sample to individual statements yielded four factors. Each of these factors represents a different dimension of the overall attitude towards saving:

Factor 1. Temperamental difficulty in saving (e.g. 'I have never been able to save').

Factor 2. Sense of solidity (e.g. 'If you've got a bit of money saved you are not so likely to be pushed around').

Factor 3. Concern with independence (e.g. 'I hate to feel I might have to ask someone for financial help').

Factor 4. Feeling of financial security (e.g. 'I feel it's unlikely I shall have any financial emergencies in the near future').

Let us consider Factor 1 more closely. There is found to be an association with five attitude statements compared with four for Factors 2 and 3 and three for Factor 4.

Factor 1
a) I have never been able to save.
b) Unless you have some specific reason to save, it's better to spend and enjoy it.
c) I believe in enjoying my money now and letting the future take care of itself.
d) I don't feel it's necessary to save just now.
e) I can't help spending all I earn.

11.6 Cluster analysis

The objective of a survey using cluster analysis is to locate homogeneous clusters of consumers, or of products as perceived by consumers. The clusters must do two things:

1. Fulfil the three conditions for market segments of 'measurability, accessibility and substantiality'. Measurability means that the size of segments can be estimated or established. Accessibility infers that it should be possible to distribute and communicate to the target market segments. Substantiality means that the segments should be large enough with sufficient demand to generate the desired profits.
2. Be sufficiently distinct one from another to offer choices in marketing strategy and marketing mix to differentiate products for specific segments. A large sample, say 1,500, and the multi-variate procedure of cluster analysis can be applied. While factor analysis examines correlations between variables across respondents, cluster analysis looks for correlations between respondents across the segmentation variables. The cluster characteristics will depend on the nature and range of the questions put to respondents (see Box 11.4). As with all survey work it is necessary to develop hypotheses before going into the field.

It would be helpful if the statistical procedure were to show a definitive association between the level of response to one particular attitude statement and membership of a particular cluster. In practice, it requires the responses recorded in answers to something like twelve statements to establish the membership of one of four or five psychographic clusters. If the psychographic questions produce psychographic types who show consistent results over time in terms of buying behaviour, or response to advertising campaigns, the reliability of the procedure used to type consumers is confirmed. Having determined attitude similarities, the groups can then be analysed against demographics, media and brands to produce an overall 'perspective'.

Box 11.4

Let us assume that we are clustering drinkers according to their use of, and attitudes towards, alcoholic drinks. Qualitative work at the exploratory stage may have suggested that there are at least four types of drinker: social, compulsive, restorative and self-compensating. Unless our questionnaire includes items which make it possible for respondents to reveal these proclivities, cluster analysis will neither prove, nor disprove, this hypothesis.

11.7 Usage and attitude studies

Research methods for usage and attitude studies generally include qualitative orientations, e.g. focus-group discussions, in-depth interviews, consumer diaries, observation studies and quantifiable results for analysis derived from rating scales, scoring and rank preferences by consumers.

Beliefs about products (e.g. brand awareness and the needs of consumers built around product use, purchase size and frequency, loyalty, prices paid, and so on) are examined in terms of the attitudinal and demographic characteristics of consumers. Respondents (as consumers) contribute to the research effort by making their preferences known through discriminating on product attributes. Product typologies on groups can be built around product characteristics with similar attributes which are deemed to be 'successful'.

Usage and attitude studies require:

1. Detailed coverage of products or brands to enable important differences between products or between brands to be identified.
2. Briefing respondents so that they understand the product or brand attributes on which they are to rate them.

11.7.1 RI natural grouping

A technique used by Research International (RI) is presented in Figure 11.1. Respondents are given various stimuli, e.g. cards with brand names or photos of products, which they separate into groups of similar items, repeating the procedure until there is no clear differentiation between the last product sub-groups.

As illustrated in Figure 11.1, faced with fifteen different products (a–o) respondents can divide those with the closest similarities into two main groups, in this case 'a b g h l m o' and 'c d e f i j k p'. Respondents' comments on why and how an allocation into groups is made are recorded at each split. Further sub-divisions occur until the respondents can no longer discriminate between the final sub-groups of varying sizes (Research International 1994).

Brands are seen by consumers to be much the same; product positioning on brand-mapping methods can help consumers to isolate or discriminate on key aspects between brands. It is possible to move brands apart so that perceived differences are maximised – price, packaging and advertising being brought into play with, possibly, product modification and a complete re-launch. If consumer perceptions of the deal carry conviction, the position of the ideal brand may suggest ways in which an existing brand might be modified in formulation and/or presentation.

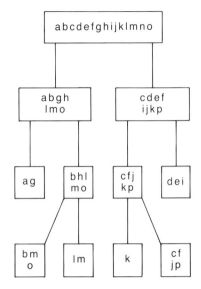

Source: Research International (1994) 'Usage and attitude studies', Position Paper 1.

Figure 11.1   Developing attributes or product groups

11.7.2 Brand mapping

At the pilot stage attitude statements are more commonly put to respondents in the form of semantic differentials than as Likert-type scales. As in consumer typing, results of the pilot are likely to be factor analysed in order to extract the most influential attitude dimensions and to reduce the criterion variables to a manageable number.

At the survey stage the main difference comes in the way in which the results are presented. In place of descriptions of consumer types we can focus attention on brand maps. It is easy to visualise brand positioning based on consumer response to one semantic differential scale. Let us assume there is a soft-drinks market containing seven brands, A–G. Consumers have been asked to rate these brands on a seven-point scale running from 'refreshing' to 'cloying'. A mean score is computed for each brand and the positions are plotted on the continuum, refreshing to cloying. If no two brands scored equally on this dimension we might get a result like this:

refreshing   A F   E G D   B C   cloying

If we had asked consumers to rate their ideal brand on the same dimension, the result might have been as follows:

refreshing   I A F   E G D   B C   cloying

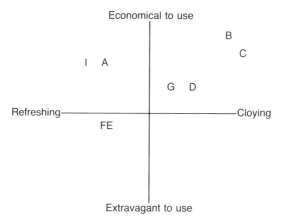

Figure 11.2 Brand positioning

The scores for the seven named brands represent their distance from the ideal. When questions related to specific attributes are asked about the ideal brand as well as about available brands, the respondent's answers are more meaningful than when a general question is asked about 'your ideal soft drink'. It is also a simple matter to plot responses to two semantic differentials assuming 'economical to use' and 'extravagant to use' for the dimensions (see Figure 11.2).

Let us assume that F and E are two brands marketed by the same company, and that strategic planning decisions are being based on responses to these two semantic differential scales. There is a clear case for re-positioning one of these two brands which consumers perceive as much the same. The re-positioning might be achieved by making one brand more economical than the other, say, by moving F closer to I, the ideal. A more 'value-for-money' image could be attached to the brand by modifying the formulation, changing the type of container used, or altering the advertising campaign (a re-launch if all three measures were taken). Figure 11.2 shows that brand A is in a strong position because of its closeness to the ideal as perceived by consumers; B scores on 'economical to use' but is seen to be 'cloying'.

In some product fields 'extravagance' can be a plus quality but perhaps not for soft drinks. Theoretically, there is a gap in this market for a cloying rather than a refreshing product which tends to be extravagant in use; but it will be a long way from the ideal. The gap is a 'non-starter' and in some circumstances this may in itself be a significant finding. In evaluating responses to attitude statements, it is necessary to take account of the fact that some attributes will count far more with individual respondents than others.

When collecting data about consumers' perceptions of products, services or brands it is essential to establish the consumer's demographic characteristics and product experience. This is because:

● The perceptual map of ABC_1 consumers may differ from that of C_2DE consumers.

- The perceptions of 'loyal' users of a brand may well differ from those of 'switchers'.
- Demographic and user groups may vary significantly in their perceptions of the ideal.
- Knowledge of the demographic characteristics of target consumers is essential for media planning.

It is possible to chart the position of brands, taking account of interaction between all the criterion variables, and for the map to show the following:

- Whether a company's existing brands are competing with each other.
- Whether there is a gap in the market waiting to be filled.

11.8 Conclusion

A segmentation study carries application of the marketing concept an important step forward; the outcome of the segmentation study is a strategic plan focused on the declared needs of a target in the market which has been carefully defined. This applies whether the study is made with the object of initiating a new product or of improving the positioning of one or more brands already in the product field, and both research approaches ('consumer typology' and 'product differentiation') yield the required data about consumers, their needs and perceptions. The segmentation study provides the blueprint for the development, or improvement, of a brand; the product as perceived by consumers being an integrated mixture of formulation, packaging, price and communication.

References

CACI (1993) CACI User Guides.
Haley, R. E. (1968) 'Benefit segmentation: a decision-oriented research tool', *Journal of Marketing*, July, pp. 30–35.
Research International (1994) 'Usage and attitude studies', Position Paper 1.
Rothman, J. (ed.) (1989) 'Special issue on geodemographics', *Journal of the Market Research Society*, Jan., vol. 31, no. 1.
Thomas, M. (1988) 'Market segmentation', *The Quarterly Review of Marketing*, Autumn.

Further reading

Green, P. and Krieger, A. (1993) 'A simple approach to target market advertising strategy', *JMRS*, vol. 35, no. 2, April, pp. 161–70.

Keegan, W., Moriarty, S. and Duncan, T. (1992) *Marketing*, Englewood Cliffs, NJ: Prentice Hall, pp. 267–89 (on market segmentation).

McDaniel, C. and Gates, R. (1993) *Contemporary Marketing Research* (USA: West Publishing Company), pp. 635–43 (on cluster and factor analysis).

Assignments

1. (a) What segmentation procedure(s) would you adopt when seeking to locate an opportunity for a new or modified product/service in the following fields:
   i) domestic laundry equipment;
   ii) packaged holidays;
   iii) cooking-oil;
   iv) car accessories.
   (b) How would you collect and process the required data?
   (c) How would you apply the results of your segmentation study?
2. (a) In what ways does the application of multi-variate statistical treatment of data collected in segmentation studies further the development of marketing plans?
   (b) How may the data be treated and to what marketing ends?
3. Does the use of these statistical techniques:
   (a) diminish the scope for using human judgement; or
   (b) enhance it?
4. Discuss the extent of the contribution to segmentation studies made by developments in information technology.

CHAPTER 12

Geodemographic profiling: MOSAIC and EuroMOSAIC

Nicholas Evans and Richard Webber

12.1 Introduction

The classification of consumers is a key issue for marketers because it enables target audiences to be defined. Once target audiences are defined in terms of market segments, it is possible to select those media that are most cost-effective in reaching them. Furthermore, it is also possible to identify local markets containing the largest numbers of the target audience.

Consumers are classified in several ways: on the basis of 'personal' demographics such as age and income; according to values and attitudes (psychographics); and on the basis of their behaviour (behaviour graphics).

Geodemographic classifications group consumers together on the basis of the types of neighbourhood in which they live. Neighbourhoods that are similar across a wide range of demographic measures will offer similar potential across most products, brands, services and media.

12.2 The benefit of geodemographics

Classifying consumers according to the neighbourhoods in which they live has a number of advantages over classifications based purely on personal details.

Coverage: Many organisations have very limited information on their customers, but as a minimum typically have name and address details. Geodemographic segments exist for every postcode in Great Britain, enabling all consumers to be classified whether they are customers, survey respondents or a name on a mailing-list.

Flexibility: Geodemographic classification systems can be applied to different types and sources of information. In this way they act as a common bridge between databases and activities which could not otherwise be related to each other. For example, they have been used to relate customers to mailing-response rates, attitudes to credit and their social values.

Speed: Classifying people by neighbourhood is quick, easy and inexpensive. Market research surveys, while more specific, are time consuming and costly.

Modelling: Geodemographic segments are homogeneous, such that two neighbourhoods of the same type will have broadly similar potential for any product wherever they occur. This provides a good basis for estimating local market opportunity.

Mapping: Retail organisations in particular often need to view the spatial distribution of their customers or potential markets. Neighbourhood classifications lend themselves to many forms of mapping and local area reporting.

12.3 The construction of geodemographic segments

Geodemographic classification systems exist for most countries in Western Europe and North America and Australia. The size of neighbourhood classified varies from 15 households on average in Great Britain to 800 in Sweden. The type of information used to classify neighbourhoods also varies but may include statistics from the following: the census; postal address files; electoral registers; consumer credit databases; personal registers; directors; mail-order purchases; market research interviews; car registrations; retail accessibility. Box 12.1 illustrates the mix of data sources used to build the Great Britain MOSAIC postcode classification system.

Cluster analysis is used to define a set of 'clusters' of neighbourhoods that are broadly similar across a wide range of different demographic data. Descriptive labels for each cluster are developed by examining their characteristics (e.g. Ageing Professionals) and each one is assigned to a smaller number of readily distinguishable groups.

In Great Britain, 80 separate measures were used to define 52 distinct MOSAIC types which were organised into twelve cluster groups.

On the basis of its postcode, each Great Britain residential address is allocated a MOSAIC code between 1 and 52. For example:

Postcode:	N6 5RZ
Grid reference – Easting:	528600
Grid reference – Northing:	187900
MOSAIC type:	34 (Chattering classes)
MOSAIC group:	8 (Stylish singles)

Box 12.1 Data sources used to build MOSAIC

Census statistics
- housing
- socio-economic data
- household and age

Demographic data
- age
- household composition
- population movement

Retail data
- accessibility

Financial data
- directors
- consumer searches
- county court judgements

Household data
- address type

12.4 MOSAIC profiling of customers

The distribution of population in Great Britain across the twelve MOSAIC groups is shown in Table 12.1. MOSAIC codes can be appended to customer files by using the postcode. This enables a distribution of customers by MOSAIC to be determined.

The first percentage column on Table 12.2 shows the MOSAIC distribution of an 'up market' customer file (for the purpose of illustration, the exact product is not important). A comparison of the Great Britain and customer distribution identifies which MOSAIC groups are over- and under-represented within the customer file.

Indices identify this degree of over- and under-representation; a value of 100 indicates that the MOSAIC proportions in the two distributions are identical. The

Table 12.1 MOSAIC distribution of population in Great Britain

MOSAIC lifestyle groups	%
L1 High-income families	9.9
L2 Suburban semis	11.0
L3 Blue-collar owners	13.0
L4 Low-rise council	14.4
L5 Council flats	6.8
L6 Victorian low status	9.4
L7 Town houses and flats	9.4
L8 Stylish singles	5.2
L9 Independent elders	7.4
L10 Mortgaged families	6.2
L11 Country dwellers	7.0
L12 Institutional areas	0.3

Table 12.2   MOSAIC profile of a customer file

MOSAIC lifestyle groups		File %	GB %	Index (Average = 100)
L1	High-income families	23.4	9.9	236
L2	Suburban semis	18.0	11.0	164
L3	Blue-collar owners	11.9	13.0	92
L4	Low-rise council	6.3	14.4	44
L5	Council flats	1.5	6.8	22
L6	Victorian low status	3.8	9.4	40
L7	Town houses and flats	11.5	9.4	122
L8	Stylish singles	5.0	5.2	96
L9	Independent elders	4.3	7.4	58
L10	Mortgaged families	4.5	6.2	73
L11	Country dwellers	9.5	7.0	136
L12	Institutional areas	0.3	0.3	100

example in Table 12.2 shows that High Income Families and Suburban Semis are particularly over-represented in this customer file. The set of indices represents a MOSAIC profile.

Profiles are a powerful analysis tool and can be built in a number of different ways:

1. Profiling the whole customer file against the Great Britain average to establish in which MOSAIC types customers are most likely to live.
2. Profiling the whole customer file against a catchment base to establish which MOSAIC types are under- and over-represented compared to the areas in which the customers live.
3. Profiling one segment of a customer file against all customers to establish which MOSAIC types buy each of a range of different products sold.
4. Profiling the average level of spend, sales, etc. to establish which MOSAIC types provide the most profitable customers.

12.5 MOSAIC profiling of survey respondents

Geodemographic codes are present on many of the industry standard market research surveys (e.g. Target Group Index, Financial Research Survey, National Readership Survey, Textile Marketing Survey). Codes can also be appended to a company's own market research surveys enabling users of specific products or media to be profiled.

Table 12.3 shows a MOSAIC profile of dishwasher owners, identified on a survey, compared to a base of all survey respondents. The benefit of such surveys is

Table 12.3 MOSAIC profile of dishwasher owners

MOSAIC lifestyle groups		File %	All respondents %	Index (Average = 100)
L1	High-income families	23.4	10.6	221
L2	Suburban semis	18.0	12.5	144
L3	Blue-collar owners	11.9	15.1	79
L4	Low-rise council	6.3	16.3	39
L5	Council flats	1.5	5.8	26
L6	Victorian low status	3.8	9.0	42
L7	Town houses and flats	11.5	10.8	106
L8	Stylish singles	5.0	4.0	125
L9	Independent elders	4.3	5.5	78
L10	Mortgaged families	4.5	4.5	100
L11	Country dwellers	9.5	5.5	173
L12	Institutional areas	0.3	0.4	75

that they reveal the nature of all users of a product, not just a company's own customers. Furthermore, surveys enable profiles of fast-moving consumer goods to be easily derived where usually names and addresses of product users are difficult to source.

The profile of dishwasher owners is sourced from the Target Group Index and reveals that the groups with the highest propensity to own the product are:

High Income Families (index = 221)
Suburban Semis (index = 144)
Country Dwellers (index = 173)

12.6 MOSAIC profiling of areas

Each postcode in Great Britain is part of a series of larger regions which include administrative areas (e.g. counties), postal areas (sectors, districts), media areas (television, radio, local press) and retail catchments and sales territories.

It is possible to determine the MOSAIC distribution of households or population for any defined area. Table 12.4 shows the MOSAIC distribution of households in Nottingham's primary shopping catchment area. The indices identify which MOSAIC types are commonly found in Nottingham compared to the rest of Great Britain.

The spatial distribution of geodemographic types in an area can be mapped and analysed because each postcode is grid referenced. Figure 12.1 (see colour section between pages 268 and 269) shows the distribution of the twelve MOSAIC groups in and around Nottingham. While the map gives an immediate indication of the location of particular target groups it is possible to use geodemographics to display a more direct measure of market opportunity.

Table 12.4   MOSAIC profiling of Nottingham

MOSAIC lifestle groups		Nottingham %	GB %	Index (Average = 100)
L1	High-income families	10.2	9.9	103
L2	Suburban semis	10.4	11.0	95
L3	Blue-collar owners	8.1	13.0	62
L4	Low-rise council	13.2	14.4	92
L5	Council flats	10.8	6.8	159
L6	Victorian low status	18.8	9.4	200
L7	Town houses and flats	4.8	9.4	51
L8	Stylish singles	10.3	5.2	198
L9	Independent elders	6.9	7.4	93
L10	Mortgaged families	3.8	6.2	61
L11	Country dwellers	2.6	7.0	37
L12	Institutional areas	0.1	0.3	33

Figure 12.2 (see colour section between pages 268 and 269) displays each MOSAIC postcode in one of five colours depending on the index for that MOSAIC group on the dishwasher profile. Red squares indicate the top 20 per cent of MOSAIC neighbourhoods where the penetration of dishwashers is more than 75 per cent above the national average. In contrast blue squares indicate the poorest 20 per cent where penetration is less than 40 per cent of the national average.

12.7 Using geodemographics to estimate local market opportunity

Market opportunity can be estimated in terms of volume for areas larger than postcodes by matching customer profiles with area profiles. This is achieved by multiplying the percentage of households in an area within each MOSAIC group by the dishwasher profile index for that group. By adding each of these 'weighted' indices, an overall index for dishwashers in Nottingham is calculated. This index might be higher or lower than the national average for dishwashers, and is dependent on the resident MOSAIC types in the area (see Table 12.4). Clearly if there is a greater percentage of MOSAIC groups with high indices, the composite index will be higher.

An estimated sales volume can be calculated by multiplying the national penetration for dishwasher by the weighted index. The resulting penetration value when multiplied by households in an area gives an estimate of volume potential for dishwashers. Table 12.5, for example, shows the estimated sales volume for dishwashers in shopping centres around Nottingham (see also Figure 12.2 in colour section between pages 268 and 269). West Bridgford has a high penetration of likely dishwasher owners while Central Nottingham illustrates the opposite. However, because of Central Nottingham's size it still represents over 32 per cent of the potential for dishwasher sales in the area as a whole.

Table 12.5   Dishwasher potential in shopping centres around Nottingham

Rank order	Primary shopping area	Potential dishwasher owners	Total HH	Index (Average = 100)
1	West Bridgford	7,978	27,437	156
2	Arnold	8,052	35,876	121
3	Central Nottingham	13,437	79,557	91
4	Beeston	8,339	49,504	91
5	Bulwell	4,010	32,016	67
Total		41,816	224,390	

Table 12.6   Daily newspapers for promoting dishwashers

Newspaper	Match index (Average = 100)
Daily Telegraph	133
The Independent	131
Guardian	128
Daily Mail	117
The Times	116
Daily Express	113
Today	100
The Sun	87
Daily Mirror	83

12.8 Profile matching

It is possible to extend the method of estimating sales volumes to assess the degree of similarity between geodemographic profiles. For example, a dishwasher manufacturer seeking to advertise in the national media would want to identify which titles were most appropriate. Profiling matching could compare the dishwasher profile against similar profiles for national daily newspapers (derived, for example, from the National Readership Survey) to assist media planning. Table 12.6 illustrates a ranking of daily newspapers according to the degree of match between their readers and dishwasher owners.

12.9 Extension of geodemographics into European markets

The emergence of a single European market has meant an increase in the number of organisations adopting integrated pan-European target marketing campaigns. A key issue for these organisations is that of maintaining centralised control of marketing through a single classification system.

EuroMOSAIC is a system that classifies 310 million individuals on the basis of the types of neighbourhood in which they live. Using EuroMOSAIC, multinational marketers are able to define their target markets and then identify local areas across Europe that offer the greatest potential for their products.

Consumers display enormous differences in behavioural and purchasing habits in each European market. For example, fashion magazines and home computers will sell well in smart apartment districts in Central Madrid. Lotteries and tobacco sell better in suburbs of Bilbao. Hunting is popular among office workers in Orebo, whilst long-haul holidays sell better in the smart singles neighbourhoods of Central Stockholm.

EuroMOSAIC identifies ten lifestyle categories that are consistent across all countries and are derived from 300 or more separate MOSAIC segments describing consumers in different European countries.

Table 12.7 illustrates how the distribution of consumer types varies across nine European countries. The development of generic geodemographic systems is now allowing marketers to use familiar market analysis techniques to promote consistent brand images to potential consumers in localised markets throughout Europe.

The availability of a consistent segmentation system crossing all European markets makes it possible, for the first time, to identify similarities and differences between markets in respect of both products and brands. A vehicle manufacturer can now establish whether the appeal of his marque differs a little or a lot between countries. A discount retailer can establish whether the visitors to his stores demonstrate a consistent or contrasting profile. A detergent manufacturer can identify whether the profile of the product category in which he competes is similar in a new market he plans to enter to its profile in the existing markets in which he already operates. A credit card operator or a subscription magazine publisher can examine his multi-country database to examine whether his customer base is more or less concentrated in exclusive upmarket suburbs or areas of trendy young cosmopolitans.

Such analysis can then be used, for example, to drive the location of new dealerships or to adjust the merchandising or promotional strategies for retail outlets; to specify to door-to-door distributors the preferred areas for the delivery of samples and coupons; to select rented names for a direct mailshot or to target existing customers with additional services to which they are most likely to respond.

In the debate on Euro-brands and the benefits of generic creative campaigns that transcend national borders, EuroMOSAIC offers a unique opportunity to establish whether a brand appeals to a consistent audience across all the markets where it is sold, and may therefore be supported by consistent positioning and appeal, or whether, as a result of local circumstances or the impact of previous advertising campaigns, it appeals to distinctly different groups in local markets, in which case separate local strategies may be more appropriate or a concerted effort to realign the brand's image so that it converges at a European level.

Table 12.7 EuroMOSAIC: national percentages

		Great Britain %	Netherlands %	Germany %	Spain %	Ireland %	Sweden %	Belgium %	Northern Ireland %	Italy %
1	Elite suburb	11.7	6.1	16.0	5.1	7.4	7.2	17.4	14.8	4.5
2	Average areas	15.8	13.4	20.9	6.6	27.4	19.4	18.9	14.3	14.3
3	Luxury flats	5.3	8.1	6.9	8.8	1.9	3.1	6.6	0.9	6.1
4	Low-income inner city	8.6	12.2	8.4	4.9	7.5	6.8	2.3	4.3	7.9
5	Hi-rise social housing	5.5	11.5	2.8	7.3	0	8.4	0	1.9	3.4
6	Industrial communities	19.4	12.2	13.0	12.4	4.9	11.9	17.0	10.8	14.6
7	Dynamic families	14.3	14.0	8.6	12.1	9.3	9.8	9.5	5.7	15.3
8	Low-income families	8.2	5.1	4.5	11.5	12.1	7.1	13.4	16.4	8.0
9	Rural/agricultural	5.5	13.6	13.7	21.4	27.1	18.6	7.9	26.8	17.9
10	Vacation/retirement	5.9	3.9	6.1	9.7	4.2	7.9	4.5	4.3	7.3

CHAPTER 13

The media: planning, monitoring and measuring

13.1 Advertising expenditure

In 1991, UK advertisers spent over £7.577 million a year on advertising. Expenditure on the national press (national newspapers and consumer magazines) was £15,559,000 and on television £2,303,000, making a national advertising total of £3,862,000. Regional press accounted for £1,628,000. As the percentage breakdown shows in Table 13.1, advertising in national and regional newspapers, consumer magazines and television accounted for 72.5 per cent (Advertising Association 1993). So it is not surprising that the advertising industry (advertisers, advertising agents and media owners) finance carefully designed and expensive research into the reading and viewing habits of the UK population. In this chapter, media planning to convey the brand message is looked at in radio, posters, cinema and cable television, as is the main national media, particularly television which has the largest percentage share in total advertising expenditure.

The media planner will need to know the advertising objectives as agreed between the client organisation and the market research supplier. Typically, the objectives include defining the target audience and reaching it by means of the most suitable and cost-effective type of media. Pastoral campaigns should be monitored and measured for their effectiveness. Such information derived with the aid of audience measurement research is intended to guide the media planners in his/her efficient purchase of media coverage from media sources.

The main sources of above-the-line audience measurement research for television, press, radio and posters are as follows:

1. The Broadcasters' Audience Research Board (BARB) for television.
2. The National Readership Surveys (NRS) for the press.
3. The Radio Joint Audience Research (RAJAR) for radio.
4. NOP Posters for 'outdoor-site classification and audience research' (OSCAR).

These sources are discussed in this order in sections 13.4 to 13.7.

Table 13.1 'Adspend' 1991

Total advertising expenditure by medium and by type (% of £7.577 million, 1991)

National press:		
National newspapers	14.8	
Consumer magazines	5.8	20.6
Regional newspapers		21.5
Business and professional magazines		9.3
Directories		6.7
Press production costs		5.5
*Television		30.4
*Poster and transport		3.5
*Radio		2.0
*Cinema		0.6 100.0

*Including production costs.
Source: AA (1993) *Advertising Statistics Yearbook*.

Socio-demographic characteristics of people within the market are of primary importance because most of the industry data are classified by sex, social grade, age, terminal education age, household size, employment or occupation of chief income-owners. Geodemographic systems for market segmentation purposes (e.g. the NRS and MEAL data) 'overlay' these data with owner and non-owner types of dwelling, regional groupings of neighbourhood types and lifestyle classifications (e.g. CACI's ACORN and CCN's MOSAIC) (see Chapter 11 on segmentation and Chapter 12 on MOSAIC). Syndicated services relate products and services to brand choice and audience profiles in market segments, for example, the British Market Research Bureau's Target Group Index (TGI), NOP's Financial Readership Survey, Tracking, Advertising and Brand Strength (TABS) and TN AGB's audience selection consumer omnibus survey 'Phonebus'.

As we saw in Chapter 11, a market segment is not viable unless it is accessible and in consumer markets this means accessible through the media. For media planning purposes it is necessary to translate psychographic and product-use classifications into demographic terms. It is necessary to record respondents' demographic and product-use characteristics when collecting data about their wants, perceptions and attitudes which is what market researchers do to aid clients in their product and media planning. Moreover, the research industry is a large and global one.

For example, A. C. Nielsen which is the world's largest information organisation has total billings worldwide which exceeded over one billion US dollars in 1992. Media Analysis and Expenditure Limited (MEAL) is a part of Nielsen and Nielsen is, in turn, a part of the Dun and Bradstreet corporation. The MEAL data on brand expenditure covers 475 product groups under 33 industry category headings. The impact that each brand achieves in advertisements on each one of six target audiences (i.e. housewives, housewives with children, men, adults, ABC1 adults and adults 16–34), is calculated.

Register-MEAL acts as an authoritative source of advertising expenditure and volume. As a guide to the size of coverage, its service report on advertising has over five hundred individual press titles. Its reports contain expenditure and brand shares for television, satellite television and radio. Its outdoor advertising expenditure reports are derived from research in partnership with the poster industry and for cinema with major service contractors throughout the country.

13.2 Considerations in media planning

A brand may be more successful in, say, London, and south-east ITV areas, than in the North-west, Yorkshire and the North-east. This may be peculiar to the brand or it may apply to the product field as a whole. Given variation in share by area the media planner needs to know whether the advertising objective is to be achieved by building on strength, counteracting weakness or by means of a judicious combination of the two. The decision will influence the allocation of the media appropriation as between areas and it may determine the choice of media category. Television and the regional press, together with radio, posters and cinema, can be scheduled on a regional basis. Given a product or service with seasonal appeal, the tactical decision 'from strength' or 'against weakness' still applies when allocating the appropriation. Should we concentrate expenditure in the high season or seek to extend demand by showing the product to be appropriate outside its season: for example, by popularising ice-cream as a year-round dessert?

If the product has a demonstrable benefit, use of the television medium is indicated. Television is a 'natural', for example, for the demonstration of gas appliances for cooking or heating. Television also 'glamorises' the process such as the BBC's Master Chef competition shown on television. On the other hand television is a less-discriminating medium than the print media, especially magazines which can be selected for the special interest, authority or ambience conveyed by their editorial content and presentation.

13.2.1 Determining the size of the appropriation

This is usually determined in advance of media planning but in the rare cases where an unmodified 'objective and task' method is being used to determine the appropriation, the media planner will play an important part in fixing the appropriation. Whether the appropriation is laid down or arrived at in consultation with the media planner, the criterion of success in media planning is the achievement of the optimum mix of:

$$\text{reach (or coverage)} \times \text{frequency} \times \text{length/size}$$

the last being influenced by creative considerations.

Data on how much the competition is spending and in what media it can be monitored are put together by subscribing to syndicated services, e.g. Media Expenditure Analysis Limited (MEAL) or the Media Register; or deduced for television from the BARB weekly reports. For a major advertiser the strategy is to plan a schedule which side-steps the competition while offering effective reach, or coverage, of the target.

13.2.2 Conversion, reinforcement or both

This basic objective will affect how the appropriation is laid out over time. When a brand is launched, frequent appearances in the media, longer commercials and larger spaces may all be used to achieve conversion and penetration of the market in the shortest possible time so that the brand breaks even and makes a profit as soon as possible. With an established brand, reinforcement of existing usage may be more critical. There may also be cases for combining conversion with reinforcement by interspersing longer appearances with shorter ones. It all depends on where the brand stands in its life cycle, the size of the appropriation and the advertising task. One part of the task may be to ensure shelf space for the brand and increase its popularity with specific market segments.

13.3 Achieving cost-effectiveness and industry changes

It will help us to appreciate the relevance of the audience research data if we consider what planning for cost-effectiveness involves before summarising the content of the reports and the methods used to collect the data. The task gets more formidable when we seek to take account of duplication between, say, television and print media, or between newspapers and magazines, or between the individual publications we are considering for a particular schedule. The National Readership Survey provides valuable input data about duplication as between the readers of different publications. As stated by the NRS, information is collected on almost 300 newspapers and magazine titles and weight of viewing and listening to television and radio. Access to teletext, subscription cable and satellite television, cinema and use of Thomson Directories and Yellow Pages are found on the NRS 'Reference source for other media'. These data indicate the intensity with which readers of specific newspapers and magazines also view television or listen to radio. But to achieve cost-effectiveness it is necessary to consider whether the opportunities being given to the target market to receive the advertising message are likely to be taken and the probabilities will vary between the broad media categories and between the specific publications and viewing times being considered. Whether or not the opportunities to see (OTS) are effective and the message is received depends on the following:

- The frequency with which the advertisement appears.
- The period of time over which it appears.
- The frequency with which target readers see the issue of publication and view the advertisement.
- The creative impact achieved by the campaign.

If the creative work effectively conveys the product benefit, and if the media planning has been successfully focused on the target consumers in the market, we can expect selective perception to work in our favour.

13.3.1 Market and media weights

We may want to refine our estimate of effective coverage by taking account of the relative importance of groups in the target market. An organisation marketing baby food might well be particularly interested in reaching women aged 15–34. But older women sometimes have babies and if experienced as mothers, older women may influence the decisions of younger women. Here it would be reasonable to apply a weight of 1 to prime target, women aged 15–34, but to discount the value of the reading/viewing of older women by applying a weight of, say, 0.5 to the reading/viewing coverage recorded for them.

The chance of an advertising campaign attracting the attention of members of the target group is clearly influenced by the readership of the publications on the schedule among members of the target group and, in the case of television, by their viewing habits. We can allow for the frequency with which respondents claim to read, view and listen when programming and can apply weights to this end.

As we shall see reading and viewing are ambiguous concepts in media research. Reading a publication can mean anything between reading it from beginning to end and glancing through it, while those recorded as viewing during our time slot may well miss our 30-seconds commercial.

We are on debatable ground when we attempt to weight media vehicles according to the probability that they will actually convey the message to the target group. In fact, it is only worth while attempting to apply weights to take account of the probability of opportunities to see being taken if sound normative data are available.

If an advertiser is established in a particular field, if campaign penetration has been monitored regularly in terms of recognition or awareness levels achieved, and if it is possible to relate this achievement to individual media vehicles, then there might be a case for giving good carriers of the message preferential weights in the computer programming. Weighting for ambience and/or authority is even more debatable since the weights are determined by judgement, unless post-exposure campaign monitoring has yielded statistical data sufficiently robust to warrant this refinement. For the print media it might pay to run the computer program using market weights only and to use the resultant ranking of newspapers and magazines as a bargaining counter. If we are advertising to a middle-class ABC_1 audience, we can ignore C_2DE readers or viewers when relating coverage to cost.

13.3.2 Inter-media relationships and changes in industries

Volatility in the broadcast and printed media has been brought about by dramatic changes in the last five years. The number of independent radio franchises has dramatically increased as well as the number of radio stations. Colour supplements and on-the-run colour in the print media has grown rapidly with a volume increase of 30 per cent in 1993 compared to 1992. By 1994 there have been seventy-six supplements with separate sections compared with the ten in 1987. Between 1987 and 1992, newspaper paginations grew by over 30 per cent (NOP 1994). Mergers and takeovers to form larger conglomerates in books, newspapers, magazines and market research (e.g. acquisitions by Dun and Bradstreet) are reflected in the broadcast and television industry (e.g. the takeover of Central television by the Carlton group in 1994). Other changes have included the replacement of the Independent Broadcasting Authority (IBA) and the Cable Authority on 1 January 1991 by the Independent Television Commission (ITC). The ITC is a public body which licenses and regulates commercially funded television services provided in and from the United Kingdom. These include Channel Three (ITV), Channel Four, public teletext and cable television, local delivery and satellite services. More than thirty new television channels have been set up. Franchises cover two-thirds of the UK population totalling around 14.2 million homes. One hundred and twenty-seven individual franchises have been awarded with coverage in size from 10,000 to 500,000 homes (ITC 1994:3).

13.4 BARB objectives and structure

The independent television companies need to monitor audiences in order to sell time to advertisers and their agents, while the publicly accountable BBC needs audience figures when negotiating the licence fee on which it still depends. The audience ratings indicate the relative popularity of programmes and aid scheduling decisions. An important requirement of the 1977 Annan Committee on the future of broadcasting which preceded the setting up of BARB had recommended a 'continued audience measurement system to remove arguments on whose audience size data was correct so that resources could be directed to research on audience reactions to programme content'. Previously, there had been different methods of data collection on audience measurement used by the BBC and ITV which had the inevitable consequence of producing different results which had caused confusion.

The Broadcasters' Audience Research Board (BARB) as an executive management body was formed in response to this in August 1980 and by 1981 a single system for television audience research was set up by the BBC and the ITV association as joint shareholders of BARB shares (BARB 1994). The system now in place is intended to provide a database common to both in reliability and acceptability in cost. A director from each of the main subscriber groups: the Institute of Practitioners in Advertising (IPA), Channel Four and BSkyB (representing satellite broadcasters), sits on the board of BARB in addition to BBC and ITV members. A similarly representative body, the Technical Advisory Group meets regularly under BARB's chairmanship to examine data quality and technical issues affecting the service.

The service consists of the provision of information to broadcasters, advertising and media buying agencies and advertisers for the television industry. The Broadcasters' Audience Research Board employs a small staff of around half a dozen and uses research suppliers on audience measurement research.

13.4.1 BARB's electronic audience measurement service

Tenders are invited from research suppliers for the BARB contract. The 1991–1998 BARB contract on audience measurement research is jointly shared by Audits of Great Britain (AGB), part of the Taylor Nelson AGB plc and RSMB Television Research. The division in responsibilities between TN AGB and RSMB and the method of metering for the BARB research are given in Box 13.1.

13.4.2 Sample design

The sample design and data-collection method used by TN AGB for BARB has three advantages:

1. Electronic observation is less susceptible to mistaken recording than 'day-after' recall.
2. Audience measurements are very soon available to those who need them.
3. When the same, or virtually the same, sample is being surveyed every day of the week the trend data are less susceptible to sampling variation than would be the case if a different sample were recruited in respect of each day's viewing.

The TN AGB design, based on area panels of television homes, makes it possible to monitor the dynamics of television viewing using comparatively small samples, always provided that the panels are representative of the survey populations area by area and that panel membership remains reasonably loyal. The cost of the

---

Box 13.1

AGB is responsible for metering, BARB software and data processing and RSMB is responsible for the Establishment Survey, address selection (from the Establishment Survey) and panel balance.

The meters utilised in the BARB contract are the AGB 4900 Peoplemeters. This meter allows panellists to enter their presence in the viewing room via a handset on a set-top meter display unit (MDU) which communicates with a master meter, the Central Data Storage Unit (CDSU). This stores the data and contains a modem which links to the home telephone socket. Overnight the AGB computer dials up each BARB panel home and draws down the evening viewing data (BARB homes are polled between 1 a.m. and 5 a.m.).

The AGB 4900 meter identifies playback recorded off-air via the video. The meter implants a 'fingerprint' onto the videotape when recording off-air takes place, and a pulsed 'fingerprint' records day/date/time/channel. When the tape is played back the meter picks up the fact that the video recorder is being used in playback mode and the day/date/time/channel 'fingerprint' of the recording being played back.

The 4900 meter also allows BARB panellists to input their guest, sex and age on the MDU via the handset.

The industry now uses 'consolidated' ratings (live + timeshift) for top programme ranking and the performance of commercial schedules.

Source: Roberts, B. (1994) Managing Director, AGB Television.

electronic methodology developed by AGB makes sample size a critical consideration.

Electronic metering means that it is possible to collect data from any number of television sets and video recorders in any one home with automatic feeding of the data each night into a central computer. This greatly enhances the speed of collection of data. Response rates from the panel are estimated by BARB (1994) to be 98–9 per cent which ensures a high degree of accuracy.

Metered records are combined with programme details and commercial broadcasts. Calculations are arrived at by computer in order to estimate audience size. The Broadcasters' Audience Research Board subscribers can purchase the raw data from the meters (for re-analysing) or the calculations on audience statistics which show the number and percentage figures watching particular programmes and commercials. BARB's Establishment Survey is based on a random sample of more than 43,000 interviews held through the year and structured according to postcode areas within the ITV regions.

The results of the survey to determine television usage and ownership across the country are combined with census data. This enables a representative sample of houses in terms of viewing habits, television and video ownership, socio-demographics, etc. to be drawn up for the audience measurement panel. A ready pool of names and addresses is drawn up in case there is a need to replace any households which drop out. The audience measurement panel consists of 4,435 homes.

A nominal incentive payment is given to panel members in return for the provision of information to BARB. The Establishment Survey contributes to the making of marketing plans because it establishes regional variations in the viewing population and 'the viewing population' is in effect 'the total population' since 98 per cent of households have television. But its primary purpose is to give credence to the data derived from the viewing panels by defining the regions they represent and providing the pool of addresses. The area panels vary in size from 100 (Border) to 500 (Central) and 475 (London).

13.4.3 BARB specialist reports

The Broadcasters' Audience Research Board issues three specialist reports – the Network report, the Astra report and the BBC report.

The 'green' weekly television audience network report gives summarised data on live and time-shift data (audiences to programmes and audiences to time segments) for the main channels for subscribers to ITV companies (see Figure 13.1), Channel Four, advertising agencies and their clients. The 'yellow' Astra satellite panel weekly television audience report is for satellite broadcasters and summarises viewing statistics on homes which receive Astra channels by cable or disk aerial. The 'grey' BBC report includes time and time-shift data and is tailored to the needs of the BBC. A weekly press release 'The week's viewing in summary' gives hours of viewing to each channel (audience share) and the most popular programmes.

The BARB Audience Measurement Service is based on a considerable investment in the electronic collection and rapid processing of viewing data. In the past, output was largely paper-based with bulky weekly reports and data tapes. A change in the 1991–8 BARB contract is that data is now transmitted daily and electronically to BARB subscribers.

Data on audience measurement research is important to ITV companies in their drive for market share and profit. Figure 13.1 shows the ITV companies and the improvement in market shares for HTV, Anglia, Central and Granada in 1993, up from 1992. The advertiser buys opportunities for his/her campaign to be seen on a particular ITV channel. However, there is no certainty that the audience recorded will be entirely present and watching when the advertisements are shown.

The introduction of the peoplemeter has improved the quality of the data relating to the viewing of panel members, for with the push-button handset the presence of the individual viewer is electronically recorded as viewing takes place. Nevertheless, there is always the chance that a panel member will leave the room during a commercial break without pressing his/her button on the handset.

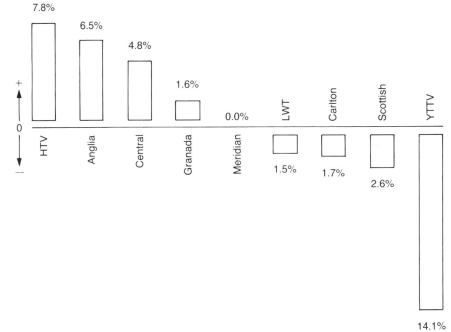

Source: HTV Group plc (1993) Report Dec., p. 6.

Figure 13.1   Improvement in ITV advertising market shares – 1993

However, a set of display lights indicates to the family what data have been recorded and is used as a reminder device to ensure that the data are correct. Any attempt to establish actual, as opposed to potential, presence necessarily involves research studies designed to measure the impact of advertising campaigns using such measures as 'recognition' and 'awareness' in *ad hoc* studies, tracking studies or by subscription to a service such as TABS.

13.4.4 BARB television opinion poll

The BBC's Broadcasting Research Department operates the television opinion panel for BARB. Electronic observation is a reliable method for counting viewers. The present system operating from 1986 consists of a national panel of 3,000, on which Channel Four and the ITV regions are represented according to population size and regional panels on which numbers are boosted to 500 for each region. The national panel complete a booklet once a week; the regional panel once every four weeks. Panellists sign on for a maximum of two years. The average response rate each week is 65 per cent and, when recruiting, it is estimated that one hundred letters will be required to generate sixty panel members. The panels are administered by post. Each respondent fills in two booklets – the 'programme diary' and 'viewpoint' designed to cover seven days' programmes from Monday to Sunday.

For the programme diary, each respondent has to rate on a scale from one (least interesting or enjoyable) to six (most interesting or enjoyable). The information which is obtained is used to calculate an appreciation index (AI) for each programme which is then compiled into a weekly 'Audience appreciation report'. Viewpoint is based on finding out what the panel members think of various programmes and their booklet contains questions to be answered about any type of programme. In addition, a 'children's panel' consisting of 1,000 respondents from the ages of four to fifteen fill in similar pairs of booklets on networked children's programmes shown up to 9.00 p.m.

The base for the television opinion panel has over 28,000 names and addresses. These names and addresses are derived from a sample of constituencies stratified by BBC and ITV region and by ACORN type. Within constituencies wards and streets are drawn with probability proportionate to size using a fixed interval from a random start, i.e. the sampling points are randomly located. Stratification by ACORN types obviates the need to set social-grade quotas. Age, sex and, for adults, working status are quota-controlled. In other words, the bank of addresses used for the television opinion panel is carefully drawn to be representative of the population – aged twelve and over.

The names drawn within each area are distributed among an eighteen-cell matrix ($3 \times 3 \times 2$):

	Groups
Total weights of viewing (hours viewed per week)	= 3
Channel preference (hours ITV/Channel Four viewed out of 10)	= 3
Social class (ABC_1/C_2DE)	= 2

This matrix controls the national panel and each of the regional panels. There are in addition four marginal controls: sex, age, presence of children and size of household. The panels are tightly controlled to ensure that they are representative of the viewing public so that they yield comparable data.

13.4.5 The appreciation index (AI)

For the 'programme diary', panellists are asked to watch as they would normally watch and to rate the programme watched (see Box 13.2). The attitude statement 'interesting and/or enjoyable' embraces two measures of appreciation and the statement is, on the face of it, asking two questions in one. The statement is flexible, because panellists may be rating an information programme (in which case 'interesting' is particularly relevant) or an entertainment programme (when 'enjoyable' is a more suitable measure of appreciation). The data are compiled for the weekly 'Audience appreciation report' for subscribers (BARB 1994). The

---

Box 13.2

6 = Extremely 5 = Very   4 = Fairly   3 = Neither 2 = Not very 1 = Not at all
interesting   interesting interesting one   interesting interesting
and/or   and/or   and/or   thing nor   and/or   and/or
enjoyable   enjoyable   enjoyable   the other   enjoyable   enjoyable

To sum the panellist's appreciation of a particular programme, positions on the scale
are scored as follows:
100   80   60   40   20   0

The AI is calculated by dividing the total score for each programme by the total
number of panellists reporting.

---

contract for the Audience Reaction Service for BARB has been held by Research
Services Ltd (RSL) since July 1994. Research Services Ltd also holds the contract
for conducting readership surveys for the NRS contract for 1992–6.

13.5 The NRS data

The NRS objective is as follows:

> to provide the common currency of readership research data for
> newspapers and magazines, using methodology acceptable to both the
> publishers of print media and the buyers of space, to the highest
> standard in a way that is cost effective and sufficiently flexible to take
> account of change and the needs of users.

The National Readership Survey data derive from a meticulously designed
probability sample representative of the adult population of Great Britain aged
fifteen and over (NRS 1994a). The fieldwork and analysis are sub-contracted to
Research Services Ltd. The data are collected throughout the year and care is taken
to timetable interviews so that seasonal and day-of-the-week fluctuations in the
reading of newspapers and periodicals are represented in the results.

Computer-assisted personal interviewing (CAPI) was introduced from 1 July
1992. Responses to questions on lap-top computers are transferred via modem to a
central computer. This facilitates speed in field surveys and enables the NRS to
report results within three weeks at the conclusion of the fieldwork.

The Joint Industry Committee for National Readership Surveys (JICNARS)
was abolished and a new company, the National Readership Surveys (NRS), was
formed. The board of directors on the NRS includes representatives from the
Newspapers Publishers Association (NPA), the Periodical Publishers Association
(PPA), the Institute of Practitioners in Advertising (IPA), the Incorporated Society

of British Advertisers (ISBA) and the Association of Media Independents (AMI). ARS Ltd is part of the MAI publishing group.

Sections 13.5.1 to 13.5.3 briefly do the following:

- Consider the probability sampling procedure used to contact readers of newspapers and magazines.
- Describe questions on readership used to establish what readers read and how frequently they do so.
- Look at readership panels.
- Describe the NRS as a source of segmentation variables.

13.5.1 Sampling procedure

The sampling procedure is described in detail in the NRS report and is a useful source for anyone studying sample design. The NRS database is available on subscription through an authorised computer bureau; monthly and half-yearly reports are published using moving averages for quarterly, half-yearly and annual bases.

The NRS data are based on a multi-stage stratified probability/random sample drawn from the postcode address file (PAF). The PAF is used as the sampling frame. A three-stage selection procedure is described in the following.

Stage 1. 2,520 enumeration districts (EDs) are used as primary sampling units; stratification of five categories of EDs is done according to ACORN type. The profile by ACORN types of the EDs drawn to represent the area in the samples is compared with the profile of all the EDs in the geographical group. Any imbalance is corrected. Each category is given differential weighting prior to point selection with booster samples for regional areas, Scotland and Wales.

Stage 2. Addresses are systematically drawn from each chosen ED, twenty-eight addresses per point are selected with a reserve list of eight addresses in case any address replacement is needed.

Stage 3. From each address an individual is selected taking into account recent changes needed for tenement, institutional and multi-household addresses. A minimum of five calls has to be made to obtain a response from a selected address before abandonment. This is done to try to ensure that all adults as far as possible have a known chance of being included in the sample. Personal interviews with the selected individual for each household chosen are conducted. Each monthly sample is balanced over time and replicates the annual sample (NRS 1994b).

13.5.2 Readership questions and panels

Questions on readership are put on forty-five prompt cards containing six grouped titles. A total of two hundred and eighty titles are measured. Box 13.3 shows the technique and typical questions asked. Weightings of results are used to estimate the numbers of readers from a total summary of 45.3 million adults.

At the beginning of 1994, a question on topic interest for magazine and newspaper readership research has been included to find out if people normally look at a list of topics when reading and looking at newspapers and magazines (NRS 1994b). Topics asked include:

UK/British news	Travel and holidays
European news and other	Property/houses for sale
Foreign news	Home ideas/furnishings, DIY
Sport	Gardening
Cars/motoring	Science/technology/computing
Food and drink/cooking	Medical/health and fitness
TV programmes	Fashion and clothes
People, personalities and	Beauty and personal
celebrities	appearance
Arts/books/music/theatre/	Relationships/emotional issues
Entertainment listings	Baby/childcare/parenting
Film and video	Jobs/appointments
Personal finance/investment	The environment
Business/company news	Women's pages generally

The questioning method has made it possible to record the penetration of a longer list of titles without increasing the length of the interview or decreasing response rates; it definitely reduces order effects and thus improves data stability. But exactly what 'reading' means to different people is open to question. Relating 'reading' to issues with specific cover dates could be done using a panel, and reading occasions could be limited to those occurring in the home where the date could be confirmed. In a volatile and highly competitive market it is useful to have data related to specific issues and to specific individuals over time, so that brand switching patterns could be extracted. In order to record the penetration of titles with modest circulations it would be necessary to set up and maintain a large panel. The cost advantage offered by the lower sampling error is more apparent than real. A solution may be to run panels for discrete periods in order to add richness to the standard data, or to monitor the effect on reading habits of a strike, promotion or new launch.

A stable print-media market, twice-a-year reporting and the size of the sample in any one month would yield data adequate to the needs of media planners. In reality, however, the print-media scene is a volatile one and the battle to maintain, let alone increase, circulations encourages the use of promotions, e.g. one-off offers, competitions and price cuts. Reading habits are in consequence disrupted. In addition there has been a proliferation of titles to meet lifestyle interests, and publications with quite modest circulations can be of importance to the media planner focusing on a closely defined target.

Average issue readership is especially in doubt where the less frequently

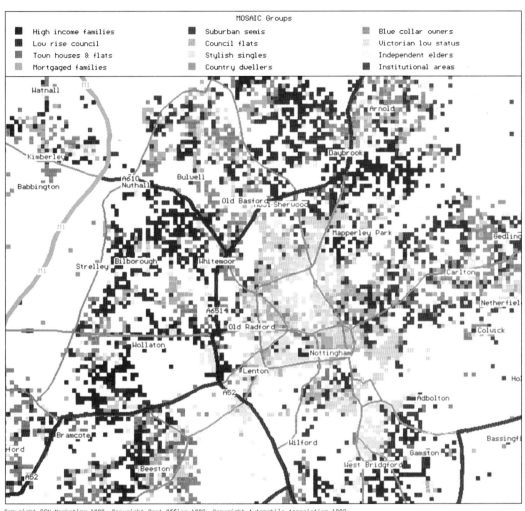

MOSAIC Groups

- ◼ High income families
- ◼ Low rise council
- ◼ Town houses & flats
- ◼ Mortgaged families
- ◼ Suburban semis
- ◼ Council flats
- ◼ Stylish singles
- ◼ Country dwellers
- ◼ Blue collar owners
- ◼ Victorian low status
- ◼ Independent elders
- ◼ Institutional areas

Scale 1:65984
Title Test map
Map Centre   455595m,   341108m
Map Size   13370m,   10708m

Figure 12.1   MOSAIC lifestyle groups around Nottingham

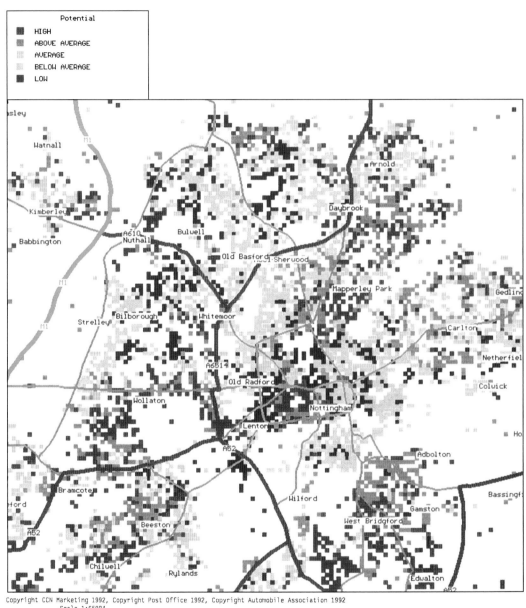

Figure 12.2   Potential for dishwasher ownership around Nottingham

---

Box 13.3 Readership questions

1. Cards are sorted into 'any publication seen in the last year' and 'no publication seen in past year'. 'Not sure' cards are put onto the 'yes' pile.
   (Typescript side of card is used)
2. Informant re-checks 'no-cards'.
3. 'Yes' cards are then dealt with one by one using the mini-masthead side of the prompt card. Each publication on the yes card is coded 'yes' or 'no' for readership in the past year.
4. For each publication read in the past year the recency question is then asked, followed immediately by the frequency question. The questions below are those for all publications except daily newspapers, which have a special question to prompt for reading 'yesterday'.

   When did you *last* read or look at any copy of ....? (Apart from today.) The response (unprompted) is coded by the interviewer as:

   Past 7 days
   (Past 2 weeks) – (Fortnightly only)
   Past 4 weeks
   (Past 2 months) – (Bi-monthly only)
   Past 3 months
   Longer ago

   And, looking at the scale on the card, which best describes how often you read or look at ....?

   Almost always (at least 3 issues out of 4)
   Quite often (at least 1 issue out of 4)
   Only occasionally (less than 1 issue out of 4)

Source: *The National Readership Survey* (1994).

published print media are concerned. Two kinds of error may occur: replicated readership, in which issues of an earlier cover date are returned as being read in the period; and parallel readership, in which more than one new reading occasion in an 'issued period' is being treated as one. A record of specific-issue readership could be achieved using a readership panel. The panel could be required to record cover dates in their diaries, but there would still be doubt as to whether publications read outside the home have been correctly dated.

13.5.3 The NRS as a source of segmentation variables

The readership penetration tables in the NRS report include the following:

- Readership among all adults.
- Readership among chief income earners (which replaces heads of households).

- Readership among men.
- Readership among women.
- Readership among housewives (female).

The social-grading system used by the NRS is a 'household' one. Prior to July 1992 the 'head of household' occupation determined the social grade of a given household. After this date, this was classified as 'chief income earner' to reflect the shift in the social-class profile of the population brought about by socio-economic changes. This re-definition was also seen as easier to administer for interviewers since it caused less confusion. The new system (see Box 13.4) gives a better up-market social-grade profile of the population in the United Kingdom. Social-grade classifications so widely used in quota sampling derives from NRS data.

In addition to establishing what kind of people read individual newspapers and magazines and the numbers reading the average issue, the NRS questionnaire also has a number of questions about television viewing and radio listening. These questions proble the intensity of viewing/listening by channel or station and (for television) the equipment in use (number of sets, video recorder, remote control, video-disc player, teletext, access to subscription cable television). The data on file make it possible to correlate readership with listening and viewing. The TGI also has on file data about mixed-media habits. The NRS and the TGI data are of value for portraying longer-term trends when media plans are being made.

Radio, posters and cinema account for over 6 per cent of total expenditure on display advertising. They are often used as local reminders of the national advertising message. As we have seen the NRS questionnaire makes it possible to sort the population into categories according to the amount of their claimed listening to radio, and to the frequency with which they say they visit the cinema. Some of the data are included in the twice-a-year report. The data are available on the computer database and this is an important source of the support media.

13.6 RAJAR

The Radio Joint Audience Research Ltd (RAJAR) was established in 1992 as a company jointly owned by the Association of Independent Radio Companies (AIRC) and the British Broadcasting Corporation (BBC). Its purpose is to operate a single audience measurement system for the radio industry comprising of the BBC, UK licensed independent radio (ILR) and commercial stations. RAJAR has a management committee to decide on policy issues and a technical advisory group to decide on technical and operational issues. Representatives on these committees are drawn from the AIRC, the BBC and the associations in the advertising industry (RAJAR 1994).

The Radio Joint Audience Research publishes detailed summaries of its research design and methodology. It publishes details on sampling, fieldwork

---

Box 13.4 Change in social grade from HOD to CIE

I			NRS Social Grade (All adults)	
			ABC_1	C_2DE
Head of Household (HOD) System				
1960			31.3	68.7
1970			35.6	64.4
1980			38.5	61.5
1990			41.9	58.1
Chief Income Earner (CIE) System				
1993 (July–December)			47.3	52.7

II
Profile Changes RSL Estimates
Est. Adults 15 + = 45,300,000

HoH Definition			
	'000	%	Index
A	1,300	2.9	100
B	6,800	15.0	100
C1	11,000	24.3	100
C2	12,300	27.2	100
D	7,900	17.4	100
E	6,000	13.2	100

CIE Definition			
A	1,400	3.1	108
B	7,600	16.8	112
C1	12,100	26.7	110
C2	11,200	24.7	91
D	7,400	16.3	94
E	5,600	12.4	94

Source: I. The NRS (1994) *Bulletin* No. 31, 23 February, p. 3.
II. The NRS (1994) *NRS Review*, Issue no. 3, p. 3.

materials, data processing and weighting and predicted cumulative audiences. The sampling methodology and analysis are very useful for those interested in research design. Its annual 'service overview and Code of Practice' publications each quarter are carried out for the National BBC and commercial services, BBC National Regional Services Greater London Region (GLR) and independent local radio (ILR) services with an adult population of over 4 million.

The stations include all BBC networked radio (Radio 1, 2, 3, 4 and 5), BBC

Table 13.2 A quarterly summary of radio listening

	Weekly '000	Research %	Average hours per head	Average hours per listener	Total hours '000	Share of listening %
Adult aged 15 and over; UK population 46,662,000						
All radio	40,642	87	18.1	20.7	842,584	100.0
All BBC	29,256	63	9.4	15.1	440,737	52.3
All commercial	27,301	59	8.1	13.9	379,993	45.1

Source: RAJAR (1994) *Quarterly Summary of Radio Listening*, January 10–March 20.

local/regional radio, all commercial radio, all national commercial radio (Atlantic 252, Classic FM and Virgin 1215), and all local commercial and other listening radio. The *Quarterly Summary of Radio Listening* gives a breakdown of the population for each of these radio channels. Table 13.2 gives a summary of the data provided for only three of these groups as an example.

The dates for this are collected from households. A 'contract' questionnaire is first administered at each household to check quota eligibility. A 'household' questionnaire is then used to collect the occupants' demographic details including the number of radio sets and car radios owned. The RAJAR diary has two sections. The first section is a self-completion questionnaire covering television viewing and newspaper readership while the second section records radio listening.

To aid identification the type of programme broadcast by each station together with its position on the waveband is included in the diary, which is small enough to carry around in a pocket or handbag. Keeping the diary is simple enough (time-slots down the side, stations across the top) and marking off quarter-hours (or half-hours between midnight and 6 a.m.). But keeping a diary does make listeners more conscious of their listening. It would be unreasonable to expect most listeners to keep a diary of their listening for more than a week so it is not possible to adopt the tactic used on consumer panels of ignoring entries until behaviour returns to normal. But some are asked to carry on for another three weeks. Twenty-four-hour recall, the method used by the BBC and by Radio Luxembourg, is cheaper to apply and free from the risk of the conditioning that is associated with keeping a diary. A sample of the general public is asked to recall its listening during the previous day and recall is aided by means of the programme. Whether or not recall is aided, the data are subject to the fallibility of the human memory and for most people listening is not a memorable activity.

Radio is still on the whole regarded as a purely tactical and local medium whose strength lies in its parochialism. It serves the following purposes:

- National advertisers can make local contact, support local distributors and local promotions.
- Local retailers and suppliers of services can advertise to their catchment areas.

13.7 Development of OSCAR

In 1983 a census of all poster sites costing £700,000 was commissioned by JICPAR for the Outdoor Advertising Association (OAA) which represents the British poster industry. Today, research for the development of this important medium for an industry standard database is carried out by NOP Posters formed as a merged operation between Associated Information Services and NOP Market Research for the Outdoor Medium in 1991.

The 120,000 outdoor site classification and audience research (OSCAR)-assessed stationary roadside panels or 90 per cent of all poster sites belong to members of the OAA. Since 1986, 10 per cent of all poster sites have been reassessed each year. These data, based on observation, serve to update OSCAR following its inception in 1981. 'Based on individual site fieldwork, OSCAR provides through statistical modelling, a gross audience estimate, pedestrian and vehicular, that is, the total possible audience passing the poster panel each week' (NOP 1994).

13.7.1 Cover and frequency in OSCAR

The poster market is a complex one. Many variously related factors influence the coverage estimated for any one campaign. Accordingly, OSCAR is in reality eleven models (see Table 13.3) varying according to day of week and the size of towns.

Inputs to OSCAR derive from a long and detailed check-list. They include the following:

- Physical characteristics of the site and of the poster panels associated with it. Pedestrian- and vehicular-visibility weightings are critical.

Table 13.3 The OSCAR model for estimating audiences

	Vehicular gross		Pedestrian gross	
	Large town	Small town	Large town	Small town
Weekday	1	4	7	9
Saturday	2	5	8	10
Sunday	3	6	11	11

Notes: Types 0–2 are large towns (Metropolis, London Borough, conurbation or major city).
Types 3–8 are small towns (County town, market town, University town, costal town, port, new town, etc.
Source: NOP Posters (1994) *OSCAR. How scores are estimated.*

Table 13.4   Monthly net coverage

	All adults %	ABC$_1$ men %	15–44 adults %
1200 average panels			
Monthly fixed	50	65	54
Rotated panels	59	73	63
3000 average panels			
Monthly fixed	71	82	75
Rotated panels	78	87	81

Source: The Outdoor Advertising Association (1994).

Box 13.5   How the model works

The OAA Poster Model is given as:

$$Cover = \frac{TAM}{TAM + (1.16T + 2.84)}$$

T = Time in weeks
A = A value
M = OTS in millions/week

A value (the probability that a person will be exposed to posters) was calculated for All Adults from the national population and actual OSCAR scores.

A Worked Example
What coverage and frequency will be achieved over one month with 1000 48s with an average of 81.8 OTS targeted against ABC1 Adults?

$$\frac{4 \times 0.0228 \times 81.8}{(4 \times 0.0228 \times 81.8) = (1.16 \times 4) + 284}$$

4 = Number of weeks
0.0228 = A value
81.8 = OTS in millions/week

$$Cover = \frac{7.46}{7.46 + 7.48}$$

Cover = 0.4993 or as a percentage 49.93%
Frequency = 7.46 + 7.48 = 14.9

Source: NOP Posters (1994) *Outdoor Cover & Frequency.*

- Estimate of pedestrian and vehicular traffic past the site.
- Type of location, for example, 'principal shopping', 'corner shop', 'residential' (nine categories).
- Special features, such as bus routes, car parks, traffic lights.

A values are available for 215 target groups taking the United Kingdom as a whole (see Box 13.5) or 23 by ISBA regions or combined regions, and conurbations (see Table 13.4). Classification within regions is limited to broad

Table 13.5   Cinema audience composition and profile

	Average audience profile	UK population profile %	Social standing	Average audience profile %	UK population profile %
Men	51	48	Class AB	26	18
Women	49	52	Class C$_1$	32	24
Age 15–24	55	17	Class C$_2$	22	27
Age 25–34	81	36	Class DE	20	31

Source: The Cinema Advertising Association (1991).

demographics. Table 13.4 gives an example of monthly net coverage from the Outdoor Advertising Association. For the United Kingdom it is therefore also possible to consider the poster audience in relation to other media (weight of viewing, listening, readership), together with more detailed demographics.

13.8 The cinema

Data relating to the number of cinema screens in the United Kingdom and the number of admissions to cinemas are published by the Department of Industry. The screen returns are published monthly broken down into the Register General's standard regions. The Cinema Advertising Association relies on NRS data for their published estimates relating to audience co-operation and to cinema-going (see Table 13.5). Cinema advertising accounts for only a fraction of advertising expenditure, 0.6 per cent in 1991, but it is a useful medium for reaching the 15–24 age group.

The Cinema Advertising Association publishes reach and frequency estimates broken down by ITV area, and by the socio-economic and media-usage characteristics of the population, based on the NRS data. Assumptions have to be made when coverage of a particular advertising campaign is estimated, for example, the need to take into account the probability of individuals visiting a particular cinema or selection of cinemas. What is being shown in the cinemas has, of course, a critical effect on the size of the audience and therefore its exposure to any advertisements shown at that time. Cinema attendance is taken to equate opportunity to see the advertising.

Data from the Cinema Advertising Association (CAA) and the National Readership Surveys (NRS) allow better-informed assumptions to be made when the coverage of a particular campaign is being estimated, because they collect data relating to the profile of audiences for specific types of film and for specific films, as well as information about the cinema-going habits of respondents.

13.9 Monitoring media planning

In summary, the backbone of the monitoring system for media is provided by BARB which monitors television buying very closely and the NRS for the print media. In addition, advertising agencies and their clients buy into services which monitor their own and competitive expenditures across all media (e.g. MEAL and the Media Register), so that comparison of own costs with those of competitors is relatively straightforward. But allowance has to be made for the fact that rates are subject to offers and bargaining so that there is a margin of error around figures necessarily based on rate-card rates. Also, ambiguities inevitably arise when advertisements relate to more than one brand, or to more than one variety of a brand.

From the monitoring/planning point of view, two important questions need to be asked:

1. Are the opportunities to receive the message being taken?
2. Is media selection based on the demographic characteristics of buyers/users as closely 'on target' (and therefore as cost-effective) as is desirable?

It is critical (in tracking studies) that sample designs, together with the asking of questions and recording of answers, should be standardised. Core tracking questions should always be asked using the same words and be put to the respondent in the same order. Three of the 'intermediate measures' used to monitor advertising effectiveness after campaign exposure concern 'recognition', 'salience' and 'attitude change'.

Recognition is more relevant to post- than pre-testing. It attempts to measure whether the opportunity to see the advertisement has in fact been taken by the respondent (see Box 13.6). This depends on both the media selection and the creative work. In a recognition check the object is first and foremost to find out whether the respondent recognises the advertisement. It is not what is remembered about it nor the respondent's attitude towards the subject of the advertisement but just whether the respondent happened to see it.

If the respondent knows the subject of the enquiry, he/she may oblige by recognising the advertisement. It is therefore necessary to use a procedure which either conceals the subject of interest, or one which makes it easy for the respondent to say 'no'.

Brand salience measures are concerned with the impact achieved by the advertising. Once this has been established the aim is to reinforce its position *vis-à-vis* the competition in the potential consumer's mental shopping-basket.

The attitude measures used to monitor the effect of an advertising campaign on brand image are less 'cut and dried' than recognition, as a measure of campaign penetration, and salience, as a measure of the 'stand-out' effect on the consumer's mind achieved for the brand by the campaign. The extent to which advertisers

---

Box 13.6

'Thinking now of just chocolate blocks and bars, please will you tell me what products come into your mind?'

The brands are recorded in the order in which they surface and their positions are ranked, the first mention out of, say, five possibles scoring 5, the second 4, and so on. Salience scores are aggregated for own brand and for main competitors, and mean scores are calculated by dividing the aggregates by the number in the sample. Trend data based on the mean scores indicate salience standing relative to the competition over time and help to measure the effect of advertising changes in scheduling, weight and creative content.

---

deliberately cultivate images for brands and the strength of belief in the added value of an appropriate image varies with the product field and the management philosophy of the client companies.

Attitude questions can take three forms:

1. Association of a list of attributes with a list of brands, a simple checking-off operation (e.g. Persil ticked for whiteness).
2. A ranking of attributes (e.g. Persil first out of x brands for whiteness), the data being processed in the way described for salience scores.
3. A rating of attributes using either Likert or semantic differential scales (e.g. 'whiteness that shows').

When collecting brand-image data it is advisable to establish what brand(s) the respondent is using/has used/is aware of. Attitude questions can be a component of a company's own 'usage and attitude' survey, carried out, say, once a year to add flesh to panel data, or a company may subscribe to a 'shared-cost syndicated' service such as TABS. Trend data are collected from a series of tracking studies, consumer panels or retail audits.

Tracking studies are increasingly being used as inputs to market models whether these be pre-launch simulation models, models designed to diagnose mix-element effects as, for example, the contribution of advertising expenditure to brand share, or 'what if we?' exercises set up to aid forward planning. For example, Burke Marketing Research uses tracking studies as inputs to their BASES and TEL-TRAC systems together with other trend sources such as consumer panels and retail audits. Burke have accumulated a considerable volume of data relating to pre-launch claims and post-launch brand performance and have developed a model which 'calibrates' consumers' claimed responses for 'over-statement and confusion'.

Economic and competitive pressures and rising costs, especially media costs, together with the existence of a wealth of expensive trend data and the computer facility to manipulate these data have encouraged companies to treat their stored data as a company asset.

13.9.1 TABS

The tracking advertising and brand strength (TABS) databank stores answers to a standardised questionnaire placed each week with 375 women and 375 men who have been contacted via the NOP omnibus survey which is based on a large probability sample. Responses to the TABS self-completion questionnaire are aggregated over four weeks and an effective response rate of 550 out of 1,000 questionnaires placed is achieved by each of the two TABS samples. The service has been in operation since 1976 and over two thousand advertising campaigns have been tracked. Respondents are questioned about their media consumption as well as their product usage. There is available normative data against which to assess responses to the key brand questions as illustrated in Figures 13.2 and 13.3.

The scales allow TABS to calculate average scores for each measure. These scores are more sensitive in monitoring advertising awareness than simply asking YES/NO questions. In the TABS questionnaire, respondents' impressions of a product or of the advertising for a specific brand are recorded on four diagrammatic scales. These are illustrated in Figure 13.2 for 'speedy spuds':

- A ladder – to show feelings about a product.
- A flowerpot – to show how much advertising for speedy spuds has been recently heard or seen. (Advertising includes magazines, newspapers, radio, posters, cinema, TV, etc.)
- An egg-timer to show whether the respondents think the price of speedy spuds has recently been high or low.
- A caterpillar – to show how interesting the advertising for speedy spuds is felt to be.

The caterpillar question is used 'for some but not all brands'. There are ten boxes in each diagrammatic scale. The respondent draws a line in pencil from one side of a box to the other. This information is then transferred to a disk by a data entry clerk. The scores are indexed on a scale 0–100. The scaled measures monitor brand goodwill (the ladder), advertising awareness (the flowerpot), price image or perception (the egg-timer) and how interesting the advertising is felt to be (the caterpillar). Comparison of these measures with actual weight of advertising in each medium helps to answer the question 'To what extent are the opportunities to see/hear/read actually making a real impact on the attitudes and behaviour of the target market?'

Answers to brand-usage questions cross-analysed with the level of goodwill give an indication of the strength of the brand. An example is given in Figure 13.3. The market is segmented into five categories:

1. Committed user – a current buyer, marking 77–99 scores at the top of the goodwill scale.
2. Enthusiastic user – a current buyer marking less-favourable scores of 66–33 on the 'for me, not for me' scale.

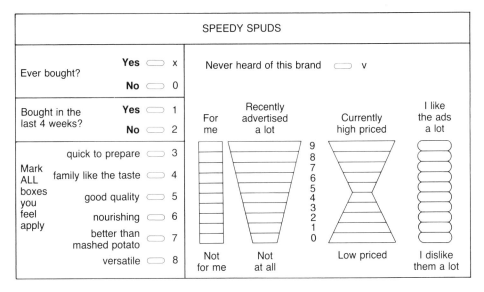

Source: TABS (1994), Extract from the TABS self-completion questionnaire, courtesy of C. Barker.

Figure 13.2 Example of the TABS self-completion questionnaire

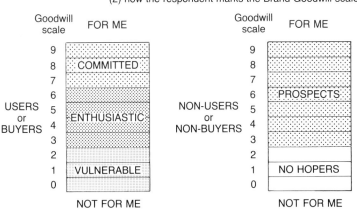

Source: TABS (1994), Extract from the TABS analysis, courtesy of C. Barker.

Figure 13.3 An example of TABS strength analysis

3. Vulnerable user – a current buyer not particularly well disposed towards the brand scoring 0–22 on the goodwill scale.
4. A prospect – a current non-buyer though favourably disposed towards the brand scoring 33–99 on the goodwill scale.
5. A no-hoper – a non-buyer with a low level of goodwill towards the brand scoring 0–22 on the goodwill scale.

Tracking advertising and brand strengths (TABS) monitors advertising awareness, and the awareness data can be related to the TVRs recorded by BARB. Awareness is dependent on creative presentation as well as 'media spend' and scheduling.

13.10 Evaluating media options for test market choice

Television is the largest single advertising medium taking 30.4 per cent of the total UK advertising expenditure in 1991. The cost of advertising on television represents a considerable marketing investment for advertisers and it can be difficult to design an experimental test launch given the disparity of size between smaller and larger ITV areas with variations in living standards, consumption habits, material practices and differences in the regional strengths and weaknesses of brands. Fortunately, for planning purposes, there is available a wealth of marketing information regularly published by the media organisations as shown in the preceding sections in this chapter.

A common practice can be to use one ITV area for an experimental launch and to treat the rest of the country as the control area. This is made possible by the availability of syndicated trend data showing competitive brand shares within ITV areas over time, in terms of both retail sales and consumer purchases. These data are used to neutralise the effect of area differences.

The development of cable television creates opportunities for the cost-effective testing of commercials. The UK cable franchises relate to small, highly clustered geographic areas of populations. The geodemographic classifications make it possible to define the social complexion of areas of this size with some precision; but it will, of course, be necessary to take account, when designing experiments, of variations in programme TVRs and in local shopping facilities.

Turning to the national press, newspapers and magazines, readership statistics are analysed on an ITV regional basis with much available syndicated data (e.g. from MEAL) relating brand and media consumption. In order to sell space to advertisers and to focus their editorial content, the provincial press also carry out their own research within their circulation areas.

It is possible to compare the effect on brand shares or different combinations of television and press advertising or to consider press alone in an ITV area. The problem is to limit the effect of the experimental treatment to the area of the experiment. It means making a special arrangement to break the print run, or, for magazines, to 'tip in'. Regional editions cover larger areas of the country. Possibilities in the extension of local-radio (LR) network to relate groups of LR stations to the ISBA sales areas create opportunities for using LR to test the sales effect of promotions to encourage local stocking-up (or to discourage de-listing).

13.11 Measuring the results of media impact on customers: store tests and retail audits

In the United States there are many small television stations serving local markets. It is comparatively easy to represent regional differences and to match ex-perimental and control areas. In an experimental design, for example, the type of commercial watched on television by consumer panels made up of housewives is related to the data obtained from laser scanning of their purchases at the point-of-sale check-out. Behaviour-scan operation panellists are represented by code numbers and these are recorded when their purchases are scanned at the check-out. In the United Kindom, Nielsen's Homescan panellists (with 7,500 people) reflect household purchasing. Data are retrieved via a modem linking their domestic telephones to the Nielsen computer. Nielsen's Scan*Pro database holds weekly scanning information from key grocery multiple stores related to informa-tion on the in-store promotional environment (Nielsen 1994). Syndicated panel services are also offered by a variety of research organisations, for example, Stats MR and TN AGB.

When an in-store experiment is being designed these data will show the following:

- Whether it is necessary to include more than one type of retail outlet in the test.
- Whether it is necessary to take account of regional differences in selecting test stores.
- Whether one or more retail organisations are of critical importance.

It may well be that one particular type of outlet (say supermarkets) is so important that the experiment can usefully be confined to this type of store, and to one dominating trade customer (say Tesco). Locations in which to stage the experiment are more likely to be made available if the negotiations are carried on with one retail organisation. In order to measure effect sales have to be recorded both before and after the test and over a period of time. In addition administration of the treatment must be controlled. In other words, the experiment depends on the co-operation of head office and of the managers of the selected stores. There is a statistical reason for basing the experiment on one particular store group, where this is practicable: the selected stores are more likely to be 'alike'. This reduces error deriving from extraneous variation. Randomised block and Latin square designs are frequently used in in-store experiments. These designs are described, with examples, in Appendix 3.

In an area test a retail audit or consumer panel is likely to be used to log brand shares, both before and after the treatment is applied. Certain elements in the mix lend themselves to 'in-store' testing whilst manipulations of pack and point-of-sale promotion are applicable for an in-store design, as the example in Box 13.7 shows.

To measure effects we need to record observations taken before, during and after introduction of the experimental treatment. The period of time to be allowed for in planning and costing a field experiment is influenced by three factors:

1. How long to allow for the experimental treatment to begin eliciting a response (penetration).
2. How quickly brand loyalty and switching patterns can be expected to develop (repeat purchase).
3. The degree of precision required in the estimate of effects.

In the case of an experimental launch the speed with which penetration is achieved will depend on the nature of the product and the creative effectiveness of the advertising campaign, together with success in achieving distribution and 'stand-out' at the point of sale.

The success of the product is reflected in its sales achievement and sales are usually reported in terms of brand shares. The research programme for a field

---

Box 13.7

In the in-store design we measure the effect of the promotional treatment by recording sales for a period before and a period after the offer is made to consumers. In the design based on consumer interviews, we use intermediate measures. We seek to establish levels of awareness of the offer, changes in use of the brand and changes of attitude towards it, but we cannot interview the same respondent before and then again after the offer has been made about awareness, use and attitude. The respondent would learn from the first interview and be more likely to notice and act on the offer.

We can use an after-only design and seek to establish past as well as present behaviour at the 'after' interview, or, more likely, use a larger number of respondents in matched groups, interviewing one group before the offer is made and the other after.

The first procedure would need three groups over all – one for each offer and one control – while the second would require at least five, preferably six (since the control group may learn) and we have made no allowance for regional differences. Simulation of the shopping context would be a cheaper and less time-consuming procedure and it would be possible to ensure that the arrangement of brands and displays remained under control.

experiment may provide for the collection of data about other marketing factors such as level of distribution achieved, awareness of advertising and response to an offer, but the critical measurement is likely to be a sales measurement. Ex-factory sales, however well recorded, suffer from three important limitations as a data source for experimentation in the field:

1. They do not tell us how competitive brands are performing in the experimental and control areas.
2. The 'pipeline' between the factory gate and the check-out makes it difficult to separate effects due to changes in sales from those due to changes in stocks.
3. It is difficult to isolate the volume and value of sales ex-factory attributable to the experimental and control areas.

These limitations may be overcome but subscription to a continuous retail audit and consumer-panel service is common practice.

13.11.1 *Retail audit and consumer-panel data*

Data relating to consumer purchases may be collected either at the point of sale or in the home. The impact of article numbering, bar coding and laser scanning on retail audits and consumer panels follows a brief discussion of the marketing significance of these two information sources. Retail audit, consumer panel or both types of data source are used to monitor brand shares (see Table 13.6). In a test area it may well be necessary to enlarge the regular, ongoing samples of retail outlets or of consumers, or to set up special *ad hoc* ones. It depends on the choice and the size of the test area. In addition, the standard reporting interval may be shortened, but the data-collection procedures are standard.

The following describe features of the retail audit and consumer panel:

- The retail audit is based on samples of retail outlets which represent the volume of business going through different categories of outlet. The sample for each Nielsen index (grocery, home improvement, health and beauty services) represents the range of outlets relevant to the products covered by the industry.
- The consumer panel will represent either private households with data collection via the housewife, or individuals. In addition to panels representing consumers in general, there are a number of specialist panels.
- The retail audit is a demanding but straightforward operation:

$$\text{Opening stock} + \text{Deliveries} - \text{Closing stock} = \text{Sales}$$

'Opening stock' was left for sale at the close of the last audit: 'deliveries' mean stock coming in since the last audit. The formula is simple, but the procedure is infinitely detailed.

Table 13.6 Data yield: retail audit and consumer panel compared

Retail audit	Consumer panel
Consumer sales and brand shares:	Consumer purchases and brand shares:
Units	Units
Sterling	Sterling
Average per shop handling	Brand penetration
	Consumer typology
	Demographic characteristics
	Psychographic characteristics
	Buying behaviour
	x amount bought
	x loyalty/switching
Retailer purchases	Where purchase made
Units (not sterling)	Type of outlet
Brand shares	
Source of delivery	
Direct/via depot/other	
Retailer stocks and brand shares	
Units	
Average per shop handling	
Stock cover	
Days, weeks, months	
Prices	Prices
Average retail selling prices at time of audit	Average purchase price
Promotion	Promotion
Display at point of sale	Offers associated purchases
Special offers	Advertising
	Media consumption by panel-members
	('Single source' data)
By type of retail outlet	
By ITV area	By ITV area

- The consumer-panel data derive either electronically via scanners or from an audit of household stores.

The retail audit is valuable in the experimental situation because, in addition to recording retail sales and brand shares, it monitors distribution achieved and signals the danger of running out of stock. The consumer panel describes the types of consumer responding to the experimental treatment and identifies repeat-purchase patterns.

13.11.2 Electronic allocation of sales data in-store

The rapid availability of marketing information made possible by electronic point of sale (EPOS) has to be set against the fact that collection of the data depends on retail co-operation and efficiency at the check-out and on the smooth running of the computer installation. Laser scanning of article numbers at the point of sale makes it possible to report consumer purchases in a short space of time, by brand within product field and by variety within brand (e.g. size, price, flavour, etc.). Article numbering (AN) has facilitated the attribution of variable costs to individual company brands. Article numbering also makes it possible to allocate shares of production, warehousing, transport and selling costs to specific sizes, scents, flavours, and types of packaging within brands. Allocation of advertising costs, often a substantial variable cost, can also be straightforward provided that the company's sales areas can be related to the ITV areas used in media planning and provided that not more than one brand or brand variety is included in the campaign.

The laser scanning of consumer sales is related to the work of the European Article Numbering (EAN) Association. The essential nature of EAN is that each article has a number assigned to it which is unique, universally recognised and can be shown in a form readable by machines as well as humans. The basic EAN is thirteen digits long, as shown in Figure 13.4.

Article numbering, bar coding and laser scanning have revolutionised the collection of sales data. The laser scanning of bar codes provides research data

Source: A. Wolfe and L. Cook (1986) *The Electronic Revolution in Store*, London: Ogilvy and Mather.

Figure 13.4 EAN thirteen-digit bar code

from a variety of sales outlets, for example, the regular scanning of records and cassettes carried out by Gallup for the music industry record charts.

13.12 Simulating exposure in the field

When a brand is exposed to the market, risks are incurred. Unless the field experiment is conducted on a limited scale, as in an in-store test, substantial production and marketing costs will accrue. The competition is also alerted and may respond in the following ways:

1. Going national on television or press with a copy or 'me-to' product.
2. Confusing experimental results by a counter-attack more intensive than would be possible on a national scale, e.g. introducing a price war.
3. Quietly monitoring the experiment while developing plans designed to spoil the national launch when it comes with a new or an improved modified product.

Other problems occur as retail buying power is increasingly concentrated so that securing effective distribution depends on the decisions of a few stores, e.g. Asda, Gateway, Safeway, Sainsburys and Tesco. Failure to perform well in the experiment area not only handicaps the brand on test, it also affects 'the manufacturer's track record' and so does longer-term damage. In addition, given that the sales/brand share targets set are achieved, for the duration of the field experiment opportunity costs are being incurred.

Generally speaking, to arrive at a valid estimate it is necessary to remain in the field for nine to twelve months. There is, therefore, a need for procedures which get closer to the verdict of the market than is possible in the lab-type experiment. The lab-type experiment depends on such intermediate measures as intention to buy. What is wanted is a sales or brand-share measure without exposure to competitors and retailers.

13.12.1 Brand-share prediction

Brand shares are the product of the historic working of the mix variables at certain fixed points in time, i.e. when the observations are taken. These data may show the relationship between area brand sales and national sales to be a volatile one. In this case the underlying relationship is revealed by averaging the readings over a period before and after the introduction of the treatment. The length of this period will depend on the frequency with which the product is bought.

The effect of marketing history up to and during the experiment is taken into account by standardising brand shares, a technique developed by Davis. When a

---

Box 13.8

If x_0, y_0 etc. are brand shares in the experimental area prior to the introduction of brand T, and if t_1, x_1, y_1 etc. are the brand shares after the introduction; and if X_0, Y_0 etc, are the brand shares in the wider market prior to the launch, then the projected share of brand T nationally will be T_1 where

$$T_1 = 100 - \left(X_0 \frac{x_1}{x_0} + Y_0 \frac{y_1}{y_0} + \ldots \right) \%$$

---

new brand is introduced into an area market, achievement in brand share is made at the expense of other brands already there. Assuming a positive result for the new entry, some brands will resist more successfully than others. If the experiment is allowed to run long enough and provided that a competitor does not succeed in muddying the water, an estimate of national share is arrived at by applying the changes to brand shares observed in the experimental area to the shares held by competing brands in the national market (see Box 13.8).

The brand-share data used when taking the standardisation approach can be derived from either a retail audit or from a consumer panel, i.e. from shares of retailer sales or from shares of consumer purchases.

The brand-share prediction model is based on three statistics:

1. Penetration: buyers of the test product as a percentage of all buyers in the product field, accumulated during the period of the test (P).
2. Repeat-purchase rate: triers of the test product buying again as a percentage of all buyers in the product field (R).
3. Buying rate factor: a weighting factor which allows for the finding that buyers of the test product consume more or less than the average – a weight of 1 – for the field (B).

$$\frac{P}{100} \times \frac{R}{100} \times B = \text{predicted brand share}$$

After a time the cumulative penetration of the brand, i.e. the number of people buying the brand for the first time, will show a declining rate of increase. Once the shape of the curve is determined and a declining rate of interest is observed, it is possible to make a reasonable estimate of the ultimate likely penetration. The repeat-purchase rate is calculated by taking the total volume of purchases in the product field made by people who have tried the brand under study and expressing the repeat purchases of the brand as a proportion of these total purchases. This repeat-purchase rate usually declines in the early weeks after a first purchase and eventually begins to level off. When the levelling-off occurs it is possible to calculate what the equilibrium market share of the brand will be.

Market modelling for brand-share prediction is discussed in more detail in Chapter 12.

13.13 Conclusion

The data sources reviewed in this chapter give a brief insight into the wealth of statistical data available to the media planner and the relationship between the media habits of consumers and brand consumption, e.g. from the Target Group Index, MEAL and the Media Register. These data are available via on-line terminals to advertising agencies from one source when they are linked to a computer bureau, e.g. Donovan Data System (DDS). Broadcasters' Audience Research Board (BARB) data are accessible on the Monday of the week following collection. Current NRS, cinema, radio and poster statistics together with data relating to competitive spending are also immediately on call. Media planning, buying and billing are integrated processes.

In advertising-media experiments, changes in brand awareness are likely to be recorded, while syndicated services which relate media exposure to product and brand consumption help to validate media planning. The main *raison d'être* of shop audits and consumer panels is the continuous monitoring of market performance. They are described in this chapter because an appreciation of the nature of the data is necessary for an understanding of the projective and predictive techniques discussed such as brand-share prediction.

References

A. C. Nielsen (1994) *Nielsen Information*, leaflet, p. 1.

Advertising Association (1993) *Marketing Pocket Book*, NTC Publications, p. 72.

BARB (1994) *Guide to the Broadcasters' Audience Research Board Ltd*, pp. 1–2.

Independent Television Commission (1994), *Cable Satellite and Local Delivery in the UK*, Leaflet, pp. 3–6.

National Readership Surveys (1994a), *The National Readership Survey*, Appendix and p.7.

National Readership Surveys (1994b) NRS Review, p. 6.

NOP Posters Ltd (1994) *OSCAR, How Scores are Estimated*, p. 1.

Radio Joint Audience Research (1994) *Service Overview and Code of Practices*, March, p. 1.

Assignments

1. A food manufacturer is planning the introduction of frozen pâtés and terrines under a 'farmhouse' label aimed entirely at the consumer market. The company has a range of pies and sausages in national distribution. The board is divided between going national with the new, more up-market range and a rolling launch; but, anticipating competitive reaction is, on the whole, in favour of an introduction throughout Great Britain.

   The media planner concerned at the advertising agency has been asked to recommend a media strategy, given an advertising appropriation of £850,000 inclusive of production costs:
   (a) what marketing information would the media planner need in order to formulate a cost-effective strategy?;
   (b) what research sources might he/she consult?

2. 'Reading a publication or looking through it is not a clear-cut unambiguous act as is, for example, buying a kilo of sugar or breaking a mirror':
   (a) explain why you agree/disagree with this statement;
   (b) how exactly may 'readership' be defined?

3. A company making dyes for the packaging industry has recently moved from the cutting of layouts by hand to the use of lasers, resulting in greater precision, a considerable saving in time and an urgent need for new business.

   An agency with industrial experience has been appointed to advertise this 'hi-tech' development:
   (a) what information would the advertising agency need in order to plan a media strategy?;
   (b) how might these data be collected?

Assume an appropriation of £100,000.

CHAPTER 14

Testing and evaluating*

A case study on 'optimising ad effectiveness – quantifying the major cost-benefits of painstaking television pre-tests'

Stephen Ashman and Ken Clarke

14.1 Introduction

A new brand with unique price advantage, creating its own new sector of a big market through easily monitored direct response, should have all the makings of an advertising success story. Indeed Direct Line Insurance is a big success. However, this article focuses mainly on how it went about making its advertising more effective than it would otherwise have been, through quantified pre-testing, modelling and 'real-life' tracking. The process of testing two separate campaigns is intimately discussed: the rough advertisements; then how these were revised; and how well the finished commercials, by comparison, performed. The improvements are claimed to have yielded media cost-benefits of well into seven figures.

The cost of television advertising productions and air-time is so large that it is important to ensure that an advertisement will be effective. It is not uncommon for an advertisement to cost half a million to produce and several more million on showing it. If similar sums were being spent on new production equipment, then a whole series of capital propositions would be produced with calculations of DCF yield and the like. Advertising budgets increasingly come under similar scrutiny.

Discriminating between good and bad in advertising calls for judgement rather than luck. But judgement, however well schooled and experienced, is difficult to exercise, for those who need to judge are themselves closely involved in the creating of that being judged. Apart from any issues of *amour propre* and protective, parental feelings, the marketing person has one thing that the intended

*This article was first published in *Admap* in February 1994, pp. 43–6. *Admap* is produced by NTC Publications Ltd, Farm Road, Henley-on-Thames, Oxon. Tel. 01491 574671. Reprinted with permission.

audience never has, the statement of advertising strategy. Ask all the right questions such as: 'Does the advertisement have one main selling proposition'? and 'Is that proposition unique to the brand, or is it expressed in a unique way?', and, with prior knowledge of the strategy, the answers become clearer and positive. The crucial problem is how to gauge how the advertisement will 'work' with those who are not privy to the strategy. No matter how hard we try, we can never wholly return to a state of ignorance, or pretend that we do not know our aims. Executives called upon to decide about an advertisement not only cannot completely divorce themselves from prior knowledge, but they are also more likely to see the advertisement successfully meeting its communication and selling objectives.

As the following case history illustrates, there may well be a feeling that we know all we need to know about our advertising and therefore have no need to test it with the public. In this instance, that would have been a disastrous mistake.

14.2 How advertisements work

So far, whenever we have talked about an advertisement 'working', we have used quotation marks; for the term needs definition. Since any company's natural objective is that advertising should help generate sales which would not otherwise have occurred, we define 'work' in terms of sales effectiveness.

Looked at from a negative point of view, it is safe to say that no advertisement is likely to be sales-effective if nobody notices it or notices what it is advertising, if it fails to communicate anything to anybody, and if nobody likes it. Alongside impact, communication and enjoyability we need to add a 'market' variable, which may best be described as 'brand elasticity'. This variable is a function of market size and maturity, brand size and development, opportunity to respond, unit price, etc. The advertisement's chances of working will be enhanced the more money is spent on showing it. For new brands and markets, the opportunity for sales effects to occur is relatively large. In mature markets, long-established brands generally find it more difficult to make sales gains, although this is by no means impossible.

A brand's elasticity of response to advertising is a given variable, and outside the control of the producer of the ad. So is media weight which is a financial decision to be taken alongside and in competition with other expenditures at corporate level. Of the three elements within the advertisement itself, two afford no great problem in research. Relevance of communication and the extent to which people understand it are not difficult to explore. Nor is enjoyability.

The third element is concerned with whether people notice the advertisement, and what it is for. What we wish to measure is an advertisement's efficiency in generating branded advertising associations – those messages and images from the advertising that spring to mind when we see the brand in a typical selling context, whether it is on the supermarket shelf, or in the *Yellow Pages*. This efficiency in generating branded advertising associations is often referred to as an awareness index (AI); it is a measure of an advertisement's productivity and is defined as a number of additional percentage points of claimed advertisement recall that would be generated by an additional one hundred TVRs.

14.3 Advertisement awareness and sales effectiveness

There is no simple relationship between sales and the measure of an advertisement's productivity. Provided there is a sales-effective message, low advertisement awareness is unlikely to be a good thing. The problem of establishing any relationship lies in the intervening stages between seller and buyer. Thus, having advertised the new wonder whitening powers of Zippo detergent, we find sales performance also being determined by Zippo's need to stand on the shelf alongside competitors' brands and subject to comparison on price, promotion, packaging, etc.

However, in instances where there is no intervening retail environment, we find that a relationship does hold. This became clear in an earlier investigation in the 1980s, similarly concerning a financial market. In this instance, our client felt very unsure about our conclusion (from an advertising tracking study) that his second campaign seemed to be much less efficient than his first in generating branded advertising associations. The second campaign had an awareness index of four as against ten for the first. The client felt that sales had actually been 'fairly buoyant' during the second campaign and certainly nothing like so bad as our work on advertising suggested. We therefore conducted an econometric analysis of sales performance. 'Sales' were here defined as new openings of the type of account featured in the advertising.

This analysis shows (see Figure 14.1) a good 'fit' between actual and model in the earlier period. Later, though, the modelled sales line became substantially higher than the actual, leaving a large negative discrepancy (see Figure 14.2). The factors in the model could not be adjusted since they were measures of reality such as interest rates, unemployment levels, and the like. Although the same could be said of advertising input in the forms of 'adstocks' (see Figure 14.3), this was not strictly true since it would assume that one 'adstock' was always of equal value to any other – in other words, that there could be no qualitative difference. This is plainly untrue.

We found that the sales model could be brought back into line with the actual sales if we down-weighted the value of the adstocks after the change in advertising campaigns. We needed to assume that the qualitative value of the second campaign's adstocks was equivalent to only 40 per cent of that in the first campaign. This brought the model back into line (see Figure 14.4) and was consistent with the findings from the tracking study about the respective levels of the awareness index.

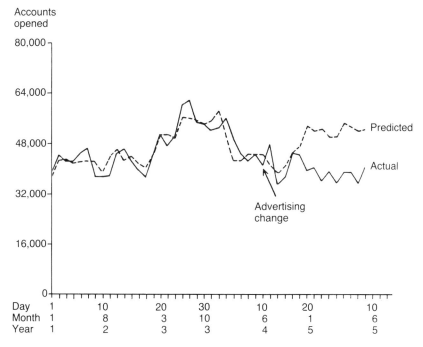

Figure 14.1   1980s financial product – actual v. predicted sales

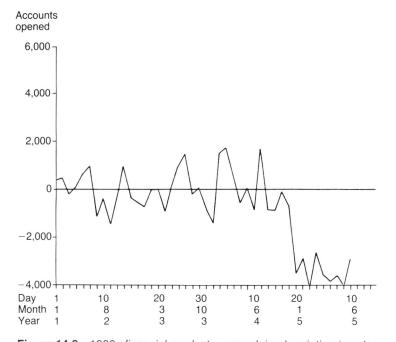

Figure 14.2   1980s financial product – unexplained variation in sales

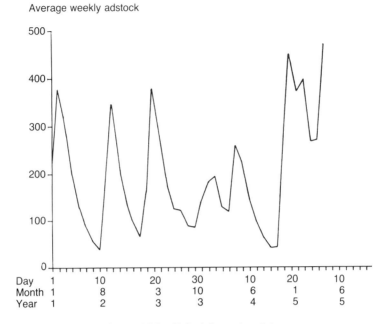

Figure 14.3 Television advertising

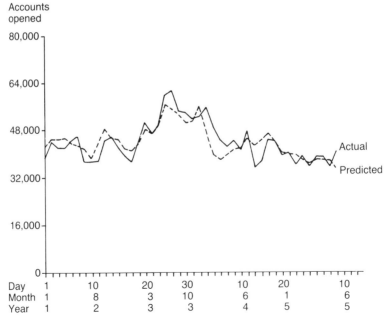

Figure 14.4 Actual v. predicted sales (if second campaign TVRs reduced by 60 per cent in the prediction)

14.4 Direct Line

In the case of Direct Line Insurance, the method of operation helps to reduce the gap – the intervening stages – between advertising and effect, for Direct Line conducts its business with its customers over the phone – not in the form of direct selling, but by responding to calls from enquirers. The first response to an enquiry is the provision of an insurance quotation. These quotations are provided as the Direct Line operator keys the insurance details into a computer which calculates and displays the quote instantly – and stores the data for sales analysis. From the customer's viewpoint, seeking a quote is the initial expression of purchase interest. The subsequent decision to purchase or not is determined by the other classic marketing Ps – price, product, packaging, etc. Advertising is therefore the stimulus which prompts the enquirer to seek a quote. Quotes provide the measure, not actual sales in the form of insurance policies taken out. The trigger to enquire about a quotation is not by seeing the products in store; there is no retail environment and no immediate competitive contrast of price and content.

In other words, Direct Line is direct marketing driven and is not part of a broker-dominated distribution system. Since there is no middleman in the operation, premiums do not have to allow for commission payments. This has given the company a very compelling pricing platform – simply, 'cheaper insurance'.

Direct Line also enjoys another considerable advantage for its marketing operations – instant access to its customer-enquiry database of quotations. As the Direct Line operator also asks each enquirer how and where they heard of the company's name (and logs the information into the computer), it is possible to build up, day by day, a picture of how well different media are performing. In the press, for example, it has been possible to test different papers and different executions comprehensively, and to identify which would produce the most acceptable levels of response in terms both of absolute numbers and cost efficiency.

Millward Brown has been commissioned to use this database, and to conduct econometric analyses in order to establish the response per pound between different media for different categories of insurance. This econometric work has also been used to develop successful forecasting models.

14.5 Direct Line's advertising history

Direct Line began selling motor insurance in April 1985. It soon found that the most cost-effective format for advertising was bottom-of-the-page strip in national newspapers. Success prompted a number of competitors to emulate Direct Line's main selling features. Some of the competitors were traditional insurance companies. This meant that there was now a new category of 'direct insurers'. The competition helped to promote the general attractiveness of arranging insurance

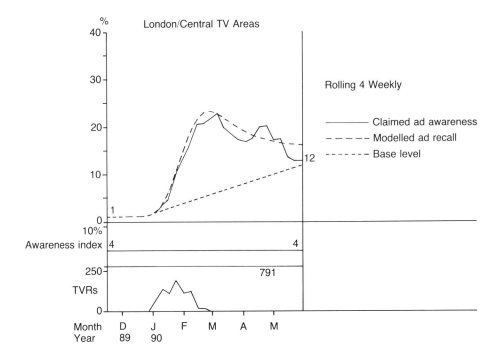

Figure 14.5   Advertisement recall model – Direct Line

direct with the insurance company, while the entry of some long-established names gave potential customers added assurance. However, all this helped to make for a much noisier, competitive market in which it would prove even more difficult for Direct Line to maintain share dominance. A new strategy was needed, designed to increase public awareness of Direct Line, its services and competitive advantages. As part of this new strategy it was decided that the brand and the product offer would best be advertised using the impact, reach and communication potential of television.

14.6 A new television campaign

On 3 January 1990 a new Motor Insurance television campaign broke in Scotland, the Midlands, London and the South. The new advertisement had been researched quantitatively via Millward Brown's recently introduced 'Link' television pre-test system. The advertisement was tested in animatic form, so that there was opportunity and time to make changes if necessary – and before too much personal prestige had been invested in a finished film. It was as well that the pre-test was conducted. It showed the following conclusions:

- The advertisement was found to be not very enjoyable.
- There was only low brand prominence.
- The focus of viewers' interest was on the little red phone which appeared in the advertisement as the endorsement of the idea that Direct Line came riding to the rescue of the harassed car insurer, but interest was low.
- The key communication point – Direct Line's price competitiveness – did not come through clearly.

From these conclusions, the following recommendations emerged:

- The red phone as the main focus of attention and attraction needed a more prominent role, stronger personality and a closer identification with Direct Line.
- The phone (and, by implication, Direct Line) needed to be more clearly positioned as the motorists' friend.
- Re-structuring of the audio and video elements was needed so that the message about competitive prices did not fight against strong visual distractions.
- Responsibility comes from the imprimatur of the Royal Bank of Scotland; this needed strengthening.

Had the advertisement been left in its original form our prediction was for an awareness index of between one and two. That is, for each additional one hundred TVRs put behind the advertisement, there would have been an extra one or two percentage points of claimed ad recall. Across the number of ads, which have been tested and then gone on to be shown on air in the same form, the correlation between prediction and actual outcome stands at 0.93. The advertisement was modified, though, in line with the recommendations, and in the event had a branded impact twice as high (see Figure 14.5). The awareness index of four shown here comes within that band of indices, 3–5, where we find the majority of advertisements.

It is very satisfactory if not spectacular; an awareness index of two or less would have been cause for concern. This is not the only measure of an advertisement's effectiveness. In the pre-test, for instance, we had found that there was a real need to improve both communication and enjoyability.

In the real-life situation the tracking study showed that the stronger role given to the phone in the finished advertisement made this branding device much stronger. For example, among those definitely recalling the Direct Line campaign, three quarters specifically recalled the red telephone and its actions – jumping into the air, the bugle call, and so on. Similarly, when a series of statements about attitudes to the advertisement were put in front of people, we found in the tracking study that there was a strongly favourable balance; in the pre-test the reverse had been true. The advertising had a number of demonstrable benefits for Direct Line.

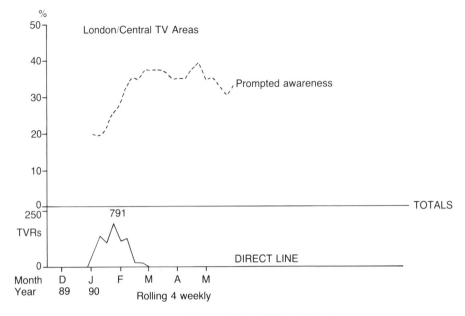

Figure 14.6   Prompted recognition of Direct Line Insurance

Index base 100 = Before advertising	
Becoming a popular choice for insurance	220
Good for people like me	170
Offer a high quality service	150

Figure 14.7   Direct Line – index of image shifts

One of the major effects looked for from the new strategy was an increase in public recognition of Direct Line and of the value in its services. In line with the strategy, prompted recognition of Direct Line rose markedly from the onset of the new campaign (see Figure 14.6); while the reputation of the company and its services rose on a number of key dimensions (see Figure 14.7). However, it was in its 'sales' effect that the advertisement was outstanding. Against a background of increasing competition, the underlying trend of Direct Line sales had been slightly downward. Once the new television advertisements began, the trend turned upward – the much-hoped-for 'hockey stick syndrome' posited in many a brand manager's forward plans yet so rarely eventualising (see Figure 14.8).

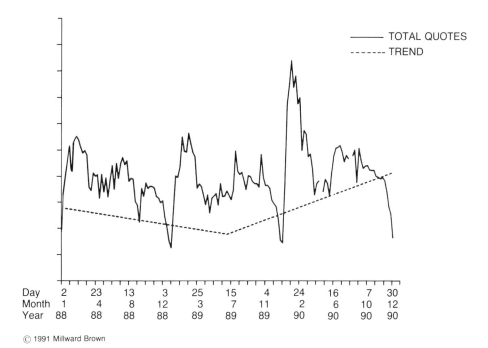

Day	2	23	13	3	25	15	4	24	16	7	30
Month	1	4	8	12	3	7	11	2	6	10	12
Year	88	88	88	88	89	89	89	90	90	90	90

© 1991 Millward Brown

Figure 14.8 Direct Line Insurance sales modelling – total quotes and underlying trend

14.7 The next opportunity – home insurance

14.7.1 The opportunity and the problem

In late 1988 Direct Line had also entered the market for home insurance. However, the press advertising policy which had initially proved so valuable for motor insurance was nothing like as successful in generating high volumes of sales of home insurance.

The reason for this relative lack of success was diagnosed as strong, consumer inertia. This comes about from the control that mortgage lenders (primarily Building Societies) hold over sales and renewal of this kind of insurance. The mortgage lender naturally insists on insurance of the property. Thus, most mortgage borrowers automatically take their insurance from their Building Society and automatically allow it to be renewed in subsequent years. There is no habit of shopping around as with motor insurance.

14.7.2 The need for new advertising

Advertising for home insurance, therefore, had to do more than just announce Direct Line. That may have worked with motor insurance, but home insurance needed something else. In particular, the advertising would need to shake up people's beliefs and opinions, so that they would begin to think of shopping around.

Direct Line had something to shake people up all right: a saving of up to 20 per cent off the annual premium paid via their Building Society (the cutting out of the middleman, again). Moreover, Direct Line had a proven format for this kind of advertising (albeit in the slightly different market of motor insurance):

- The buyers of house insurance, like the buyer of the new car in the advertisements previously tested, face a major problem – in this instance, the cost of the insurance on offer from the Building Society manager. Again, the little red telephone could come to the rescue with a saving of up to 20 per cent of their previous premium.
- Within the advertising, the stronger role and clearer characterisation given to the little red phone in the earlier ad could be maintained, together with its friendly character as once again it rode to the rescue.

14.7.3 Any need for new research?

To answer 'no' could be strongly defended. After all, the new advertising would have the same structure as the earlier advertisement. There was an adequate understanding of the basic cost problem facing the insurer. The Direct Line answer was clear, simple to grasp and strong – a saving of 20 per cent. Furthermore, the mechanics of the advertisement, the desired characterisation of the red phone and its slightly 'cheeky chappie' appeal, had been learnt from the earlier advertisement testing and tracking.

Nor could the cost of testing the new advertisement be overlooked: almost £10,000 for research and as much again, and possibly up to twice as much, on producing an animatic – a total cost of £20–30,000 plus extra time to be built into the planning and production schedule for the new campaign. In these circumstances many would have argued that there was little to be gained by further testing, and that we have by now learnt quite enough to judge advertising for home insurance. It was as well that the new home advertisement was put through a pre-test.

14.7.4 Pre-testing the new home advertisement

The advertisement, like its predecessor, did not rate well among the target audience on either enjoyability or on the scale of subjective assessment of brand prominence (see Figure 14.9). The only key rating on which the advertisement performed noticeably better than average was 'ease of understanding'. This, however, begs the important question of whether people actually understood the message correctly.

It had been concluded from the original motor insurance advertisement test that the phone must be given greater prominence, as the embodiment of the Direct Line service. Unfortunately, in the later animatic for home insurance, the red phone achieved even less prominence than it had in the earlier test (known as 'showroom') (see Figure 14.10). The role of the red phone in the advertisement proved, in fact, to be the nub of the problem. This became clear when respondents were asked: 'Would you please tell me what was happening in the advertisement . . . what was shown, what was said, the story being told and how it all fitted together?'

The verbatim reports of replies from people indicated that no less than 60 per cent clearly misunderstood the message. Worse, they got the message completely the wrong way round. Rather than the telephone, people saw the principal character as the Building Society manager and thought that it was he – not the

	Rating	Diff. from average
Enjoyment	2.57	−0.62
Subjective 'attention getting'	2.72	0.05
Subjective brand prominence	2.71	−0.98
Ease of understanding	3.59	0.31

Figure 14.9 Direct Line 'dream mortgage' – ratings summary

'What is the main thing you will notice when you see the ad repeatedly on television?'	Home	'Show-room'
% mentioning phone	38	47

Figure 14.10 Focus of the advertisement

phone – who offered the cost saving. As a result, the identity and role of the little red phone became something of a mystery, indeed a source of irritation, being dismissed as 'silly', 'a gimmick', and the like.

It was recommended that the finished film needed crucially to identify the red phone as the main agent and provider of the solution. The sudden appearance of the phone inside the Building Society office in the animatic was contributing to the audience's misconceptions. The telephone, therefore, needed to be seen clearly as coming to the rescue from outside the building; making its way to the side of the couple worried about the cost of home insurance; causing consternation to the Building Society manager, and finally as the agent removing worries and enabling the couple to get 'one up' on the manager.

These recommended modifications were put into effect in the finished film, which was itself put through a Link pre-test. Critically, it was found that the misunderstandings and misconceptions found with the animatic had been completely eradicated in the finished film.

14.8 The home insurance advertisement in real life

As with the earlier campaign, the start of the new home campaign saw a dramatic increase in prompted recognition of Direct Line (see Figure 14.11). Similarly,

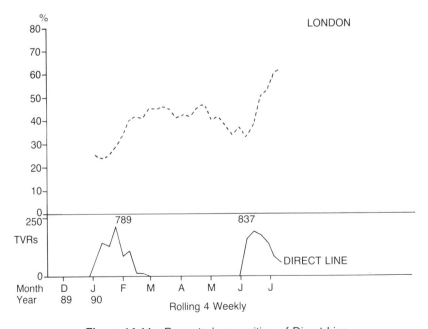

Figure 14.11 Prompted recognition of Direct Line

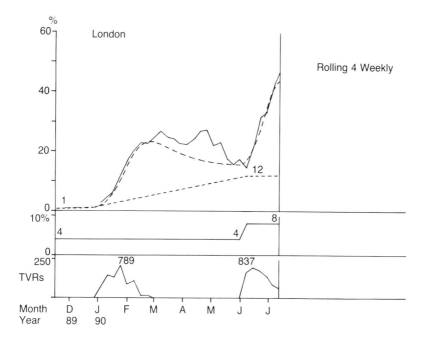

Figure 14.12 Direct Line modelled television advertisement awareness

claimed awareness of television advertising showed a second spurt, some 50 per cent of the target audience claiming to have seen advertising for Direct Line on television recently – twice the peak level achieved with the earlier motor campaign for virtually the same level of TVRs.

Therefore, the productivity of the second advertisement must have been considerably greater. This is confirmed by the awareness index. The earlier advertising was highly satisfactory, with an AI of four, but the new advertisement's AI of eight placed it as an unusually stronger performer (see Figure 14.12).

In passing we should also note that the vast majority of people (80 per cent) found that the advertisement told them something of interest. This 'something' was the offer of a 20 per cent saving, undercutting Building Societies, cheapest and competitively priced. It is clear from the testing programme that had the advertisement stayed in its original form there would have been nothing like this communication success.

14.9 Sales effects

We suggested earlier that in the case of Direct Line there would be a more direct relationship between advertising efficiency and sales than would be the case with

	Motor	Home
Sales uplift		
Index base 100 = year-on-year uplift in		
motor quotations after advertising	100	210
Ad efficiency		
Awareness index	4	8

Figure 14.13   Sales uplift = advertisement efficiency

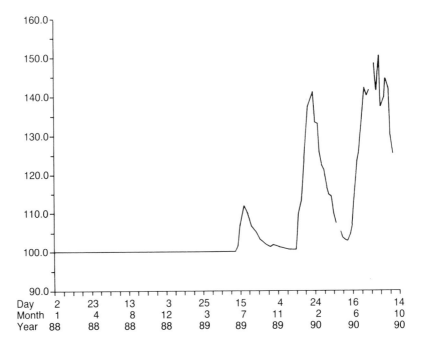

Figure 14.14   Direct Line Insurance sales model – index of sales during advertised periods

fmcg. For one thing, there is a direct connection with the potential buyer and no intermediary such as a retailer or distributor. For another, the basic sales datum is the quotation rather than a purchase which is influenced by the most crucial factor of price.

Thus when set side by side, we see how closely matched the two key indicators of performance of the Motor and House campaigns are: sales uplift and efficiency for the advertising as measured by the awareness index (see Figure 14.13).

We can also note the marked effect which television advertising has had on the number of quotes requested. The econometric modelling had enabled us to say that television advertising had added over 40 per cent of motor quotes in those regions with advertising after allowing for longer-term trends (see Figure 14.14).

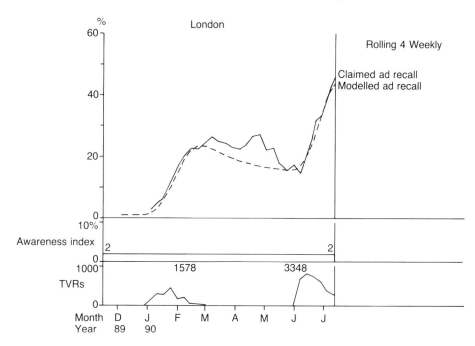

Figure 14.15   Advertisement recall model – Direct Line

14.10 Contribution of the research to sales and profitability

The acid test of the value of the pre-test research lies in the question: 'What would have happened if the original animatics had not been tested and had not been amended in the finished film?'

As a first step we would need to take the predicted value of the awareness indices as shown in the Link tests of the animatics. Then we would need to substitute the predicted value for the actual values in the ad recall model (see Figure 14.12). The tests on both animatics produced predictions for the awareness indices of between one and two.

Giving the advertisement the benefit of any doubt and adopting the high end of the range for our estimate, we have substituted the actual awareness indices of four and eight with a uniform index of two for both campaigns. In order to bring back the modelled line of recall to fit with the actual, we have had to compensate for the loss of advertising efficiency by increasing the number of TVRs in the model. The resulting model is shown in Figure 14.15. Over the whole period, then, there would have needed to be massively more TVRs to make up for poorer efficiency – 4,930, rather than 1,630.

Note that we have not made any allowance here for the fact that the original animatic for home insurance caused great confusion in communication and some irritation over the role of the red phone; these would undoubtedly have further impaired the effectiveness of the advertising. Therefore, the benefit of having improved the advertising was equivalent to at least some 3,300 TVRs in the first half of 1990. This may be translated through to a 'bottom line benefit' to Direct Line's profitability of some £5 million. Looked at the other way round, had the animatics not been improved, and extra money not been spent to compensate, fewer quotations would have been sought.

It can be said that these models indicate a loss of some tens of thousands on home insurance quotations, equivalent to a loss of two-thirds of business generated by the television advertising.

14.11 Conclusions

1. Direct Line's first move into television advertising in support of motor insurance would have been much less effective had it not been for the pre-testing of the advertisement.
2. At that point it would have been easy to say that the decision-maker's judgement had benefited from learning about consumer reactions: therefore, there would be no need to pre-test the next phase of the advertising for home insurance.
3. That would have left us showing a commercial which our target audience would not have readily associated with Direct Line; which would not have been readily understood – and indeed would have created confusion; and which would not have been enjoyable.
4. The loss to sales from having less-efficient advertising would have been very large.
5. The value to Direct Line in having improved advertising was equivalent to £5 million of extra media expenditure.

CHAPTER 15

Quality issues in market research

Phyllis Vangelder

The application of marketing research to measurements of quality perception and customer satisfaction is not new. In a sense marketing research has always been about this. What has been different in the past few years is the formal recognition of quality standards and customer satisfaction as company necessities, written into procedures and professionally monitored.

Consideration of quality is not just about the efficiency of a product or service, but the nature of the transaction between the manufacturer or provider of the good or service and the customer.

Market research can help companies and their customers to identify their needs and this is an opportunity for the researchers to be involved in the management process. The same techniques that were applied to fmcg are now also applied to services. As Peter Mouncey has written:

> the new generation of mass produced, highly packaged services creates
> a degree of familiarity through frequent usage, much the same as can
> be gained from the purchase and usage of many products . . . the same
> basic concept underlies the successful marketing of both products and
> services – gain as in-depth an understanding of the consumer and his
> needs as is possible and then develop and market the 'product'
> accordingly. This role is the property of the market research industry.
> (1987:23)

Closely linked with the concept of how the manufacturer or provider of services views his/her customer, is the way consumers are changing. They are becoming increasingly sophisticated, with knowledge and understanding of marketing techniques. The shift of emphasis is from the manufacturer to the consumer – the 'prosumer'. One result of this sophistication is the vulnerability of the brand: today's customers are cynical about television commercials – they want to be amused rather than instructed to buy a particular brand. At the Market Research Society Conference in 1993, Steve Chinn of Saatchi and Saatchi quoted a male lager drinker at a discussion group:

What you don't seem to realise is how much we know about what
you're doing and what role you need us to play. You think what
you're doing is clever and remote, but we understand it. (Chinn 1993:
1–5)

Customers not only understand the marketing process, they are aware of their
rights. They have expectations and knowledge of products and services, reinforced
by articles in the press and programmes on television. Research International have
a Service Expectations model which illustrates the series of expectations about the
service new customers expect they will receive from the service provider (Banks
1993).

The brand, whether a service or product, has to work hard for its survival, but
it has never been more important. The manufacturer needs to stay close to his/her
customer to understand his/her relationship with his/her brand to strengthen the
appeal and relevance of his/her communications. Steve Chinn suggested that 'We
can take the "consumers" into our confidence and recognise their role as partners
in marketing development.' However a barrier to this is 'the acceptance by the
broad marketing community that relationship marketing, in which the consumer
and the manufacturer are genuinely treated as equal partners in a mutually
beneficial process, will be necessary' (Chinn 1993).

15.1 Relationship research

The rationale for relationship marketing lies in the change from a transaction focus
to a relationship focus. Christopher *et al.* (1991) show transaction marketing to be
a focus on a single sale and orientation on product features for a short time-scale.
Relationship marketing focuses on customer retention, with orientation on product
benefits with high customer service emphasis, commitment and contact. In
transaction marketing quality is primarily the concern of production, in relationship marketing it is the concern of all areas.

Relationship research is the close monitoring of customer needs in order to be
able to provide the right levels of service and quality over the longer term. In the
case of service institutions like banks and building societies, this means seeing the
customer is serviced through various life stages, buying different products perhaps,
but remaining loyal to the company in a lifetime bond. In the case of the
manufacturing company this relationship is through the brand.

Retention marketing in which every effort is made to retain long-term
relationships with customers is cost-effective. Financial institutions, for instance,
attempt to cross-sell other financial products to their customer base.

Maritz Marketing Research refer to the relationship development process as
'proactive relationship management' (Cottrell 1993). Their PRM approach is a
proactive and ongoing communication with their customer via telephone throughout the product/service ownership or use-period for the purpose of enhancing the

potential of long-term loyalty. British Telecom's Customer Satisfaction Monitor, described in more detail on page 318, can be compared.

These research approaches highlight the importance of proactive insight into customer attitudes rather than a reactive infrastructure that only comes in contact with customers who complain. Philip Kotler refers to this proactive customer relationship management structure as 'wrap-around marketing'. It gives the company an opportunity to gain continuous feedback.

15.2 Total quality management

Total quality management (TQM) is what it says – a totality that applies as much to the internal organisation of a company as to its relationships with its customers and its suppliers or other links in the channel. Total quality management implies a change in management style where managers have to let staff have power to 'own' a problem. It also means a greater attention to customer needs in markets that have become increasingly competitive. Xerox, IBM, Royal Mail, British Telecom, Shell, McDonald's, John Lewis Partnership and British Airways are just some examples of companies that have used a customer care approach and examined the needs of end users. Through careful training and rigid disciplines, such companies can produce a consistent interaction between their staff and their customers.

Customer care and customer satisfaction surveys have become a very important part of the research suppliers' repertoire as companies realise that researching both the customer and non-customer is an essential part of TQM. Total quality management includes many aspects which research methods can measure – staff performance, the effectiveness of complaints procedures, the efficiency with which information is disseminated, speed of operations, personnel training, service response times, etc.

15.3 Employees

Customer care must take into consideration employees' attitudes about the companies in which they work. Employees must be willing and able to deliver the desired levels of service which customers require. Role ambiguity and conflict are issues that management must face in TQM. Research among employees is a specialised task and several research companies have dedicated departments conducting this work.

The British Petroleum (BP) Exploration Operating Company have published a case where they show that a voyage of self-discovery was the key to getting a new message of changed values over to staff (Jones 1993).

15.4 Service encounters

Albrecht and Zemke (1985) speak of the concept of 'service encounters' or moments or truth and 'critical incidents': the actual encounter between customer and company. The need to measure this encounter and track its continuing efficiency is paramount, because it is this encounter which is important and salient to the customer.

When measuring quality in services, we are measuring quality which is relative to expectations – it does not necessarily mean the service is of low quality. Consumers have what Parasuraman *et al.* (1991) refer to as zones of tolerance, the difference between desired and adequate expectations.

There are many examples of research of this kind carried out in the following service areas both in the public and private sectors:

- Banks and building societies.
- Package holidays.
- Airlines.
- Utilities.
- Car owners.
- Gambling casinos.

15.5 Public sector

We shall begin by discussing research in the public sector. The non-competitive environment in which the public services and private utilities operate has tended to reduce their responsiveness to their customer needs. However, both public and privatised services have utilised customer satisfaction research to examine these needs.

In Britain restraint is supplied by the regulatory bodies set up to control suppliers' behaviour. Offer and Oftel regulate the electricity and telecommunication industries and Ofwat and Ofgas regulate the water and gas industries. By incorporating measures of customer satisfaction in their assessment of suppliers' performance, the regulators can encourage them to alter their service in a way that best meets customers' needs. Utilities are concerned to discover the service improvements that will produce the most cost-effective method of improving satisfaction.

The Competition and Service Utilities Act 1992 states 'The Director General (of Gas Services) may make regulations prescribing such standards of performance in connection with the provision of gas supplying services . . .' they 'may only be made . . . after arranging for such research as the Director considers appropriate, with a view to discovering the views of a representative sample of persons likely to be affected and considering the results'.

One result of this has been a proliferation of 'performance indicators' attempting to quantify the delivery of specific standards of service. A highly important function of customer satisfaction research is to aid public sector managers in choosing the most appropriate performance indicators. An example of this process is the work undertaken by MORI on behalf of the Audit Commission, the body responsible for monitoring the performance of local government in England and Wales (Burns 1993). Public sector management is recognising that the public has a role to play in determining the manner that service is provided. With this has come the recognition that the public should be consulted.

15.6 The Citizen's Charter

The Government's Citizen's Charter launched in 1991 is an official recognition of the rights of people to good service in the public sector, 'to make public services answer better to the wishes of their users and to raise their quality overall'. In other words, providers of public services should identify their customer's needs and expectations and provide appropriate services. The Citizen's Charter White Paper also stressed the role of the customer:

> The public sector should provide choice wherever practicable. The
> people affected by services should be consulted. Their views about the
> services they use should be sought regularly and systematically to
> inform decisions about what service should be provided.

The revenue section of the Citizen's Charter White Paper included a clear commitment from the Revenue to 'seek people's views about the service they receive' and among government departments in the United Kingdom, the Inland Revenue has been among the first to engage in a large-scale, multi-stage programme of customer service research in accordance with the Citizen's Charter initiative. The Charter, with its emphasis on the needs and empowerment of the ordinary citizen, clarified both the target of the study and the underlying rationale of the research. The department found that the value of research lies not just in the provision of statistics, but in providing rich data about the 'customers' of the department.

A new government department – the Office of Public Service and Science – was created to oversee and co-ordinate the charter's implementation. Separate charters have been published covering the Health Service, London Underground, the Post Office and many other public services as well as local councils which launched their own versions. In all cases the use of research approaches underlies the effectiveness of these charters. In the 1993 edition of London Underground's Charter 'Aiming Higher' the Managing Director Denis Tunnicliffe writes:

> We know from regular customer research, that you attach particular
> importance to clear and up-to-date information, helpful and courteous

staff, working lifts and escalators and clean trains and stations. In this 1993 edition of our Customer Charter we explain how well we have performed against the commitment we made to you in Summer 1992.

The publication quotes figures on the percentage of customers rating as acceptable or better the various dimensions of importance. A paper by Mark Hodson and Robert Falconer to an ESOMAR Seminar on Customer Satisfaction described London Underground's continuous customer attitude research programme – the Customer Satisfaction Index – in detail (Hodson and Falconer 1993).

15.6.1 *Market research and the Citizen's Charter*

Cynthia Pinto and Susannah Quick presented a paper at the Market Research Society Annual Conference in 1993 where they discussed the role of market research and the Citizen's Charter (Pinto and Quick 1993), particularly some of the work they undertook for local authorities and district health authorities. They stressed in their paper that before standards can be set, providers of public services need to understand exactly what the expectation of their users and potential users are. They illustrate their paper with examples from surveys on patients' expectations about the amount of warning for admittance to and discharge from hospital and their views on their accommodation while in hospital and on customer perception of the quality of service from local councils. Their conclusion headed 'The role of research in a customer-led social climate' identifies the contribution that market research can make in developing customer-generated definitions of quality; in developing better ways to measure the importance of different services and aspects of service delivery to users in order to provide guidance on the allocation of resources; and in terms of monitoring perceptions of quality over time. Pinto and Quick also stress the need for professional, high-quality, objective and usable market research in this sector. They point to the danger of poor-quality, biased surveys commissioned by inexperienced buyers.

Market and Opinion Research International (MORI) have also undertaken hundreds of surveys in the public sector. It has been their experience that customers find it easier to respond to specific questions rather than general satisfaction questions. The resulting measures must then be reduced. An initial method of data reduction is to look for the level of correlation between different satisfaction variables. Multi-variate analysis and data inspection allow selection of surrogate measures and reduce the number of measures required for future surveys. Market and Opinion Research International have devised a satisfaction attainment scoring system that relates the level of importance of a given service attribute to the quality of service being delivered. This scoring system allows the client to appreciate the contribution made by each service attribute to the overall level of customer satisfaction.

A 'PATSAT' system is conducted by CASPE Consulting, developed to obtain feedback from patients on all aspects of care they receive. Questionnaires are tailored to the needs of each hospital, speciality, ward or clinic and combine the issues proven to be those that patients most wish to comment on plus local topics of particular reference or the user. One-off surveys are sometimes more appropriate, for instance, among the elderly (French 1993).

A PhD thesis by A. G. H. Thompson at the Manchester School of Management, quoted by Lewis (1993), looked at the measurement of patients' perceptions of the quality of hospital care. He developed a substantive survey questionnaire to measure the expectations and satisfactions of hospital in-patients from admission to discharge. Thompson concluded that expectations were an important element in reported levels of satisfaction and he developed indices of patient satisfaction and dissatisfaction as well as identifying dimensions in need of improvement (Thompson 1983).

Another project at the Manchester School of Management, funded by the Health Service, is investigating general practitioner services. Data have been collected from GPs and other health service personnel, examining the service they provide and their perceptions of patients' needs. A large survey of patients (n = 6,800) is also being conducted. Areas covered include: accessibility of care; the nature of care and doctor–patient interaction. A major part of the questionnaire is a ServQual section covering fifty-five dimensions of service. Factor analysis of the pilot study found three major factors: responsiveness (i.e. time pressure, willingness to assist patients, time for emotional problems and prompt service); reliability (i.e. GP effectiveness, home visits, effectiveness of other practice staff, dealing with emotional problems) and empathy (i.e. individualised attention from GPs, nurses and receptionists) (Lewis 1993).

15.6.2 *Improving the level of customer satisfaction*

The problems of measuring patient satisfaction were highlighted in another MORI survey conducted on hospitals in Leeds. Despite high satisfaction about hospitals, users felt there were improvements that needed to be made, with each user suggesting an average of three improvements. The researchers' problem was to detach the positive overall attitudes to the hospital as an institution, from significant criticism on issues such as waiting time and information provision (Burns 1993).

Many local councils undertake residents' surveys to ensure that their resources are spent in the optimum way and people are getting what they want. As well as assessing perceptions of the quality and effectiveness of services, such surveys can save money for councils. For instance, surveys undertaken by MORI show that a small change to its meals-on-wheels service saved the London Borough of Lewisham several thousands of pounds.

Information provision is an extremely important aspect of public service. Research undertaken by MORI shows quite conclusively that an improvement in communications can have a major impact on the level of customer satisfaction. The case of Warwick District Council's housing services was an example of this. A

1988 MORI survey showed that the housing services were well regarded but the tenants were dissatisfied with the information provided to them. A tenants' handbook detailing their rights and responsibilities and giving contact points for various services resulted in an increase in the proportion of tenants who felt the Council kept them informed and a significant rise in the, already high, level of overall satisfaction with the housing service.

Very often council newsletters, providing a means of communication to residents, are a result of research. Surveys are quoted by MORI from East Hampshire where research led to increased customer care training, changes in the refuse collection service, more recycling facilities, improved distribution of the council newspaper and publication of a conservation strategy.

In Richmond Borough Council a corporate PR strategy, computerised council house waiting-list, new telephone network and more user-friendly reception areas plus extra services for handicapped people were all initiatives taken on the basis of MORI surveys.

15.7 Customer service

Assessment of customer service may take a number of forms: management audit; evaluation of customers' complaints; sample surveys; customer exit surveys; mystery shopping surveys. Mystery shopping techniques are often used, for instance, to check on the performance of a salesperson. The role of the interviewer undertaking mystery shopping is quite different from the interviewer in a standard survey and training is necessary in observational and memory skills. Mystery shopping as a research technique has been utilised for a long time. Restaurant critics or *Which?* have used this approach consistently. The Market Research Society's Code of Conduct allows the technique provided that certain sensible conditions are met (Clause A15).

There are several techniques to help clients increase their understanding of customers' needs. For instance, benchmark measures where, for example, an electricity company may compare itself with other utilities.

15.7.1 The GAP model

This has been developed from the extensive work of Berry and his colleagues (Parasuraman *et al.* 1990). They defined service quality as a function of the gap between consumers' expectations of a service and their perception of the actual service delivery by an organisation. They suggested that this gap was influenced by four other gaps:

1. Managers' perceptions of customers' expectations may be different from actual customer needs and desires, i.e. managers do not necessarily know what customers expect from a company.
2. Even if the needs are known, they may not be translated into appropriate service specifications/standards and systems.
3. The service performance gap when the service that is delivered is different from management's specifications for service, due to variations in the performance of personnel, i.e. employees not being able or willing to perform at a desired level.
4. What is said about the service in external communications, i.e. advertising and promotion which is different from the service that is delivered.

Gap 5 is consumers' actual expectations and perceptions of service.

15.7.2 *ServQual*

This approach to measuring the quality of service was developed by Berry (Berry and Parasuraman 1991; Parasuraman *et al.* 1990). In addition to the service quality gap he and his colleagues developed from the dimensions of service quality the ServQual questionnaire (Parasuraman *et al.* 1990). This has twenty-two pairs of Likert-type scales. The first twenty-two items are designed to measure customer expectations of service for a particular service industry and the following twenty-two are intended to measure the perceived level of service provided by a particular organisation. ServQual is used to trace service quality trends and improve service; categorise customers; compare branches/outlets of an organisation and compare an organisation with its competitors. It is limited to current and past customers as respondents need knowledge and experience of the company. There are considerations relating to weighting of variables and the use of negative statements which are discussed in the literature on ServQual.

15.7.3 *SIMALTO*

Simultaneous multi attribute level trade-off (SIMALTO) is a profile and trade-off approach used to collect data on the zone of tolerance (expectations and unacceptable levels, perceptions, of a company and its competitors, and priorities for improvement (Green 1977). Forms of SIMALTO, presenting the respondent with all aspects of the service and different levels of service for each attribute, are completed by each respondent. As many as fifty attributes can be included in such an exercise, though in practice twenty-five attributes or less are used.

Chudy and Sant (1993) illustrated an application of SIMALTO in an ESOMAR seminar on customer satisfaction. Taylor Nelson, their company, have developed a sophisticated choice-modelling technique for the manipulation of quantitative data on customers' needs, expectations, perceptions and values. Key outputs from this model include benchmarks and standards, relative importance of service aspects, improvement priorities, needs and value segmentation, service and price sensitivity and customer risk profiling. A combination of gap analysis, relative importance and improvement priorities is used to highlight the most critical aspects of a service from the customer's point of view. A scenario-testing facility can be used to identify the impact of improved quality initiatives on customer loyalty and increased brand preference.

SIMALTO PLUS is a more sophisticated version of SIMALTO.

15.7.4 SMART

A paper to the 1988 Market Research Society Conference illustrated the 'SMART approach to customer service' with a case describing Research International's research for the National Westminster Bank for its UK Quality Service programme (Baird *et al.* 1988). Salient, multi-attribute research technique (SMART) is a conjoint analysis approach which faces up to the need to measure both the tangible elements of service, such as length of queues, and the intangibles, such as being treated as an individual. It allows for the involvement of all interested parties (in this case, bank, quantitative and qualitative researchers) in the final analysis and interpretative phase. The initial part of the exercise is to derive those attributes which are of most importance to the individual respondent, i.e. the salient issues. From this point on, respondents concentrate on only the eight attributes at the top of their list. The next exercise is profiling involving respondents stating which of the attribute levels they feel best describes the standard of service perceived from the provider in question. A SMART barometer elicitation measures the relative importance of their set of attributes. Analysis of the data collected in the barometer grids are undertaken using conjoint analysis and cluster analysis. A switching question is also used to determine whether a respondent would switch from his/her existing bank to an alternative at any stage.

There are several problems relating to the measurement of consumer expectations and satisfactions. For example, the 'option' technique adopted in the SIMALTO or SMART approach, asking people to choose between different levels of behaviour, appears to be directly actionable. One of the problems is the relative distance between levels and of making scales realistic to the respondent. The measurement and relevance of importance are also very difficult.

Customer satisfaction surveys are not easy and in a seminal paper Mary and Peter Bartram (Bartram and Bartram 1993) have identified some of the reasons why they fail to satisfy clients. One reason is that they provide feedback on people's personal performance. They identify nine issues of concern: the management commitment; the focus of the research; the development of the research design which discusses the advantages and disadvantages of several approaches (e.g. SMART, SIMALTO, ServQual) and points out some of the problems (e.g.

distance measures, realistic scales, the measurement and relevance of 'importance'); the problems of continuous measurement; the sensitivity of the data; the need for re-assessment of the tracking survey; the presentation of the data and their application. The Bartrams present some very important guidelines for this type of research, suggesting that the key to success in this area is complexity in preparation followed by simplicity in delivering results. They also point to some trends. They suggest that there is an increasing recognition that research must measure what differentiates, rather than what is important. There will be more studies focusing on retention and on defecting customers, and the rapidly changing expectations of new customers. They also highlight the need for better ways of measuring psychological satisfactions, to complement the functional ones and stress the importance of measuring the contribution of customer satisfaction programmes to the improvement of market penetration, market share, business volume and profitability. Finally, they conclude by pointing out that the search for ways to meet customer expectations will be accompanied more and more by the search for ways to exceed them.

15.8 Profitability

Customer care is not altruistic – the price/quality relationship is often affected by service. Research can identify the elements of the service mix most important to the customer. It is also important to demonstrate the link between customer satisfaction measures and improved income.

Roger Banks in an article in *MRS Research Plus* (1993) quotes Arthur Redmond in a paper about Pepsi's Taco Bell restaurant chain to the American Marketing Association meeting:

> We tracked the business results of . . . focused effort and compared bottom line results with customer satisfaction performance. . . . Talk about an impressive relationship: those stores delivering the highest customer satisfaction scores also showed the highest growth and profit results. . . . Of equal importance, the growth rate in the highest scoring stores was almost double the lowest scoring. The difference on operating profit was almost as significant. (Banks 1993)

The success of British Airways' shift in image was reflected in its improved profitability. Research has shown that 85–90 per cent of people who complain do not buy again, unless their complaint is dealt with satisfactorily. Procter & Gamble now have a hotline for complaints – there are more complaints, but more sales. Alexander Biel has said 'there is now a preponderance of evidence from a variety of sources that even in the toughest economic times, the consumer is unwilling to sacrifice justifiable perceived quality for price' (1992: 1–16).

15.9 Examples

Customer satisfaction research is about measuring performance, evaluating people and both the tangible and intangible services they offer.

There are numerous examples in both the private and public sectors of company and service industries engaging in this type of research process. There are many other organisations which have an ongoing customer-monitoring process, but the following are presented as examples because they are in the public domain and papers and case studies have been presented by their representatives:

- Stork NV, a large Dutch conglomerate, has developed a methodology for the measurement and improvement of client satisfaction (de Vos 1993).
- IBM is another company dedicated to the concept of customer satisfaction. IBM Personal systems implemented their 'Customer First' programme in fourteen countries in Europe in 1991. Surveys are conducted in between eight and fourteen countries and this is being extended. Customer satisfaction consultants have been appointed in eight countries to help interpret the results of the research for dealers and provide requisite training (Mutz *et al.* 1993).
- British Airways' 'Putting People First' programme used market research to shape the campaign with an intensive programme of both qualitative and quantitative approaches among both passengers and staff. Research was used as input, not only to business strategy, but formed the basic input for staff training programmes. Writing in summer 1986, Mary Bartram, then market research manager for BA, described the Customer Services Standard Monitor, the Catering Monitor, the advertising tracking programme and staff surveys (Bartram 1986).
- British Telecom have been involved with customer care and quality for over a decade. Their TELCARE programme has now evolved into the Customer Satisfaction Monitor, a large-scale research programme, monitoring customer satisfaction at every level in which they are in contact with BT. Taylor Nelson, BMRB and FDS are among the research companies taking part in one of the largest ever telephone research projects. The close co-operation between British Telecom and the market research profession is another example of performance measures giving management a vital awareness of the needs and expectations of its customers.
- Royal Mail has for some time been engaged in a total quality management programme known as 'Customer First', based on the needs of external and internal customers. 'Hard measures' of service quality such as Research International's ongoing 'end-to-end' programme, measuring the time taken from 'pillar box to doormat' as well as 'softer' measures such as the extent to which Royal Mail is associated with attributes such as 'reliable and 'trustworthy' are covered by research. The 'end-to-end' measure (Banks *et al.* 1992) resulted in an overall improvement of 11 per cent in three years. A paper to the

ESOMAR Seminar on Customer Satisfaction Research (White and Banks 1993) described Royal Mail's attempt to measure the key 'intangible' aspects of the customer/staff interface. The Customer Perception and Satisfaction Index (CPSI) programme uses Research International's SMART technique which has now been used worldwide for over eighty customers. For Royal Mail each month some 200 self-completion questionnaires are despatched to members of the general public and 175 to small business customers within each of 120 postcode areas. The survey seeks to determine the level of service that customers perceive is currently being offered by Royal Mail on a range of relevant tangible and intangible attributes using the SMART profiling approach. Part of the process is communicating the concept and findings of the CPI to Royal Mail's districts around the United Kingdom.

- It is not only large companies like BT and British Gas who undertake customer satisfaction surveys. For instance, BEM Research conducted research for Victoria Wine. Customers' views were distilled into thirty-four service aspects, ranging from politeness, product knowledge and sales skills. Respondents' most important service aspects were traded off. Each was then assigned as 'expected as a matter of course', 'especially impressive', 'not bothered' or 'disliked' enabling the company to establish 'moments of truth' and prioritise staff training to customers' real wishes. Mystery shopping was used to assess customer handling skills and product knowledge. A weighting system derived from the customer survey ensured that the final results of the mystery customer programme reflected the importance of each element (Hurst 1993).

Data from customer satisfaction surveys are used as management tools and findings are being made available to staff.

15.10 Retailers

For many companies, the customer who is the most important to their business is the retailer responsible for selling the products to the customers, and a large growth area in customer satisfaction studies is in studies amongst retailers on subjects such as products, representatives, ordering, delivery, marketing and merchandising support, technical support, and training and accounts.

Linked with satisfaction studies amongst retailers, is the concept of 'category management' whereby the retailer and manufacturer have a close relationship, working together to improve a product category. This is a consumer-led process that involves managing product categories as business units and segmenting them by store clusters or on a store-by-store basis to satisfy customer needs. Nielsen have developed a customised process of category management and presented a paper at an ESOMAR Seminar on Retailing (Buckingham 1993).

15.11 BS 5750

As part of total quality management many companies are registering with the British Standards Institution for the accreditation standard BS 5750. In Europe the standard is ISO 9000. The standard is implemented by a company designing its own quality system and then having an assessment carried out by an independent accredited body. Each company therefore implements the standard in its own way. The BS 5750 standard requires a system of internal quality auditing, corrective action and management review to be in place. When buyers of research become accredited, research companies also consider the pros and cons of their own accreditation. Some buyer companies indeed look to research companies, not only to be a member of the Interviewer Quality Control Scheme (IQCS), thereby ensuring a minimum standard of interviewing, but also to have BS 5750 accreditation. Essentially a management system, BS 5750 sets out the procedures for a company's organisation and resources, the responsibilities of key personnel, the working methods employed in the day-to-day management and operation of the company to ensure that a service appropriate to the needs of the client is provided. The main benefit for a research company is that it identifies, reviews and formalises procedures and in documenting them strengthens and enhances them. The discipline of well-documented, clear and systematic procedures, properly thought through and subjected to regular inspection, can do much to improve and maintain standards and performance in many parts of the total research process. Standards such as BS 5750 do not determine quality, they simplify, record and monitor the systems and procedures to be followed in carrying out work to a quality standard already determined and set.

15.12 Social marketing

There was an awareness of social marketing in the 1970s. In 1979, Keith Crosier identified Type I social marketing as involving the transfer of marketing management practice and market research practice into new fields characterised frequently, but not exclusively, as not for profit. Type II social marketing involved giving consideration to the social implications and consequences of marketing practice – socially responsive and responsible marketing (Crosier 1979). In the 1990s we are only too aware that organisations which had been non-profitable are now being held to account – charities, hospitals, local government departments must now show profits. What we are conscious of in the 1990s is the need for all organisations, be they in the commercial or public sectors, to be socially responsible.

Michael Frye, Chairman of the Royal Society of Arts, gave a stirring paper to the 1992 Market Research Conference in which he identified a twenty-first-century perception of ethics for the individual, the community and business which encouraged people to operate in the 'domain of manners'. Issues for the decade included environmental responsibility and encouragement of people's potential in the workplace. In 'the age of community, when ethics, perception, values, choices, standards are applied to any organisation, the conclusions become self-evident. . . . If we are to sustain such an organisation, we need to replenish it and the wider community' (Frye 1992).

There has been a good deal of research about 'green products' and consumer response to them (see the *MRS Survey* issue on 'Green issues'). While there is more cynicism about 'green' nappies and detergents, there remains a great deal of concern that companies respect the environment and care for their employees and their customers.

15.13 Conclusion

The mind set of companies and customers is changing in the 1990s and the research profession has the techniques to measure this. But in any measuring system it is essential that the information is relevant and actionable. Research has an important practical responsibility in tracking and monitoring this change and a social responsibility in ensuring its results are used effectively and honestly.

References

Albrecht, K. and Zemke, R. (1985). *Service America: Doing business in the new economy*, Homewood IL: Dow Jones-Irwin.

Baird, C., Banks, R., Smith, P. and Morgan, R. (1988) 'The SMART approach to customer service', Proceedings of the Market Research Society Conference.

Banks, R. (1993) 'Putting total quality on the bottom line', *MRS Research Plus*, April.

Banks, R., Brown, D. and Jones, S. (1992) 'From pillar box to doormat: Royal Mail's 'end-to-end' survey and its impact on the bottom line', *AMSO Effectiveness Awards 1991*, Henley-on Thames: NTC Publications.

Bartram, M. (1986) 'Putting people first', *MRS Survey*, Summer.

Bartram, P. and Bartram, M. (1993) 'Satisfied or satiated? How the appetite for customer satisfaction can be sustained', Proceedings of the ESOMAR Seminar on New Perspectives in Customer Satisfaction Research.

Berry, L. L. and Parasuraman, A. (1991) *Marketing Services: Competing through Quality*, New York: The Free Press Division of Macmillan.

Biel, A. L. (1992) 'Anticipating expectations: what will tomorrow's customers want? Proceedings of the ESOMAR Congress, Madrid.

Buckingham, C. (1993) 'The Category Management revolution', Proceedings of the ESOMAR Seminar on Maximising Retail Sales in a Recession', Amsterdam.

Burns, T. (1993) 'Customer research in a non-competitive environment', Proceedings of the ESOMAR Seminar on New Perspectives in Customer Satisfaction Research, London.

Chinn, S. (1993) 'Inventing, re-inventing and circumventing the future: a new role for research', Proceedings of the Market Research Society Conference.

Christopher, M., Payne, A. and Ballantyne, D. (1991) *Relationship research*, Oxford: Butterworth-Heinemann in association with the Chartered Institute of Marketing.

Chudy, B. and Sant, R. (1993) 'Customer driven competitive positioning: an approach towards developing an effective customer service strategy', Proceedings of the ESOMAR Seminar on New Perspectives in Customer Satisfaction Research', London.

Cottrell, R. J. (1993) 'Proactive relationship marketing: the next step to long-term customer loyalty', Proceedings of the ESOMAR Seminar on New Perspectives in Customer Satisfaction Research, London.

Crosier, K. (1979) 'How effective is the contribution of market research to social marketing?', *Journal of the Market Research Society*, vol. 21, no. 1, Jan.

de Vos, A. D (1993) 'Satisfied clients: a methodology for the measurement and improvement of client satisfaction', Proceedings of the ESOMAR Seminar on New Perspectives in Customer Satisfaction Research, London.

French, A. (1993) 'Researching the NHS: first break a leg', *MRS Research Plus*, April.

Frye, M. (1992) 'Who walked among the stones of fire?', Proceedings of the Market Research Society Conference.

Green, J. L. (1977) 'SIMALTO: a technique for improved product design and marketing', Proceedings of the ESOMAR Congress, Oslo.

Hodson, M. G. J. and Falconer, R. (1993) 'Myth or reality? The truth about customers' satisfaction with London's Underground', Proceedings of the ESOMAR Seminar on New Perspectives in Customer Satisfaction Research, London.

Hurst, S. (1993) 'Setting the standards for a vintage show', *MRS Research Plus*, April.

Jones, S. L. (1993) 'Self-discovery: the key to successful quality measurement', Proceedings of the ESOMAR Seminar on New Perspectives in Customer Satisfaction Research, London.

Lewis, B. R. (1993) 'Measuring consumer expectations and satisfactions', Proceedings of the ESOMAR Seminar on New Perspectives in Customer Satisfaction Research, London.

Mouncey, P. (1987) 'Are you being served?', *Survey*, Summer.

MRS Survey (1989) 'Green issues', Winter.

Mutz, G., Greig, I. and Howell, S. (1993) 'Customer, dealer and employee satisfaction: prerequisites for market driven quality in IBM', Proceedings of the ESOMAR Seminar on New Perspectives in Customer Satisfaction Research, London.

Parasuraman, A., Berry, L. and Zeitaml, V. A. (1991) 'Understanding customer expectations of service', *Sloan Management Review*, vol. 32, no. 3.

Parasuraman, A., Zeithaml, V. and Berry, L. (1990). *Achieving Service Quality: Balancing perceptions and expectations*, New York: The Free Press Division of Macmillan.

Pinto, C. and Quick, S. (1993) 'Meeting local needs: the role of market research and the Citizen's Charter', Proceedings of the Market Research Society Conference.

Thompson, A. G. H. (1983) 'The measurement of patients' perceptions of the quality of hospital care', The Manchester School of Management.

White, P. and Banks, R. (1993) 'Royal Mail's customer perception and satisfaction index (CPSI): an object lesson in communicating with the end user', Proceedings of the ESOMAR Seminar on New Perspectives in Customer Satisfaction Research, London.

APPENDIX 1

Access to secondary sources

A1.1 Electronic desk research

Desk researchers are increasingly using in-office computer, or their own desktop micros to gain access to secondary data. This development is being encouraged by the proliferation of host bureaux which make it possible for the desk researcher to consult a range of data sources through one supplier. Prestel, Infoline, Data-Star, Dialogue and Textline are examples of host bureaux.

The information filed may be numeric, bibliographic or both:

- British Telcom's Prestel service contains around 200,000 pages of information on subjects ranging from accounts of companies to statistics on zinc production. Prestel is a numeric service.
- Pergamon Press's Infoline is a bibliographic service hosting abstracts of articles published in business directories such as Dun and Bradstreet, Who Owns Whom.
- Data-Star hosts both numeric and bibliographic information.
- Textline from Finsbury Data Services abstracts articles from eighty British and European newspapers, plus 'journals such as *Marketing* and *Marketing Week*'.

Many University Libraries, e.g. Loughborough University of Technology, have on-line public access catalogue (OPAC) systems available at terminals in their libraries and via their campus network. The outline OPAC system makes it easy to search for references to books and other library materials. The system features an action bar at the top of the screen, function key prompts at the foot, pull-down menus and a series of window-like screens which overlap each other so that the information searched for on 'authors' and 'title(s)' appears on one screen.

A1.2 Government statistical service

Government departments generate a wealth of statistical data critical to strategic planning. The Central Statistical Office databank offers 'regularly updated macro-economic and related statistical data in computer-readable form'. The data are available 'to host bureaux for incorporation in their client services' as well as to end users.

Of particular interest to market researchers are the following:

- Statistics and Market Intelligence Library of the Department of Industry and Trade, 1 Victoria Street, London SW1H 0ET (0171-215 4895)
  Provides up-to-date and comprehensive trade statistics for all countries, and general statistical publications from all over the world.
- The OPCS Reference Library
  Office of Population Censuses and Surveys
  St Catherine's House, Kingsway, London WC2B 6JP (0171-242 0162); for library (0171-242 2235/2237)
- Business Statistics Office
  Cardiff Road, Newport, Gwent NPT 1XG (01633 222973) (for general enquiries)

There are numerous government publications, and examples of these are the *Annual Abstract of Statistics, Business Monitor Surveys, Census of Production, Census of Population (1991), Department of Employment Gazette, Economic Trends, Financial Statistics, Family Expenditure Surveys, General Household Survey, Material Income and Expenditure Surveys, Monthly Digest of Statistics, Regional Trends, Social Trends, British Business and Monopolies Commission Reports* which are obtainable from HMSO bookstores. Information on these publications are obtainable at the following addresses:
The *Central Statistical Office*, Press and Information Office, Room 65C/3, Great George Street, London SW1P 3AQ. Tel: 0171-270 6363/6364.
(The CSO publishes *Government Statistics, A Brief Guide to Sources*, free from the CSO.)

Association of British Chambers of Commerce (ABCC), 9 Tufton Street, London SW1P 3QB. Tel: 0171-222 1555.

The *Department of Trade and Industry* (DTI), Ashdown House, 123 Victoria Street, London SW1E 6SW. Tel: 0171-200 1992.

The DTI's *Business in Europe Hotline*, Tel: 01272 444888 for contacts and information on the single European market (address as above).

The DTI's *European Community Information*, Tel: 0171-200 1992 (address as for DTI, London).

The DTI's *Export Intelligence*, Prelink Ltd, Export House, 87a Wembley Hill Road, Wembley, Middlesex HA9 8BU. Tel: 0181-900 1313.

The DTI's *Export Marketing Information Centre*, Tel: 0171-215 5444/5 (address as DTI, London).

For expert help and publications, contact the nearest DTI regional office or *DTI Export Publications*, PO Box 55, Stratford-upon-Avon, Warwickshire CV37 9GE. Tel: 01789 296212.

For the DTI's *Export Marketing Research Scheme*, contact ABCC at 4 Westwood House, Westwood Business Park, Coventry CV4 8HS. Tel: 01203 694484.

British Standards Institute (BSI), Linford Way, Milton Keynes, Bucks. Tel: 01908 221166.

Independent Television Commission (ITC), 70 Brompton Road, London SW1. Tel: 0171-584 7011.

International Chamber of Commerce (ICC), 14–15 Belgrave Square, London SW1X 8PS. Tel: 0171-823 2811.

Office of the Data Protection Registrar, Springfield House, Water Lane, Wilmslow, Cheshire SK9 5AX. Tel: 01625 535777.

A1.3 Banks

Some DTI services are informed to companies and individuals via the 'Commercial Banks', e.g. National Westminster, Barclays, Midland and Lloyds Bank, which also provide services through their international divisions for exporters or those wishing to research overseas markets. Banking reviews published regularly include *Barclays Economic Review*.

A1.4 Sources of marketing data

The 1994 *MRS Yearbook* also contains sources of marketing data under the following headings:

- Demographics and basic statistics.
- Classification and lifestyle.

- Products and services.
- Finance.
- Retail trade.
- Media.
- Industry statistics.

Shared-cost services and databanks mentioned in 'The marketing research process' feature in this section of the *Yearbook*. Research suppliers, i.e. organisations and individuals in the United Kingdom, Republic of Ireland and overseas providing marketing research services are set out in this section.

A1.5 Business sources of information

A1.5.1 Associations and institutes (UK):

Advertising Agency Registrar Services, 26 Market Place, London W1N 7AL. Tel: 0171-437 3357.

The Advertising Association, Abford House, 15 Wilton Road, London SW1V 1NJ. Tel: 0171-828 2771.

Advertising Standards Authority (ASA), Brook House, 2–16 Torrington Place, London WC1E 7HN. Tel: 0171-580 5555.

Agency Assessments, 7th Floor, Brettenham House, Lancaster Place, London WC2 7EN. Tel: 0171-836 4416.

Association for Survey Computing the formerly known Study Group on Computers in Survey Analysis (SGCSA), 4 Mansel Drive, Rochester, Kent ME1 3HX. Tel/Fax: 01634 846092.

Association of British Market Research Companies (ABMRC), IDA Ltd, Victory House, 99–101 Regent Street, London W1R 7HB. Tel: 0171-439 3971.

Association of European Market Research Institutes (AEMRI), Travel and Tourism Research Ltd, 39c Highbury Place, London N5 1QP. Tel: 0171-354 3391.

Association of Independent Radio Companies (AIRC), Radio House, 46 Westbourne Grove, London W2 5SH. Tel: 0171-727 1646.

Association of Market Survey Organisations (AMSO), Martin Hamblin Research, 36 Smith Square, London SW1P 3HL. Tel: 0171-222 8181.

Association of Qualitative Research Practitioners (AQRP), The HPI Research Group, 8 Buckingham Street, London WC2N 6BU. Tel: 0171-939 8111.

Association of Users of Research Agencies (AURA), c/o ISBA, 44 Hertford Street, London WIY 8AE. Tel: 0171-499 7502.

Audit Bureau of Circulation (ABC), Black Prince Yard, 107–9 High Street, Berkhamsted, Herts HP4 1AD. Tel: 01442 970880.

British Direct Marketing Association, Grosvenor Gardens House, 35 Grosvenor Gardens, London SW1 0BS.

British Institute of Management (BIM), 3rd Floor, 2 Savoy Court, The Strand, London WC2R 0EZ. Tel: 0171-497 0580, Fax: 0171-497 0436, *Administrative HQ*, Management House, Cottingham Road, Corby, Northants NN17 1TT. Tel: 01536 204222.

British List Brokers Association, The Pines, Broad Street, Guildford, Surrey GU3 BH. Tel: 01483 301311.

British Merchandising Association, Suite 12, 4th Floor, Parkway House, Sheen Lane, East Sheen, London SW14 8LS. Tel: 0181-878 0825/0738.

British Promotional Merchandise Association (BPMA), Suite 12, 4th Floor, Parkway House, Sheen Lane, East Sheen, London SW14 8LS. Tel: 0181-878 0738.

British Quality Foundation, 120 Walton Road, Victoria, London SW1 1JZ. Tel: 0171-931 0607.

British Rate and Data (BRAD), Maclean Hunter Limited, Maclean Hunter House, Chalk Lane, Cockfosters Road, Barnet, Herts EN4 0BU.

Broadcasters' Audience Research Board Ltd (BARB), Glenthorne House, Hammersmith Grove, London W6 0ND. Tel: 0181-741 9110.

Chartered Institute of Marketing (CIM), Moor Hall, Cookham, Maidenhead, Berkshire SL6 9QH. Tel: 01628 524922.

Cinema and Video Industry Audience Research (CAVIAR), 127 Wardour Street, London W1V 4AD. Tel: 0171-439 9531.

Communications Advertising and Marketing Education Foundation (CAM Foundation), Abford House, 15 Wilton Road, London SW1V 1NJ. Tel: 0171-828 7506.

Confederation of British Industry (CBI), Centre Point, 103 New Oxford Street, London WC1A 1DU. Tel: 0171-379 7400, Fax: 0171-240 1578.

Direct Mail Services Standards Board, 26 Eccleston Street, London SW1 9PY. Tel: 0171-824 8651.

Direct Marketing Association (UK) Ltd, Haymarket House, 1 Oxendon Street, London SW1Y 4EE. Tel: 0171-321 2525.

Direct Marketing Centre, 1 Park Road, Teddington, Middlesex TW11 0AR. Tel: 0181-977 5705.

European Pharmaceutical Market Research Association (EPHMRA), 9 Paterson Drive, Woodhouse Eaves, Leicester LE12 8RL. Tel: 01530 510718, Fax: 01508-981080.

Federation of European Marketing Research Associations (FEMRA), Secretariat Studio 38, Wimbledon Business Centre, Riverside Road, London SW17 0BA. Tel: 0181-879 0709, Fax: 0181-947 2637.

Incorporated Society of British Advertisers (ISBA), 44 Hertford Street, London W1Y 8AE. Tel: 0171-499 7502.

Independent Television Association (ITVA), Knighton House, 56 Mortimer Street, London W1N 8AN. Tel: 0171-612 8000.

Industrial Marketing Research Association (IMRA), 11 Bird Street, Lichfield, Staffs WS13 6PW. Tel: 01543 263448.

Institute of Customer Care, St John's House, Chapel Lane, Wescott, Surrey RH4 3PJ. Tel: 01306 876210.

Institute of Packaging, Sysonby Lodge, Nottingham Road, Melton Mowbray, Leicestershire LE13 0NU. Tel: 01664 500055.

Institute of Practitioners in Advertising (IPA), 44 Belgrave Square, London SW1X 8QS. Tel: 0171-235 7020.

Institute of Public Relations (IPR), The Old Trading House, 15 Northburgh Street, London EC1V 0PR. Tel: 0171-253 5151.

Institute of Sales and Marketing Management, National Westminster House, 31 Upper George Street, Luton, Bedfordshire LU1 2RD. Tel: 01582 411130.

Institute of Sales Promotion (ISP), Arena House, 66–68 Pentonville Road, London N1 9HS. Tel: 0171-837 5340.

Institute of Statistics, 43 St Peter's Square, Preston, Lancashire PR1 7BX. Tel: 01772 204237.

Joint Industry Committee for regional Press Research (JICREG), Bloomsbury House, 74–77 Great Russell Street, London WC1B 3DA. Tel: 0171-636 7014.

Market Research Society (MRS), The Old Trading House, 15 Northburgh Street, London EC1V 0PR. Tel: 0171-490 4911.

Market Society, Stanton House, 206 Worpole Road, London SW20 8PN. Tel: 0181-879 3464.

Media Expenditure and Advertising Ltd (MEAL), Registrar House, 3 Holford Yard, Cruikshank Street, London WC1X 9HD. Tel: 0171-833 1212.

National Quality Information Centre, PO Box 712, 61 Southwark Street, London SE1 1SB. Tel: 0171-401 7227.

National Readership Surveys Ltd (ARS), 11–15 Betterton Street, Covent Garden, London WC2H 9BP. Tel: 0171-379 0344.

Outside-Site Classification and Audience Research (OSCAR), NOP Posters, Tower House, Southampton Street, London WC2E 7HN. Tel: 0171-612 0100.

P R Consultancy Registrar Services, 26 Market Place, London N7 AL. Tel: 0171-437 3357.

Publication Relations Consultants Association (PRCA), Willow House, Willow Place, Victoria, London SW1P 1JH. Tel: 0171-233 6026.

Radio Joint Audience Research (RAJAR), 44 Belgrave Square, London SW1X 8Q5. Tel: 0171-235 0004.

Royal Statistical Society, 25 Enford Street, London W1H 2BH. Tel: 0171-723 5882, Fax: 0171-706 1710.

Sales Promotion Consultants Association (SPCA), PO Box 1578, London W1 9FR. Tel: 0171-702 8567.

Social Research Association (SRA), Chairman Justin Russell, The Mental Health Foundation; Administrative Officer Genevieve Gosschalk, 116 Turney Road, London SE21 7JJ. Tel: 0171-736 6503.

Strategic Planning Society, 17 Portland Place, London W1N 3AF. Tel: 0171-636 7737, Fax: 0171-323 1692.

Technical Assistance Research Programme (TARP), 4–6 Denbeigh Mews, London SW1V 1HQ. Tel: 0171-630 1277.

A1.5.2 *Useful Publications and Sources (UK and Overseas):*

Advertising Age, 740 N. Rush Street, Chicago, IL 60611, USA. Tel: (312) 649-5200.

Advertising Research Foundation, 3 East 54th Street, New York, NY 10022, USA. Tel: (212)751-5656. For *Journal of Advertising Research*.

Adweek, 820 Second Avenue, New York, NY 10017, USA. Tel: (212) 661-8080.

American Academy of Advertising, The Citadel, Charleston, SC 29409, USA. Tel: (803) 792-7089. For *Journal of Advertising*.

American Marketing Association (AMA), for Annual Conference proceedings and the *Journal of Health Care Marketing*, *Journal of Marketing*, *Journal of Marketing Research*, and *Marketing News*, 250 S. Wacker Drive, Chicago, IL 60606-5819, USA. Tel: (312) 648-0536.

Blackwell Publishers Ltd, 108 Cowley Road, Oxford. OX4 1JF, England. For *EC Direct – A comprehensive Directory of EC Contents* (1992) by Hons Martend.

Bowker Saur Ltd, 40 Grosvenor Street, London W1X 9DA, England. Tel: 0171-493 5841. Titles include *Directory of European Business* (1992).

CBD Research Ltd, 15 Wickham Road, Beckenham, Kent, BR5 2JS, England. Tel: 0181-650 7745. Titles include *Current British Directories*, and *The Directory of British Associations*.

Centaur Publications, St Giles House, 49–50 Poland Street, London, England, W1V 4AX. Tel: 0171-439 4222. Titles include *Creative Review*, *Direct Marketing*, *Design Week*, *Leisure Industry Journal*, *Marketing Week* and *Precision Marketing*.

Croner Publications Ltd, Croner House, London Road, Kingston upon Thames, Surrey, KT2 6SR, England. Tel: 0181-547 3333. Titles include the *European Business Information Sources*.

Dow Jones & Co Inc, 199 Liberty Street, New York, NY 10281 USA. Tel: (212)416-0200. For the *Wall Street Journal*.

Dun and Bradstreet Corporation, 99 Church Street, New York, NY 10007-0300, USA. Tel: (212)553-0300. Its subsidiary *Moody's Investors Services*, publishers on banking, finance, bonds and stocks.

Dun and Bradstreet Ltd, Holmers Farm Way, High Wycombe, Bucks HP12 4UL, England. Tel: 01494 422000. Titles include *Who Owns Whom* and *Key Business Enterprises.*

The Economist, 25 St James Street, London SW1A 1HG, England. Tel: 0171-830 7000. For *The Economist* and *Business Surveys.*

Editions Delta, 55 Rue Scailquin, B-1030, Bruxelles. Tel: 02-217 5555. For the *Yearbooks of the European Communities and of other European Organisations* (1993).

EMAP Business Publications, 33–39 Bowling Green Lane, London EC1R 0DA, England. Tel: 0171-404 5513. Titles include *Media Week.*

Euromonitor, 87–88 Turnmill Street, London EC1M 5QU, England. Tel: 0171-251 8024. For the *European Directory of Marketing Information Sources* (1990).

Eurostudy Publishing Co Ltd, Ludgate House, 107 Fleet Street, London EC4A 2AB, England. Tel: 0171-583 1025. For international reports on world financial markets and economies.

Extel Financial Ltd, Fitzroy House, 13–17 Epworth Street, London EC2A 4DL, England. Tel: 0171-251 3333. Titles include *The European Handbook*, and the *Handbook of Market Leaders.*

Financial Times Business Information Ltd, Tower House, Southampton Street, London, England, WC2E 7HA. Tel: 0171-240 9391. For business, international trade and financial surveys.

General Agreement on Tariffs and Trade (GATT). Information and Media, les Tarifs Douaniers et les Commerce, Centre William Rappard, 154 rue de Lausanne, 1211 Geneva 21, Switzerland. Tel: 022-7395111. For data on international trade statistics.

Haymarket Publishing Services Ltd, 12/14 Ansdell Street, London W8 5TR, England. Tel: 0181-943 5000. Titles include *Business Express*, *Campaign*, *Conference and Incentive Travel*, *Management Today*, *Marketing*, *PR Week*, *Promotion and Incentives.*

ICC Business Publications Ltd, Hampton, Middlesex TW12 1BR, England. Tel: 0181-783 0922. Titles include *Macmillan's Unquoted Companies.*

International Monetary Fund (IMF), Publication Services, 700 19th St, NW, Washington, DC 20431. Tel: (202)623-7430. For IMF publications on world economic and financial surveys.

Jordan and Sons Ltd, 21 St Thomas Street, Bristol BS1 6JS, England. Tel: 0117 9230600. For market surveys and 'Britain's Top Foreign Owned Companies'.

Market Research Society (MRS), The Old Trading House, 15 Northburgh Street, London EC1V 0PR, England. Tel: 0171-490 4911. For annual conference papers, *MRS Yearbook*, *MRS Newsletters* and the *International Directory of Market Research Organisations*.

Mintel Publications Ltd, KAE House, 7 Arundel Street, London WC2R 3DR, England. Tel: 0171-836 1814/379 3536. For market surveys.

NTC Publications Ltd, Farm Road, Henley-on-Thames, Oxfordshire RG9 1EJ, England. Tel: 01491 574671. Titles include *The Advertising Statistics Yearbook* (1994), *Advertising Works 7*, *Directory of Continuous Market Research* (1994), *The European Advertising and Media Yearbook* (1994), *European Media Cost Comparison* (1993), *World Advertising Expenditures 25th Survey*, *The Advertising Forecast*, *The European Advertising and Media Forecast*, and the *Quarterly Survey of Advertising Expenditure*.

Predicasts, A 2 IFF Communications Company, 11001 Cedar Avenue, Cleveland, Ohio 44106, USA. Tel: (800)321-6388. For Predicasts, US and international data on markets, industries and forecasts.

Reed Information Services Ltd, Windsor Court, East Grinstead House, East Grinstead, West Sussex RH1G 1XD, England Tel: 01342 326972. Titles include *Kompass Business Directory* (1994–1995), *Kellys Business Directory* (1994), *Regional Sales Guide* (1994–1995), *Advertisers Annual (3 volumes) – The Blue Book*.

Standard and Poor's Corporation, 25 Broadway, New York, NY 10004, USA. Tel: (212)208-8000/8650. For directories on US and international corporation records, directors, executives and commodities.

Taylor and Francis, 4 John Street, London WC1 2ET, England. Tel: 0171-405 2237 for the *Encyclopedia of the United Nations* (1990).

Thomas Publishing Company, Five Penn Plaza, 250 West 34th St, New York, NY 10001, USA. Tel: (212)695-0500. For directories on US and international manufacturers.

APPENDIX 2

The principles of analysis

John Bound

A2.1 Introduction

When quantitative data have been collected by marketing research methods, the data have to be analysed to turn them into information which will help in making marketing decisions. The data which may be recorded on paper forms or in a computer file have to be summarised so that their meaning may be understood. This is analysis.

This appendix treats both principles which remain unchanged, and practice which is changing rapidly. Computers enable all sorts of analysis procedures to be carried out easily, and there are at the time of writing 200 program packages available in Britain for doing different parts or sorts of these tasks, using big or little computers. We shall try to discuss methods made practicable by computing advances rather than those methods already becoming outdated, though perhaps still widely used.

The task of analysis needs a knowledge of techniques as well. For anyone who has not met the problem before, it is daunting to be confronted with a large pile of paper questionnaires, or even a computer file containing already captured data. Marketers and planners are not usually called upon to do this, but may well be expected to operate simple computing packages which make it easy to produce results providing the user knows what is wanted. Even if a specialist analyst is employed, a knowledge of the possibilities of analysis is necessary.

Our field here is an enquiry set up to answer a particular problem, or the *ad hoc* enquiry, as it is often called.

A2.2 What analysis is trying to do

The purpose of statistical analysis is to find patterns in data, and show them clearly in comparison with any previous expectations. There are thus two parts: the first is

334

finding the patterns, and the second is seeing how well they fit any expectations. If there is previous experience of certain patterns, then the easiest thing to do is straightway to see whether the new data are the same. To take a simple marketing research example: if it has previously been found that big dogs eat more of a test product than do small dogs, then we look to see if the same is true, and to what extent. To say whether any patterns we find are of practical interest we need to bring in other knowledge.

The basic tool for statistical analysis is the table with rows and columns of figures. The table of this kind is one of mankind's great discoveries, enabling patterns to be readily seen and compared. Yet when a pattern is complex, involving many factors, it becomes impossible to find it or to summarise it by tables. Then multi-variate statistical methods may be used. These produce approximately correct mathematical or pictorial descriptions of complex data in terms of just a few factors. These methods also produce measures of how well the description works. Some of these procedures are mentioned below. The idea is simple: we replace a complicated explanation with a simpler one which is roughly correct, just as giving an average might make a statement which was more or less true about a lot of people, but perhaps not exactly correct about any one of them.

A2.3 Techniques

A2.3.1 General

There are some well-established routines for survey analysis. The main approach is the use of tabulations of various kinds, that is, counting the number of answers in various categories (or perhaps averaging any answers which are in the form of numbers) and putting the figures into tables.

The usual path is to start with one-way, then to go on to two-way tables, and after that to many-way tables. After this the use of multi-variate techniques may be considered. All these terms will be defined shortly. How far along this route to go depends on the objectives, the simplicity of the patterns revealed, and the amount of data.

When conclusions have been reached, suitably designed tables can then enable other people to understand both the conclusions and the way they have been derived. The tables for this are different from those we use in the initial search for patterns.

A2.3.2 One-way tables

The first step is to produce these. A one-way table is a simple table for a question or observation giving the number and percentage of the different answers. A set of

Table A2.1   A one-way table

Base: all respondents	460
	(100)
Prefer new	269
	(58)
Prefer old	175
	(38)
Don't know/no preference	16
	(3)

these is sometimes called a 'code-book' or 'top-line results'. Table A2.1 is an example of how this may look.

The heading refers to the question number and topic of the question on which the table is based. The base is the description and number of the respondents on which the table is based. Percentages to whole numbers are usual.

These results for all questions are often shown compactly in the form of a 'hole-count', which is just what it was in the days of punched cards. A hole-count is a summary table showing the code numbers representing the possible answers across the top, and the questions down the side. The entries are then the number of times each answer code occurs for any question, handily with percentages. See Table A2.2.

In Table A2.2, the heading 'Col' for column on a punched card indicates which question in tabulated. There may be more than one card or computer file record for one questionnaire, so the 'card of type 0' heading identifies which is in use. Some questions in the table have multiple responses, so the 'Sums' column shows the total number of responses. The layout, although based on the original punched card operation, is equally applicable to computer files.

Another useful way to present these answers is to write in the percentages for each question onto a blank questionnaire.

For some enquiries these figures give key results. In our example of a product test comparing two products, the key result might be the percentage preferring each, as shown in Table A2.2.

A2.3.3 Two-way tables

Such one-way tables are seldom enough. The results need to be shown separately for sub-groups of the sample in the form of two-way tables.

Even in the product-test example above, we would clearly want to know what sort of people preferred each product, and would have collected data about this too. So we take our one-way table of 'Product preferred', and add two other columns, one headed perhaps 'Users of A', and the other 'Users of B'. So now we have a rectangular or two-way table that looks like Table A2.3.

Table A2.2 A typical hole-count

COL	0	1	2	3	4	5	6	7	8	9	Blank	Single	Multiple	Sums
1	0	0	0	72	0	0	0	0	0	0	0	72	0	72
				100.0								100.0		1.00
2	0	72	0	0	0	0	0	0	0	0	0	72	0	72
		100.0										100.0		1.00
3	0	0	0	0	72	0	0	0	0	0	0	72	0	72
					100.0							100.0		1.00
4	72	0	0	0	0	0	0	0	0	0	0	72	0	72
	100.0											100.0		1.00
5	9	10	10	10	10	10	10	3	0	0	0	72	0	72
	12.5	13.9	13.9	13.9	13.9	13.9	13.9	4.2				100.0		1.00
6	7	8	8	7	7	7	7	7	7	7	0	72	0	72
	9.7	11.1	11.1	9.7	9.7	9.7	9.7	9.7	9.7	9.7		100.0		1.00
7	23	20	29	0	0	0	0	0	0	0	0	72	0	72
	31.9	27.8	40.3									100.0		1.00
8	3	6	6	9	8	9	9	8	9	5	0	72	0	72
	4.2	8.3	8.3	12.5	11.1	12.5	12.5	11.1	12.5	6.9		100.0		1.00
9	0	5	11	6	3	25	22	0	0	0	0	72	0	72
		6.9	15.3	8.3	4.2	34.7	30.6					100.0		1.00
10	0	20	27	23	1	1	0	0	0	0	0	72	0	72
		27.8	37.5	31.9	1.4	1.4						100.0		1.00
11	20	44	8	0	0	0	0	0	0	0	0	72	0	72
	27.8	61.1	11.1									100.0		1.00
12	19	42	11	0	0	0	0	0	0	0	0	72	0	72
	26.4	58.3	15.3									100.0		1.00
13	0	35	36	28	31	18	22	24	30	20	0	25	47	244
		48.6	50.0	38.9	43.1	25.0	30.6	33.3	41.7	27.8		34.7	65.3	3.39
14	20	36	36	24	29	17	16	27	20	18	22	4	46	243
	27.8	50.0	50.0	33.3	40.3	23.6	22.2	37.5	27.8	25.0	30.6	5.6	63.9	3.38
15	0	33	24	17	25	4	24	19	0	0	4	30	38	146
		45.8	33.3	23.6	34.7	5.6	33.3	26.4			5.6	41.7	52.8	2.03
16	0	16	14	8	14	0	0	0	0	0	20	52	0	52
		22.2	19.4	11.1	19.4						27.8	72.2		0.72
17	0	12	20	11	10	0	0	0	0	0	19	53	0	53
		16.7	27.8	15.3	13.9						26.4	73.6		0.74
18	0	5	4	1	3	2	0	3	5	0	49	23	0	23
		6.9	5.6	1.4	4.2	2.8		4.2	6.9		68.1	31.9		0.32

'STAR' DDP Report WASHING POWDER: There were 72 (unweighted) cards of type 0, selected for = Total Sample. Source: Demotab Ltd.

Table A2.3   A two-way table showing both unweighted
and weighted bases

	Total	Use brand A	Use brand B
Base: all respondents			
unweighted	460	224	236
weighted	476	220	256
	(100)	(100)	(100)
Prefer new	269	79	194
	(58)	(36)	(76)
Prefer old	175	126	60
	(38)	(57)	(23)
Don't know/no preference	16	15	2
	(3)	(7)	(1)

These sub-group figures give a very different aspect to the figures for the total sample: a marketing decision is called for to decide whether the existing users of the brand or the users of a competitive brand are the more important in choosing the new formula. Quite a few existing users show little preference, so we shall want to look at the results for people who feel strongly, if we have thought to ask about this.

Note that we conventionally show as 'base' a description of whatever group the table is based upon, and the sample size for this total and each sub-group. Since we have different weighted and unweighted bases we show both: the distinction between the two is explained below. The percentages are worked out on the weighted base.

In the body of the table we show both the numbers of responses and their percentage of the total sample size. Sometimes we show the average of numerical answers, and perhaps the standard deviation as well. The various sub-groups we put across the page, and the possible answers down the side. The typical survey computer printout looks like Table A2.4 – useful for study, but not for communication results. However, the two-way table is only part of the story: we may well need more complex many-way tables.

A2.3.4 Many-way tables

These tables come in sets. Each table is based upon only part of the sample. They are needed to see the patterns when there is interaction between analysis breaks.

Interaction arises if different parts of the sample, such as people in the town and in the country give different patterns of answers to a question. We then need a set of tables, one table for the town, and one for the country. From them we might perhaps see that people in the country with large families have different opinions

Table A2.4   A typical two-way table with several analysis breaks on the one page

		Total	Area		Age			Sex	
			North	South	Under 25	26–40	Over 40	Male	Female
Total		72	35	37	16	9	47	36	36
		100%	100%	100%	100%	100%	100%	100%	100%
Agree strongly	(5)	0	0	0	0	0	0	0	0
		–	–	–	–	–	–	–	–
Agree	(4)	2	2	0	0	0	2	0	2
		3%	6%	–	–	–	4%	–	6%
Neither	(3)	6	0	6	1	1	4	4	2
		8%	–	16%	6%	11%	9%	11%	6%
Disagree	(2)	21	13	8	7	2	12	11	10
		29%	37%	22%	44%	22%	26%	31%	28%
Disagree strongly	(1)	43	20	23	8	6	29	21	22
		60%	57%	62%	50%	67%	62%	58%	61%
No answer		0	0	0	0	0	0	0	0
Mean score		1.54	1.54	1.54	1.56	1.44	1.55	1.53	1.56

Source: Demotab Ltd.

from people in the country with small families, whereas in the town there is no difference between opinions according to size of families. Similarly, in discussing one example, Table A2.4, we have suggested that the way in which preferences vary between users of brands may be different for people with strong preferences.

Such sets form a three-way, or three-dimensional table, but since paper has only two dimensions for printing, we have to make a set of tables. The third variable is sometimes called a filter variable. The number of tables in all the different possible sets escalates. In our example of a twenty-question survey, there are 380 possible two-way tables, and 6,840 three-way sets. The problem of selection is obvious. But even this is not the end: the answers people give may vary in our example not only between town and country, but also this variation may itself be different in various parts of Britain.

So we need a four-way table, and even more multi-way tables as we find more complicated patterns. We may also derive new variables: for example, we might count the number of questions for which each respondent said 'don't know', and use this as a measure of involvement with the topic. This would enable yet more tables to be formed.

There are three things which stop this process going on indefinitely. The first is that we are willing to accept a simple explanation that fits roughly, but which everybody can understand. An exact but complicated explanation might well fit only data collected in exactly the same circumstances; indeed, perhaps not even then. We would like to think our answers had a chance of applying more widely, and the simple explanation may have a better chance of this.

The second reason is that the usefulness in marketing of complicated answers is limited. You usually just cannot sell a different product in each part of the country, or to people in the town against people in the country. If you can, then such knowledge is useful.

The third reason is that we run out of sample size for the bases of the many-way tables. There may be only a handful or even none at all in some of the tables for sub-sub-groups of even the biggest sample survey. That is why the government conducts a population census of all the 55 million people in Britain: the results need to be broken down in great detail. In practice three-way tables are often as far as we go.

So there are a great many tables that can be produced, and we need a way to choose which to look at.

A2.4 The selection of tables

Thus for each table we have to decide the column headings. For two-way tables this is all. For many-way tables we have also to decide the filter variables for each value of which a separate table is to be produced.

Consider first two-way tables. The headings for the columns are sometimes called 'analysis breaks', 'independent variables' or 'predictor variables'. They may or may not vary from question to question: often a block of questions on the same topic will have the same breaks, and important predictor variables like age may be used for every question. A crude technique is to use the same group of analysis breaks for every question.

There are two ways of deciding which column headings to use. The better is to know already from other research or experience what sort of sub-groups are likely to vary. Age, sex and social class are most commonly found to make a difference between sub-groups. If you know the age, sex and social class of someone in Britain it is generally true that you can say much about what they buy, read and think. The advantage of this method is that if differences are *not* shown in the particular enquiry, that is a matter for comment. There is a snag: the possible predictors may not be known, or some predictors may not have been discovered.

This leads to the second method, which is often used indiscriminately. This is to try out a large number of variables, and to see which of them makes a difference, perhaps deciding on this by some statistical significance test such as the chi-squared test. But 'hunting', as it is called, has snags.

If you look at a lot of variables as potential analysis breaks, pure chance will make some of them appear important. There is no guarantee at all that any of the breaks you discover will apply to any other similar survey. What we are trying to do is to say something about the market in general, rather than to give an exact description of the particular sample. So if we come in with a theory then we can use our data to see if it is supported by the particular enquiry.

The use of significance tests also has technical problems: these do not theoretically apply if used repeatedly on different aspects of the same data, and most of them apply only to simple unrestricted probability samples which few market research surveys are. Having said this, we cannot deny that many people have used tests such as the chi-squared to find tables in which sub-groups vary and have found the results practically useful.

When we go beyond the two-way tables to three-way and many-way tables, it becomes quite impossible to produce more than a few out of the thousands which could be generated. Some theory is necessary to select which two-way tables to split further. A problem here is that a two-way table which shows no difference between sub-groups may show differences if such a table is produced separately for each sub-group of a third variable.

For instance, consumption of porridge varies little between homes with older and with younger housewives. Consumption also varies little between homes with children and homes without children. However, consumption varies a great deal between young homes with children and young homes without children. The three-way tabulation here is clearly essential to understand the market.

The selection of filter variables for many-way tables thus follows the same principles as for two-way tables. It has to be done with care to avoid producing too many tables.

We have not referred at all to graphical methods. These are of little use for understanding data based on counts of answers. On the other hand, a good chart can convey a particular point forcefully in presentation.

A2.5 Table bases

Each table should show its base: that is, a description of the part or whole of the sample it covers, and the size of the sample. The size of each sub-group is also shown.

These bases vary because the table may be based upon only part of the data, and because the sub-groups analysed in the columns of tables may vary. As we said when discussing two-way tables, all tables based on samples should have this base or sample size shown for each sub-group, and also the size and description of the sample on which the table total is based. This sounds simple enough, but raises two other points which often cause confusion. They are weighting and multiple response.

Weighting is the process of giving some responses greater weight relative to others in totalling the numbers of responses to a question. It is done because, by accident or design, there are too many or too few of some types of respondent. The effect may be to make the total number of responses shown in the table fewer or more than the number of respondents. Percentages are correctly worked out on this different 're-weighted' total, but of course it is the original number of people that forms the 'unweighted base' and enables estimates of the sampling variability of the figures in the table. Both types of base should be shown if they are at all different.

In the example in Tables A2.1 and A2.3 above, the weighting calculation makes little difference to the percentages in the total columns. This is as usual: indeed, big differences would raise queries. All the same, since weighting improves estimates at little effort now that the computer does the calculations, it should normally be carried out.

Questions which have more than one simultaneously valid answer are known as multiple-response questions and require suitable software for recording and tabulation. The number of answers tabulated may exceed the number of respondents. The table may be based either on the number of respondents or the number of responses.

If we ask what newspaper was read yesterday, the answer may be to name none, one or several. If we want to know the number of people reading each paper, then the total of the numbers in each category will be greater than the total number of respondents, and the percentages add to more than a hundred. This may look odd, but is all right.

We might prefer to have the table based on the total number of newspapers read, so that the percentages would give the share of readership rather than readers. Most software packages designed for marketing research surveys will readily handle these multiple-response questions, and tabulate them on whichever base is required. Not all packages are designed to handle data in this form, and, if not, both questionnaire design and tabulation are made more complicated.

A2.6 Multi-variate analysis

When the methods of tabulation starting with one-way tables, going on to two-way tables, and finally three- and more-way tables, have been fully explored we may turn to multi-variate analysis. The techniques all provide a simplified explanation of the data which is more or less correct. The results may appear as mathematical descriptions or as graphic maps.

How do we know when this point has been reached? First, the bases for the tables we want to examine may be reduced to a handful of respondents or even none at all. Second, we may be tired of examining hundreds of tables, but believe relationships exist which we have not been able to find by using either our existing theory or by 'hunting'. Third, we may suspect that relationships are too complex to be presented by tables. If our trouble is sample size we should remember that multi-variate analysis done on small samples will vary greatly in its results from sample to sample, just as will the results from tables with small bases.

Multi-variate analysis is nowadays invariably done by computer packages. These can normally be run on microcomputers, provided the data sets are not too big. They are easy to run with little knowledge of either computing systems or the statistical reasoning behind them. This does not matter very much (many people will disagree with this) if the results are taken as hypotheses, to be checked from other data gathered in other circumstances. Some understanding is required, though, if any useful insights are to be generated.

These techniques all provide a simplified explanation of the data which is more or less correct. There is almost always a trade-off between the exactness of the explanation and its elaborateness. The simpler the explanation and the more it is consistent with, or based upon, what is already known, the more likely it is that we have found something which is of more general interest than giving an exact description of the particular data which we have by chance collected. Whenever we create a model from data, we should recall that there are innumerable *other* models we might have found which would fit nearly as well, or even better if we changed our criterion of what is a good fit.

There are two sorts of these techniques. The first is the analysis of dependence, when we know which variable or variables we want to predict given the others. The second is the analysis of inter-dependence, when we want to see how all the variables affect one another. This often takes the form of drawing a map to show how people, attitudes or brands stand in relation to one another, according to some criterion.

A2.6.1 *Analysis of dependence*

Multiple regression is the commonest form, but has limited use in survey analysis. It predicts a number, such as the number of packets of tea purchased, given various other numbers, such as the number of children in a family, and the income per week.

The answer takes the form of an algebraic equation, from which it may be seen how important are the various predictors, and what would happen if they were changed in value in a particular instance. For survey data multiple regression has problems. The data are usually just not in the form of numbers which can be manipulated, but are the counts of various categories. Very different results can often be produced by a slight change in technique.

This problem of categorical or ranked data may be overcome by the use of the generalised linear model, applied by, for example, the GLIM package. Although this produces complicated models, it enables individual discrepant observations to be seen. The use of the generalised linear model with appropriately transformed data is, however, not common in marketing research, but is likely to become more so.

Conjoint analysis takes the results of choices by respondents between hypothetical possibilities varying in a number of factors to estimate the relative importance of each of these factors.

Respondents might, for example, be asked whether they preferred a small car with medium acceleration or a large car with poor acceleration, and a series of similar questions. A deduction would then be made about the relative importance of size and acceleration. One problem of the technique is that it usually needs extensive questioning of each respondent, although programs have been developed to shorten later questions as data are successively entered on the keyboard. The appropriate questions are then presented on the screen at each stage.

A2.6.2 Analysis of interdependence

If we have three observations about each of a number of entities such as people, or brands, or attitude scales, we may think of each entity as a point in three-dimensional space. We could construct a model with little balls on wires from which we could see the general relationships, grouping and outlying observations. If, though, we had more than three observations about each we should require many-dimensional space which we could not represent. However, mathematical procedures have been developed which do effectively the same thing.

Principal component analysis (PCA) is widely used. It constructs a number of factors which are weighted averages of the original measurements. A few of these factors, ignoring the rest, will often give a good description of the whole data set.

Sometimes it is called 'factor analysis', after a particular type used more often at one time. There are many variations of the method. PCA is often used with numerical responses from a sample of respondents to a series of attitude scales for each of a number of brands. The process produces uncorrelated factors each of which is a weighted combination of a number of scales. As the factors are brought in they give an increasingly good explanation of the total pattern. The factors are then regarded as an underlying structure from which each of the scales is built up. Although there are as many factors as scales, only the first few factors are usually considered (there are rules of thumb for deciding which).

An example often quoted is that of measuring nearly rectangular parcels: if for each parcel the girth, diagonal of each side, and volume were recorded, PCA would show as major factors the underlying dimensions of length, breadth and height.

The technique has been criticised as showing little more than can be seen from looking at the correlations between each attitude scale. It is widely used as a method of reducing the number of attitude scales to be employed in further enquiries.

Cluster analysis seeks to put entities into groups on the basis of similarities on a number of measures. The number of groups, and the process of their formation (do you start with many groups and see what happens when some are amalgamated, or start with one group and split it successively?), are arbitrary. If the groups are distinct enough, the choice of method makes little difference, and subsequent analysis by group membership may be rewarding. The technique is applied to produce classification methods for databanks (such as the TGI) appropriate for particular product fields rather than generally. Life-stage or lifestyle variables may be used as a basis for forming clusters.

A number of techniques under the heading of multi-dimensional scaling reduce data from many dimensions to an approximate representation to fewer, in practice, to two or three. These depend on measures of difference between the entities.

These measures may take many forms, such as the difference in the number of people saying a scale applies, whether a particular scale is thought to apply at all, or whether a particular brand is seen as having more of a characteristic than another. The resulting maps, which may include points not only for each brand, but also for scales and people, require interpretation, since the meaning of the dimensions on which they are plotted must be inferred from the positions of the entities, a somewhat circular process. Correspondence analysis is a form which takes categorical data, thus needing minimal assumptions about the form of the data.

A2.7 Practical processing

The application of all these ideas in practice depends on the size of the job, the time available and the hard- and software. Specialised agencies will take data from the questionnaire stage and process it to specification, and can make many helpful suggestions. They cannot, of course, work without an analysis specification as it is called. Deriving this from knowledge of the objectives and methods of the enquiry is normally the job of the research executive concerned. An experienced analyst can take a questionnaire and a set of data and turn out what is usually required, but this is akin to asking the librarian to suggest a book to read. Particularly if the survey is large and complicated, the expertise of the professional analysts and the versatility of their equipment are often a good buy. They can work with great speed.

On the other hand, for small enquiries a personal computer or even a large flat surface can be an adequate tool. The researcher who analyses his/her own data comes to understand it in detail, and can explore it interactively. Whichever way analysis is done, it is necessary to know something about the practical considerations which the following section goes through.

Most survey data are still recorded on paper questionnaires in handwriting. This may well change.

The other possibilities are electronic recording at a visual display unit, use of a hand-logging device where data are keyed or bar codes swept as questions are asked or observations made, or paper questionnaites on which marks are made to be read electronically (optical-mark recognition). Techniques for reading handwriting are at the time of writing experimental.

The paper questionnaire requires a separate data-capture process if electronic processing is, as usual, to be used. Paper does, though, carry information beyond the words and figures it bears. All questionnaires on receipt should be examined one by one for completeness, consistency and the more elusive quality of meaningfulness. Whether there are major misunderstandings, if the document is carelessly completed, even facetious or fraudulent, may be seen by the human eye, particularly if a batch of documents from the same source is together. Rejection or correction of the data is then necessary. Personal editing is thus always needed, as well as the checks that may be made electronically.

Data capture or keying takes data from paper questionnaires to a computer. Some software is necessary to do this: many analysis packages provide a checking process. This sets up the recording so that only acceptable answers to a particular question will be read. For example, if adults are indicated at a particular point by the code 1, and non-adults by 2, any attempt to record any other code will be rejected. If multiple-response data are to be recorded, provision is made.

The layout of the questionnaire makes a great difference to the labour of data capture. If codes are clearly shown, preferably by being ringed, or clearly written in, with answers consisting of large numbers written in boxes, the work will be done faster and more accurately. In the same way the detailed design of the questionnaire affects the work of the interviewer.

The data capture may be checked. Some packages provide a verification procedure, in which some or all of the data may be re-keyed, and discrepancies shown up.

The data in a questionnaire may require coding. That is, the answers have to be put into numerical categories, when they have been received in words. This may be done by the interviewer, with the categories set out on the questionnaire, or later in the office. The categories may not be set until after the office has received the data. These will then be in the form of a summary in words of what a respondent said, the words themselves verbatim, if not too many, or a description of what was observed (if new packaging were being offered to respondents, interviewer might record, 'broke finger-nail'). Such material is not simple to record on VDU or data-logger, so paper has an advantage. It typically arises as the answer to an open-ended question such as 'What makes this magazine article particularly interesting?'

The process of setting the categories is known as 'making a coding frame'. Usually for an open-ended question for which responses are recorded more or less verbatim, the responses in a sample of the questionnaires are examined, and meaningful categories determined. Too many are confusing, but categories can be combined later, while creating new ones during the coding process means re-coding questionnaires already processed. Not more than a dozen categories usually result. A separate frame has to be made and coding done for each open-ended question. Open-ended questions are therefore a costly form.

The next stage is to go through the questionnaires and write on each one at the answer to the particular question the number of the category. This is coding. Coding needs to be done carefully: it is easy to miss a category of mentions occurring only infrequently, but which is none the less important.

It is not necessary to have electronic equipment to analyse data. For a sample of a hundred or two, simple analysis may be done by a hand-count. This may be a preliminary operation to get top-line figures. The questionnaires are sorted into piles, each representing a combination of desired classifications. Thus if the data are to be analysed by three age groups and two sexes, there will be six piles. It is much easier if the same analysis breaks are used for every question. For each question in turn, the questionnaires are sorted into further piles, one for each answer. The piles are counted, the answers noted, and a check made that the total number of answers or respondents is correct.

An alternative is to work through each questionnaire in turn, putting a tick on a sheet in a box for the particular answer. Even more care is needed to get the totals correct. The totals have to be carefully written into tables and percentages worked out.

An intermediate stage, using a spreadsheet on a microcomputer, is suitable for small data sets where the answers consist mainly of numbers. These might be the answers to an industrial market research enquiry, where a limited number of respondents give estimates for various usages and market sizes. Such data can be incorporated in a spread-sheet. This enables ratios to be calculated for each respondent, and the original figures and the ratios compared between respondents by running the eye down the page. Totals and averages for all respondents may then be shown. Division of respondents into sub-groups may be troublesome though.

The one-way tables or hole-count will show any 'out-of-range' codes such as those denoting people aged 124, but not errors arising from the answers to two or more questions together. If a computer is being used, programs are available to carry out logical checks to find such errors. When inconsistencies are found, they may be identified for querying and correction, or the data may be automatically modified. For example, if only those saying yes in question 2 about whether they use the product are to be asked in question 8 what they think of it, the combination of the code representing no in question 2 with any code except that for not applicable in question 8 shows an error.

An arbitrary correction may then be thought best, by changing the answer to question 8 to 'not applicable'. On the other hand, a detailed examination of the questionnaire and perhaps reference to the respondent may show where the error lies. Large surveys are open to hundreds of checks of this kind, and thousands of minor inconsistencies may be revealed. Automatic correction is then almost inevitable.

It is important to 'clean' the data. Not only is accuracy desirable, but discrepancies have a way of appearing in the finished tables in a prominent and embarrassing position.

A2.8 The use of computer packages

These are many. Some are menu-driven and others, usually the more powerful, require the preparation of computer files of instructions using some specialised language. They may provide a selection of data entry, data checking, data manipulation, tabulation in various forms, graphical presentation, calculation of summary statistics and tests of significance. They may further provide one or more modelling or multi-variate techniques. The data-entry modules include some for CATI (computer-aided telephone interviewing) assisting in sample selection as well as data collection. As with all software, the more widely applicable and more flexible packages are more complex to use.

The Study Group for Computer Survey Analysis publishes every two years a catalogue of software for statistical and survey analysis: the 1987 edition lists 207 items, 83 British, 112 American, and 12 from other parts of the world. Most are micro-computer based under the PC/MS-DOS operating system.

The most complete service is provided by the specialist analysis houses referred to above. Many names appear in the Market Research Society organisations book. They will take questionnaires, code and key them, then produce tables to specification, doing all or part of these jobs as needed. They will apply multi-variate techniques to the data as directed. Their staff can give valuable guidance in all this; as always, executive involvement costs more. We emphasise the use of these agencies because the mechanics of the earlier stages of analysis are complicated and time-consuming for those who are not practised in their use.

Time spent this way is a diversion from the main purpose of marketers. For them, *intelligent* employment of specialists is likely to be an economy in both time and money. The specialists cannot work without a knowledge of the background, objects and methods of the enquiry, so they have to be directed by people who have some ideas of the problems and possibilities of analysis. There is, though, no reason why the individual researcher or student should not do it all, given time and access to equipment. The software is a more important part of this than the actual machine.

Out of the 207 packages, many of which are intended for specialist statistical purposes outside survey research, we have selected as examples two commonly met with, which illustrate some of the possibilities. This is not to say that they are the best.

SNAP (Mercator Computer Services Ltd, Bristol) is a micro-computer tabulation package which is largely menu-based. At each stage in operation the possible alternatives are shown on the screen, and all that is needed is to select between them. The package does tabulation, and limited data manipulation. There is a module for data entry which produces a picture on the screen of a 'card' containing the responses for one respondent, and the entries at any point may be checked for being in the legitimate range. The ability to manipulate data is limited, except by linking to other packages. There are few summary statistics or significance tests, and no multi-variate or modelling facilities at all. As in all menu-driven programs the ease of initial use soon becomes tedious: there is, however, a batch option which enables large numbers of tables to be produced by entering a few commands.

SPSS (SPSS UK Ltd, Walton-on-Thames) is a suite available either for micros or larger machines, capable of handling and manipulating large and complicated data sets on the bigger machines. It has facilities for a wide range of modelling and multi-variate techniques as well as summary statistics and numerous statistical tests. The layout of tables is not satisfactory for scanning or presentation unless the complex add-on module is used. There is also an add-on graphics module. There are no special data-entry or logical-check facilities, but data can be manipulated in many ways.

The program is driven by creating command files in a specialised language, described in a large manual needed to cover the numerous possibilities. *SPSS* is popular among social scientists, who use it for prolonged examination of their data sets.

Of the many other program packages some specialise in flexible tabulation, others in model building, some in time-series analysis, some in graphics display; some are designed to produce large volumes of repetitive output, some to generate tables one by one. Some link in input and output with others, while some store their data only in forms unintelligible to any other package. The choice is wide and expanding: the only catalogue available is the listing of the SGCSA referred to above. Costs vary widely. Type of machine is not normally a restriction, although complicated operations on large data sets usually mean a bigger machine than the micro.

The computer has made analysis both easier and more difficult. It can produce great volumes of tables: little is achieved, however, by transposing 250 question-naires into 275 tables. Skilfully used, the computer can enable thorough and thoughtful study of data, and the eventual production of the tables which communicate in a report. The way data become information needs understanding if the marketer is to appreciate the potential and the limitations of his/her research.

Bibliography

Association for Survey Computing (eds. B. C. Rowe, A. Westlake and P. Rose) (1995) *Software for Statistical and Survey Analysis is 1994–95*, London: The Association for Survey Computing.

Ehrenberg, A. S. C. (1985) *A Primer in Data Reduction*, Chichester and New York: John Wiley.

Green, P. E., Tully, D. S. and Albaum, G. (1988) *Research for Marketing Decisions* (5th edn), Englewood Cliffs, NJ: Prentice Hall.

Hague, P. N. and Jackson, P. (1987) *Do Your Own Market Research*, London: Kogan Page.

Further reading

One of the few books which deal with the principles of tabulation for both investigation and reporting is Ehrenberg's *A Primer in Data Reduction*. Practical guidance on data collation and analysis of wider application than the title suggests is given in Hague and Jackson's *Do Your Own Market Research*. The principles of multi-variate analysis are covered by Green, Tull and Albaum.

A special issue of the *Journal of the Market Research Society* (vol. 36, 3, 1993) entitled 'Special issues on research and computing' expands on many technical issues.

APPENDIX 3
Statistical tests

E. J. Davis

A3.1 The null hypothesis

When dealing with the results of experiments or surveys carried out on samples of people, shops, or whatever, it is seldom possible to *prove* results. Instead, we usually attempt to assess which of two mutually exclusive hypotheses is more likely to be true on the basis of our observed results. The general forms of these two hypotheses and the symbols attached to them are:

H_0: the hypothesis that our results do not show any significant differences between population groups over whatever factors have been measured; and

H_1: the hypothesis that differences shown in our results reflect real differences between population groups.

The first of these hypotheses, H_0, is known as the null hypothesis. If it is true it indicates that our results show nothing except chance differences between our measurements. If we can obtain sufficient evidence to refute this hypothesis with an acceptable level of confidence, then we are justified in accepting the alternative hypothesis, H_1. In effect we begin by assuming that any difference between two sample measurements is not significant and is due to chance until we can find a good basis for rejecting this assumption. If we can reject the null hypothesis we say that our result is 'significant'.

A3.2 Errors of the first and second kind

In addition to setting down our hypotheses, we need also to decide on the degree of risk we can accept of being wrong in taking a result as significant when it is not. For most market research purposes we work with a level of risk of 1 in 20 of being

351

wrong, often referred to as the 95 per cent limit or the 5 per cent level of significance. In terms of the experiments discussed in Chapter 8, this means that we devise our experiments so that we can apply tests of significance such that if they indicate a real difference, this will be a correct evaluation 95 times out of 100. As we do not normally carry out our experiments often enough to be able to think in terms of being right on 95 per cent of occasions we change the words slightly, and say that we have a 95 per cent chance of being right. From this it follows that we have a 5 per cent chance, or probability, of being wrong, and our tests are operating at the 5 per cent or 0.05 level of significance.

The level of significance here indicates the level of risk of our being wrong in rejecting the null hypothesis when it is true, and thus of accepting our experimental difference as real when it is not. Being wrong in this way is known as a Type 1 Error.

There is a converse risk – that of failing to detect or to accept a positive experimental result because our experimental measurements are too crude. If, say, a change in some measure, such as consumption of some food product from 30 grams per head to 35 grams per head per day would show a profitable return on some marketing expenditure, then an experiment capable only of showing a change of 10 grams or more as significant will leave the company open to such a risk.

An opportunity to take profitable marketing action may be lost because an experiment is set up which is not powerful enough to measure results with the precision needed in the particular situation. Being wrong in this way is known as a Type II Error.

Two further elements which should be taken into account when assessing the levels of significance to be used are the size of the benefits expected if successful action is subsequently taken, and the penalties expected from taking a wrong decision. In situations such as the final stages of the development and launch of a new brand, the potential benefits and potential losses resulting from decisions based on the experimental results are high. This normally calls for the design of experiments giving high levels of precision and low risks of wrongly rejecting the null hypothesis – such as 1 chance in 100 (the 1 per cent level), as opposed to the 1 chance in 20 (the 5 per cent level). But such experiments are themselves costly, and should not be used in less risky situations where the costs would not be justified. Initial testing of ideas and products is often better undertaken based on the use of significance levels of 10 per cent or more, simply because in the early stages of testing it is often unreasonable (and probably unprofitable) to insist on the more rigorous levels of significance appropriate to high-risk situations.

The problems then of interpreting the statistical results of experiments are by no means simple, nor confined merely to the use of prescribed formulae yielding magic numbers to be labelled 'significant' or 'not significant'. However, with these reservations the following statistical tests can be applied with care to a range of statistical results.

A3.3 Differences between sample measurements

The range of uncertainty surrounding a measurement obtained from a sample is indicated by the 'standard error' of that measurement.

To calculate the standard error of a measurement, such as the mean price respondents say they would pay for a new product, their mean foot measurements, and so forth, we first calculate the arithmetic mean and use that as a basis for calculating the standard error. The standard error of a mean can then be calculated from this formula:

$$se_m = \sqrt{\frac{\Sigma(x - \overline{x})^2}{n^2}}$$

where n = sample size (assumed here to be at least 30);
$\quad\quad x$ = each individual measurement taken in turn;
$\quad\quad \overline{x}$ = the mean of all values of x; and
$\quad\quad \Sigma$ = indicates all values of $(x - \overline{x})^2$ added together.

When dealing with attributes such as whether a person smokes or not, whether they like the test product or whether they think they would buy the test product in preference to their usual brand, we can use a more simple version of this formula. In these cases we can put $x = 1$ whenever the respondent smokes, prefers, would buy, or whatever, and $x = 0$ if he/she does not. It is then easy to show that under these conditions the standard error of the percentage having the stated attribute can be calculated by the formula below:

$$se_p = \sqrt{\frac{p(100 - p)}{n}}$$

where p = the percentage scored 1 (preferably between 10% and 90%); and
$\quad\quad n$ = sample size (assumed to be at least 30).

When using proportions instead of percentages substitute $(1 - p)$ for $(100 - p)$ in the formula.

A3.4 Testing experimental differences involving percentages

Experimental designs such as those used for rating new products (see section 8.7.4 on page 175) may involve monadic tests using independent matched samples each reporting on one variant, or comparative tests where the same sample of people report on two or more variants of the product. The procedures for testing the results vary, and are described separately.

A3.5 Monadic results from independent samples

The hypotheses:

H_0:   that any difference between readings p_1 and p_2 from two
         independent random samples of n_1 and n_2 respondents is the
         result of chance alone;

H_1:   that the difference between the readings must be attributed to
         the experimental conditions.

Note that these hypotheses do not stipulate any direction for any difference, i.e. whether p_1 or p_2 is the higher percentage. Hence a two-tailed test is used, and finding a significant difference in either direction would lead to the rejection of H_0.

First calculate p, the overall percentage given by combining both samples, on the assumption that they are both drawn from the same population. This is given by:

$$p = \frac{n_1 p_1 + n_2 p_2}{n_1 + n_2}$$

Then calculate the standard error of the difference $(p_1 - p_2)$:

$$se_d = \sqrt{p(100 - p)\left(\frac{1}{n_1} + \frac{1}{n_2}\right)}$$

In the special case where $n_1 = n_2$:

$$p = \frac{p_1 + p_2}{2}$$

$$se_d = \sqrt{p(100 - p)\frac{2}{n}}$$

Now calculate the absolute value of the test statistic, t, ignoring its sign, where t is defined as:

$$t = \frac{p_1 - p_2}{se_d}$$

If $t \geqslant 1.64$ the difference is significant at the 10 per cent level; if $t \geqslant 1.96$ the difference is significant at the 5 per cent level; and if $t \geqslant 2.58$ the difference is significant at the 1 per cent level.

If a significant difference is found at the required level it suggests that the difference between the readings p_1 and p_2 is not simply due to chance, but reflects a real difference in preferences for the test items.

In some circumstances the direction of any difference is important, as in experiments with a new version of a product expected to be preferred by more people than the old. Here we are not testing whether there is a difference in *either* direction, but whether there is a difference in *one* direction only. In such cases a one-tailed test is used and rejection of H_0 follows only if the test is significant in the appropriate direction.

Assume that p_1 measures acceptance of the old product, and that p_2 measures acceptance of the new version when they have been tested on two independent samples. Then our hypotheses become the following:

H_0: that p_2 is no greater than p_1; and
H_1: that p_2 is greater than p_1.

We calculate se_p and t as before, but now we are only interested in t if p_2 exceeds p_1. The test is now concerned with only one tail of the distribution of error, and the values of t associated with different levels of significance are changed.

If $t \geqslant 1.29$ the one-way test is significant at the 10 per cent level; and if $t \geqslant 1.64$ the one-way test is significant at the 5 per cent level; and if $t \geqslant 2.32$ the one-way test is significant at the 1 per cent level.

A3.6 Comparative readings from the same sample

If we measure preferences for A, B, C, etc. in the same sample, then there are problems of correlation. As p_a increases so p_b may well diminish, and vice versa. Now to establish whether any difference is significant we have to take account of correlation in our formula for se_p. Our hypotheses become the following:

H_0: there is no difference between the proportions p_a and p_b preferring A and B, measured within a single sample;
H_1: there is a difference between preferences for A and B.

Now the formula for the standard error of the difference becomes

$$se_d = \sqrt{\frac{p_a(100 - p_a) + p_b(100 - p_b) + 2p_a p_b}{n}}$$

$$t = \frac{p_a - p_b}{se_d} \text{ as before,}$$

and the values of t apply as before for either one-tailed or two-tailed tests.

A3.7 More complex tests of preference scores

Sometimes we wish to examine more complex situations, such as a preference test where the sample is broken down by some other attribute such as social class. Then the χ^2 or chi-squared test is a more useful way of proceeding.

Suppose we have the following results from a sample of 195 housewives who have each tested products X and Y and stated their preferences. Information on social class has also been collected from each respondent. The results were as follows:

	ABC_1	C_2D	
Prefer X	55	45	100
Prefer Y	35	60	95
	90	105	195

A t-test on the overall split between preferences for X and Y has shown that this is not significant. It appears that there may be differences in preferences between social classes. While it would be possible to carry out a t-test for each class a χ^2-test is more powerful and economical. Here

H_0: there is no difference between the pattern of preferences by social class;
H_1: the pattern of preferences differs between the two social classes.

If there is no difference between classes, then we would expect the same proportion of housewives in each class to prefer X, and the same proportion to prefer Y. The overall estimate of the preference of X is 100 out of 195. Applying this ratio to the 90 ABC_1 housewives, we would expect 46.2 to prefer X, i.e. $100/95 \times 90$. Similarly we would expect $95/195 \times 90$ ABC_1 housewives to prefer Y; $100/195 \times 105$ C_2D housewives to prefer X, and $95/195 \times 105$ to prefer Y

	Observed	Expected	$O - E$	$(O - E)^2$	$(O - E)^2/E$
X/ABC_1	55	46.2	8.8	77.44	1.68
Y/ABC_1	35	43.8	−8.8	77.44	1.77
X/C_2D	45	53.8	−8.8	77.44	1.44
Y/C_2D	60	51.2	8.8	77.44	1.51
	195	195.0	0		6.40

In fact, once we have calculated one of the four expected values in a 2×2 table such as the above the other three values are fixed because of the need for columns and rows to add to their original totals. In technical terms we have only 'one degree of freedom' in such a table.

For each cell we now have an observed (O) and an expected (E) value. We then calculate $(O - E)^2/E$ and add.

We can now consult Table A3.2 of values of χ^2 for our number of degrees of freedom and level of significance, and see whether our sample value exceeds the tabulated value or not. If it does, the differences are significant at that level.

Comparing the calculated value of 6.40 with Table A3.2 for one degree of freedom, the results are seen to be significant at the 5 per cent level but not quite at the 1 per cent level.

In general, when using χ^2:

- Use frequencies, not percentages.
- Cells should preferably contain five or more cases.
- Degrees of freedom = (rows − 1) × (columns − 1), e.g. a table of two rows and three columns has $(2 - 1) \times (3 - 1) = 2$ degrees of freedom.

A3.8 Differences involving variables

The same general procedure is followed for comparing means of variables as for proportions. In these cases, for independent samples calculate a pooled estimate of the *se* thus:

$$se_d = \sqrt{\frac{n_1}{n_2} \cdot se\frac{2}{x_1} + \frac{n_2}{n_1} \cdot se\frac{2}{x_2}}$$

$$t = \frac{\bar{x}_1 - \bar{x}_2}{se_d}$$

Null hypotheses and alternative hypotheses are set up as before, and the links between values of t and levels of significance for one-tailed and two-tailed tests are the same as for testing proportions.

Table A3.2 Some values of χ^2

| | Degrees of freedom | | | |
	1	2	3	4
10%	2.7	4.6	6.3	7.8
5%	3.8	6.0	7.8	9.5
1%	6.6	9.2	11.3	13.3

Where pairs of readings are taken from the same sample, such as numbers of cigarettes smoked by individuals before and after an experiment or weights of slimmers before and after treatment, etc. the situation is most easily handled by calculating the difference, d, for each individual and $\bar{d}$, the average value of d. Then calculate se_d:

$$se_d = \sqrt{\frac{\Sigma(d - \bar{d})^2}{n}}$$

Then our hypotheses become the following:

H_0: that the value of d is not significantly different from zero; and
H_1: that the observed differences are significant.

The tabulated values of t at different levels of significance and for one-tailed and for two-tailed tests apply as before.

A3.9 For more complex situations 'analysis of variance' is used

Consider the experiment described in section 8.6 with results in volume of sales by outlets in three areas, North, Midlands and South and with three pack designs or treatments on test (see Table A3.3).

The regional differences in sales are clearly seen, and on visual inspection they appear to be greater than the differences in sales between the experimental packs. It therefore becomes logical to try to separate the variation or 'variance' between treatments (pack designs in this case) from the variance between regions. Hence we undertake an analysis of variance.

Table A3.3

		Shop sales in a pack test			
	T1	T2	T3	Total	Average
N	150	220	180	550	183.3
M	90	100	110	300	100.0
S	60	70	70	200	66.7
Total	300	390	360	1050	
Average	100	130	120		116.7

Now the overall variance is given by

$$s^2 = \frac{1}{n-1} \Sigma (x - \bar{x})^2$$

where n = number of cells in the analysis;

x = the average sales level over all stores in all regions, namely

$$\bar{x} = \frac{1050}{9} = 116.67$$

Within the total variance some part will be due to the following:

- Variations in sales between areas.
- Variations in sales between pack designs.
- Chance variations in sales between stores.

The statistic F is used to assess whether any observed differences in the variance contributions are significant, or probably due only to chance, and hypotheses H_0 and H_1 are set up as before.

The calculations necessary to analyse the overall variance from the experimental results into the parts due to each of these sources are as follows:

r = numbers of rows (areas)
t = number of treatments (packs)

Add up total sales and calculate average sales ($\bar{x}$)
For each area find total sales and average sales (rows) – $\bar{A}_i$.
For each pack find total sales and average sales (cols) – $\bar{P}_j$.

Calculate $\displaystyle\sum_{1}^{r} \sum_{1}^{t} (x_{ij} - \bar{x})^2$ = sum of squares total (SST)

Calculate $r \displaystyle\sum_{1}^{r} (\bar{A}_i - \bar{x})^2$ = sum of squares, areas (SSA)

Calculate $t \displaystyle\sum_{1}^{t} (\bar{P}_j - \bar{x})^2$ = sum of squares, packs (SSP)

As a check on arithmetic one more figure may be calculated:

$$\sum_{1}^{r} \sum_{1}^{t} (x_{ij} - \bar{A}_i - \bar{P}_j + \bar{x})^2 = \text{error/residual sum of squares} = \text{(SSE)}$$

Calculate degrees of freedom (d.f.) and follows:

Total d.f.	= no. of areas × no. of treatments − 1
	= $(r \times t) - 1$
Between areas d.f.	= no. of areas − 1
	= $(r - 1)$
Between treatments d.f.	= no. of treatments − 1
	= $(t - 1)$
Residual/error d.f.	= $(r - 1)(t - 1)$

Note that the degrees of freedom between areas + between treatments + residual = total degrees of freedom. Then complete the following table:

Analysis of variance for random block design

Source of variance	Sum of squares	d.f.	Mean square	Value of F
Between packs	SSP	$t - 1$	MSP = SSP/$(t - 1)$	MSP/MSE
Between areas	SSA	$r - 1$	MSA = SSA/$(r - 1)$	MSA/MSE
Error/residual	SSE	$(r - 1)(t - 1)$	MSE = SSE/$(r - 1)(t - 1)$	
Total	SST	$rt - 1$		

For the shop sales data from the pack test:

r = areas = 3
t = packs = 3

$$\sum_1^r \sum_1^t (x_{ij} - \bar{x})^2 = 24,400.0$$

$$r \sum_1^r (\bar{A}_i - \bar{x})^2 = 21.666.7$$

$$t \sum_1^t (\bar{P}_j - \bar{x})^2 = 1,400.0$$

$$\sum_1^r \sum_1^t (x_{ij} - \bar{A}_i - \bar{P}_j + \bar{x})^2 = 1,333.3$$

The table then becomes the following:

Source of variance	Sum of squares	d.f.	Mean square	Value of F
Areas	21,666.7	2	10,833.3	32.5
Packs	1,400.0	2	700.0	2.1
Error	1,333.3	4	333.3	
Totals	24,400.0	8		

We can now consult tables of the values of F to test whether either of the F values is significant. We enter the tables with 2 d.f. for areas and 2 d.f. for packs (the numerators in the F ratios) and 4 d.f. for the mean square error (the denominator). In tables of the values of F the degrees of freedom for the numerator are denoted by v_1, and those for the denominator by v_2.

Using $v = 2$ and $v = 4$, the tables show the following significant values for F:

1% level $F = 18.00$
5% level $F = 6.94$
10% level $F = 4.32$
25% level $F = 2.00$

This result shows, as we suspected, that there are very strong area differences, with the between-areas value of F being significant well beyond the 1 per cent level. The value of F for the packs, however, is only significant at the 25 per cent level – that is, we could expect such observed differences in the sales of the different packs in one experiment in four, just by chance even if the packs had no differential effects on sales levels.

The action to be taken on this result would depend on other factors in the situation, such as the relative costs of the three packs, the time pressures for a decision, and so forth. Broadly we could do the following:

- Adopt pack 3, accepting the low level of significance of the experimental result.
- Continue with the existing pack (if there is one).
- Carry out further experiments to get a more specific indication of the effects of packs on sales.

Analysis of variance is such a widely used method of assessing the significance of experimental results that it is included in most computer statistical packages. The programs vary in detail, but the raw data are fed in as responses to promptings by the computer program, and the completed calculations printed out or displayed in a form similar to the table above. Some programs stop at the calculation of the F values, but others go on to indicate the associated levels of significance.

It is important to appreciate what calculations are taking place to produce the analysis of variance from a set of data, but seldom necessary to carry through the arithmetic by hand.

The facilities are also normally there for handling the calculations arising from more complex experiments quickly and accurately, for taking account of more factors, and for investigating possible interactions between levels of factor. At each stage of increasing complexity the calculations expand, but following the patterns shown above.

For example, the Latin square design discussed in section 8.6 leads us to the tables on page 363.

The similarity in structure between the tables is seen, with the inclusion of an additional line in the Latin square results. The error/residual calculation is now

$$\sum_{1}^{t} \sum_{1}^{r} (x_{ij} - \bar{A}_i - \bar{P}_j - \bar{O}_k + 2\bar{x})^2$$

Analysis of variance for Latin square

Source of variance	Sum of squares	d.f.	Mean square	Value of F
Between packs	SSP	$t - 1$	$MSP = SSP/(t - 1)$	MSP/MSE
Between areas	SSA	$t - 1$	$MSA = SSA/(t - 1)$	MSA/MSE
Between outlets	SSO	$t - 1$	$MSO = SSO/(t - 1)$	MSO/MSE
Error/residual	SSE	$(t - 1)(t - 2)$	$MSE = SSE/(t - 1)(t - 2)$	
	SST	$t - 1$		

where the $\bar{A}_i$s are the averages of the areas;
    the $\bar{P}_j$s are the averages of the packs; and
    the $\bar{O}_k$s are the averages of the outlet types.

A3.10 Worked example of the use of a Latin square

This example follows the design set out in section 8.6, with three packs being tested in three outlet types in three areas. The sales figures are shown in the table below.

Raw sales data from pack test

Region	Type of retail outlet			Total	Average
	Grocer	Chemist	CTN		
North	122^2	114^3	139^1	375	125
Midlands	108^1	115^2	104^3	327	109
South	91^3	110^1	114^2	315	105
Total	321	339	357	1,017	
Average	107	113	119		113

The indices against cell sales indicate the pack version used.

To facilitate the calculation of the pack averages the figures may be rearranged thus:

				Total	Average
Pack 1 sales	139	108	110	357	119
Pack 2 sales	122	115	114	351	117
Pack 3 sales	114	104	91	309	103

It is now possible to calculate all the sums of squares required and to fit them into the analysis of variance table below.

Analysis of variance

Source of variance	Sum of squares	d.f.	Mean square	Value of F
Packs	456	2	228	25.3
Areas	672	2	336	37.3
Outlets	216	2	108	12.0
Error	18	2	9	–
Totals	1,362	8		

These values of F can be compared with the tabulated values for v_1 and v_2 both at two degrees of freedom:

at the 5% level $F = 19.0$; and
at the 1% level $F = 99.0$.

Hence both pack figures and the area figures show significant differences at the 5 per cent level.

The fact that the figures show significant variations by pack needs careful interpretation, and reference back to the averages by pack indicates that the variation arises from one pack performing less well than the other two. There is still doubt about which of the three packs may sell best – but some progress has been made in finding that one version sells less well than the other two.

Further reading

Bagozzi, R. (1994) *Advanced Methods of Marketing Research*, Cambridge, MA: Blackwell Publishers.

Kinnear, T. and Taylor, J. (1991) *Marketing Research: An applied approach*, New York: McGraw-Hill.

Parasuraman, A. (1991) *Marketing Research*, Reading, Mass: Addison-Wesley.

Tull, D. and Hawkins, D. (1990) *Marketing Research: Measurement and method*, New York: Macmillan.

APPENDIX 4

Market Research Society publications

A4.1 Serials

Research (monthly)
This was re-launched in October 1992, with a new title and focus on the news and issues of the market research industry with coverage of the Society's own activities.

Journal of the Market Research Society (quarterly)
JMRS is a refereed academic journal.

Market Research Abstracts (bi-annual)
Market Research Abstracts covers all fields of marketing and advertising research, as well as relevant papers in statistics, psychology and sociology. Over 400 papers and articles are abstracted each year from some 40 different English language journals.

Field Newsheet (quarterly)
This has articles and information of particular interest to interviewers.

Research Plus (monthly)
This mid-monthly publication, following the re-launch of *Research*, now focuses on a different industry sector each month, through a range of feature articles by leading practitioners.

A4.2 Annuals

Market Research Society Yearbook
The *Yearbook* contains lists of members together with their affiliations, and details of organisations and individuals providing market research services in the United Kingdom and Republic of Ireland. It also includes details of Society activities, services and useful addresses in the United Kingdom and overseas.

International Directory of Market Research Organisations (11th edition)
The 11th edition of the *International Directory* published in 1993 gives details of facilities of market research organisations in over 70 countries worldwide.

A4.3 Other publications

Country Notes
These provide a basic guide on demographics, sampling methods, research procedures and sources of information in different countries. They are available in regional volumes as follows: Western Europe, Far East, North America, Eastern Europe and Latin America.

Dictionary of Market Research
The *Dictionary of Market Research* has been compiled by Philip Talmage as a joint publication of The Market Research Society and The Incorporated Society of British Advertisers (ISBA).

Guide to Sources of Samples for Telephone Research
Thirty-three information sources are listed, with full details about the type of data they provide.

Issues in Political Opinion Polling
The chapters cover the basic techniques of opinion polling, interviewing for opinion polls, the accuracy of opinion polls, bias and sample re-weighting, the publishing of poll findings, the electoral effects of opinion polls, and a glossary of technical terms used in survey research.

Guide to the Practice of Market and Survey Research
The MRS has published this guide in order to explain to those outside the survey research industry what market researchers do and what market and survey research in general is about.

Occupation Groupings: A job dictionary
An A–Z of common and not so common occupations by socio-economic gradings – a valuable tool in the classification of respondents.
Recommended Papers for the Diploma of The Market Research Society
A comprehensive collection of papers covering all aspects of market research, including reprints from the *Journal of the Market Research Society* and Annual Conference Papers; ESOMAR conference and seminar proceedings; the *Journal of Consumer Research*, *Journal of Advertising Research* and *Journal of Marketing Research*.

Standardised Questions
This publication was originally produced in July 1972. A new edition was published in October 1984. It examines the most commonly used methods of asking certain types of question and of recording the answers and is still used today.

Glossary of media terminology

Average issue readership (AIR)   The number of people who claim to have read or looked at a publication in the last issue period, i.e. 'yesterday' in the case of the *Daily Mirror*, and 'in the last week' in the case of *Woman's Weekly*.

Average listening hours   The average number of hours listened to a radio station. Calculated by dividing total listening hours in a week by weekly reach (total number listening in a week).

Cost per hundred (CPH)   The average cost of achieving 100 TVRs against a specified audience. (See TVR.)

Cost per thousand (CPT)   Used with reference to a specific audience, cost per thousand is a measure of the average cost of reaching 1,000 members of this audience. For example: if a spot on Thames TV reaches 400,000 men and costs £4,000, then the cost per thousand men is £4,000 ÷ 400 = £10.00.

Cover (sometimes termed **reach** or **net coverage**)   The proportion of the audience having an opportunity to see the advertising one or more times. Usually measured as a percentage, but can be expressed in thousands.

Cumulative cover   The increased cover resulting from taking space in more than one issue of a particular publication.

Effective reach (sometimes termed **effective cover**)   The percentage of the target audience who have the opportunity to see the desired number of TV spots (or hear radio spots, or see press ads). For example: if it is desired that the target audience see between two and eight spots, then the effective reach of the schedule is the percentage with between two and eight OTS.

Equal impacts   A strategy for regional allocation giving equal number of TVRs to all regions.

Frequency   The average number of times the target audience has an opportunity to see the campaign measured in OTS. (OTH for radio.)

Calculated as frequency = gross OTS ÷ net cover
           or = TVRs ÷ net cover (for TV)

Source: J. Walter Thompson Company, Media Research Unit, 'Media glossary'

Gross rating points   The total number of OTS achieved by a campaign expressed as a percentage of the universe. For TV this would be equivalent to total TVRs. For press, it would be the sum of individual average issue readerships. For example: a campaign achieving 70 per cent cover at 4 OTS would yield 280 gross rating points.

Impacts   Impacts (sometimes termed gross impressions or messages) are the total number of separate occasions a commercial(s) is viewed by a specific audience, measured in thousands.

MPX (magazine-page exposure)   MPX scores the number of times an average issue reader of a publication looks at an average page.

Net homes   Describes the number of homes in a TC area, exclusive of overlap. (See TV overlap.)

OSCAR (outdoor-site classification and audience research)   Provides classifications of site visibility/quality and traffic past site. Does not provide demographics of audience.

OTH (opportunity to hear)   The radio equivalent of OTS – the average number of times an audience is exposed to a radio commercial. 'Exposure' is defined as any listening within the clock quarter-hour.

OTS (opportunity to see)   The opportunity to see a TV commercial or a press, cinema or poster advertisement, defined as follows:

Press:	Read or looked at any issue (for at least two minutes), within the publication period (e.g. last week, for a weekly).
Cinema:	Measured in actual cinema admissions.
Posters:	Traffic past the site.
TV:	Presence in room with set switched on at turn of clock minute to one channel, providing presence in room with set on is for at least fifteen consecutive seconds.

Average OTS is measure of frequency of exposure to an advertisement: if an audience is exposed to an advertisement on average three times each, then this is equivalent to an average OTS of 3.

Page traffic   The percentage of readers who 'look at' a specific page within a publication.

Pass-on readership (sometimes termed **secondary readership**)   Readers of a publication other than the purchaser or his/her immediate household. For example: readership which takes place in a doctor's waiting-room.

Penetration   Refers to the proportion of a population who are reached by a medium.

Pre-empt   A system of buying TC air-time similar in principle to an auction. The rate card may consist of a range of many different rates. The buyer will elect the rate desired to pay for a spot but he/she can lose the spot if 'pre-empted' by another buyer subsequenty paying more for that spot. Pre-emption can occur up to midday on the day of transmission.

Primary readership   The first reader of a publication or members of his/her immediate household.

Readers per copy (RPC)   The average number of readers seeing each copy sold. Calculated as average issue readership ÷ circulation.

Share deals   A method of negotiation designed to increase ITV contractors' share of television revenue. Discounts are given to advertisers investing a share of their budget equivalent to the TV areas' net homes share or sales share, whichever is the greater. Used until December 1987.

Timeshift   Practice of recording programmes on VCR and viewing later.

TV overlap   TV overlap areas consist of districts falling within the boundaries of more than one TV area; 18 per cent of householders are currently in overlap areas.

TVR (television rating)   Expressed in terms of a specific audience, e.g. adult TVRs, home TVRs, etc. For a single TV spot twenty-one housewife TVRs means that 21 per cent of all housewives were recorded as viewers of that spot. For more than one spot, TVRs represent the sum of individual spots. For example, a campaign of twenty spots, each of fifteen TVRs, is equivalent to 300 TVRs.

Glossary of sampling terms

Probability (random)

Disproportionate stratefied random sample Where there is a marked variation in the sizes of the strata in a population, it is more efficient to use a variable sampling fraction. To calculate the sample estimates for the population as a whole, estimates driven from individual strata are weighted according to their relative size. A disproportionate sample is also used when the characteristic to be studied is markedly variable across the population, e.g. unemployment.

Multi-stage area sample The sample is drawn in more than one stage, usually after stratification by region and type of district. Three-stage drawing is quite common; first, constituencies; second, ward or polling districts; third, electors using the register of electors as a sampling frame. This form of cluster sampling has more than two segmental stages of random sampling.

PPS With probability proportionate to size of population/electorate; used in multi-stage drawing and associated with the use of systematic interval. A range of numbers, equivalent to its population, is attached to each item on the list (e.g. each constituency, each polling district) before the draw is made. A number between one and the total population, divided by the number of sampling points, is drawn at random (or generated by computer). This indicates the starting-point; the list of items is then systematically sampled, the probability of selection being proportionate to the size of each item.

Probability sample Each member of the population has a known (and non-zero) chance of being selected into the sample.

Proportionate stratified random sample A uniform sampling fraction is applied to all the strata, i.e. the proportion of n (the number in the sample) to N (the number in the population) is the same for all strata.

Sampling frame A specification of the population which allows for the identification of individual items. The frame should be completed, up to date and without duplication of items.

Simple cluster sample One stage over sampling in which the population is divided into clusters of units (sub-populations) from which a random sample of a few clusters can be chosen. All units in the chosen clusters can then be selected from a study.

Simple random sample　All the population members are listed and numbered and the sample is drawn in one stage.

Stratification　The population is divided into homogeneous groups (strata) whose relative size is known. Strata must be mutually exclusive. A random sample is taken in each stratum.

Systematic sample　The sampling interval is calculated (let $N/n = k$). The first member of the sample is drawn at random from a numbered list; k is added to the number of the randomly selected member. This identifies the second member and the procedure is repeated. (N = number of items in the population and n = number of items in the sample.)

Two-stage area sample　Instead of selecting all units, a random selection of the chosen clusters is studied. This form of cluster sampling allows a more representative examination of a wider geographic area.

Purposive (non-random)

Convenience sample　Sample units are chosen according to what is conveniently available to the researcher.

Judgement sample　A method of purposive sampling based on subjective judgement. Assumes the researcher is knowledgeable about the population in choosing the sample units.

Purposive sample　A non-probability sampling method selection of sample members is dependent on human judgement.

Quota sample　A method of stratified sampling in which selection of sample members within each stratum is non-random. The population is divided into cells or segments subjectively on the basis of having certain control characteristics for each population cell, a quota of units is chosen based on the judgement of researchers. Sample units are selected for study to fill the quota in each cell.

Glossary of abbreviations

AA	Advertising Association
ABMRC	Association of British Market Research Companies
ACORN	a classification of residential neighbourhoods
AGB	Audits of Great Britain, part of TN AGB
AI	appreciation index
AIDA	attention, interest, desire, action
AIR	average issue readership
AMSO	Association of Market Survey Organisations
AMTES	area marketing test-evaluation system
AN	article numbering
APG	Account Planning Group
API	advertising-planning index
AQRP	Association of Qualitative Research Practitioners
AURA	Association of Users of Research Agencies
BARB	Broadcasters' Audience Research Board
BBC	British Broadcasting Corporation
BI	behavioural intention
BMRB	British Market Research Bureau
BPTO	brand/price trade-off
BRD	Broadcasting Research Department
BSB	British Satellite Broadcasting
CAPI	computer-assisted personal interviewing
CATI	computer-assisted telephone interviewing
CAVIAR	cinema and video industry audience-research
CIE	chief income earner
CRN	classified residential neighbourhoods
CSO	Central Statistical Office

372

DAGMAR	defining advertising goals for measured advertising results
DCF	discounted cash flow
DDS	Donovan Data Systems
DIY	do-it-yourself
DK	don't know
DSB	Direct Satellite Broadcasting
EAN	European article numbering
EC	European Community
EDP	electronic data processing
EML	extended media list
EPOS	electronic point of sale
ESOMAR	European Society for Opinion and Market Research
GSS	Government Statistical Service
HOH	head of household
ILR	independent local radio
IPA	Institute of Practitioners in advertising
IQCS	Interview Quality Control Scheme
ITC	Independent Television Commission
ITCA	Independent Television Companies Association
ITV	Independent Television
JMRS	Journal of the Market Research Society
LR	local radio
MEAL	Media Expenditure Analysis Ltd
MIS	marketing information system
MLH	minimum list heading
MORI	Market and Opinion Research International
MR	market research
MRDF	Market Research Development Fund
MRS	Market Research Society
NBD/LSD	negative binomial distribution/logarithmic series distribution
NOP	National Opinion Poll
NPD	new product development
NRS	National Readership Survey
OPCS	Office of Population Censuses and Surveys
OR	operational research
OSCAR	outdoor-site classification and audience research
OTS	opportunities to see

PAF   postcode address file
PIN   Pinpoint Identified Neighbourhoods
PPI   personal purchases index
PPS   probability proportionate to size

RAJAR   Radio Joint Audience Research Ltd
R&D   research and development
RBI   Research Business International
RI   Research International
RSGB   Research Services of Great Britain
RSL   Research Services Limited

SCPR   Social and Community Planning Research
SIC   standard industrial classification
SN   subjective norm
SRA   Social Research Association

TABS   tracking advertising and brand strength
TAT   thematic apperception test
TCA   television consumer audit
TCPI   toiletries and cosmetics purchasing index
TEA   terminal education age
TGI   Target Group Index
TN AGB   Taylor Nelson Audits of Great Britain
TV   television
TVR   television rating

USP   unique selling proposition

VCR   video cassette recorder
VDU   visual display unit
VIP   valued impressions per pound

Index